The State of Capitalism

T0265698

EReNSEP Writing Collective

Nicolás Aguila researches the Political Economy of Money and Finance at the Department of Politics, Philosophy, and Economics, Universität Witten/Herdecke. His research covers topics in money, credit, central banking, and subordinate financialisation. His publications include: 'Not all zombies are created equal. A Marxist-Minskyan taxonomy of firms', *International Review of Applied Economics* and 'From Individual Wage to Household's Labor Income', *Review of Radical Political Economics*.

Carla Coburger is Junior fellow for Economic and Monetary Sovereignty at the Excellence Cluster Africa Multiple, University of Bayreuth, Germany. She researches global financial networks, currency regimes and their relation to the development of productive capacities. Her publications include: *Kapitalismusanalysen. Klassische und neue Konzeptionen der Politischen Ökonomie* and 'The West African CFA Franc Zone as a Double Monetary Union'.

Sergi Cutillas teaches global political economy at the Faculty of Economics and Business of the University of Barcelona. His research interests include money, debt, digitalization, and financial regulation. He has also actively participated in campaigns to promote debt audits and the cancellation of illegitimate debts. His publications include 'National states, transnational institutions, and hegemony in the EU', *Evolutionary and Institutional Economics Review*.

Juan J. Duque is doing research in contemporary capitalist finance. His training is in philosophy and his current research focus is on cryptofinance. His publications include 'State involvement in cryptocurrencies. A potential world money?', *Japanese Political Economy*.

Matteo Giordano is doing research in Economics and Political Economy at the Department of Economics, SOAS. His main areas of interest are European Political Economy, financialisation, international macroeconomics, and history of economic thought.

Costas Lapavitsas is Professor of Economics at SOAS. He has published widely on the Political Economy of Money and Finance and his research during the last few years has focused on the financialisation of capitalism. He served as a Member of Parliament in Greece in 2015. His most recent books include *Capitalism in the Ottoman Balkans, The Left Case Against the EU* and *Profiting Without Producing*.

Spyros Marchetos is Assistant Professor at the Political Sciences School of the Aristotle University of Thessaloniki. His research focuses the history of ideas from the Enlightenment to the present, the history of European labour, radical movements and the Extreme Right, the history of medicine and public health, and the history of debt. His works include *'How Did I Kiss Mussolini!' The First Steps of Greek Fascism*. He served as a member of the Debt Truth Committee of the Hellenic Parliament (2015).

Thanos Moraitis conducts research at the Department of Economics at UMass Amherst on issues relating to Political Economy and Macroeconomics. His publications include 'Modelling opportunity cost effects in money demand due to openness'.

Marie Hyllested is researching the Political Economy of Money and Finance. She has also been actively involved in social movements. Her current interests include feminist economics, financial imperialism and political economy of banking and financial markets.

Yuning Shi pursues research at the Department of Economics at SOAS on financialisation, Chinese State-Owned Enterprises, and the political economy of China. She is also actively involved in policy-related work on the US financial system. Her publications include 'China versus the US in the pandemic crisis', *Canadian Journal of Development Studies / Revue canadienne d'études du développement*.

Aylin Soydan is Professor of Economics at Istanbul Okan University. Her research interests include financialisation, internationalisation of capitalist production, economic development, and (de)industrialisation. Her publications include 'Financialisation in Developing Countries: Approaches, Concepts, and Metrics', *International Review of Applied Economics*.

The State of Capitalism

Economy, Society, and Hegemony

Costas Lapavitsas and the
EReNSEP Writing Collective

VERSO

London • New York

The authors would like to thank the Rosa Luxemburg Foundation and
its West Africa office in Dakar for financial and intellectual support in
undertaking the necessary research on peripheral countries for the book.

First published by Verso 2023
© Costas Lapavitsas and the EReNSEP Writing Collective 2023

1 3 5 7 9 10 8 6 4 2

Verso
UK: 6 Meard Street, London W1F 0EG
US: 388 Atlantic Avenue, Brooklyn, NY 11217
versobooks.com

Verso is the imprint of New Left Books

ISBN-13: 978-1-83976-784-5
ISBN-13: 978-1-83976-785-2 (US EBK)
ISBN-13: 978-1-83976-786-9 (UK EBK)

British Library Cataloguing in Publication Data
A catalogue record for this book is available from the British Library

Library of Congress Cataloging-in-Publication Data
Names: Lapavitsas, Costas, 1961- author.
Title: The state of capitalism : economy, society and hegemony / Costas
    Lapavitsas and the EReNSEP Writing Collective.
Description: New York : Verso, 2023. | Includes bibliographical references
    and index.
Identifiers: LCCN 2023016770 (print) | LCCN 2023016771 (ebook) | ISBN
    9781839767845 (paperback) | ISBN 9781839767852 (US EBK) | ISBN
    9781839767869 (UK EBK)
Subjects: LCSH: Capitalism. | Economics. | Hegemony.
Classification: LCC HB501 .L267 2023 (print) | LCC HB501 (ebook) | DDC
    330.12/2--dc23/eng/20230503
LC record available at https://lccn.loc.gov/2023016770
LC ebook record available at https://lccn.loc.gov/2023016771

Typeset in Minion Pro by Hewer Text UK Ltd, Edinburgh
Printed and bound by CPI Group (UK) Ltd, Croydon CR0 4YY

Contents

Part III

1
Perilous Times

A historical interregnum

Covid-19 ushered in a bout of great economic, social, and political turbulence across the world, and exacerbated strains that had been accumulating for several years. The health emergency disrupted economies and societies, catapulting national states into unprecedented prominence. This was followed in 2022 by the telling geopolitical event of the times, Russian military intervention in Ukraine leading to a war with the involvement of the USA and its main European allies, and then an escalation of US–Chinese geopolitical tensions.

The early 2020s could be called the Pandemic Crisis, marked by changing configurations of society and politics, both domestically and internationally. Three decades after the crumbling of the Soviet Bloc, capitalist relations dominate life across the world, giving rise to enormous social tensions and new hegemonic contests. Landmark events of that period include the Great Crisis of 2007–09 and the successive wars launched by the USA and its allies in the Middle East, Afghanistan, and elsewhere. The advent of Covid-19 and the war in Ukraine greatly intensified global instability.

The roots of the turmoil lie, however, in capitalist accumulation. In this respect, the period since the Great Crisis of 2007-09 represents a historical interregnum in the well-known Gramscian sense that the old is dying but the new cannot be born, thus giving rise to morbid symptoms.[1] Core economies across the world are marked by weak production and predatory finance.[2] Financialisation is entrenched, and finance remains the chief beneficiary of government policies as well as the source of fabulous wealth for an oligarchic sliver of society. At the historic sites of advanced capitalism, growth is feeble, employment is precarious and poverty endemic, while income differentials continue to widen, creating vast social fractures. Neoliberal financialised capitalism, dominant for more than four decades, is showing signs of exhaustion.

The health emergency also brought to the fore the persistently flawed relationship between hours of paid work and hours of tedious and unpaid reproductive work. It shone a light on what kind of work is essential for core capitalist societies to survive, and how much of it is performed by female workers as well as workers from ethnic and racial minorities. The venerable struggle against the glass ceiling for women at work, conducted by feminists for decades, looked hollow as reproductive labour tasks were again largely imposed on women within the home, while domestic violence increased.

In the periphery of the world economy, meanwhile, new centres of capitalist accumulation have emerged, leading to a global rebalancing of economic activity, while endless tracts of humanity remain trapped in conditions of low income and poor employment. The subordinate integration of peripheral countries into the world economy has taken on new and pernicious forms, including interpenetrating networks of production, trade and finance. At the same time, the global expansion of capitalism has had a catastrophic impact on the natural environment. The health emergency adduced fresh evidence of the noxious

---

1 Exactly what Gramsci meant by his pithy phrase remains, nevertheless, unclear. See G. Achcar (2022) 'Morbid Symptoms: What Did Gramsci Really Mean?', *Notebooks: The Journal for Studies on Power*, 1 (2), 379–87.

2 The distinction between core and periphery is deployed throughout this book but we have consciously avoided giving a formal definition. The field is laden with fierce debates – several of which are briefly reviewed in subsequent chapters – and we sought to avoid sterile terminological arguments. Uneven development has characterised the capitalist mode of production from its very beginning, but the analytical and geographical boundaries of core and periphery are constantly shifting. The key point is that current unevenness is entirely the result of the domination of the globe by capitalist economic relations, lacking significant 'pre-capitalist' or 'non-capitalist' features. This makes the contemporary division between core and periphery far more complex than its previous variants. We establish its analytical content incrementally in the subsequent chapters.

relationship between humanity and nature fostered by the search for profit.

As the interregnum unfolded after 2007–09, capitalist economies in both the core and periphery came to depend even more heavily on the mechanisms of state. A salient aspect of the Pandemic Crisis was the ability of core states to influence economic activity and the reliance of economies on state support. After decades of neoliberal ascendancy in policy and ideology, it is well-nigh impossible to conceive of enduring capitalist accumulation without the crutches of the state. In this respect, there is no comparison between core and peripheral states, the enormous power of the former deriving in large part from their command over domestic fiat money.

The more the state becomes integral to the functioning of the economy, the greater is the power of a narrow capitalist oligarchy over state mechanisms. The institutions of democracy have steadily atrophied, particularly the intermediate layers connecting working people and local communities to political life. Mainstream politics exudes failure and irrelevance, while popular sovereignty is effectively absent, including in core countries.

And yet, despite the corrosion of economy, society, and politics at the core, the ceaseless rebalancing of global production, trade, and finance, and the extraordinary levels of state economic intervention, there is no evidence that capitalist accumulation is entering a new and dynamic phase. At the core of neoliberal financialised capitalism, deep structural change is meticulously avoided, leaving class power firmly in the hands of a narrow layer of fabulously wealthy property owners. The new order appears unable to be born.

The hazards are apparent at the global level. The years following the Soviet collapse were marked by the hegemonic supremacy of the USA, in truth the most powerful empire the world has ever known. As the interregnum took shape, however, unipolar US supremacy came to an end. Fresh hegemonic struggles have been unleashed across the world, with the eruption of war in Ukraine in 2022 signalling the heightened risk of generalised military conflagration.

In the years of neoliberal ascendancy, the underlying drivers of hegemony and imperialism were, on the one hand, multinational enterprises constructing global production networks and, on the other, internationally active financial enterprises permeating domestic economies. The USA took the lead in erecting an institutional framework conducive to the profit making of this exceptionally aggressive nexus of private capitals. It exercised its hegemonic power across the world economy, seeking the compliance of the core and the subordination of the periphery. Crucial to its power was control over the dominant form of world money – that is, the US dollar.

But the USA has squandered its pre-eminence by allowing its domestic productive accumulation to weaken, while engaging in endless wars. The independent centres of capitalist accumulation that have emerged during this period – above all, in Asia – rely critically on their national states. A challenge to US hegemony has gradually taken shape, primarily from China but also from other powers, all seeking to influence the institutional framework of the world economy in line with their own interests.

The risks to humanity are potentially lethal, since hegemony rests on military as well as economic and ideological power. Following the invasion of Ukraine in 2022, the USA and its allies took unprecedented actions to exclude Russia from the institutional framework of the world economy, including from the mechanisms of the dollar as world money. The message was taken by China and other powers, which intensified the search for alternative mechanisms.

The USA will not abandon its hegemonic position without a fight. Despite the exhaustion of neoliberal financialisation, the hegemon can command enormous economic, political, and military resources. Opposing alliances are hastily formed and hardened across the world. Contestants for hegemony will seek to accrue further military power in the years ahead, including conventional and nuclear weaponry. The interregnum is pregnant with lethal risks for humanity.

Confronting the challenge from the left

The manifest failures of capitalist relations and the prominence of the state during the health emergency entailed forceful social reactions. Heavy-handedness by state authorities in core countries included cultivating intense political sentiments – even interpersonal enmity and fear – and infringing on rights and liberties. In peripheral countries, it was often the inability of the state to ensure protection of life and health that ignited animated responses. The domination of the media by corporate interests and the stifling uniformity of public discussion in core countries also gave rise to criticism. Above all, the social determinants and implications of the health emergency caused deep concern.

Unfortunately, the left, the historical voice and force of political opposition to capitalism, has failed to rise to the occasion. Despite castigating capitalism, it lacks a strong narrative for radical change grounded in the experience of working people and addressing in plain language their needs, hopes, and fears. The roots of the left among workers and the poor in core countries have become even more attenuated, leaving it adrift in the political storms of the times.

The exhaustion of neoliberal financialised capitalism and the aggravation of hegemonic contests call for fresh proposals from the left. Economic strategies are required to boost public investment and employment, support the livelihood of workers, and deal with debt and inequality. The property rights of the capitalist elite ought to be challenged, reasserting the virtues of the social over the private and the collective over the individual. Radical economic strategies require democracy and popular sovereignty to be re-established while countries engage in a coherent struggle for peace and equality.

In this light, this book examines the underlying forces of the interregnum since 2007–09 by weaving in different disciplines.[3] Analysis is pursued primarily from the standpoint of Marxist political economy, while remaining open to other heterodox approaches to contemporary capitalism and acknowledging their political parameters. A prime concern is to confront the responsibility of the left as a historical political current.[4] Structural arguments are offered for opposing and overthrowing capitalism, and for gauging the stance of states and other institutions and forces, including political parties. The work draws on the rich materials on the evolving capitalist transformation during the last several decades as well as on the pronouncements of political actors across various levels of public discourse.[5]

The task is necessarily synthetic, its remit is very extensive, and the requirements are complex and multifaceted, calling for a joint effort.

---

3 Taking a cue from the writings of Immanuel Wallerstein; see I. Wallerstein (1996) *Open the Social Sciences: Report of the Gulbenkian Commission on the Restructuring of the Social Sciences*, Mestizo Spaces / Espaces Metisses, Stanford University Press: Stanford.

4 The distinction between the historic political currents of mature capitalism remains crucial in this regard, particularly in relation to policies and public discourse; see N. Bobbio (1996 [1994]) *Left and Right: The Significance of a Political Distinction*, University of Chicago Press: Chicago.

5 See the remarks on methodology in J. G. A. Pocock (2009) *Political Thought and History: Essays on Theory and Method*, Cambridge University Press: Cambridge; see also Q. Skinner (2002) *Visions of Politics*, vol. 1: *Regarding Method*, Cambridge University Press: Cambridge.

This book is the outcome of collective writing that combines different types of knowledge and experience, while still finding a common voice. For several years, the European Research Network on Social and Economic Policy (EReNSEP) has sustained itself through the voluntary efforts of its members, and has maintained its academic and political integrity in conditions that have become increasingly unbearable for heterodox voices. The present volume is the product of long-standing discussions and research, all authors taking collective responsibility for the final product as a matter of methodological and political choice.

To provide structure to its broad content, the work is split into three parts. Part I comprises chapter 2 and discusses the social, economic, and political dimensions of the health emergency. The pandemic posed profound questions regarding the social and economic aspects of public health and medicine in contemporary capitalism, not least the power of Big Pharma originating in core countries.

Part II – from chapter 3 to chapter 8 – turns to the extraordinary role of the state in contemporary capitalism, as was evidenced during the pandemic. In substance, part II discusses domestic capital accumulation in core countries, paying close attention to the weakness of the side of production and the transformation of financialisation since the Great Crisis of 2007–09. The role of the state is examined partly in terms of fiscal and monetary policy, and partly through the implications of state command over fiat money.

The turmoil of the early 2020s, however, stretched across the world economy. Thus, part III – from chapter 9 to chapter 17 – turns to the international dimensions of capitalist accumulation and considers the interaction of non-financial enterprises, financial institutions, and states in the world economy. Capitalist hegemony and imperialism are rooted in economic activities, continually redefining the division between core and periphery across the world. Contemporary capitalist hegemony and imperialism rest on the aggressive nexus of internationalised production and global finance. Part III further examines the emerging hegemonic frictions by considering China and the European Union.

Chapter 17 concludes by sketching an outline of alternative economic, social, and political strategies to exit the interregnum turning left. Working people have the power to change the world, but achieving this task requires the overthrow of the malign capitalist relations that dominate it. A firm grasp of these relations is the first prerequisite.

PART I

Unforeseen Health Emergency

2

An Inequitable and Diverging World

The health risks of neoliberal capitalism

According to the World Health Organization (WHO), excess mortality associated with Covid-19 stood at 15 million across the world in 2020–21.[1] Other research suggests that the pandemic's true toll may be one order of magnitude greater than official death counts.[2] The calamity had a greater impact on Europe and the USA than most of Asia and Africa – a novel imbalance when it comes to public health – the probable reasons for which are discussed below.[3]

1 See WHO (2022) 'Global Excess Deaths Associated with COVID-19, January 2020–December 2021', at who.int.

2 See, selectively, A. Karlinsky and D. Kobak (2021) 'The World Mortality Dataset: Tracking Excess Mortality across Countries during the COVID-19 Pandemic', *medRxiv* (published 4 June). For the burden of disease, see M. Roser and H. Ritchie (2016) 'Burden of Disease', at ourworldindata.org; GBD 2015 Mortality and Causes of Death Collaborators (2016) 'Global, Regional, and National Life Expectancy, All-Cause Mortality, and Cause-Specific Mortality for 249 Causes of Death, 1980–2015: A Systematic Analysis for the Global Burden of Disease Study 2015', *The Lancet* 388, 1459–544; see also GBD 2015 Disease and Injury Incidence and Prevalence Collaborators (2016) 'Global, Regional, and National Incidence, Prevalence, and Years Lived with Disability for 310 Diseases and Injuries, 1990–2015: A Systematic Analysis for the Global Burden of Disease Study 2015', *The Lancet* 388, 1545–602.

3 The infection/fatality rate (IFR) of the disease fluctuated across countries according to demographic factors, public policy, and the quality of medical treatment; see Swiss Policy Research (2021) 'Studies on Covid-19 Lethality', November update, at swprs.org. By the end of 2021 – before the seemingly less serious Omicron variant had

Covid-19 caught the core of global capitalism entirely unprepared. Even powerful and wealthy countries lacked the necessary medical equipment and skilled personnel – not to mention the institutional mechanisms of health provision – to protect those most vulnerable, especially the elderly. In both core and peripheral countries, health systems found themselves at risk of being overwhelmed, and governments saw their legitimacy threatened. This lack of preparedness was hardly due to an absence of warning, as several viral epidemics marked the preceding decades with increasing frequency – HIV/AIDS, SARS-Cov-1, Avian Flu, Ebola.[4] The policy failures of 2020–22 reflected primarily the institutional biases and systemic malfunctions of the state machinery of contemporary capitalism.

The main cause of the Covid-19 illness is the SARS-Cov-2 virus, but viral interactions with human and other animal hosts constitute extremely complex systems, making it difficult to ascribe the pandemic to a single factor. The disease raised profound questions about human life and nature in contemporary neoliberal capitalism. Capital treats nature, the elemental terrain of human existence and foundation of all wealth, as occupied territory to be exploited ruthlessly. The outcomes of this inherently predatory attitude are highly dangerous and unpredictable, affecting both the climate and biodiversity. It is plausible that the pandemic was related to global biosafety risks arising from the spoliation of natural ecosystems and reproductive cycles by capitalist production and trade.[5]

The epidemiological and clinical features of Covid-19 were largely unknown in early 2020, and thus adequate diagnostic and therapeutic

---

spread across the world – the IFR had significantly fallen among the elderly and was minimal for younger age groups; see C. Axfors and J. P. A. Ioannidis (2021) 'Infection Fatality Rate of COVID-19 in Community-Dwelling Populations with Emphasis on the Elderly: An Overview', *medRxiv* (published 23 December). The decline was partially attributable to extensive vaccination campaigns.

4 Critical Marxists, such as David Harvey, gave prescient warning of a 'global infectious disease pandemic that halts all trade'. See Harvey's synthetic work that lucidly dissects the antinomies of capitalism: D. Harvey (2014) *Seventeen Contradictions and the End of Capitalism*, Profile Books: London, p. 10.

5 From the broad literature on this issue see, for instance, J. W. Moore (2015) 'Anthropocene or Capitalocene? On the Nature and Origins of Our Ecological Crisis', in *Capitalism in the Web of Life. Ecology and the Accumulation of Capital*, Verso: London, New York, ch. 7; see also A. Malm (2020) *Corona, Climate, Chronic Emergency: War Communism in the Twenty-First Century*, Verso: London; and R. Wallace (2016) *Big Farms Make Big Flu: Dispatches on Influenza, Agribusiness, and the Nature of Science*, Monthly Review Press: New York.

mechanisms were not readily available. As the health emergency worsened, however, it became clear that the virus tended to kill people with underlying – often long-term – ailments. Most vulnerable were the workers, the poor, and the old, already marginalised by the health systems of even the richest countries and heavily exposed to persistent long-term health complaints frequently associated with unhealthy work and living conditions.

Covid-19 was aptly described as a 'syndemic'.[6] This notion, developed by medical anthropologists in the 1990s, highlights biological and social interactions important for prognosis and treatment, as well as for the design of health policy, which are in sharp contrast to one-size-fits-all approaches toward public health.[7] In the case of Covid-19, the acute respiratory impact of the virus combined with an array of non-communicable diseases clustering in social groups according to deeply embedded patterns of inequality. In contemporary neoliberal capitalism, the combination proved catastrophic.

To be more specific, medical experts quickly realised that the pandemic was linked to other environmental and medical factors, including malnutrition, air pollution, obesity, vitamin D deficiency, hypertension, chronic respiratory diseases, and so on.[8] These were particularly acute for several ethnic and racial groups in core countries. The disease steadily acquired a class character, amplifying entrenched patterns of income and wealth inequalities as well as racial discrimination. The policies to confront it, furthermore, shone fresh light on the relation of state to society.

Since the health emergency resulted from a broad array of interconnected environmental, medical, political, moral, economic, and social factors, confronting it required a multidisciplinary approach.[9] And yet,

---

6 See R. Horton (2020) 'Offline: COVID-19 Is Not a Pandemic', *The Lancet* 396 (10255): 874.

7 H. Baer, M. Singer, and I. Susser (eds) *Medical Anthropology and the World System*, Praeger: Westport, CT and London, p. 15.

8 See H. E. Mark et al. (2020) 'Malnutrition: The Silent Pandemic', *BMJ* 371: m4593. See also L. L. Benskin (2020) 'Perspective Article: A Basic Review of the Preliminary Evidence that COVID-19 Risk and Severity Is Increased in Vitamin D Deficiency', *Front Public Health* (10 September); see further G. Gerotziafas et al. (2020) 'Guidance for the Management of Patients with Vascular Disease or Cardiovascular Risk Factors and COVID-19: Position Paper from VAS-European Independent Foundation in Angiology/ Vascular Medicine', *Thromb Haemost* 120 (12): 1597–628.

9 The complex approach required is reminiscent of the 'undisciplinary' method

contrary to previous practice, as, for instance, during the Ebola epidemic of 2014–15, social scientists were largely excluded from the formation of strategies to confront Covid-19. In the most powerful countries of the world, policy was dominated by the extraordinary ideological construct of 'hard science', largely sidelining the insights of child psychologists, mental health professionals, economic historians, political scientists, and others.[10] This deeply problematic approach was not fully remedied even after it was incontrovertibly demonstrated that early measures were based on inaccurate data projections.

Within a few months of its outbreak, the pandemic morphed into a global social and economic crisis reflecting the noxious relationship between neoliberal capitalism and public health. The protagonists of the turmoil were the states of contemporary capitalism, demonstrating deep-seated weaknesses as well as colossal strengths. The pandemic took a varied course across the world as different states adopted separate policies. Several core countries were unable to prevent, detect, and adequately respond to the viral threat, and their health systems were shown to be in a dilapidated and retrogressing condition. Above all, the hegemonic USA proved woefully inept at protecting the health of its population.[11] Peripheral states were obliged to confront the shock with far more limited resources at their disposal, but on occasion deployed more effective strategies, as is shown below.

Strategy and policy to confront Covid-19

The strategic decisions of core states, with the USA in the lead, set the broad parameters of the medical response to the pandemic, within a framework determined by biomedicine and epidemiology. Modern biomedicine, despite its great advances, is not socially neutral and subsists in tension with the multiple traditions of epidemiology, as is

advocated by Immanuel Wallerstein; see Wallerstein (1996) *Open the Social Sciences*; and (2004) *World-Systems Analysis: An Introduction*, Duke University Press: Durham, NC; London. For a particularly clear statement of the importance of an approach that combined disciplines, see G. Vanden Bossche (2021) 'Some Guidance to Separating the Wheat from the Chaff', 14 August, at voiceforscienceandsolidarity.org.

10 T. Green (2021) 'Introduction', in *The Covid Consensus: The New Politics of Global Inequality*, C. Hurst & Company: London.

11 J. A. Bell and J. B. Nuzzo (2021) 'Global Health Security Index: Advancing Collective Action and Accountability Amid Global Crisis', at ghsindex.org.

shown in the rest of this chapter.[12] Social conflicts and political choices ultimately decide which individuals benefit from biomedicine and which social groups have their health bolstered by epidemiologically informed public action.[13]

Choosing a strategy to confront Covid-19 was exceptionally complex, and time pressure was extreme. All strategies would, obviously, include restrictions of social interaction, lockdowns, and vaccinations, but the weight of each of these factors would not be determined by medical considerations alone. In practice, state policies depended heavily on non-medical factors, reflecting economic interests and imbalances of social and political power. Crucial to choosing was balancing the economic reproduction of capital against the needs of society.

Putting the needs of society first would have required ample resources to be made available rapidly to health systems, with the aim of developing therapeutic treatments for the disease. It would also have required increased provision of primary care, and widely available local medical resources. Such an approach would also have included restrictions, lockdowns, and vaccinations, but these would not have been its mainstay. The impact on established economic interests – particularly the large enterprises heavily involved in public health and biomedicine – would have been substantial, since this approach would have altered the backbone of health provision.

Furthermore, socially minded strategies would have required rapid construction of an effective system of testing and tracing. Resources would also have to be made available for safe transport to work and adequate protection at the workplace, obviously varying among offices, factories, building sites, and so on. In addition, students and teachers would have required protection across the education system. Above all, there would have to have been active participation by the population in controlling the disease; simply demanding the passive endurance of people as the disaster unfolded did not go far enough.

---

12 See C. E. Rosenberg (1992) *Explaining Epidemics and Other Studies in the History of Medicine*, Cambridge University Press: Cambridge. See also Baer, Singer, and Susser (eds) (2003) *Medical Anthropology and the World System*.

13 For a more detailed presentation, see S. Marchetos (2022) 'Epidemics and Syndemics in Historical Perspective', in P. Mossleh (ed.) *The Corona Phenomenon: Philosophical and Political Questions*, Value Inquiry Book Series/Social Philosophy, vol. 376, Brill: Leiden, pp. 233–69.

The strategies chosen by core countries, despite their differences, were generally remote from such considerations. The typical response was to adopt exceptional measures, including society-wide lockdowns and vaccination mandates. The counterpart to restrictive measures was to rely on giant pharmaceutical corporations to develop vaccines. In effect, leading states placed a bet on mitigating the impact of the disease through restrictions, in the hope that pharmaceutical corporations would rapidly develop vaccines that could be made widely available.

Given the strategy of mitigation and vaccine development, the pandemic proved a severe shock to the political culture at the core of contemporary capitalism, with some states choosing to shroud sensitive data in secrecy instead of promoting scientific openness.[14] Leading states even foisted invasive and divisive policies on their societies with scant epidemiological rationale or scientific legitimation. It is no exaggeration to say that the spirit of the Enlightenment, the historical legitimation of capitalist political power, took a severe blow during the health emergency.[15]

In practice, moreover, state responses across the world varied considerably depending on institutional structures, history, geopolitical perspectives, command over resources, and class priorities. A range of policy options soon materialised, varying from Zero Covid to herd (or community, or population) immunity, all of which were contestable in their effectiveness and debatable in their meaning. There would be no unified approach to confronting the threat to humanity posed by Covid-19. Divergence ruled, and that was far from accidental in the contemporary world.

Several countries, including China, opted for variants of the Zero Covid policy either in its strict sense (eradication) or its wider one (elimination).[16] These policies evidently included very restrictive

---

14 BMJ Editorial (2002) 'Covid-19 Vaccines and Treatments: We Must Have Raw Data, Now', *BMJ* 376: 102.

15 See D. Hind (2008) *The Threat to Reason: How the Enlightenment was Hijacked and How We Can Reclaim It*, Verso: London. Nonetheless, authoritarian impulses continue to be contested and occasionally rolled back. A case in point is the decision of a federal American judge to make public the data submitted to license Pfizer's Covid-19 vaccine; see A. Siri (2022) 'Instead of FDA's Requested 500 Pages Per Month, Court Orders FDA To Produce Pfizer Covid-19 Data at Rate of 55,000 Pages per Month!' *Injecting Freedom* (7 January), at aaronsiri.substack.com.

16 There is no internationally agreed definition of the elimination of the SARS-CoV-2 virus, but the concept falls short of eradication, with which it is frequently

measures, and seemed appealing to countries with natural protective barriers to the spreading virus, such as Australia and New Zealand. Zero Covid did not necessarily denote an intensive preoccupation of governments with the wellbeing of workers and the poor. But it did seek to protect life, particularly among ageing populations, since elderly people were highly susceptible to Covid-19.

On the other side of the spectrum lay the policy of herd immunity, defined by the WHO as the indirect protection from infectious disease occurring when a population becomes immune either through vaccination or previous infection (natural immunity).[17] Several countries with variable political configurations were attracted to versions of this policy, notably Japan and Sweden, but also less affluent countries, such as Belarus and Nicaragua.[18] Aiming for herd immunity entailed restrictions much less severe than Zero Covid's, allowing for free movement and keeping schools, parks, and businesses open.

As different approaches to restrictions took shape, the political contours of the pandemic emerged sharply. The policies implemented in practice by most core states fell between the two extremes of the spectrum. Meanwhile, across vast tracts of the periphery of the world economy, countries also chose a place in the spectrum according to the

---

confused. Eradication stands for the permanent reduction of the incidence of a disease to zero across the world, an objective that has been practically achieved only for smallpox. Elimination may be understood as accepting that some community transmission would still occur but taking maximal action rapidly to limit such transmission. See D. C. G. Skegg and P. C. Hill (2021) 'Editorial. Defining Covid-19 Elimination', *BMJ* 374: n1794. For the Chinese approach to controlling the pandemic, see C. Martinez (2020) 'Karl Marx in Wuhan: How Chinese Socialism Is Defeating COVID-19', *International Critical Thought* 10 (2): 311–22.

17 WHO (2020) 'Coronavirus Disease (COVID-19): Herd Immunity, Lockdowns and COVID-19', 31 December, at who.int. Herd immunity – the precise meaning of which kept changing depending on political considerations – had practically disappeared from official discourse by 2022, as is shown by a simple Google search.

18 The debate engendered by these choices was fierce, and at times vicious: see A. Tegnell (2021) 'Review Article: The Swedish Public Health Response to COVID-19', *World Medical and Health Policy, APMIS: Journal of Pathology, Microbiology and Immunology* 129 (7): 320–3; A. Heydarian Pashakhanlou (2021), 'Sweden's Coronavirus Strategy: The Public Health Agency and the Sites of Controversy', *World Medical and Health Policy* 14 (3): 507–27; A. Baldizón (2021) 'Nicaragua's Social Policy Response to Covid-19: Business as Usual at All Costs', *CRC* 1342, Covid-19 Social Policy Response Series 29, Bremen; J. Capelán (2020) 'Nicaragua – The Country That Didn't Swallow the Covid Blue Pill', *Off-Guardian*, 30 September, at off-guardian.org; K. Karath (2020) 'Covid-19: How Does Belarus Have One of the Lowest Death Rates in Europe?' *BMJ* 370: m3543; H. Sakamoto (2021) 'Japan's Covid-19 Strategy', Social Science Research Council, 1 April, at items.ssrc.org.

capacity of their health systems and the strength of their state mechanisms. In this highly pressurised context, the public debate on Covid-19 policy in core countries took on a technocratic aspect, relying heavily on medical and epidemiological inputs. Scientists occasionally, but not always, engaged in cost–benefit analysis of feasible options by counting deaths and assessing the economic costs of alternative policies.[19] The most intractable issues of the pandemic, however, were neither technical nor scientific – they were social and deeply political.

The strategic gamble was simply immense. If an effective vaccine did not materialise within a short space of time, social costs would escalate rapidly, and so would political risks. Developing a new drug or vaccine is an uncertain process that normally takes years of research and frequently leads to failure. Barely one in a thousand among potential pharmaceutical compounds reaches the stage of clinical human trials, and even fewer are marketed. Of these, as few as three may account for 70 to 80 per cent of a producer's total sales, while occasionally a single medicine could provide three quarters of a corporation's profits.[20]

As the search for a vaccine intensified, restrictive measures multiplied without precedent. Curfews were enforced on vast metropoles; domestic and international travel were restricted; face-to-face meetings were tightly regulated or banned, including within families; places of worship were shut; even open-air activities were restricted or forbidden; the functioning of hotels, restaurants, bars, coffee shops, gyms, shopping malls, supermarkets, pharmacies, and hairdressers was placed under heavy control or stopped altogether; schools and universities were shut or heavily restricted. Restrictive policies evidently had military aspects amounting to the coercive isolation of huge sections of society or even shutting down entire economic sectors.

The restrictions had a profound impact on families and individuals. Lockdowns disrupted family, social, and work interactions, affecting broad layers of the population, especially the old. The loss of contact at the workplace – that is, the loss of a fundamental constitutive element of working people's lives – transformed at a stroke the practices of labour.

---

19 See, for instance, P. Thomas (2020) 'J-Value Assessment of How Best to Combat Covid-19', Nanotechnology Perceptions, 16 (1): 16–40.

20 OECD (2001) *Competition and Regulation Issues in the Pharmaceutical Industry*, Policy Roundtable 2000, p. 8, at oecd.org.

A new sociality was imposed, especially on large urban centres, comprising physical isolation, invasion of personal space by work done remotely, and heavy reliance on mass media and the internet. At the same time, several forms of solidarity emerged spontaneously as communities came together to support weak and isolated members. But the longer the restrictions lasted, the greater the exhaustion and frustration of working people.

Chaotic and diverging responses across the world

Faced with the common threat of the pandemic within the strategic parameters outlined in the preceding section, the world forbore any attempt at unity. States competed against each other by drawing on different political priorities and ideological concerns, class structures, institutional mechanisms, and international alliances. A veritable policy mosaic emerged, with states taking disparate positions while simultaneously invoking 'hard science'. Borders became harder, international travel shrank abruptly, and foreigners were forcibly kept out even from countries traditionally advertising a cosmopolitan outlook, such as Belgium and the Netherlands.

The hegemonic USA proved pitifully under-resourced as well as disorganised and slow in implementing restrictive measures. Official US Covid-19 deaths had already reached world record levels by 2020–21 and kept rising.[21] Belated calls, issued at the highest level, for a 'comprehensive, permanently funded system for testing, surveillance, and mitigation measures that does not currently exist' went largely unheeded.[22]

The EU response in the early stages of the pandemic was slow and disorganised, with poor results for public health.[23] Tensions soon emerged within the EU as members insisted on following divergent strategies. Britain also jumped from a liberal and disorganised approach toward a severe application of restrictions after suffering a heavy death

---

21 E. J. Emanuel, M. Osterholm, and C. R. Gounder (2022) 'A National Strategy for the "New Normal" of Life with COVID', *JAMA* 327 (3): 211–12.

22 D. Michaels, E. J. Emanuel, and R. A. Bright (2022) 'A National Strategy for COVID-19: Testing, Surveillance, and Mitigation Strategies', *JAMA* 327 (3): 213–14.

23 M. Anderson, M. Mckee, and E. Mossialos (2020) 'Covid-19 Exposes Weaknesses in European Response to Outbreaks', *BMJ* 368: m1075.

toll.[24] Japan followed a policy broadly similar to Sweden's until late 2021, avoiding full lockdowns and aiming at herd immunity and voluntary social distancing. But as cases surged in August 2021, the country was forced to change course.[25] Conjunctural factors also influenced government choices – for instance, the experience that East Asian countries had accumulated from recent viral outbreaks, such as swine flu and avian flu, as well as previous (and different) coronavirus epidemics such as SARS-CoV-1.

Purely contingent political events also intervened, as, for instance, in Sweden and New Zealand, which sat at either end of the policy spectrum.[26] In the early stages of the pandemic, Swedish public health opinion was divided, but the government soon opted for a herd immunity approach.[27] Avoiding obligatory measures, this essentially liberal approach revolved around non-binding recommendations on family, social, and work interactions. This contrasted sharply with New Zealand, where public health opinion was also divided during the earliest stages of the pandemic, until the government was panicked into an extreme 'fortress' policy in March 2020 that lasted until late 2021. At about the same time, Sweden also made an abrupt change but in the opposite direction, as it introduced some restrictive measures in response to a spike of cases in late 2021.

Events and processes were even more complex across the vast terrain of peripheral countries in Latin America, Africa, the Middle East, South Asia, and elsewhere. Cuba achieved formidable results by pioneering and implementing a national emergency plan based on popular mobilisation and community-based response. The Cuban approach included border closure, testing, tracing, aggressive early treatment with a range

---

24 K. Rankin (2021) 'Covid19 Premier League: Spectrum of Public Health Choices', *Scoop*, 14 October, at scoop.co.nz.

25 There was even a turn toward using ivermectin, an antiparasitic and antiviral 'miracle drug' that is available in generic form. Ivermectin was developed in Japan but has attracted heavy criticism in other countries: see TrialSite Staff (2021) 'Chairman of Tokyo Metropolitan Medical Association Declares During Surge, Time for Ivermectin is Now', *TrialSite News*, 16 August, at trialsitenews.com. On ivermectin's general properties and safety, see A. Crump and S. Ōmura (2011) 'Ivermectin, "Wonder Drug" from Japan: The Human Use Perspective', *Proc. Jpn Acad. Ser. B Phys. Biol. Sci.* 87 (2): 13–28. On its contested performance against Covid-19, see Swiss Policy Research (2021) 'The Ivermectin Debate', at swprs.org.

26 Rankin (2021) 'Covid-19 Premier League'.

27 See the responses of A. Tegnell, in M. Paterlini (2021) 'Feature: What Now for Sweden and Covid-19?', *BMJ* 375: n3081.

of locally produced medicines, isolation, and development of a range of vaccines.[28]

But human catastrophes also unfolded in several peripheral countries, which were directly attributable to the callousness and short-sightedness of their rulers. In India, the extreme right-wing government failed to provide basic support and protection to vast numbers of poor people, contributing to an estimated 2 to 4 million excess deaths by the end of August 2021.[29] The right-wing government of Brazil presided over a public health disaster, taking the opportunity further to undermine the country's underfunded health system and primary care.[30] The president, Jair Bolsonaro, refused to implement a national lockdown, publicly criticised provincial governors who had imposed local lockdowns, kept changing health ministers, concealed statistical evidence, and preposterously called the disease a 'little flu' that could be dealt with by drinking hydroxychloroquine.[31]

China, the strategic competitor to the USA for global hegemony, took a highly distinct path by adopting a Zero Covid policy until the beginning of 2023, which resulted in far fewer deaths, even if it had severe costs of social isolation and economic disruption. It is incontestable, furthermore, that several Asian countries, such as Thailand and Vietnam, protected human life and economic activity more effectively than either the USA or the EU by applying severe restrictions, providing basic medical support, and relying on communal mobilisation. Finally, it appears that large parts of Africa were hit less harshly by the pandemic than the USA and Europe, perhaps due to relatively younger populations and, possibly, weaker links between the urban and rural parts of African countries. Several African countries, such as Nigeria and Senegal, were also able to implement effective restrictions, in part drawing on the accumulated experience of previous epidemics.

The mitigation and vaccine strategies followed by several core states

28 M. Bermejo et al. (2021) 'Special Report: Equity and the Cuban National Health System's Response to COVID-19', *Pan American Journal of Public Health* 45: e80.

29 See C. T. Leffler et al. (2022) 'Preliminary Analysis of Excess Mortality in India During the COVID-19 Pandemic', *American Journal of Tropical Medicine and Hygiene* 106 (5): 1507–10.

30 R. de Oliveira Andrade (2020) 'Covid-19 Is Causing the Collapse of Brazil's National Health Service', *BMJ* 370: m3032.

31 See A. Saad-Filho (2021) 'Brazil: Inequality and Catastrophe', in *The Age of Crisis. Neoliberalism, the Collapse of Democracy, and the Pandemic*, Palgrave Macmillan: Cham, pp. 135–49.

had significant costs in terms of mortality, economic activity, and the wellbeing of populations.[32] Popular reaction gradually grew, often led by right-wing forces suspicious of the media and other forms of managing public opinion. The pandemic piled up inflammable material engendering great risks for capitalist rule, which were exacerbated by the economic crisis sparked by the health emergency, as is shown in part II.

The ideological and institutional aspects of the public health crisis, therefore, call for closer examination in the rest of this chapter. Despite the chaotic and divergent responses by core and peripheral states, the tone across the world was set by Western precepts, particularly the technocratic emphasis on 'science'. A revealing light was cast on the relationship between contemporary capitalism and public health.

The rise and fall of public health

Covid-19 focused reflection on the idea of health, often taken as self-evident but whose historically specific character is increasingly recognised by both the medical community and the public.[33] Its roots can be traced to the ancient Greeks, who were probably the first to break with supernatural conceptions of health and disease.[34] Western ideas about medicine evolved alongside the conceptions of the Enlightenment regarding hygiene, and even further with the development of biomedicine in the late nineteenth century.[35]

---

32 T. Green (2021) *The Covid Consensus*.

33 See I. Badash et al. (2017) 'Redefining Health: The Evolution of Health Ideas from Antiquity to the Era of Value-Based Care', *Cureus* 9 (2): e1018.

34 A physiocratic school of thought, linked to Hippocrates, defined health as a state of dynamic equilibrium between the internal and external environments of human beings, thus positing an intricate connection between health, human behaviour, and the physical and social environment; see Y. Tountas (2009) 'The Historical Origins of the Basic Concepts of Health Promotion and Education: The Role of Ancient Greek Philosophy and Medicine', *Health Promotion International* 24 (2): 185–92. During the Middle Ages, the Greek heritage was submerged in Europe but permeated the great Arab and Persian medical traditions of classical Islam; see H. Edriss et al. (2017) 'Islamic Medicine in the Middle Ages', *The American Journal of the Medical Sciences* 354 (3): 223–9.

35 See G. Vigarello (1988) *Concepts of Cleanliness: Changing Attitudes in France since the Middle Ages*, translation J. Birrell, Past and Present Publications, Cambridge University Press, Editions de la Maison des Sciences de l'Homme: Cambridge and Paris. For a celebrated exposition of the mainstream liberal perspective, see R. Porter (1999) *The Greatest Benefit to Mankind: A Medical History of Humanity from Antiquity to the*

The material infrastructure of health that people in Western countries often take for granted is based upon ideas and social and intellectual struggles that took shape more than a century ago. The notion of public health crystallised in the mid-nineteenth century and its scope has waxed and waned over time, shrinking visibly in recent decades.[36] By the late nineteenth century, public health movements had sprung up in several core capitalist countries. Medics, scientists, administrators, and activists with varied backgrounds joined these movements, intent on confronting the social problems thrown out by urbanisation, industrialisation, and large-scale immigration. Fully aware of the pernicious effects of class and social decay, they were morally committed to improving the health of the population.

Public health movements generated social and political pressures to which governments had to respond, even if reluctantly, before the First World War. From the late nineteenth century to the 1920s, public health policy typically aimed to replace the loss of workers' income due to illness and injury, and only partially to prevent infectious diseases.[37] The Russian Revolution and the growth of labour and socialist movements across the world forced capitalist states to implement a range of further reforms. Public health was finally acknowledged as a legitimate policy concern by several core countries, although the colonies were a different matter altogether.[38]

The new policy priorities partly coincided with reforms demanded by

---

Present, Fontana: London. At the turn of the twentieth century, public health institutions in the West promoted and applied fundamental tenets developed by medical pioneers, including the germ theory of disease and the understanding that 'preventing disease in the weakest elements of society ensured protection for the strongest (and richest) in the larger community'. L. Garrett (2001) *Betrayal of Trust: The Collapse of Global Public Health*, Oxford University Press: Oxford, p. 10.

36 A pioneer was the German polymath and political radical Rudolf Wirchow, a central figure in nineteenth-century medicine and arguably the founder of biomedicine and epidemiology, as well as a keen supporter of therapeutics and prevention of disease on a society-wide scale; see R. H. Shryock (1936) *The Development of Modern Medicine: An Interpretation of the Social and Scientific Factors Involved*, University of Pennsylvania Press: Philadelphia, p. 206.

37 Public health measures included 'water purification, sanitation, housing standards, food inspection, and inoculation; hospital care and medical service providing for sick persons who could not pay fees; and subsidising research that promised to identify the causes of and cures for infectious disease'; see A. L. Fairchild et al. (2010) 'The EXODUS of Public Health: What History Can Tell Us About the Future', *Am. J. Public Health* 100 (1): 54–63.

38 On the creation of hygienic spaces exclusively for colonists in twentieth-century colonial capitals, see G. Picker (2017) *Racial Cities: Governance and the Segregation of Romani People in Urban Europe*, Routledge: Abingdon and New York.

the socialist left, but the objectives of capitalist states in pursuing public health were very different. Above all, they aimed 'to maintain the supply of workers for industry and commerce and ensure a steady source of healthy recruits for military service'.[39] Other goals, their salience varying among countries, included insulating the more affluent classes from the diseases of the poor and assuring the stability of regimes. The difference from the idealism and the aspirations of the earlier movements was striking.

In practice, interwar health policy meant supporting disease prevention and therapy, plus providing income replacement for sick workers. There was strong belief in the effectiveness of medical care based on confidence in its scientific foundations. Hierarchical networks of teaching hospitals and research laboratories were built in big cities, systematically producing new knowledge that was then diffused across geographical areas through medical schools and health professionals.[40] This system, which replicated and strengthened existing class structures, was well adapted to the needs of both nation and empire.

In the USA, the Great Depression encouraged alliances between specialists in the provision of sanitary services, organised labour, and local reformers. The professionalisation of medicine and the heavy emphasis on science and technology, however, eroded commitment to public principles of health. Roosevelt's National Health Act in 1939 continued to echo socially minded conceptions of public health, but medical care after the Second World War was entrusted to 'insurance companies, hospitals, physicians, and other interest groups that did not understand (or actively opposed) the role public health could or should play'.[41] The public health movement effectively imploded as academics, public health professionals, and social reformers were sidelined. Scientific progress and medical expertise took centre stage, deployed instrumentally by the big businesses that came to dominate the field.

Beyond the USA, however, the idea of public health continued to gain ground, spurred by revolutions and anti-colonial movements. Several leading European countries developed welfare states that promoted public health provision. The WHO was founded as a United Nations (UN) agency dedicated to global health and safety, aiming to guide the

---

39 D. M. Fox (1998) 'Health Policy and the History of Welfare States: A Reinterpretation', *Journal of Policy History* 10 (2): 239–56, at p. 245.

40 Ibid.

41 Fairchild et al. (2010) 'The EXODUS of Public Health'.

public health services of member states on the use of pharmaceuticals, vaccines, and non-drug medicines. Under Halfdan Mahler, its Danish Director-General from 1973 to 1988, the World Health Organization (WHO) promoted primary health care plus universal education, proper nutrition, and access to safe water, sanitation, immunisation, and essential medicines, as well as maternal and child health care.[42] This socially responsible approach to public health – loathed by national and international bureaucracies connected to capitalist interests – was overturned following Mahler's departure.[43]

The abandonment of public health policies in recent decades has been spearheaded by the USA, where corporate interests closely connected to private hospitals and universities have steadily shaped a market-dominated approach to health. The mainstay was advanced biomedical research, drawing heavily on leading universities and commercial institutions that enjoyed abundant state and private funding.[44] Antibiotics, vaccines, psychotropic drugs, and a host of other new medical technologies and clinical interventions appeared to provide the means of attacking disease without disrupting the social order. Presented as apolitical, these methods had deeply political and social consequences – health became increasingly based on 'hard science' and divorced from disruptive popular movements.

Health management in the ascendant

The economic crisis of the early 1970s, signalling the end of the long post-war boom and the rise of neoliberalism, led the governments of several core countries to shrink their health budgets.[45] Long before the demise of the Soviet Union, public health spending had been slashed in all the states of the USA, except for clinical care provision.[46] When the Cold War came to an end, the USA lacked even the semblance of a coherent health care system, and one in five of its citizens was

---

42 See A. Snyder (2017) 'Halfdan Mahler Obituary', *The Lancet* 389 (10064): 30.

43 S. Ventegodt (2015) 'Review Article: Why the Corruption of the World Health Organization (WHO) is the Biggest Threat to the World's Public Health of Our Time', *Journal of Integrative Medicine & Therapy* 2 (1): 1–5.

44 See Fox (1998) 'Health Policy and the History of Welfare States'.

45 Ibid., p. 251.

46 Garrett (2001) *Betrayal of Trust*, p. 7.

uninsured. The global hegemon relied on 'health management' entrusted to a hodgepodge of insurers, physicians' organisations, and managed care companies, all seeking private profit.

During this period, a new discourse gradually emerged in the USA, linking health to individual responsibility. The true culprits of poor health were, apparently, individual choices, pernicious habits, and irrational excesses, rather than social structures, class-riven institutions, and corporate and government policies. A state-supported but market-driven approach came to dominate health provision. It was up to health buyers to check the price and quality of the 'commodities' provided by health sellers.

The neoliberal wind blowing from Washington in the 1980s did not produce a consensus on health, but the perspective of health management steadily gained ground across the world.[47] In Europe, where the state had acted as primary health provider for decades, the new perspective seemed to offer a way of cutting, or restraining, health budgets. Even in peripheral countries, where people frequently lacked clean water, safe sewage, adequate food, good housing, clinics, and hospitals, the global multilateral organisations of US hegemony – above all, the World Bank – proclaimed the merits of the health management perspective.[48]

Ironically, the US health system is notoriously inefficient: its costs are high, and it ranks last 'on access to care, administrative efficiency, equity, and health care outcomes'.[49] Its defects are a veritable litany – perverse doctor–patient relationships, a lack of services in several geographical areas, malpractice by providers, exclusion of the weaker members of society, and emphasis on profit making by the insurance and pharmaceutical industries alike.[50] These glaring flaws were replicated in several

---

47 The official US body charged with the task of generating a consensus produced a platitude remarkable only for its circular logic: 'The committee defines the mission of public health as fulfilling society's interest in assuring conditions in which people can be healthy': Committee for the Study of the Future of Public Health (1988) 'The Future of Public Health', National Academy Press: Washington DC, p. 1. For more on this issue, see Garrett (2001) *Betrayal of Trust*, pp. 5–17.

48 See Garrett (2001) *Betrayal of Trust*, p. 8.

49 See E. C. Schneider et al. (2021) *Mirror, Mirror 2021: Reflecting Poorly. Health Care in the U.S. Compared to Other High-Income Countries*, The Commonwealth Fund Report 2021, p. 2, at commonwealthfund.org.

50 D. Callahan and S. B. Nuland (2011) 'How American Medicine Is Destroying Itself', *The New Republic*, 19 May, at newrepublic.com.

low- and middle-income countries, particularly as the privatisation of health services made bold steps, supported by the entry of financial enterprise into the field of health provision.[51]

Neoliberal strategists and administrators have effectively redefined health, basing it on individual biological characteristics and a personally acquired potential for 'wellbeing'. The balance between health and disease presumably varies across the life cycle, but the responsibility for health falls squarely on the shoulders of each person. Treatment strategies strive to augment the biologically inherited or personally acquired endowment of the virtuous – and preferably wealthy – individual.[52] This conception of health has gradually dominated the relevant institutions, providing the basis for a widespread individualistic approach to health.

It is important to note that socially minded medics have continued to advocate a different approach that demands 'upending the medical hierarchy, putting public health, primary care, and community care at the top and downgrading (or maybe I should write revering less) specialists'.[53] The necessary changes should not be the exclusive concern of the medical profession but also involve the broad public.[54] Unfortunately, the pandemic made things even worse, as Big Pharma hijacked the fight against Covid-19 with the connivance of the governments of core countries.

The medical context: Biomedicine and epidemiology

The rise of the health management perspective has occurred within parameters established by biomedicine and epidemiology, two distinct scientific disciplines which have never been devoid of social determinants. Modern biomedicine seeks primarily to treat the ailments of individuals.[55] Epidemiology, on the other hand, considers entire populations with the aim of preventing illness from spreading, assesses the

51 See R. Janssen and J. van der Made (1990) 'Privatisation in Health Care: Concepts, Motives and Policies', *Health Policy* 14 (3): 191–202, p. 192.

52 All citations in this paragraph come from J. Bircher (2005) 'Towards a Dynamic Definition of Health and Disease', *Med Health Care Philos.* 8 (3): 335–41.

53 See R. Smith (2018) 'How Medicine Is Destroying Itself', *BMJ Opinion*, 19 February, at blogs.bmj.com.

54 Callahan and Nuland (2011) 'How American Medicine Is Destroying Itself'.

55 Rosenberg (1992) *Explaining Epidemics and Other Studies in the History of Medicine.*

distribution of diseases, and identifies risk factors that ultimately affect morbidity.[56]

At the risk of oversimplification, biomedicine treats health in biological terms, proposing physical remedies for conditions ascertained through medical tests and prescribing mostly medicinal or surgical therapeutic interventions. It became dominant in most Western countries after the Second World War, helped by the rise of health insurance and the growth of pharmaceutical corporations.[57] During the Cold War, it dominated clinics and university curricula, securing its ascent by obtaining state and private funds that were previously unimaginable in the medical sciences.[58] At present, it is the standard intellectual framework for health work, and rests on global institutions that exercise a decisive influence over medical and health policy.[59]

Fundamental to biomedicine is the confluence of molecular life sciences, modelling, and clinical experimentation. On this basis, the biology laboratory became the locus of discovery, causal explication, manipulation, and control of pathological processes, while marginalising the pathology clinic.[60] Medicine began increasingly to look like biology.[61] Critics soon pointed out that biological sciences were quite distinct from medicine, while both had important interactions with other sciences.[62]

---

56 Baer, Singer, and Susser (eds) (2003) *Medical Anthropology and the World System*, p. 25.

57 On the rise of biomedicine, see V. Quirke and J.-P. Gaudillière (2008) 'The Era of Biomedicine: Science, Medicine, and Public Health in Britain and France after the Second World War', *Medical History* 52: 441–52, p. 442. Its historical origins lie in German scientific laboratories, where the foundations of cell theory, tumour theory, and cellular pathology among others were elucidated; see P. Keating and A. Cambrosio (2004) 'Does Biomedicine Entail the Successful Reduction of Pathology to Biology?' *Perspectives in Biology and Medicine* 47: 357–71, p. 361. See also I. Löwy (2011) 'Historiography of Biomedicine: "Bio," "Medicine," and in Between', *Isis* 102 (1): 116–22, p. 117.

58 W. G. Rothstein (1987) *American Medical Schools and the Practice of Medicine: A History*, Oxford University Press: Oxford and New York, pp. 220–80.

59 S. Valles (2020) 'Philosophy of Biomedicine', in E. N. Zalta (ed.) *The Stanford Encyclopedia of Philosophy*, at plato.stanford.edu.

60 Jean-Paul Gaudillière (2002) *Inventer la biomédecine: La France, l'Amérique et la production des savoirs du vivant (1945–1965)*, La Découverte: Paris, p. 369.

61 'Medicine, as we all know, is one of the branches of biology. It is applied biology, like agriculture', see M. Stoker (1980) 'New Medicine and New Biology', *BMJ* 281: 1678–82. For another institutionally powerful scientist, biomedicine aspired to reduce 'the problems of disease to problems of molecular science': see K. A. Dill (1999) 'Strengthening Biomedicine's Roots', *Nature* 400 (6742): 309–10.

62 A. Schechter (1999) 'Medicine and Biology Are More Than Biomedicine', *Nature* 401: 424.

Health provision ought to aim at continually realigning medicine with biology rather than reducing medical practice into (lavishly remunerated and hierarchically produced) biology.[63]

A radical critique of received biomedical wisdom was formed in the 1970s by Thomas McKeown, the 'founder of social medicine'.[64] For McKeown, a leading British physician with rich clinical experience, declining mortality in recent centuries was due to rising living standards and better nutrition, rather than biomedical progress. Biomedical ideas were informed by a mechanistic conception of the human body associated with capitalist ideologies and practices. Medicine is wider than clinical care, and broad social factors are the primary historical determinants of health.[65]

In the 1970s, it was still possible to believe that the scientific establishment was dedicated to the pursuit of knowledge independently of other considerations.[66] In truth, that was never the case, and the research agendas of several scientific fields reflected Cold War considerations. Since the 1970s, however, as corporate business became dominant, an entirely different world emerged in medical scientific work. Molecular biology became a gigantic business across several fields, including pharmaceuticals, chemistry, agriculture, information systems, and veterinary medicine. Laboratories and academic health centres proliferated at universities, while scientists made fortunes by actively commercialising their research. The traditional norms of scientific research died a long time ago, as jobs, teaching posts, and access to private and public funding became appendages to commercial success.[67]

---

63 Keating and Cambrosio (2004) 'Does Biomedicine Entail the Successful Reduction of Pathology to Biology?' p. 368.

64 See A. Deaton (2015) *The Great Escape: Health, Wealth, and the Origins of Inequality,* Princeton University Press: Princeton, New York, p. 91. McKeown's main arguments can be found in T. McKeown (1979) *The Role of Medicine: Dream, Mirage, or Nemesis?* Princeton University Press: Princeton, NJ. On the early reception of McKeown's and Cochrane's ideas among medics, see C. Alvarez-Dardet and M. T. Ruiz (1993) 'Thomas McKeown and Archibald Cochrane: A Journey through the Diffusion of their Ideas', *BMJ* 306: 1252. See also J. Lawson (2003) 'Rethinking McKeown', *Am. J. Public Health* 93 (7): 1032.

65 A complementary perspective on the same issues is presented in another seminal work: S. Federici (2004) *Caliban and the Witch: Women, Body, and Primitive Accumulation,* Autonomedia: New York. On McKeown's legacy, see Alvarez-Dardet and Ruiz (1993) 'Thomas McKeown and Archibald Cochrane'.

66 S. Krimsky (2019) *Conflicts of Interest In Science: How Corporate-Funded Academic Research Can Threaten Public Health,* Hot Books: New York, p. 1.

67 Things worsened considerably once US law recognised patents for genetic

When Covid-19 struck, its characteristic features were largely unknown, and biomedicine was of little immediate use. As deaths mounted, particularly among the old, there was an urgent need to protect the victims, thus opening space for epidemiology. This scientific discipline also took shape in the nineteenth century but remains a 'multi-site tradition' with a disputed status and in constant tension with biomedicine.[68] Epidemiology is typically mobilised by governments to decide which individuals would benefit from biomedicine as well as which social groups would have their health bolstered through public action.[69]

Deploying several scientific traditions and practices, epidemiologists focus primarily on the occurrence of diseases in populations and their health outcomes. The field has steadily broadened from communicable diseases and epidemics to cover all phenomena relating to health in populations.[70] Dissent is an integral part of this discipline, and controversies relate even to the definitions of its fundamental notions. Epidemiology is a diverse and eclectic discipline that seeks to integrate social practice and scientific analysis.[71]

---

constructions; see A. Kaplan, 'Foreword' to Krimsky (2019) *Conflicts of Interest in Science*.

68 See J. Breilh (2021) *Critical Epidemiology and the People's Health*, Oxford University Press: New York, pp. 13–14; on Virchow's towering presence in this field too, see also R. Taylor and A. Rieger (1985) 'Medicine as Social Science: Rudolf Wirchow on the Typhus Epidemic in Upper Silesia', *International Journal of Health Services* 15 (4): 547–59. For an overview of Chinese epidemiology, see L. Huigang et al. (2020) 'A Brief History of the Development of Infectious Disease Prevention, Control, and Biosafety Programs in China', *Journal of Biosafety and Biosecurity* 2 (1): 23–6. See primarily Rosenberg (1992) *Explaining Epidemics and Other Studies in the History of Medicine*, ch. 13. As regards the historical and relative meaning of this term, see also J. N. Hays (2009 [1998]) *The Burdens of Disease: Epidemics and Human Response in Western History*, Rutgers University Press: New Brunswick, NJ, p. 4ff.

69 For further detail, see Marchetos (2022) 'Epidemics and Syndemics in Historical Perspective'.

70 See R. H. Friis (2018) *Epidemiology 101*, Jones & Bartlett Learning: Burlington, MA, p. 22. See also Term 'Epidemiology, demarcation of', in *A Dictionary of Epidemiology* (2014) edited for the International Epidemiological Association by M. Porta, Oxford University Press: Oxford, New York, p. 96. See further the lemma 'Epidemiology', in M. Porta (ed.) (2014) *A Dictionary of Epidemiology*, p. 95. Moreover, epidemiology as a professional discipline can be considered anomalous, its characteristics evoking those of traditional liberal arts; see D. W. Fraser (1987) 'Epidemiology as a Liberal Art', *N. Engl. J. Med.* 316: 309–14, p. 309.

71 See C. Victora, N. Pearce, and J. Olsen, preamble to Porta (ed.) (2014) *A Dictionary of Epidemiology*, p. v. See also M. Porta, 'Preface' to Porta (ed.) (2014) *A*

When Covid-19 struck, epidemiologists reviewed the handling of previous epidemics, particularly AIDS. For decades, AIDS prevention and treatment among the rich had received lavish funding, while the disease continued to spread mainly among the poor.[72] Instead of providing focused care for the sick, resources were squandered on puritanical propaganda campaigns for primary prevention. The mantra of 'limited resources' facilitated the spread of AIDS among the weak, while the socially privileged layers enjoyed treatments whose wider application was deemed 'not sustainable' for their 'inferiors'. The importance of this result by epidemiologists became clear when Covid-19 struck and medical resources for workers and the poor were in short supply, while Big Pharma took charge of the overall medical response.

The pathology of Big Pharma

The pharmaceutical sector in advanced capitalist economies essentially comprises two tiers. At the lower level there is a galaxy of generally smaller enterprises that focus on manufacturing and trading of medicines that are often off-patent (generic) or licensed by patent holders. At a higher level stands Big Pharma: a handful of giant corporations dominating biomedicine and possessing enormous economic and political clout across the world.

Big Pharma is essentially unaccountable to society, even if its regulation by the state appears strong on paper. Its close links (financial and otherwise) with government health agencies make its regulation practically ineffectual. Despite an appalling record regarding public health, Big Pharma continues to extract vast profits by drawing on state-protected patents, tax breaks, and systematic exploitation of publicly funded research. Political reactions to its disastrous impact on public health are generally lame, and social scientists, who should have been

---

Dictionary of Epidemiology, p. xiv. Irrespective of its stance on the pandemic and the use of vaccines, the recent polemic by R. F. Kennedy Jr is especially poignant on AIDS policy; see R. F. Kennedy Jr (2021) *The Real Anthony Fauci: Bill Gates, Big Pharma, and the Global War on Democracy and Public Health*, Skyhorse Publishing: New York.

72 See 'Preface to the Paperback Edition', in P. Farmer (2008) *Infections and Inequalities: The Modern Plagues*, University of California Press: Berkeley, CA. See also P. Mayaud, S. Hawkes, and D. Mabey (1998) 'Advances in Control of Sexually Transmitted Diseases in Developing Countries', *The Lancet* 351, Supplement III: 29–32, p. 31.

putting forth critical analyses of its doings, are 'too busy scrambling for their piece of the pie'.[73]

Big Pharma plays a decisive role in the direction of biomedical research by orchestrating the activities of publicly funded research laboratories, prominent research universities, and venture capitalists. It holds the bulk of the intellectual property rights (patents) that allow medicines to be commodified.[74] It dominates the global production networks of medicines, aggressively trades biomedical provision, and extracts profits at the expense of public budgets, research institutions, and consumers.[75] Despite its record, or perhaps because of it, Big Pharma emerged as a winner from Covid-19.

Moreover, the pharmaceutical sector is highly financialised, and the deeper significance of this point will become clearer in parts II and III. Suffice it to say that Big Pharma tends to focus on accumulating huge liquid reserves while limiting investment in its physical capacity to produce medicines. Its exposure to capital markets has increased substantially, as have its financial pay-outs to shareholders, which typically exceed spending on research and development.[76] Big Pharma operates globally, invests modestly, interacts closely with financial markets, and ruthlessly exploits intellectual property rights in medicines.[77] Its very existence is a historical singularity and an epochal disgrace.

The overpowering presence of Big Pharma has created multiple pathologies in health provision. For one thing, there is systematic neglect of the medicinal needs of poorer parts of the world that are unable to produce drugs due to general lack of research funding, adequate regulatory and ethical frameworks, and appropriate technical infrastructure and personnel.[78] Across peripheral countries, it is

---

73 See Farmer (2008) *Infections and Inequalities*, p. xxii.

74 D. Brown et al. (2019) 'Working Paper: Democratic Public Ownership in the UK Pharmaceutical Sector', The Democracy Collaborative, Global Justice Now, Working Paper, p. 3, at globaljustice.org.uk.

75 See R. Fernandez and T. J. Klinge (2020) *Private Gains We Can Ill Afford: The Financialisation of Big Pharma*, Stichting Onderzoek Multinationale Ondernemingen (SOMO) (The Centre for Research on Multinational Corporations), Amsterdam, p. 16. See also C. Rikap (2019) 'Asymmetric Power of the Core: Technological Cooperation and Technological Competition in the Transnational Innovation Networks of Big Pharma', *Review of International Political Economy* 26 (5): 987–1021.

76 Fernandez and Klinge (2020) *Private Gains We Can Ill Afford*, pp. 21–9.

77 Ibid., pp. 29–30.

78 See C. H. Barrios and M. S. Mano (2021) 'Is Independent Clinical Research Possible in Low- and Middle-Income Countries? A Roadmap to Address Persistent and New

practically impossible to engage in research in medical provision that is not controlled by Big Pharma. The result is that pharmaceutical research tends to focus on the needs of relatively better-off populations rather than on global health problems.

In addition, Big Pharma's dominant position in medical research favours the production of 'persistently one-sided studies that can no longer be questioned by studies from other sides'.[79] Evaluating pharmaceutical data is based on studies published in scientific journals that belong to private profit-making enterprises. Well-meaning regulations notwithstanding, journals are far from shining beacons of academic freedom.[80] An editor of *The Lancet*, a leading medical journal, called the periodicals 'information laundering operations for the pharmaceutical industry'.[81] The reason is not hard to ascertain. Publishing favourable studies of medicinal trials brings substantial benefits to journals, as Big Pharma appreciates good publicity.[82]

Published medical papers that become a matter of public record meticulously hide their one-sidedness, often with catastrophic results for genuine scientific inquiry. The problem could, perhaps, be attenuated by having obligatory clinical trial registrations and making public all data submitted to regulatory authorities, but Big Pharma does not accept this practice. A more radical remedy to ease the stranglehold of the pharmaceutical industry on medical research programmes would be independent funding for clinical research.[83]

With the support of governments, Big Pharma took charge of core country responses to Covid-19 in conjunction with biomedical research laboratories and other private agents. Not surprisingly, Covid-19 proved the inequality virus *par excellence*, disproportionately impacting the

---

Barriers and Challenges', *American Society of Clinical Oncology Educational Book* 41: 221–30.

79 See J. P. Vandenbroucke (2005) 'Rapid Response: Without New Rules for Industry-Sponsored Research, Science Will Cease to Exist', *BMJ* 331: 1350.

80 P. C. Gøtzsche (2013) *Deadly Medicines and Organised Crime: How Big Pharma Has Corrupted Healthcare*, Radcliffe Publishing: London, New York, p. 62.

81 R. Horton (2004) 'The Dawn of McScience', *The New York Review of Books* 51 (4), 11 March, at nybooks.com.

82 R. Smith (2005) 'Medical Journals Are an Extension of the Marketing Arm of Pharmaceutical Companies', *PLoS Med.* 2 (5): e138. See also See M. Egger, C. Bartlett, and P. Jüni (2001) 'Are Randomised Controlled Trials in the BMJ Different?' *BMJ* (Clinical research ed.) 323 (7323): 1253–4.

83 Barrios and Mano (2021) 'Is Independent Clinical Research Possible in Low- and Middle-Income Countries?' pp. 221–30.

weak in terms of both health and economic wellbeing.[84] In the USA, for instance, life expectancy declined precipitously between 2018 and 2021, and the fall affected mostly poor communities that also suffer from racial discrimination.[85] The pandemic also caused devastation in several peripheral countries that increasingly relied on the provision of vaccines produced by Big Pharma. Poverty escalated sharply across the world.[86]

In sum, the health emergency was a historic moment in the development of mature capitalism, displaying in condensed form the deep class inequalities within and across the countries of the world. The policy response to the epidemic made clear that far from converging as capitalism became global, countries are increasingly diverging, while internal social divisions have become deeper. Moreover, medicine is not a classless human achievement but a scientific and practical endeavour that has become a field of capitalist profit riven with class divisions. The pandemic thus raised pivotal issues about the character of contemporary capitalist accumulation and the resulting state contestations in the world economy. These are considered in the rest of this book.

84 See S. Ali, M. Asaria, and S. Stranges (2020) 'COVID-19 and Inequality: Are We All in This Together?' *Can. J. Public Health* 111: 415–16. Even liberal charities summarised in damning terms the resultant inequalities: see Oxfam International (2021) The Inequality Virus, at oxfamilibrary.openrepository.com.

85 S. H. Woolf et al. (2021) 'Effect of the Covid-19 Pandemic in 2020 on Life Expectancy across Populations in the USA and Other High Income Countries: Simulations of Provisional Mortality Data', *BMJ* 373: n1343; R. K. Masters, L. Y. Aron, and S. H. Woolf (2022) 'Changes in Life Expectancy between 2019 and 2021 in the United States and 21 Peer Countries', *JAMA Network Open*.

86 G. Therborn (Ljungbyholm) (2020) 'Opus Magnum: How the Pandemic is Changing the World', *Thesis Eleven*, 6 July, at thesiseleven.com. See also the estimates by World Bank staff in D. G. Mahler et al. (2022) 'Pandemic, Prices, and Poverty', *World Bank Data Blog*, 13 April, at blogs.worldbank.org.

PART II

The State and Domestic Accumulation at the Core

When Covid-19 arrived, the world economy was already in precarious circumstances, and once lockdowns and other restrictions were imposed by core and peripheral states, a global economic crisis began to take shape.

Lockdowns and restrictions resembled war, since they entailed curfews, forcible interruption of economic activity, and direct state intervention in production, the financial sector, and the labour market. They also severely disrupted supply chains across the world, making it difficult for producers to access manufactured and other inputs. Together with the great uncertainty caused by the rapid spread of the disease, the measures led to a collapse of private investment, propelling mature capitalist economies toward an unprecedented fall in output in the first half of 2020. Household consumption also fell precipitously and saving increased, exacerbating recessionary pressures. To cap it all, in early 2020, conditions in financial markets became extremely tight, and a sharp financial crisis was in the offing.

The extraordinary contraction of output in early 2020 brought rapid increases in unemployment and exacerbated poverty, creating conditions of severe material deprivation across core and peripheral countries. Workers, the poor, and the marginal layers of society bore the heaviest burden of the lockdowns. Labour was undertaken 'at distance' across broad swathes of enterprises and public institutions, further expanding the already broad grey area of neither work nor leisure in contemporary capitalism.

Yet, the similarities between Covid-19 and war do not go very far. The economic impact of lockdowns bore no relation to what normally happens after the outbreak of war, typically including wholesale redirection of productive capacity and restriction of private consumption to make resources available for military purposes. Instead, lockdowns sparked off an economic crisis that had several features in common with other crises of financialised capitalism seen during the last four decades.

When the magnitude of the emerging economic disaster became clear, core states took unprecedented actions to confront it. The first port of call was monetary policy. Central banks in the USA, the European Union (EU), and Japan engaged in massive liquidity injections, pushing interest rates toward zero. The authorities relied on creating fiat money backed by state power, the counterpart of which was gigantic acquisition of public (and private) debt by the central banks. State-created liquidity relaxed the tight conditions in the financial markets, setting off an extraordinary boom in stock markets in 2020–21, at a time when core economies faced a deep recession.

Loose monetary policy had already been implemented in the Great Crisis of 2007–09. However, in the early 2020s, fiscal policy also expanded enormously across core countries, creating huge budget deficits as public spending rose and the tax intake initially fell due to contracting output. The fiscal expansion in the USA, the EU, and elsewhere took the form of subsidies for corporations to cover wage bills and keep workers in employment, deferrals of tax and social security payments, debt holidays, loan and credit guarantees for companies, direct subvention of money to households, and so on.

In the Pandemic Crisis, the state emerged as an overriding economic agent in contemporary capitalism, capable of generating gigantic economic crises as well as rescuing capitalist accumulation. State intervention briskly set aside the precepts and prescriptions of austerity and deregulation, and even led to nationalisation of fundamental components of capitalist accumulation.[1] Central banks positioned themselves

---

1 State-imposed restrictions and economic intervention in core countries gave a broad reach to the hypothesis of 'techno-feudalism', originally denoting the spontaneous creation of hierarchical power networks around firms seeking to 'protect our own first'. In these networks, capitalist giants act unchecked, while the figure of the citizen is eclipsed as identities are organised around market links; see, C. Durand (2020) *Techno-féodalisme: Critique de l'économie numérique*, La Découverte: Paris.

as the leading public institutions in the economic arena, relying on absolute command over the final means of payment.

As several of the policy shibboleths of the last four decades were swept aside, it was easy to imagine that the end of neoliberalism had arrived. But that was premature. The state has always been at the heart of neoliberal capitalism, guaranteeing the rule of the dominant corporate and financial bloc of the capitalist class through selective interventions at critical moments. The monetary and fiscal policies of core states in 2020–21 defended primarily the interests of big business, intensifying inequality and sowing the seeds of further economic disturbance. Above all – indicating the persistence of neoliberalism – core states resisted actively reshaping the sphere of production by challenging private property rights and shifting the balance of power in favour of labour and against capital.[2]

Despite also pursuing extensive intervention, peripheral states were largely unable to replicate the monetary and fiscal expansion implemented by core states. Middle- and low-income countries faced limits in boosting fiscal spending as well as encountering international currency constraints when it came to monetary expansion. The rapid accumulation of public debt in the early 2020s posed a major threat to peripheral countries compared with the core states. Divergence characterised state economic intervention across the world, as it also did for state policies to confront the health emergency.

State measures allowed neoliberal capitalism to cope with the economic blows of the pandemic, but its condition remained deeply precarious and became even worse as the turmoil of the 2020s grew. At the root of this lay the weakness of capitalist accumulation in core countries, exacerbated by the advance of financialisation for several decades; the writing had been on the wall since the Great Crisis of 2007–09, as shown in the following chapters.

---

2 State actions fit the hypothesis of a steady drift of Western societies away from liberal values in favour of conceptions of group identity that increase divisions and political frictions. This hypothesis is not far removed from another, namely that liberal hegemony is giving way to a resurgence of a conservative extreme right, a trend that started before the pandemic and accelerated through the agency of powerful oligarchies. Such debates proliferated in the circles of radical critics of contemporary society at the time of the pandemic; see, for instance, N. Ahmed (2020) 'White Supremacism and the Earth System: The Protests, the Pandemic, and the Planet from Systemic Decline to Civilizational Renewal', Insurge Intelligence, at medium.com/insurge-intelligence.

3

Financialised Capitalism and the Quake of 2007–09

The Great Crisis of 2007–09 is a landmark in the development of contemporary capitalism. Its fundamental features have been extensively discussed in the social sciences, and there were certainly several causes that led to it.[1] But there is little doubt that the gigantic shock sprang out of the aggressive financialisation of core countries during the preceding two decades. The 1990s and 2000s were the golden era of financialisation, especially in the USA. Marked by the US real estate bubble of 2001–06, that period came to an end in 2007–09.

Equally important is that the crisis laid the ground for the protracted weakness of accumulation at the core of the world economy in the 2010s. The collapse of financial markets and the precipitous decline in economic activity in 2020, as well as the extraordinary policies implemented by

---

1 The immediate causes of the crisis in the USA are to be found in the burst of the housing bubble of the 2000s; see, for instance, R. Dodd (2007) 'Subprime: Tentacles of a Crisis', *Finance & Development* 44 (4): 15–19, at imf.org. Crucial to the bubble was the proliferation of mortgage-backed securities on the balance sheets of financial enterprises. For a coherent mainstream account, see V. Acharya and M. Richardson (2009) 'Causes of the Financial Crisis', *Critical Review* 21 (2): 195–210. Indeed, the crisis reflected deep changes in the operations of financial capitals that are examined in the rest of part II. The Great Crisis also made apparent the pernicious role of big banks, which posed a systemic threat to contemporary economies; see D. Duffie (2011) *How Big Banks Fail and What to Do about It*, Princeton University Press: Princeton, NJ. Fundamentally, however, the crisis of 2007–09 reflected the changing balance of capitalist accumulation across the world and the associated pre-eminence of finance in the USA and Western Europe; see P. Gowan (2009) 'Crisis in the Heartland: Consequences of the New World System', *New Left Review* 55: 5–29.

core states to deal with the shock, have their roots in the crisis of 2007–09. The turmoil of the early 2020s accelerated the unravelling of financialised capitalism that began in the late 2000s.

This chapter highlights the significance of financialisation for the operations of financial enterprises in core countries, particularly regarding securitisation and the rise of shadow banking.[2] The latter phenomena characterised the 2010s, shaping the role of the state in core countries – especially of central banks – and contributing to the flagging of capitalist accumulation. They are prominent features of financialised capitalism and will be further considered in subsequent chapters.

Financialisation of core countries

The vast literature on financialisation in the social sciences has not produced an agreed meaning for the term.[3] The approach taken in this book treats financialisation as a historical transformation of mature capitalism reflecting, first, the extraordinary growth of the financial sector relative to the rest of the economy and, second, the spread of financial practices and concerns amid non-financial enterprises and other fundamental agents of capitalist accumulation.[4]

To be more specific, in recent decades, large non-financial enterprises have become less reliant on banks for the financing of investment, and indeed possess huge volumes of temporarily idle funds available for

---

2 This analytical account of the crisis of 2007–09 and its aftermath in this section draws heavily on C. Lapavitsas and I. Mendieta Muñoz (2018) 'Financialization at a Watershed in the USA', *Competition & Change* 22 (5): 488–508; and (2019) 'The Historic Rise of Financial Profits in the U.S. Economy', *Journal of Post Keynesian Economics* 42 (3): 443–68. It also draws on the brief discussion of current economic trends in C. Lapavitsas et al. (2020) 'A Pandemic Basic Income to Confront the Crisis', Rosa Luxemburg Stiftung Policy Paper No. 2020/2. December.

3 The lack of clear meaning was noted by B. Christophers (2015) 'The Limits to Financialization', *Dialogues in Human Geography* 5 (2): 183–200. For key definitions, see G. Krippner (2005) 'The Financialization of the American Economy', *Socio-Economic Review* 3: 173–208; T. I. Palley (2007) 'Financialisation: What It Is and Why It Matters', The Levy Economics Institute Working Paper No. 529; C. Lapavitsas (2011) 'Theorizing Financialization', *Work, Employment and Society* 25 (4): 611–26. A still useful survey is N. van der Zwan (2014) 'Making Sense of Financialization', *Socio-Economic Review* 12 (1): 99–129.

4 For a fuller discussion, see C. Lapavitsas (2013) *Profiting without Producing: How Finance Exploits Us All*, Verso: London.

lending. Banks, on the other hand, have broadened their profit-seeking activities by providing mediation services in open financial markets, a process that has also encouraged the growth of shadow banking. Finally, workers and households from other social classes have been drawn into the networks of finance as debtors but also as holders of financial assets, for instance, pension policies. One of the most striking features of financialisation is the penetration of finance into the economic activities of workers and the middle classes, transforming both the outlook and the conventional practices of housing, education, health, and other areas of social life.

The sustained rise of financialisation during the last four decades is attested – to varying extents – across core capitalist countries, with the USA and UK as paradigmatic countries.[5] Debt has grown across most of the core economies, although with significant fluctuations indicating major shifts in financialisation, as is considered in this and subsequent chapters. Since the early 2000s, financialisation was also observed – with even more variation – in developing countries, exacerbating the phenomena of international financial subordination discussed in chapter 13.

Perhaps the most pervasive structural feature of financialisation, however, is the shift of financial systems across the world in a market-based direction. The distinction between market-based and bank-based financial systems arose in the early days of capitalist industrialisation and is considered in detail in subsequent chapters, including in

5 For an early mainstream analysis of the altered role of intermediaries within domestic markets, see T. Adrian and H. S. Shin (2010) *The Changing Nature of Financial Intermediation and the Financial Crisis of 2007–09*, Federal Reserve Bank of New York Staff Reports No. 439. A discussion from a critical perspective and in broader terms can be found in E. Stockhammer (2010) 'Financialisation and the Global Economy', PERI Working Paper Series No. 240. The financialisation of non-financial corporations, the shift toward shareholder value, and the changes of corporate behaviour in line with financial interests were discussed by O. Orhangazi (2007) 'Financialization and Capital Accumulation in the Non-Financial Corporate Sector: A Theoretical and Empirical Investigation of the U.S. Economy: 1973–2003', Political Economy Research Institute (PERI) Working Paper Series No. 149; see also O. Orhangazi (2008) *Financialization and the US Economy*, Edward Elgar: Cheltenham, UK, and Northampton, MA. For the financialisation of households – both the rise of indebtedness and the proliferation of pensions and financial assets owned by households – see P. L. dos Santos (2009) 'At the Heart of the Matter: Household Debt in Contemporary Banking and the International Crisis', *Ekonomiaz* 72: 54–77. For a mainstream view on this topic, see also R. Rajan (2011) *Fault Lines: How Hidden Fractures Still Threaten the World Economy*, Princeton University Press: Princeton, NJ.

connection with shadow finance. To give a rather ruthless summary, market-based financial systems rely on open markets for finance, and at the same time banks tend to operate with relatively short horizons and at arm's length from their borrowers. A bank-based system, in contrast, assigns much less prominence to open financial markets, while banks maintain a close (and even controlling) influence over their borrowers.

Among core countries, the classic twentieth-century instances of market-based systems are found in the UK and the USA; for bank-based systems, the reference countries are Germany and Japan. Peripheral countries across the world, including those in which powerful concentrations of capitalist accumulation have emerged, still have primarily bank-based systems. In the decades of financialisation, however, financial sectors across the world increasingly adopted market-based practices, including in countries that have bank-based systems. This development reflects the underlying transformation of capitalist accumulation and has profound implications for the role of the state in the economy.

The financialisation of capitalism is sometimes considered to be the return of the rentier, or the rise of the rentier economy.[6] In the traditional and historical sense of the word, a rentier is a holder of loanable money capital who makes it available at interest rather than investing it directly to produce profit. This traditional image is probably what Keynes had in mind when he suggested that suppressing interest rates would be 'the euthanasia of the rentier'.[7] But the traditional rentier is not particularly relevant to financialised capitalism.

---

6 For a recent rendition of this view, see B. Christophers (2020) *Rentier Capitalism: Who Owns the Economy, and Who Pays for it?* Verso: London. For the rentier as money owner shifting funds from the productive to the financial sector, see, selectively, J. Crotty (1990) 'Owner–Manager Conflict and Financial Theory of Investment Stability: A Critical Assessment of Keynes, Tobin, and Minsky', *Journal of Post Keynesian Economics* 12(4): 519–42; F. Demir (2007) 'The Rise of Rentier Capitalism and the Financialization of Real Sectors in Developing Countries', *Review of Radical Political Economy* 39 (3): 351–9; R. Pollin (2007) 'The Resurrection of the Rentier', *New Left Review* 46 (July/August): 140–53; and G. Epstein (ed.) (2005) *Financialization and the World Economy*, Edward Elgar: Northampton, MA. For the role of the rentier in extracting financial profits, see G. Epstein and A. Jayadev (2005) 'The Rise of Rentier Incomes in OECD Countries: Financialization, Central Bank Policy and Labor Solidarity', in G. Epstein (ed.) *Financialization and the World Economy*, pp. 46–74. See also G. Epstein (2001) 'Financialization, Rentier Interests, and Central Bank Policy', Paper prepared for PERI Conference on Financialization of the World Economy, 7–8 December, University of Massachusetts, Amherst, MA.

7 J. M. Keynes (1973) *The General Theory of Employment, Interest and Money*, Macmillan: London.

The golden era of financialisation exhibited declining and generally low rates of interest, which reached extraordinarily low levels in recent years. And yet, despite low interest rates, the oligarchic upper layer of the capitalist class continued to accumulate fabulous wealth. The secret of such wealth accumulation has lain with capital gains and direct profit extraction from the income and money holdings of others. Wealth has indeed accrued from property in capital, taking the form of financial assets and allowing capitalists to appropriate, first, surplus value generated domestically as well as abroad and, second, parts of the money holdings and income of working people and other classes. Wealth accrual took advantage of proliferating financial expropriation, a characteristic feature of predatory financialised capitalism.[8]

Rentiers that draw income from advancing loanable capital at interest do not form a distinct layer within the capitalist class of contemporary core countries. Rather, surplus value and money holdings – including those belonging to other classes – are constantly reallocated primarily within and across the capitalist class through a range of financial enterprises and markets. The reallocation depends on property rights over financial assets but also on the hierarchical positions within the management structures of financial and non-financial enterprises. The privileged layer that dominates social and political life is the main beneficiary; its role proved instrumental to the bubble that eventually led to the disaster of 2007–09.

The bubble of 2001–06: International capital flows and domestic speculation

The immediate processes that led to the bubble of 2001–06 can be traced to the burst of the earlier dot.com bubble in the US stock market that occurred in the late 1990s. In response, the Federal Reserve, the central bank of the USA, lowered interest rates rapidly and decisively in 2001. Soon after that, household debt in the USA began to expand enormously, mostly in the form of housing mortgages. The growth of housing debt occurred in conjunction with furious financial speculation pivoting on the securitisation of mortgages.

---

8 See Lapavitsas (2013) *Profiting without Producing.*

In sharp contrast to the preceding dot.com bubble, that of 2001–06 was not driven by the stock market.[9] Borrowing by non-financial enterprises was also a secondary feature of the financial expansion during those years. The rise in financial asset prices had a limited impact on investment, which remained generally modest in the USA and other core countries during that period. Moreover, the easy availability of household credit kept consumption at high levels, but there was no consumer boom in either the USA or Europe in the 2000s, particularly as real wage growth remained subdued.

Rather, the bubble – and the ensuing crash – of the 2000s pivoted on the mortgage market and its related financial processes, bringing together the underlying strains of financialised capitalism. It reflected the ascendancy of market-based finance, including commercial and shadow banking in core economies, with disastrous implications for both economy and society.

It is instructive to note that in the first half of the 2000s, as the bubble was forming in the USA, there was widespread discussion among mainstream economists and state officials regarding a putative savings glut (that is, an excess of savings over investment) in developing countries (particularly East Asian and oil-exporting countries). The glut of funds was presumably directed toward the USA and other core countries, inducing the expansion of US finance.[10]

---

9 See C. Whalen (2007) 'The U.S. Credit Crunch of 2007: A Minsky Moment', Public Policy Brief No. 92, The Levy Economics Institute, for an analysis of financial innovation (securitisation) and the burst of the preceding dot.com bubble, which pushed financial operators to consider real estate as a safer option in a period of low interest rates.

10 This view was articulated by Ben Bernanke, the Governor of the Federal Reserve; see B. S. Bernanke (2005) 'The Global Savings Glut and the U.S. Current Account Deficit', Sandridge Lecture, Virginia Association of Economics, March 10, at bis.org. See also B. S. Bernanke (2015) 'Why Are Interest Rates So Low, Part 3: The Global Savings Glut', Brookings, 1 April, at brookings.edu. The presumed glut was obviously related to current account imbalances; see, for instance, O. J. Blanchard and G. M. Milesi-Ferretti (2009) 'Global Imbalances: In Midstream?' IMF Staff Position Note SPN/09/29. The USA as receiver of the foreign funds and a safe haven is discussed by R. J. Caballero, E. Farhi, and P. O. Gourinchas (2008) 'Financial Crash, Commodity Prices and Global Imbalances', NBER Working Paper No. 14521. The importance of capital flows from developing countries to finance the US current account deficit is highlighted in M. Obstfeld and K. Rogoff (2009) 'Global Imbalances and the Financial Crisis: Products of Common Causes', Paper prepared for the Federal Reserve Bank of San Francisco Asia Economic Policy Conference, Santa Barbara, CA, 18–20 October.

It became clear, soon after the crisis of 2007–09, that there was little substance to this argument.[11] The financial bubble and the ensuing crash were primarily an affair of core capitalist countries, particularly those bordering the North Atlantic. Net international fund flows from developing countries were supportive of the explosive growth of finance in core countries, not least by helping interest rates stay low. But the main external culprit of the US financial bubble was gross capital flows from European to US banks. German and French banks were an integral part of the escalating securitisation of mortgages.[12] They were also further cogs in the emerging mechanisms of shadow banking.

Global flows aside, the 2001–06 financial explosion in the USA was sustained primarily by domestically generated credit. The bubble was fundamentally due to financial speculation by private US financial institutions involving the securitisation of mortgages – that is, the pooling of mortgage loans to be sold as new financial instruments, instead of being kept on the books of the issuer. Flushed with cheap liquidity supplied by the Federal Reserve, commercial and investment banks, as well as a range of shadow financial institutions, created complex transaction chains involving the origination, pooling, and securitisation of mortgages. Securitisation was based on credit enhancing, rating, and insuring of the new assets available for sale. Financial institution profits came primarily from continuous transacting in such assets rather than from making mortgage loans.

The pooling of mortgages into securitised assets was supposed to isolate and price risk, particularly as mortgages were bunched into distinct groups of varying risk levels. Investors would presumably buy the new assets by making informed choices according to their own risk preferences.[13] On this convenient assumption, financial institutions

---

11 See C. Borio and P. Disyatat (2011) 'Global Imbalances and the Financial Crisis: Link or No Link?' BIS Working Papers No. 346, who rightly stress the difference between net and gross capital flows as well as that between 'financing' and 'savings'. For further elaboration, see C. Borio and P. Disyatat (2015) 'Capital Flows and the Current Account: Taking Financing (More) Seriously', BIS Working Papers No. 525 and Y. Akyüz (2017) 'Inequality, Financialization and Stagnation', South Centre Research Paper No. 73.

12 See Gowan (2009) 'Crisis in the Heartland'.

13 See Acharya and Richardson (2009) 'Causes of the Financial Crisis'. The worsening of loan quality due to securitisation is discussed in A. Berndt and A. Gupta (2008) 'Moral Hazard and Adverse Selection in the Originate-to-Distribute Model of Bank Credit', Working Paper, Tepper School of Business, Carnegie Mellon University; see also B. Keys et al. (2008) 'Did Securitization Lead to Lax Screening? Evidence from Subprime Loans', Quarterly Journal of Economics 125 (1): 307–62.

moved aggressively into the subprime mortgage field – that is, into providing mortgages to the poorest and most deprived sections of the US working class with a view to rapid securitisation. Loans were effectively pushed onto families that were highly unlikely to be able to service their housing debts in the future.

Financial speculation involving the working class of the USA – often its poorest metropolitan layers – and pivoting on shadow finance, was the prime culprit of the huge bubble that led to the collapse of 2007–09 and the ensuing global crisis. The uniqueness of this development in the history of capitalism cannot be overstressed.

Pernicious shadow finance: Securitisation and repo markets in the bubble of the 2000s

Securitisation has long existed in the US housing market, operating under the aegis of the government-sponsored enterprises (GSEs) that sustain housing provision in the USA.[14] The 2000s, however, witnessed the widespread entry of private financial institutions into mortgage securitisation, giving it an aggressively financialised character and changing the outlook of the GSEs.

The entry of financial speculators into the housing market also encouraged the growth of shadow finance, a rather imprecise term capturing a broad range of activities by several financial intermediaries, such as money market funds, mutual funds, hedge funds, and many others. Their functioning as specific forms of financial capital is considered in more detail in the following chapters, but suffice it to note here that they have a simple distinguishing feature, namely they are not commercial banks.[15] Even though they are often referred to as shadow banks, these institutions are more akin to financial portfolio managers, as is shown in chapter 5.

Shadow banks were instrumental to the financial bubble of 2001–06 for several reasons, key among which is that, since they are not

14 Namely, the Government Federal Home Loan Mortgage Corporation (Freddie Mac), the Federal National Mortgage Association (Fannie Mae), and the Government National Mortgage Association (Ginnie Mae).

15 See T. Lane (2013) 'Shedding Light on Shadow Banking', remarks by Mr Timothy Lane, Deputy Governor of the Bank of Canada, to the CFA Society Toronto, Toronto, Ontario, 26 June, at bis.org.

commercial banks, they are not allowed to take regular deposits from the public – that is, deposits that would normally count as money backed by a state guarantee. For the same reason, shadow banks do not have direct access to liquidity created by the central bank. Rather, they normally obtain wholesale funding in open financial markets by collecting loanable capital from pension funds, insurance companies, large corporations, rich capitalists, and others. The collected loanable capital is subsequently invested in a wide range of securities, including public and private bonds, corporate shares, derivatives, and more.

Securitisation is an integral aspect of shadow banking, allowing for loanable capital to be collected and lent again in open financial markets. It amounts essentially to the systematic creation of new securities based on existing securities – that is, new promises to pay that rest on delivering existing promises to pay. To engage in this practice, shadow banks must have regular access to abundant short-term funding, particularly as their complex portfolio strategies require large holdings of cash or other liquid funds. The implications of this development are profound, as is shown in subsequent chapters, but a brief discussion is necessary at this point – particularly of the repo market – to place the crisis of 2007–09 in appropriate context.

Reliance on short-term liquid funds characterises most financial institutions. Commercial banks, for instance, require short-term funds to meet obligations for immediate payments, such as deposit withdrawals. Banks obtain short-term funds by trading with each other in the money market, and ultimately with the central bank, which is the dominant bank of the money market. Shadow banks, however, cannot operate in the same way, particularly as they do not have direct access to central bank funds. Consequently, the sustained growth of shadow banking has been accompanied by the rise of new forms of short-term lending, including, above all, repurchase operations (repos). The growth of the repo market has placed its stamp on financialised capitalism.

Repos have become standard practice for both commercial banks and shadow intermediaries in the money markets of core countries.[16]

---

16 A simple introduction to the functions and applications of repos can be found in M. Choudhry (2006) *An Introduction to Repo Markets*, 3rd edition, Wiley: New York. Further, P. Hördahl and M. R. King (2008) 'Developments in Repo Markets during the Financial Turmoil', *BIS Quarterly Review*, December: 37–53, discuss the behaviour of repo markets relative to the size of financial shocks and the availability of risk-free collateral. For an integrated analysis of repo operations within the infrastructure of the

Essentially, they are transactions in loanable capital, in which a short-term loan takes place, with a security acting as collateral. The borrower sells to the lender a security (for instance, a public bond, or publicly backed mortgage debt). Simultaneously, the seller is contractually obligated to buy back the security after a short period of time – for instance, one to five days – at a price that is specified at the start of the transaction.[17] In effect, the seller borrows money from the buyer for a short period of time, and the buyer earns interest as the difference between the price at which the security is originally sold and the price at which it is repurchased.

Repo loans depend, crucially, on the quality of the collateral security, and the buyer typically seeks further protection for the loan through a so-called 'haircut' of the value of the security relative to the going market price. Indeed, the lender is often more interested in obtaining the security as collateral than in receiving interest. The reason is that the same security could subsequently be used again as collateral in further borrowing, allowing the original lender to engage in ever more complex forms of speculation. Public securities are fundamental to these transactions, and typically provide the best collateral.

Repos have become a standard way for central banks to operate in the money markets of financialised capitalism. They are fundamental to the wholesale liquidity that sustains the securitisation activities of a range of financial institutions, while also ensuring the overall liquidity of financial markets.[18] Some participants in the money market – for instance, the asset managers of investment funds, pension funds, hedge funds,

---

shadow banking system, see Z. Poszar et al. (2010) *Shadow Banking*, Federal Reserve Bank of New York Staff Report No. 458. A detailed evaluation of repo markets in core countries is offered by the Study Group of the Committee on the Global Financial System of the BIS (at BIS (2017) 'Repo Market Functioning', CGFS Papers No. 59). The Study Group suggested that reduced use of repos would improve financial stability by limiting liquidity risks and thus the vulnerability of financial institutions. For the heightened role of central banks in repo markets in the 2010s, see H. E. Ennis and J. Huther (2021) 'The Fed's Evolving Involvement in the Repo Markets', Economic Brief', *Federal Reserve Bank of Richmond*, pp. 21–31.

17 A reverse repo is the same set of transactions but seen from the perspective of the borrower, i.e. of the seller of the security who would buy it back. For more analytic descriptions, see BIS (2017) 'Repo Market Functioning'.

18 For an early analysis from a mainstream perspective, see M. K. Brunnermeier and L. H. Pedersen (2007) 'Market Liquidity and Funding Liquidity', *The Review of Financial Studies* 22 (6): 2201–38; see also G. Gorton and A. Metrick (2010) 'Regulating the Shadow Banking', *Brookings Papers on Economic Activity* 41 (2): 261–312.

and insurance companies – borrow by providing securities as collateral; others – for instance, the managers of money market funds and large corporations – lend.

It is vital to note that the repo market pivots on the state. Public bonds are the most important form of collateral, and, if they are in short supply, the repo market begins to malfunction. Furthermore, central banks intervene heavily in repo markets to regulate the overall liquidity of the financial system as well as to influence the short-term rate of interest. In these respects, the repo market reflects the tight interweaving of state, banks, and shadow intermediaries that has become particularly prominent during the last two decades.

The pernicious role of shadow banks together with commercial banks came to the fore during the US housing bubble in the 2000s, amply supported by the central bank. Shadow banks grew enormously by originating and securitising mortgages during 2001–06, drawing profits in the form of fees, commissions, and capital gains. The wholesale funding for these activities largely came from short-term markets, including the repo market. Investment banks, which are basically financial intermediaries that specialise in providing expertise and services to facilitate transactions in the stock market, enthusiastically got in on the action. Both commercial and investment banks established a range of shadow intermediaries promoting mortgage securitisation by seeking funds through the repo and other short-term markets.

Profits were made from subprime mortgages sold to the poorest sections of the US working class, only to be securitised and then quickly resold to a range of other intermediaries that constantly rebalanced their portfolios.[19] For US banks in particular, the chains of securitisation facilitated the sidelining of existing regulatory controls. By securitising mortgage debt and thus removing it from their balance sheets, banks appeared to hold an adequate proportion of capital as security against losses.[20] In practice, however, banks were continually

19 See V. Constâncio (2012) 'Shadow Banking: The ECB Perspective', at ecb.europa.eu.

20 Mainstream economists were quick to spot the importance of securitisation as a tool for moving assets off balance sheets, thus freeing up bank capital; see C. W. Calomiris and J. R. Mason (2004) 'Credit Card Securitisation and Regulatory Arbitrage', *Journal of Financial Research* 26 (1): 5–27. In the context of the Great Crisis, V. Acharya, P. Schnabl, and G. Suarez (2013) 'Securitisation without Risk Transfer', *Journal of Financial Economics* 107 (3): 515–36 focused on securitisation as a means for evading regulatory capital requirements. A deeper discussion on the regulatory framework of securitisation in the years prior to the Great Crisis was offered by A. Jobst (2005) 'The

expanding transactions in mortgage-related assets on an increasingly risky basis.

US banks managed to present an image of solidity, even though they were heavily exposed to assets that had been created by lending to destitute layers of the working class for housing purposes. European banks also played a vital part by providing liquid funds to US banks and purchasing securitised assets across the Atlantic. The profitable merry-go-round resting on slender speculative foundations continued for several years before the inevitable comeuppance arrived.

The storm breaks

Financial expansion in core countries faltered in 2006 as the US housing market went past its peak. A significant proportion of the subprime mortgages backing securitised assets became 'delinquent' as the Federal Reserve began slowly to raise interest rates after 2004. The poor and marginal layers of the working class, to which a gaggle of banks and shadow financiers had sold mortgages aggressively, could no longer make regular payments. The first major tremors hit the US money market in 2007, as the securitisation mechanisms based on mortgage debt started to unravel in the money market. Financial institutions seeking wholesale liquidity to fund further securitisations began to find that liquid funds were no longer obtainable.

The money market is pivotal to the capitalist credit system, since it provides the locus for wholesale trading of short-term liquidity among financial institutions, thus allowing for the determination of the market rate of interest.[21] It is this market that ultimately registers the systemic interconnectedness of the various private and public components of finance. For this reason, the money market is typically the site at which capitalist crises first appear, while also providing channels of contagion across the economy. In all these respects, the role of shadow banks and their close relationship with regular banks proved critical in 2007–09.

The bubble burst in 2008, when it became apparent that several major

---

Regulatory Treatment of Asset Securitisation: The Basel Securitisation Framework Explained', *Journal of Financial Regulation and Compliance* 13 (1): 15–42.

21 For a discussion of the emergence and role of money markets from a Marxist perspective, see C. Lapavitsas (2003) *Social Foundations of Markets, Money and Credit*, Routledge: London.

banks (both investment and commercial) had enormously overextended the provision and trading of housing-related securitised loans, with little capital to cover the losses that emerged among the mortgages provided to the poorest, who could no longer service their housing debts. Shadow banks were unable to obtain short-term funding in the repo and other markets to support their speculative portfolios, including their securitised assets.

In August–September 2008, liquidity disappeared in the US financial markets, as huge losses loomed for those who held subprime-mortgage-backed assets. The providers of wholesale funds withheld supply, and even prioritised the return of their loaned capital from the markets, thus giving rise to a 'silent bank run', including in the repo market.[22]

The ensuing financial crisis led to a collapse of both international credit and trade flows, triggering a synchronised recession across the world economy in 2008–09. Peripheral countries were hit hard due to the shrinking of trade and the reversal of capital flows, including portfolio and foreign direct investment. Nonetheless, they began to recover soon after the initial shock, since they were marginal to the speculative mechanisms of the bubble that primarily involved US and European financial institutions, and had accumulated substantial international reserves. Events in Europe, however, took a very different turn for two fundamental reasons.

German, French, and other banks were heavily involved in the US bubble through credit flows associated with the securitisation of mortgages. Moreover, following the launch of the euro in 1999, the dysfunctional structures of the European Economic and Monetary Union (EMU) created fresh divisions of core and periphery in Europe, intensifying the financial pressures from the collapse of the US housing bubble.[23] The global crisis of 2007–09 morphed into the Eurozone crisis of 2010–12 that directly threatened the survival of the euro, while forcing Greece, Ireland, and Portugal to accept bailouts with severe conditions.

As this vast and complex disturbance unfolded, it became clear that the final guarantor of financialised capitalism is the state. Decisive state

---

22 See G. Gorton and A. Metrick (2012) 'Securitized Banking and the Run on Repo', *Journal of Financial Economics* 104 (3): 425–51.

23 For a historical description of this process, see A. Tooze (2018) *Crashed: How a Decade of Financial Crises Changed the World*, Penguin: London.

intervention, particularly in the USA, brought a measure of stability to the world economy, acting as a harbinger of the state's response to the Pandemic Crisis. Crucially, however, state intervention did not bring structural change, nor did it place the financialised core of contemporary capitalism on a dynamic growth path. On the contrary, accumulation flagged, and production remained weak throughout the 2010s.

Intervention by core states in the crisis of 2007–09 resulted in further bolstering of the ruling capitalist elites. The primary means was expansionary monetary policy, while much less weight was placed on fiscal policy. Indeed, the core countries of the world economy suffered from fiscal austerity in the 2010s, once the immediate shock of the crisis had passed. The poor performance of accumulation during that decade, summed up in weak profitability, as is shown in the next chapter, was compounded by the sustained deficiency of aggregate demand emanating from the private sector and exacerbated by fiscal austerity. Following heavy state intervention in the crisis of 2007–09, financialised capitalism entered a decade of weak accumulation in core countries.

4

Core Economies Falter after 2007–09

Weak capitalist accumulation

States played a pivotal role in core economies throughout the 2010s, with the burden of intervention falling mostly on monetary policy in line with the development of financial markets and institutions summed up in the previous chapter. During the same period, fiscal austerity generally prevailed, though with significant differences among countries, shifting the costs of the gigantic turmoil of 2007–09 onto working people and the poor.

Despite intervening heavily, core states avoided structural reforms, concerned to protect the interests of the privileged layer at the top of the capitalist class. The crisis of 2007–09 did not function as a cleansing process of capitalist accumulation, nor did it establish new foundations for dynamic growth. Property rights over productive resources did not come under threat, and when failing financial institutions received capital injections from the public purse, the influx of funds was not accompanied by an infusion of public spirit. Speculative profit making remained the guiding principle of the financial sector. There was no creative destruction ushering in a fresh phase of capitalist accumulation – only plain destruction of labour skills, resources, and livelihoods.

The historical weakness of accumulation during 2010–19 is apparent in the low average growth rates registered by the core regions of the world economy: 1.3 per cent in Japan, 1.6 per cent in the EU, and 2.3 per cent in the USA.[1] Even in China, where the average was 8.5 per cent, growth weakened notably in the second half of the 2010s. Feeble accumulation is also evidenced by poor profitability and productivity growth despite sustained technological advances throughout this period. Mainstream economists became alarmed by the persistent misfiring of capitalist accumulation, and arguments of 'secular stagnation' proliferated.[2]

The anaemic performance of accumulation in the 2010s was partly due to the suppression of aggregate demand as core states implemented austerity policies, but even more significant was the underlying weakness on the side of production. At the same time, the profound income and wealth inequalities of financialised capitalism became even worse. When the pandemic struck, the core of the world economy was not only unprepared for a health emergency but ripe for economic disaster.

To obtain insight into these developments, this chapter and the next examine the performance of core countries from the perspective of aggregate demand and supply before and after the Great Crisis of 2007–09, focusing on USA, Germany, France, the UK, and Japan. To be sure, China has emerged as a giant locus of capitalist accumulation, and its hegemonic contest with the USA is considered in chapter 14. For the purposes of this chapter, however, suffice it to focus on five core countries of the world economy, with a particular emphasis on the hegemonic USA.

A word of warning is necessary before considering aggregate demand and supply, since, for Marxist political economy, the two sides cannot be strictly separated. Private enterprises plan production by forming expectations of demand and produce output based on costs deriving heavily

---

1 Estimated from World Bank data.

2 Proposed notably by Lawrence Summers in a speech made in 2013 at a conference of the IMF and published as L. Summers (2015) 'Have We Entered an Age of Secular Stagnation?' IMF Fourteenth Annual Research Conference in Honor of Stanley Fischer, Washington, DC', IMF Economic Review 63 (1): 277–80; see also L. Summers (2014) 'Reflections on the 'New Secular Stagnation Hypothesis', in C. Teulings and R. Baldwin (eds), Secular Stagnation: Facts, Causes and Cures, CEPR Press: London; and (2015) 'Demand Side Secular Stagnation', American Economic Review 105 (5): 60–65. Summers claimed that weak investment combined with a glut of saving by an ageing population has created long-term deflationary pressures. There is no doubt that in recent decades both investment and productivity growth have been poor, while loanable capital has flourished in core countries. These developments are crucial to the trajectory of financialised capitalism, but they are also inextricably linked to its exploitative social structure. Economic theory ought to be casting light on the latter. For a historical overview of the idea of 'secular stagnation', see R. Backhouse and M. Boianovsky (2016) 'Secular Stagnation: The History of a Macroeconomic Heresy', European Journal of the History of Economic Thought 23 (6): 946–70.

from real wages and technology. Enterprise plans help determine aggregate demand in the form of both investment and consumption, but if expected demand does not materialise, production is curtailed. Moreover, the drive to innovate and adopt new technologies is negatively affected when demand is weak over a long period of time. Aggregate demand and supply are inextricably linked in capitalist economies.

Nonetheless, capitalist economies rest primarily on production, where value and surplus value are generated.[3] The side of production is ultimately the determining factor in the overall performance of capitalist accumulation. The variable that most usefully sums up the underlying condition of aggregate supply is the average rate of profit, particularly that of non-financial enterprises. The point of departure for the analysis of accumulation weakness in the 2010s is the conduct of profitability before and after the Great Crisis of 2007–09.

Average rate of profit and real wages

The average rate of profit depends on real wages, while also reflecting the growth of labour productivity, which obviously relies on technological change. Labour productivity is the driving engine of capitalism, the means through which profits rise and enterprises win the battle of competition in the medium to long run. To facilitate analysis, it is instructive to deploy the simplest formulation of the average rate of profit in Marxist political economy:[4]

$$r = (S/V) / [1 + (C/V)],$$

where S is surplus value, V is variable capital, and C is constant capital (in money terms: profit, the real wage bill, and investment in fixed and

---

3 This is one of the best-known precepts of Marxist political economy, deployed by Marx throughout his work. It underpins, for instance, his discussion of the distinction between price and value; see K. Marx (1981) [1894], *Capital*, vol. 3, Penguin Books: Harmondsworth, Middlessex, ch. 10.

4 It is important to bear in mind that the average rate of profit contains considerable dispersion and may disguise significant variation on the supply side. A substantial proportion of enterprises in core countries, for instance, have low, or even very low, profitability, reflecting profound competitive frailty. The presence of these 'zombie firms' underscores the weak performance of accumulation since the Great Crisis and is considered more fully in later chapters.

variable goods, respectively). The numerator varies directly with the rate of exploitation of labour, S/V (that is, with surplus value relative to the value of the wage basket), while the denominator varies inversely with the value composition of the capital invested, C/V (that is, with the value of the investment goods relative to the value of the wage basket).

If real wages (V) fell, other things being equal, both the numerator and the denominator would rise, the former raising the rate of profit and the latter lowering it. The overall effect, however, within reasonable assumptions about magnitudes, would probably be to raise the rate of profit. It stands to plain economic reason that the average rate of profit falls when real wages rise.

If labour productivity rose, other things being equal, both V and C would fall, as the value content of the wage basket and the investment goods would decline. Since V would fall, the rate of exploitation in the numerator would rise, as would happen with a fall in real wages. However, the impact on the value composition of capital in the denominator would be ambiguous: if C fell by more than V, the value composition would fall; if, on the other hand, V fell by more than C, the value composition would rise.

Therefore, the overall impact on the average rate of profit would be ambiguous. The rise in the rate of exploitation would boost the rate of profit, and the impact might be even bigger if the value composition fell. If, on the other hand, the value composition rose, it would give a downward push to the rate of profit that could potentially exceed the boost from the rising rate of exploitation, thus bringing the rate of profit down. Once again, however, within reasonable assumptions about magnitudes, a rise in productivity would probably raise the average rate of profit.[5]

Consequently, the trajectory of the average rate of profit, which reflects the underlying strength of accumulation, could be usefully analysed through the movement of real wages and the productivity of labour. Their interplay could be considered as the 'internal mechanism'

---

5 The drive to increase productivity would typically rest on a rising technical composition of capital – that is, on more machinery and other inputs per worker, or an increasing capital/labour ratio in physical terms. A rising technical composition would push up the organic composition of capital – that is, the simple value reflection of the technical composition. If the organic composition rose, the rate of profit would fall – a standard result in Marxist analysis. In short, for productivity to rise, the technical composition of capital must also rise, and that would exercise downward pressure on the rate of profit. What matters for our purposes, however, is the effect of rising productivity *per se* on profitability. If productivity is not rising rapidly, despite increases in the technical composition of capital, profitability is unlikely to register a sustained increase.

of capitalist accumulation determining the rate of profit.[6] If labour productivity tended to increase slowly, profitability would be unlikely to rise in a sustained fashion. The overall outcome for the rate of profit would, however, depend on real wages, since profitability could still be sustained through downward pressure on real wages.

Frail profitability, weak productivity growth, rising inequality

Consider now some evidence on the operation of the 'internal mechanism' in recent years in core countries, particularly the hegemonic USA. The trajectory of the profit rate of non-financial enterprises in the USA since the early 1980s and up to the pandemic shock is shown in figure 4.1.[7]

The chart indicates that Covid-19 arrived at a time of distinct feebleness of productive accumulation in core countries. Over the last four decades, the profit rate of non-financial enterprises in the USA exhibited a rather level trend – perhaps rising gently – while following a cyclical path, broadly in line with the overall fluctuations of the economy. After the Great Crisis of 2007–09, the profit rate recovered mildly, peaked in 2014, and then began to decline again. Covid-19 struck the US economy when profitability was weak and the already frail accumulation showed signs of exhaustion. Broadly similar points hold for capitalist accumulation in the EU, which was further weighed down by the malfunctioning of the euro and was lodged in stagnation for most of the 2010s, as is shown in chapter 15.

---

6 Always bearing in mind the impact of changes in the organic composition of capital, discussed in note 5, as well as the impact of changes in the intensity of labour. Both of these factors are integral parts of the 'internal mechanism'. In particular, changes in the intensity of labour could alter the rate of exploitation independently of the value of the wage basket or the division of the working day into a necessary and a surplus part.

7 The calculation is based on the method of G. Duménil and D. Levy (1994) 'The U.S. Economy Since the Civil War: Sources and Construction of the Series' Paris, CEPREMAP: Paris, at CepreMap.fr. The pre-tax rate of profit for the corporate sector was also computed following the adjustment proposed by A. Shaikh (2010) 'The First Great Depression of the 21st Century', in L. Panitch, G. Albo, and V. Chibber, *Socialist Register 2011: The Crisis This Time*, The Merlin Press: Wellingborough, pp. 44–63. The results were similar. For further detail on the method of calculation, see C. Lapavitsas and I. Mendieta-Muñoz (2016) 'The Profits of Financialisation', *Monthly Review* 68 (3): 49–62.

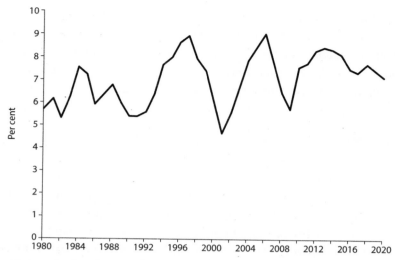

Figure 4.1. Profit rate of non-financial enterprises, USA, 1980–2020.
Source: Authors' calculations; Data from BEA and NIPA.

Further insight into the operation of the 'internal mechanism' can be gained by considering labour productivity during this period. The important factor in this respect is not the absolute level of labour productivity, which typically tends to rise over time in capitalist economies, but its rate of growth.

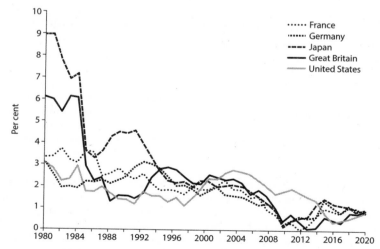

Figure 4.2. Rate of growth of labour productivity,
five-year moving average.
Source: Authors' calculations based on OECD data.

Figure 4.2 shows the trajectory of productivity growth in the five core countries during the last four decades, a period of cataclysmic technological change, particularly in telecommunications, information technology, and artificial intelligence. For most of this period, core countries were plagued by declining rates of productivity growth, despite sustained technological innovation. Poor productivity growth has been particularly striking since the Great Crisis of 2007–09, especially in the USA and the UK but also in Germany, France, and Japan.

Weak productivity growth, a well-known feature of capitalism in recent decades, has been extensively discussed in the mainstream literature.[8] Its causes are a matter of debate, but there is no doubt that the relentless technological advances in information and communications technology have not resulted in productivity gains comparable to previous historical periods, such as the introduction of the railways, or electrification.[9] It remains to be seen how the latest wave of technological change, particularly artificial intelligence, will impact on productivity growth in the coming years.

During the decades of financialisation, flimsy productivity growth attenuated the 'internal mechanism' in core countries. Confronted by poor productivity growth during this period, capitalist oligarchies supported profitability by applying downward pressure on real wages,

---

8 Mainstream economists typically refer to the slowdown of productivity growth in the period after the Great Financial Crisis as the 'productivity puzzle'. A detailed discussion of the factors that might have contributed to the slowdown in the USA over a longer period of time can be found in R. Gordon (2016) *The Rise and Fall of American Growth*, Princeton University Press: Princeton, NJ. For empirical evidence on productivity growth trends worldwide, see P. Ollivaud, Y. Guillemette, and D. Turner (2016) 'Links between Weak Investment and the Slowdown in Productivity and Potential Output Growth across the OECD', OECD Economics Department Working Papers No. 1304; see also K. Young Eun and N. Loayza (2019) 'Productivity Growth: Patterns and Determinants Across the World', World Bank Policy Research Working Paper No. 8852; and A. Dieppe (ed.) (2021) *Global Productivity: Trends, Drivers, and Policies*, World Bank: Washington DC.

9 It is plausible that the weak growth of productivity in core countries also reflects the relative contraction of their manufacturing sectors along the lines of 'induced technological change' proposed by Kaldor in his sharp critique of neoclassical growth theory. Shifting manufacturing capacity abroad – especially to Asia – and applying sustained downward pressure on real wages might have boosted profits in the short term in core countries but has not helped productivity growth in the longer term. See N. Kaldor (1957) 'A Model of Economic Growth', *Economic Journal* 67 (268): 591–624; and (1961) 'Capital Accumulation and Economic Growth', in F. A. Lutz and D. C. Hague (eds), *The Theory of Capital*, St Martin's Press: New York, pp. 177–222.

particularly as 'de-localisation' of production entailed the loss of hundreds of thousands of manufacturing jobs and trade union organisation weakened.[10]

There were, however, significant differences among core countries in this respect. After 2007–09, real wages remained broadly stagnant in the UK and Japan, but rose in the USA, Germany, and France. Even in countries in which real wages rose during the 2010s, there were great variations among different strata of wage earners. In the USA, for instance, most of the growth in real wages was concentrated in the upper deciles of the wage earners' distribution, while median earners faced stagnation.[11] The rise amounted to worsening inequality rather than to improved conditions for the working class. Similar points hold for Germany, where real wages showed some upward movement but only after an extended extraordinary wage freeze which had lasted since the 1990s.[12]

Moreover, core countries also supported profitability through what might be called the 'external mechanism' of capitalist accumulation – that is, by importing cheaper wage and other goods from abroad. As global trade expanded during the decades of financialisation, core countries took advantage of the enormous expansion of wage labour in China and elsewhere in East Asia, which went together with rapid increases in productivity.[13] Core countries also moved industrial

---

10 See Ö. Onaran et al. (2015) 'Working for the Economy: The Economic Case for Trade Unions', Greenwich Political Economy Research Centre Policy Brief No. 05-2015; and T. Auvray et al. (2020) 'Financialization's Conservation and Transformation: from Mark I to Mark II', Université de Genéve, Political Economy Working Papers Université de Genève No. 2.

11 The income of chief executives and other managers, which has increased rapidly in recent years, is accounted as wages, thus artificially boosting the wage share even in the face of increasing income inequality. See J. Behringer and T. van Treeck (2021) 'Varieties of Capitalism and Growth Regimes: The Role of Income Distribution', Socio-Economic Review 20(3): 1–38.

12 See the hard-hitting Congressional Research Service Report, 28 December 2020, at fas.org. For a recent German account on income inequality and the role of housing, coupled with a historical analysis of the changes in the last two decades, see C. Dustmann, B. Fitzenberger, and M. Zimmermann (2022) 'Housing Expenditure and Income Inequality', The Economic Journal 132 (645): 1709–36. For a comparative study of income inequality in Britain and the USA, see R. Blundell et al. (2018) 'Income Inequality and the Labour Market in Britain and the US', Journal of Public Economics 162: 48–62.

13 For a recent analysis of East Asian economic growth and gains in productivity, see A. D. Mason and S. Shetty (2019) 'A Resurgent East Asia: Navigating a Changing World', World Bank East Asia and Pacific Regional Report, World Bank: Washington, DC.

capacity to East Asia, Central America, and Eastern Europe, thus benefiting from lower wages and laxer labour regulations, as is shown in chapter 12.

Downward pressure on real wages and importing cheap wage goods from abroad allowed capitalists in core countries to appropriate most of the gains in productivity – modest as these were – leaving little for workers. The result was deepening, acute, inequality. Figure 4.3 confirms the relentless worsening of the functional distribution of national income for labour in the years following 2007–09.

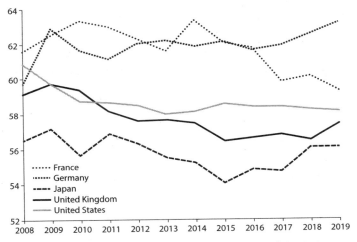

Figure 4.3. Labour income share as % of GDP.
Source: Authors' calculations based on ILOSTAT.

Steadily escalating inequality has been a prominent feature of capitalist economic, social, and political development in recent decades, fully reversing the gains made by workers in the years after the Second World War.[14] The escalation of inequality corresponds to the emergence of hugely powerful and wealthy oligarchies across core countries, the weakening of the middle strata, and the frequently catastrophic decline in the material conditions and life prospects of the working class. The precise causes of rising inequality vary from country to country, but

14 The literature on this issue is very extensive, most notably T. Piketty (2013) *Capital in the Twenty-First Century*, Harvard University Press: Cambridge, MA, but see also B. Milanovic (2016) *Global Inequality: A New Approach for the Age of Globalization*, Harvard University Press: Cambridge, MA.

there is no doubt that profits have commanded an increasing portion of domestically produced output compared with wages, thus compressing labour's share in national income.[15]

'Zombie' firms and their prospects

The underlying weakness of production in core countries is further indicated by the existence of broad swathes of 'zombie' firms – that is, enterprises whose profits are so low that they cannot even service their debts. Economic theory would expect unprofitable firms to exit production, since they would fail in competition. However, zombies avoid demise by running down cash balances, selling assets, raising additional equity, or becoming still more indebted. Financialised capitalism has greatly facilitated the survival of zombies through easy credit and low interest rates for decades.[16]

Zombie firms are typically less productive than other enterprises and their investment levels are lower, thereby depressing aggregate productivity and growth. In general, there are two types of zombies: first, those that face very low profitability after paying interest and other financial charges, and, second, those that have negative profitability even before meeting financial obligations.[17] While the difficulties of the former are largely financial, those of the latter are fundamentally related to production and prevent the accrual of a positive rate of profit. The former face problems of profitability because of financial obligations, but the latter face financial problems because of low profitability.

The overwhelming majority of zombie firms in the US economy

---

15 In recent years, there has been a surge of research into inequality by both mainstream and heterodox authors. While the focus of mainstream economists has been directed at personal inequality measures at both the national and international levels, including gender and race disparities, heterodox scholars have typically focused on functional inequality. For inequality in the countries in our sample group, see, for example, A. Guschanski and Ö. Onaran (2018) 'Determinants of the Wage Share: A Cross-Country Comparison Using Sectoral Data', *CESifo Forum* 19 (2): 44–54.

16 See M. Adalet McGowan, D. Andrews, and V. Millot (2017) 'The Walking Dead? Zombie Firms and Productivity Performance in OECD Countries', OECD Economics Department Working Papers No. 1372; see also R. Banerjee and B. Hofmann (2020) 'Corporate Zombies: Anatomy and Life Cycle', BIS Working Papers No. 882.

17 N. Águila and J. Graña (2022) 'Not All Zombies Are Created Equal: A Marxist-Minskyan Taxonomy of Firms: United States, 1950–2019', *International Review of Applied Economics* 37(1): 3-22.

belong to the second type, registering negative profitability even before making interest payments. Furthermore, their numbers have steadily risen; indeed, the second type has become prevalent since the early 1980s.[18] The malaise of US capitalist accumulation is deeply rooted, originating primarily in production and only secondarily in finance.

Zombies survive by using their meagre profits to repay debt and are thus heavily dependent on high demand. However, zombies typically respond to enhanced demand by overstretching existing production capacity rather than by investing or innovating. Once the limits of capacity are reached, they increase prices, contributing to inflationary pressures. Moreover, falling revenue may force zombies to close doors.[19]

Far from being a theoretical curiosity, zombies have become a staple at the core of the world economy. When the pandemic struck, small and medium enterprises in core countries faced a collapse of revenue and profits, accompanied by cash shortages and difficulties in meeting financial commitments.[20] Zombies survived by drawing on state support and obtaining additional loans from banks, often with state guarantees. Extraordinarily loose credit conditions further postponed the rationalisation of weak enterprises along the normal lines of capitalist competition.

The heavy presence of zombies indicates that confronting the weakness of accumulation would require far bolder steps than merely providing cheap credit or boosting aggregate demand. The weakness of production is unlikely to be assuaged without sustained public intervention to rationalise production, protect employment, and redeploy resources into socially useful activities. This necessarily means challenging private property rights, engaging in substantial public

---

18 Thus, while in 1969 the proportion of enterprises registering negative profitability before the payment of interest was roughly 3 per cent, by 2001 it had risen to 33 per cent, despite enterprise indebtedness being relatively low. See Águila and Graña, 'Not All Zombies Are Created Equal'.

19 See J. Baines and S. B. Hager (2021) 'The Great Debt Divergence and its Implications for the Covid-19 Crisis: Mapping Corporate Leverage as Power', *New Political Economy* 26 (5): 885–901.

20 See M. Osada et al. (2021) 'Quantifying the Impact of the COVID-19 Pandemic on Firms' Default Probability in Japan', VoxEU, CEPR at cepr.org/voxeu; A. De Vito and J. P. Gómez (2020) 'Estimating the COVID-19 Cash Crunch: Global Evidence and Policy', *Journal of Accounting and Public Policy* 39 (2): 106741; T. Didier et al. (2021) 'Financing Firms in Hibernation during the COVID-19 Pandemic', *Journal of Financial Stability* 53: 100837; Baines and Hager (2021) 'The Great Debt Divergence'.

investment, and shifting the balance of power in favour of labour. Rather than going down that path, core countries compounded the frailty of accumulation by persistently undermining aggregate demand in the 2010s.

Deficient aggregate demand: Investment, consumption, and government expenditure

Aggregate demand in core countries was persistently weak throughout the 2010s as the private sector registered poor results in both investment and consumption, and as several governments pursued policies of fiscal austerity. Evidence of the weakness of aggregate demand is given by investment as a percentage of gross domestic product (GDP) across the group of five core countries, as is shown in figure 4.4:

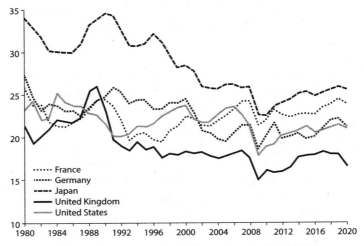

Figure 4.4. Gross capital formation as % of GDP.
Source: Authors' calculations based on World
Bank World Development Indicators.

The Great Crisis of 2007–09 brought a synchronised collapse of investment across core countries, and recovery was very slow during the ensuing decade. By the late 2010s, investment as a proportion of GDP had not even reached the levels attained before 2007, further worsening the poor record of productivity growth among core countries. Indeed, investment in core countries has been generally weak since the early 1980s.[21] Low investment is associated with the rebalancing of productive capital globally as industrial capacity shifted to East Asia and elsewhere. Not least in this respect is the emergence of global production chains, discussed in chapter 12, making it possible for large multinational enterprises of core countries to engage in manufacturing without expanding – or even directly possessing – productive capacity. Weak investment is also associated with the sustained downward pressure on real wages, which has made labour power cheaper.

The deficiency of private aggregate demand was also visible in consumption as a proportion of GDP, although that varied considerably among the five core counties, as figure 4.5 shows.

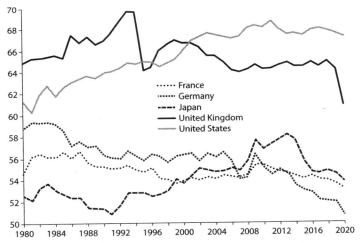

Figure 4.5. Consumption as % of GDP.
Source: Authors' calculations based on World
Bank World Development Indicators.

21 There is an extensive empirical literature on this issue. R. Döttling, G. Gutiérrez, and T. Philippon (2017) 'Is There an Investment Gap in Advanced Economies? If So, Why?' at ssrn.com; G. Gutiérrez and T. Philippon compare weak private fixed investment in Europe and the USA in (2016) 'Investment-less Growth: An Empirical Investigation', NBER Working Paper No. 22897; R. Banerjee, J. Kearns, and M. Lombardi (2015) '(Why) Is Investment Weak?', BIS Quarterly Review March, 67–82, discusses the low level of investment after the Great Crisis; empirical analysis of the decline of investment in advanced countries can also be found in M. A. Kose, et al. (2017) 'Weakness in Investment Growth: Causes, Implications and Policy Responses', World Bank Policy Research Working Paper No. 7990.

In the 2010s, and until Covid-19 struck, consumption generally fell or remained flat in the five core countries, since real wages faced downward pressure and household borrowing tended to decline in relative terms. The advent of Covid-19 dramatically reduced consumption. The striking characteristic of consumption in core countries (except for Germany) in the years of financialisation has been reliance on private debt. Most notably in the USA and the UK, consumption was supported by mounting household indebtedness in the face of downward pressure on real wages and a persistent decline of the share of GDP accruing to labour, as is shown in subsequent chapters.[22] Even in these countries, however, the bubble of the 2000s was not due to escalating consumption expenditure. The driving mechanism lay in the financing of housing, which is certainly a part of household expenditure but is highly peculiar, insofar as it involves one large transaction typically made to obtain a part of the existing social stock of houses.

Weak consumption together with poor investment translated into a sustained deficiency of private domestic aggregate demand across core countries. External demand, on the other hand, presented a more complex and varied outlook, as shown in figure 4.6.

The USA and UK – as well as France, although on a more modest scale – registered persistent current account deficits; in contrast, Germany and Japan had persistent surpluses. There is a structural difference among core countries in this respect that has become entrenched in the course of financialisation. Namely, Germany and Japan rely far more heavily on external demand to support accumulation than the USA and the UK.[23]

---

22 For a mainstream analysis of consumer debt rising to offset stagnating or decreasing real wages thus keeping consumption stable, see R. G. Rajan (2010) *Fault Lines: How Hidden Fractures Still Threaten the World Economy*, Princeton University Press: Princeton, NJ. The 'Rajan Hypothesis' – essentially the notion that there is a positive relation between income inequality and credit bubbles – has been examined empirically in different institutional contexts. See, for example, T. van Treeck and S. Sturm (2012) 'Income Inequality as a Cause of the Great Recession? A Survey of Current Debates', International Labour Organization Conditions of Work and Employment Series No. 39; see also S. Yamarik, M. El-Shagi, and G. Yamashiro (2016) 'Does Inequality Lead to Credit Growth? Testing the Rajan Hypothesis Using State-Level Data', *Economics Letters* 148: 63–7; and M. A. Destek and B. Koksel (2019) 'Income Inequality and Financial Crises: Evidence from the Bootstrap Rolling Window', *Financial Innovation* 5: 1–23, p. 21.

23 Typically referred to as export-led as opposed to debt-led (or profit-led) financialisation by post-Keynesian economists; see, for instance, E. Stockhammer (2012) 'Financialization, Income Distribution and the Crisis', *Investigación Económica*,

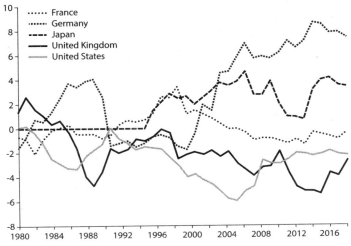

Figure 4.6. Current account balance as % of GDP.
Source: Authors' calculations based on World
Bank World Development Indicators.

The decades of financialisation have been marked by the external deficits of the USA, putting a particular complexion on the role of the dollar as world money, as is discussed in subsequent chapters.

It is important to note that Germany is proportionately a far greater exporter than Japan and has a much larger surplus relative to GDP. Indeed, Germany is an outlier among core countries, registering enormous current account surpluses since roughly the time of the introduction of the euro. The exporting strength of German capital is closely related to the workings of the monetary union of the EU and the emergence of the euro, as is shown in chapter 15. Nevertheless, Germany's external strength was undermined by the poor performance of its domestic investment and consumption throughout the 2010s.

In view of the deficiency of private demand after 2007–09, the role of governments proved crucial in core countries. Figure 4.7

Escuela Nacional de Economía, Universidad Nacional Autónoma de México 71 (279): 39–70. A similar distinction is also offered by the Regulation School along the so-called 'axes' of financialisation, namely productive–financialised accumulation, extensive–intensive accumulation, and introversion–extraversion (See J. Becker and R. Weissenbacher (2015) 'Changing Development Models: Dependency School Meets Regulation Theory', paper presented at International Conference: Research and Regulation, 10–12 June, Paris.

shows that substantial fiscal deficits emerged across the core in 2008, immediately after the outbreak of the Great Crisis. It is also apparent that a dramatic escalation of deficits occurred after the blow dealt by the pandemic in 2020. The deficits of 2008–09 mostly reflected the impact of so-called automatic stabilisers, briefly discussed in the following chapters, as government spending softened the impact of the crisis, while tax revenue declined. As soon as the immediate impact of the financial shock faded, however, governments restrained deficits and implemented austerity through-out the 2010s.

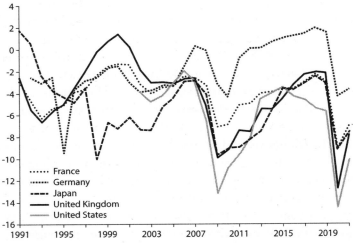

Figure 4.7. Government budget balance as % of GDP.
Source: Authors' calculations based on World
Bank World Development Indicators.

The champion of austerity in the 2010s was Germany, chalking up fiscal surpluses soon after 2007–09 and for most of the decade. The posi-tive boost of external demand to the German economy through exports was effectively countermanded by government policy. The fiscal approach of Germany was summed up in the debt brake policy, introduced in 2009 and given constitutional status.[24] The debt brake

---

24 On the 'debt brake' and its effects, see A. Truger and W. Henner (2013) 'The German "Debt Brake": A Shining Example for European Fiscal Policy?' *Revue de l'OFCE* 127 (1): 153–88; see also K. Rietzler and A. Truger (2019) 'Is the "Debt Brake" behind Germany's successful fiscal consolidation?', *Revue de l'OFCE* 2: 11–30. The 'debt brake' was suspended during the pandemic to allow for a sizeable fiscal response by the

required regional governments to target zero structural (that is, non-cyclical) deficits, while the federal government was allowed a minimal structural deficit. The declared aim was to reduce public debt toward the level of 60 per cent of GDP that was formally imposed in 1992 by the EU Maastricht Treaty, which effectively launched the euro.

The rigid framework of the EMU also meant severe restrictions on fiscal expenditure and deficits for other member states. Caught in this trap – and without a system of fiscal transfers among states to compensate for current account imbalances – the EMU was dominated by austerity in the 2010s, in an attempt to eliminate fiscal deficits and reduce public debt. The costs were ultimately borne by working people through downward pressure on wages and salaries, as well as through reduced public spending on social infrastructure and welfare.

The UK also implemented a severe policy of austerity, an egregious example of self-harm with a negative impact on growth and workers' livelihoods. The macroeconomic data of the UK for the period since 2007–09 is arguably the worst among core countries. In contrast, the US government expanded fiscal deficits in the second half of the 2010s, particularly as the Trump administration cut taxes for the richer layers of the population. Setting aside the deeply inequitable outcomes of this strategy, fiscal policy in the USA at least did not systematically exacerbate the underlying feebleness of private demand.

Given the prevalence of fiscal austerity, the main burden of government intervention fell on monetary policy, thus casting further light on the evolution of financialisation. This is a critically important aspect of economic policy by core states during the 2010s, which is briefly considered in the rest of this chapter.

Unconventional monetary policy and quantitative easing

In the summer of 2008, as the US financial system became enveloped in a systemic crisis, the Federal Reserve intervened through the repo markets to provide short-term liquidity. Essentially, the US central bank bought securities from private banks (such as publicly issued bills and bonds, or publicly backed mortgage debt) subject to a contractual

---

German state. It was also amended following the outbreak of the Ukraine war to enable the massive rearmament planned by Germany.

agreement to resell these at a specified date. Repos were the main method through which central banks generally controlled the short-term rate of interest and proceeded to lower it dramatically. The intervention boosted liquidity available to banks and shadow intermediaries, thus sustaining and promoting financialisation in ways that will be examined more fully in the next chapter.

Moreover, for several years after 2008, the Federal Reserve engaged in large-scale purchases of financial securities. These purchases were the main component of the policy of quantitative easing, which characterised core countries in the 2010s and signalled the further transformation of financialised capitalism. The outright purchase of public and private securities allowed the US central bank to supply private banks with massive additional reserves, further supporting shadow intermediaries and lowering medium- and long-term interest rates. A large proportion of the liquidity created by the central bank as it bought securities was kept by the financial institutions in the form of interest-earning deposits with the central bank.

It is common to call monetary policy based on quantitative easing (and the accompanying extremely low interest rates) 'unconventional'. Quantitative easing originated in Japan after the decade of stagnation that followed the burst of the country's huge financial bubble in the late 1980s.[25] The Bank of Japan broke new ground among core central banks by adopting a zero-interest-rate policy in 1999. In 2001, it also adopted quantitative easing and pursued this with few interruptions during the following years. However, quantitative easing across core countries after 2007–09 was largely determined by the Federal Reserve, confirming the role of the dollar as world money and buttressing US hegemony.[26] The

25 See R. Miyao and T. Okimoto (2017) 'The Macroeconomic Effects of Japan's Unconventional Monetary Policies', Research Institute of Economy Trade and Industry Discussion Paper 17-E-065, at rieti.go.jp. See also T. Okimoto (2019) 'Trend Inflation and Monetary Policy Regimes in Japan', *Journal of International Money and Finance* 92: 137–52.

26 For an overview of the Federal Reserve's quantitative easing programme and its consequences in the early years following the crisis, see G. D. Rudebusch (2018) 'A Review of the Fed's Unconventional Monetary Policy', Federal Reserve Bank of San Francisco Economic Letter No. 2018-27. For a technical analysis of the effects of quantitative easing in the UK, see G. Kapetanios et al. (2012) 'Assessing the Economy-Wide Effects of Quantitative Easing', *The Economic Journal* 122 (564): 316–47. For the effects in the EU, see M. Mandler and M. Scharnagl (2020) 'Estimating the Effects of the Eurosystem's Asset Purchase Programme at the Country Level', Deutsche Bundesbank Discussion Paper No. 29/2020; and L. Gambetti and A. Musso (2017) 'The

Bank of England followed suit in 2009, while the European Central Bank (ECB), which was initially constrained by the rigid regulatory framework of the EMU, changed its stance gradually and adopted quantitative easing after 2015.

Quantitative easing casts further light on financialised capitalism. The technical methods deployed vary from country to country, depending on the historical and institutional framework of each country's financial system. Significant differences often surface in the assets that central banks choose to buy, but the thrust of policy is similar across core countries: central banks purchase huge volumes of public and private financial instruments (typically bonds) by creating equally enormous amounts of essentially fiat money on their own balance sheets. The money is typically kept by commercial banks in deposits with the central bank (that is, as bank reserves) and sometimes it is also kept by the state as its own deposits with the central bank. In effect, commercial banks sell one type of asset (securities) and acquire another (deposits with the central bank).

The path of financialisation has been tightly bound up with quantitative easing since the Great Crisis of 2007–09. Through vast purchases of securities, central banks were able to push nominal and real interest rates toward zero in the 2010s, and even into negative territory. They supplied copious reserves of liquidity to banks and shadow intermediaries, thus providing scope to engage in fresh speculations based on extremely low interest rates. The expansion of liquidity and low interest rates supported financial asset prices for several years, leading to a sustained rise of the stock markets in the 2010s, especially in the USA.

The boost to financial asset prices after the Great Crisis of 2007–09 signalled the further transformation of financialised capitalism, marked by the growth of shadow banking. There was no financial bubble in the 2010s similar to that of the 2000s, but financial growth was sufficiently broad to sustain speculative mechanisms pivoting on securities trading by shadow banks. The resulting sources of instability and potential crisis became apparent in early 2020, when the financial sector of the USA and other core countries went through a tremendous spasm. Rising financial asset prices, meanwhile, guaranteed the income and wealth of the privileged layer at the top of the capitalist class and exacerbated inequality.

Macroeconomic Impact of the ECB's Expanded Asset Purchase Programme (APP); ECB Working Paper No. 2075.

Quantitative easing supported accumulation in the years after 2007–09, but its impact on productive investment was mediocre at best, as is clear from the analysis in the preceding sections. Moreover, financial institutions came to rely on easy and cheap provision of liquidity by the central bank, making a reversal, or abandonment, of the policy a difficult proposition, since it would raise the spectre of financial collapse. Central banks confronted that dilemma again in the 2020s after a further – and even more aggressive – deployment of unconventional monetary policy.

Finally, in 2008, the Federal Reserve deployed monetary policy to protect the global pre-eminence of the dollar as reserve currency. Above all, it provided dollar liquidity to other central banks through bilateral foreign exchange swaps, as is discussed in later chapters.[27] Suffice it to note that the Great Crisis of 2007–09 caused an acute dollar shortage internationally, and intensified demand for the dollar as a reserve currency and means of payment across the world. Foreign exchange swaps among central banks were a crucial means of buttressing the role of dollar as world money, and thus a pillar of US hegemony. Similar phenomena were observed in 2020, and the strategic use of dollar liquidity by the Federal Reserve emerged as an indisputable lever of US hegemonic power during the war in Ukraine in 2022.

Central bank discretion and mildly regulated finance

The Great Crisis of 2007–09 was overcome largely through the deployment of extraordinary monetary policy by central banks. In core countries, central banks became veritable behemoths ensconced in the heart of the economy. These public institutions are run by unelected

---

27 Swap lines have been used repeatedly by central banks in recent decades, and extensively during the Great Crisis of 2007–09 and the Pandemic Crisis. They are characteristic of the transformation of international finance and reflect the global hierarchy of currencies with the dollar at the pinnacle. For technical and institutional expositions, see, selectively, R. N. McCauley and C. R. Schenk (2020) 'Central Bank Swaps Then and Now: Swaps and Dollar Liquidity in the 1960s', BIS Working Papers No. 851; S. Murau, F. Pape, and T. Pforr (2021) 'The Hierarchy of the Offshore US-Dollar System: On Swap Lines, the FIMA Repo Facility and Special Drawing Rights', Boston University Global Development Policy Center, GEGI (Global Economic Governance Initiative) Study; and M. Choi et al. (2021) 'The Feds Central Bank Swap Lines and FIMA Repo Facility', Federal Reserve Bank of New York Staff Report No. 983.

technocrats who manage money and finance ultimately to support and reproduce the capitalist status quo. For the privileged layer at the top of financialised capitalism it is of paramount importance to prevent financial collapse, but also to avoid rapid inflation that could potentially destroy the value of debt and disrupt the extraction of financial profit.

The disaster of 2007–09 modified the broad ideological framework within which central banks implement monetary policy. In the 1990s and 2000s, the golden era of financialisation, the dominant approach, whether openly acknowledged or not, was inflation targeting. The aim of central banks was to avoid the acceleration of inflation by controlling short-term interest rates.[28] The theoretical foundations of inflation targeting are not directly relevant for our purposes but suffice it to mention that the theory rests on the ancient Quantity Theory of Money plus the assumption that any trade-off between unemployment and inflation would be limited and temporary. On these grounds, the aim of the central bank should be to keep prices stable, while allowing the economy to find its 'natural' level of output and employment.

Given this ideological framework, the independence of central banks had already become an article of economic policy orthodoxy by the 1990s. The prevalent view was that an independent central bank should be run by bureaucrats impervious to electoral cycles and freed from the constraints of political systems. The expert technocrats would not be subject to the demands of a fickle electorate and would not attempt to raise employment or achieve better growth outcomes through monetary policy. They would focus solely on keeping inflation under control.

28 For official mainstream arguments in favour of central bank independence, see S. Fischer (2015) 'Central Bank Independence', remarks by Stanley Fischer, Vice Chairman Board of Governors of the Federal reserve System at the 2015 Herbert Stein Memorial Lecture National Economists Club, Washington, DC; and B. S. Bernanke (2010) 'Central Bank Independence, Transparency, and Accountability', Speech of Chairman Ben S. Bernanke at the Institute for Monetary and Economic Studies International Conference, Bank of Japan, Tokyo, Japan, 25 May. For a trenchant heterodox critique of inflation targeting, see P. Arestis and M. C. Sawyer (2003) 'Inflation Targeting: A Critical Appraisal', Levy Economics Institute Working Paper No. 388. For a critique of the theoretical case for independence, stressing the distributional effects of monetary policy, see J. E. Stiglitz (2013) 'A Revolution in Monetary Policy: Lessons in the Wake of the Global Financial Crisis', Lecture at the Reserve Bank of India, at gsb. columbia.edu/faculty/jstiglitz. See also R. Wray (2007) 'A Post-Keynesian View of Central Bank Independence, Policy Targets, and the Rules-Versus-Discretion Debate', *Journal of Post Keynesian Economics* 30 (1): 119–41.

Independent central banking is integral to the attenuation of democracy in financialised capitalism. The management of interest rates and the creation of fiat money by the central bank are policy tools used exclusively by unelected experts linked to the capitalist elite. State power, drawing on command over the final means of payment, enables central banks to exercise control over interest rates. In short, the backbone of monetary policy is public credit embodied in the central bank and deployed by unelected technocrats.

The Great Crisis of 2007–09 revealed a fundamental flaw in the theoretical and policy framework of inflation targeting. Namely, when monetary policy focuses exclusively on controlling inflation via short-term interest rates, it effectively ignores the conduct of financial markets and the instability that might arise as a result. For, even if commodity prices were stable, monetary policy could destabilise the economy by encouraging inflation of financial assets, including real estate and the stock market. The crisis of 2007–09 and the ensuing recession put paid to the notion that an independent central bank focusing closely on inflation control would stabilise capitalist accumulation. After 2007–09, the rigid framework of inflation control was in practice replaced by a loose discretionary approach to managing credit and interest rates.

Far more critical than the trials and tribulations of inflation targeting, however, was the elevation of central banks into the paramount economic institutions of financialised capitalism after 2007–09. In the 2010s, core central banks steadily acquired more power, not least through a range of controls over the financial system. Supervisory control over financial institutions of the USA took the form of the so-called Volcker constraints.[29] The main aim was to prevent renewed bouts of speculation by US banks via limiting proprietary trading – that is, speculative trading in securities and other financial assets on the banks' own account. Banks were also constrained in transacting with, or investing in, shadow intermediaries, such as hedge funds. These constraints did not ensure the overall stability of the financial system, as

---

29 For further detail on the impact of regulating proprietary trading by banks in the USA and in the EU, see J. P. Krahnen, F. Noth, and U. Schüwer (2017) 'Structural Reforms in Banking: The Role of Trading', *Journal of Financial Regulation* 3 (1): 66–88. On the rules regarding proprietary trading by banks in the USA, see US Department of the Treasury (2013) 'Prohibitions and Restrictions on Proprietary Trading and Certain Interests in, and Relationships with, Hedge Funds and Private Equity Funds', at GPO.gov.

became obvious in 2020, but imposed stronger regulation on large private banks and rebounded in favour of shadow banking.

Equally important in this respect were the so-called macroprudential policies adopted by core countries, which amounted to the reintroduction of some controls over credit provision by private banks.[30] Limits were placed on the growth of banks and other credit institutions, for instance by imposing 'loan to value' ratios and similar small-scale controls. Macroprudential policies did not signal a systemic reversal of financial liberalisation but strengthened the discretionary powers of central banks. They constrained large commercial banks without eliminating the tendency toward financial instability, and the main beneficiary was again shadow finance, which grew steadily throughout the 2010s.

Taking advantage of central bank intervention and quantitative easing, stock markets in the USA and other core countries registered sustained rises throughout the 2010s. Shadow intermediaries, drawing on state support for finance, discovered fresh fields of speculation, while commercial banks came under pressure through regulatory controls. During that period, shadow banking created new sources of instability, which threatened wholesale collapse when the Pandemic Crisis broke out in early 2020. Once again, state intervention saved the day along similar lines to 2007–09 but on a far greater scale. To analyse the role of the state and the profound problems that resulted from its interventions, it is necessary to consider the evolution of financialisation in the 2010s more closely.

---

30 A review of the literature on macroprudential policies can be found in G. Galati and R. Moessner (2013) 'Macroprudential Policy: A Literature Review', *Journal of Economic Surveys* 27 (5): 846–78. The shift from microprudential to macroprudential regulation aimed at avoiding system-wide crises is discussed by S. G. Hanson, A. K. Kashyap, and J. C. Stein (2011) 'A Macroprudential Approach to Financial Regulation', *Journal of Economic Perspectives* 25 (1): 3–28. See also S. Claessens, S. Ghosh, and R. Mihet (2013) 'Macro-Prudential Policies to Mitigate Financial System Vulnerabilities', *Journal of International Money and Finance* 39 (C): 153–85.

5
The Travails of Financialisation

The 2010s were a watershed for financialisation in core countries, marked by the comparative retreat of commercial banking. In relative terms, private debt, and notably household debt, waned in several countries as the disastrous impact of the crisis of 2007–09 percolated through society. The decline of private debt was counterbalanced by rapidly increasing public debt, most clearly seen in the USA and the UK, the paradigmatic countries of financialised capitalism. Feeble accumulation in core countries was accompanied by growing dependence on the state, manifested in the historic swelling of central bank balance sheets.

In this environment, shadow banks were able to grow further by engaging in new types of speculation. Stock markets rose steadily throughout the decade, especially in the USA, drawing on easy central bank liquidity. Large commercial banks in the USA had fewer opportunities to make profits than in previous decades, particularly as they were also constrained by regulatory controls.

The rebalancing of financialisation between commercial banks and shadow banks confirmed the historic shift of mature financial systems in a market-based direction, with profound implications. On the one hand, the privileged layer at the top of society became even more powerful as extraordinary wealth was concentrated in the hands of portfolio managers. On the other, fresh instability was created, becoming starkly evident in early 2020 as the health emergency induced a precipitous stock market collapse. That near calamity further enhanced the dependence of market-based finance on permanent support by core states.

Financialisation weakened: Financial profits and household debt

The relative weakening of financialisation after 2007–09 can be gauged by comparing the path of non-financial profits to that of financial profits. The most distinctive features of financialised capitalism – summed up in chapter 3 – relate to changes in profit extraction that favoured financial relative to non-financial profits. Figure 5.1 presents the historic trajectory of the two forms of profit in the USA.

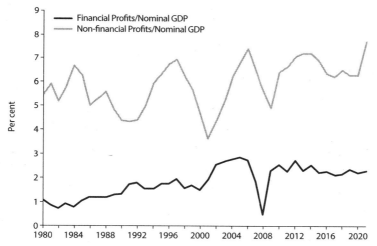

Figure 5.1. Financial and non-financial profits relative to GDP, USA.
Source: Authors' calculations using NIPA data.

Non-financial profits have been measured using the same method as for the calculation of the average rate of profit in chapter 4. However, non-financial profits in this chapter have been standardised relative to GDP – rather than the capital invested – to enable comparison with financial profits by overcoming data problems that are particularly severe regarding capital invested in the financial sector. Nevertheless, the trajectory of the ratio of non-financial profits to GDP since the early 1980s has obvious similarities with the trajectory of the average rate of profit during the same period.

Financial profits, on the other hand, were estimated by summing up the profits of commercial banks in the USA for reasons of data availability, and were also standardised relative to GDP. Commercial bank profits are a reasonable proxy for financial profits during the decades of financialisation, although they leave out shadow banking, which is discussed in the following sections.[1]

Three important points are clear from figure 5.1. First, financial profits began a sustained increase relative to GDP in the early 1980s, which lasted for the next two decades. During this period, the ratio of financial to non-financial profits also moved decisively in favour of the former, becoming extraordinarily high during the bubble of the early 2000s. The profitability of US commercial banks was underpinned primarily by the spread between the interest rate on loans and the interest rate on deposits. It also depended on fees and commissions charged by banks to mediate financial transactions among enterprises, households, and other financial firms – a characteristic feature of financialisation.[2] That period was the golden era of financialisation in the USA.

Second, financial profits collapsed in 2007–09, and non-financial profits also declined sharply as the Great Crisis took hold of the US economy.[3] The banking sector of the USA was severely shaken as the crisis ravaged the speculative mechanisms that had created the bubble. State intervention after 2008–09 restored financial profits to a historically high level in ways discussed in this and the following chapters, and bank profits remained high throughout the 2010s, but there was no upward trend. The Federal Reserve kept interest rates generally low throughout that decade, thus compressing bank spreads. Income from fees and commissions also came under pressure as the volume of financial transactions shrank and banks were constrained by the regulations introduced after 2009. The balance between financial and non-financial profits stopped moving in favour of the former.

Third, the Pandemic Crisis, in sharp contrast to 2007–09, did not

---

1 For further detail on the method of calculation, see Lapavitsas and Mendieta Muñoz (2019) 'The Historic Rise of Financial Profits in the U.S. Economy'.

2 Ibid.

3 For an empirical analysis of the collapse of bank profits in 2007–8 after a sustained expansion in the 2000s, see M. E. Detragiache, M. T. Tressel, and R. Turk-Ariss (2018) 'Where Have All the Profits Gone? European Bank Profitability Over the Financial Cycle', IMF Working Paper No. 18/99. A comparative study of the twenty largest banks in the USA, European Union (EU), and Japan by R. A. Weigand (2016) 'The Performance and Risk of Banks in the US, Europe and Japan Post-Financial Crisis', *Investment Management and Financial Innovations* 13 (4): 75–93, found that Japanese and European banks still remained severely impaired even in 2015.

reduce profits either in the non-financial or in the financial sector of the US economy. Despite causing immense economic disruption, the crisis did not originate directly in capitalist accumulation. Profits were sustained by the state intervening rapidly in 2020 to prevent a collapse of both sectors as the health emergency worsened. Even more striking, however, was the rapid escalation of non-financial profits in 2021 compared with stable financial profits. Fundamental to this development was the rise in inflation, which shifted income from labour to non-financial enterprises, as is shown in subsequent chapters. A profound change had taken place compared with previous decades.

The shock to the financial systems of core countries due to the crisis of 2007–09 is also apparent in the trajectory of household debt, shown in figure 5.2.

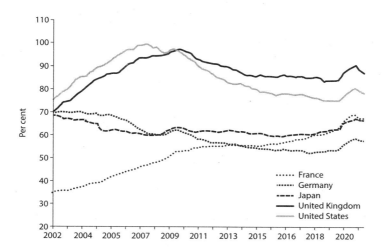

Figure 5.2. Household debt as % of GDP.
Source: Authors' calculations based on Bank for
International Settlements credit-to-GDP gaps.

Household debt differs qualitatively from the debt of enterprises, which largely reflects the economic functioning of capitalist accumulation. In contrast, household debt depends on a broad range of non-economic factors, including the legal framework and the institutional mechanisms of housing provision. It varies according to whether households and individuals have access to formal financial mechanisms, and its social and moral dimensions are prominent.[4] In core countries, household debt is determined primarily by mortgages and much less by unsecured consumer debt. In peripheral countries, the order is reversed, and consumer debt (including credit card debt) is the main form of household debt.[5]

The enormous shock of 2007–09 in both the USA and the UK resulted in a relative contraction of household debt. In Germany and Japan, on the other hand, which did not experience a housing bubble in the 2000s, household debt continued to decline as a proportion of GDP. France was the exception, reflecting a determined shift in favour of financialisation that has marked the country for decades. Caught in the trap of the EMU and unable to compete with Germany, France went down the path of further boosting its financial sector domestically and internationally.

The relative retreat of financialisation in the 2010s can also be seen in figure 5.3, which tracks the debt of non-financial corporations in core countries.

Financialisation in the USA has never been characterised by strong growth of corporate debt, but rather by rising household and interbank debt, resulting in profits through the corresponding financial expropriation.[6] Following the crisis of 2007–09, the debt of non-financial enterprises

4 The complex factors underpinning consumer debt are discussed in depth in A. Barba and M. Pivetti (2009) 'Rising Household Debt: Its Causes and Macroeconomic Implications: A Long-Period Analysis', *Cambridge Journal of Economics* 33 (1): 113–37. Barba and Pivetti note especially the contradiction of household debt rising at a time when real wages were under sustained pressure. Precisely this contradiction lay at the root of the Great Crisis of 2007–9; see also footnote 20 in chapter 4.

5 For an analysis of household debt in developing countries focusing on the role of foreign bank lending, see H. Cho (2010) *South Korea's Experience with Banking Sector Liberalisation*, The Centre for Research on Multinational Corporations: Amsterdam; see also C. Lapavitsas and P. L. Dos Santos (2008) 'Globalization and Contemporary Banking: On the Impact of New Technology', *Contributions to Political Economy* 27 (1): 31–56; and E. Correa and G. Vidal (2012) 'Financialization and Global Financial Crisis in Latin American Countries', *Journal of Economic Issues* 46 (2): 541–8. For the role of domestic banks in lending to support consumption, see E. Karacimen (2016) 'Consumer Credit as an Aspect of Everyday Life of Workers in Developing Countries: Evidence from Turkey', *Review of Radical Political Economics* 48 (2): 252–68; see also L. Rethel (2010) 'Financialisation and the Malaysian Political Economy', *Globalizations* 7 (4): 489–506.

6 See A. Mian, L. Straub, and A. Sufi (2020) 'Indebted Demand', NBER Working Paper No. 26940, for some remarkable measurements of debt and associated income transfers in the USA. See also J. Graham, M. Leary, and M. Robert (2015) 'A Century

in the USA declined relative to GDP. The proportion began to rise again in the second half of the 2010s as corporations took advantage of low interest rates to channel profits to shareholders through stock buybacks, but did not escalate rapidly. Stagnating corporate debt in the 2010s was also observed in Japan and Germany, while in the UK corporate debt even contracted relative to GDP. The exception, as was already noted, was France, where corporate debt rose substantially.

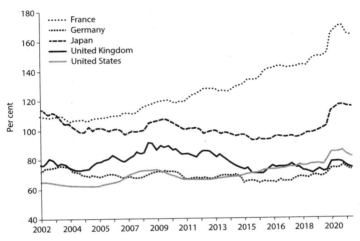

Figure 5.3. Non-financial corporate debt as % of GDP.
Source: Authors' calculations based on Bank for
International Settlements credit-to-GDP gaps.

The trajectory of corporate debt is consistent with the feebleness of accumulation in core countries during the 2010s. Corporate debt increased dramatically only in 2020, as central banks truly loosened monetary conditions in the face of the pandemic shock, giving a fresh boost to financialisation.

of Capital Structure: The Leveraging of Corporate America', *Journal of Financial Economics* 118: 658–83 for an analysis of trends in US corporate indebtedness. A recent review of corporate debt dynamics by L. A. de Almeida and M. T. Tressel (2020) 'Non-Financial Corporate Debt in Advanced Economies, 2010–17', International Monetary Fund, finds strong heterogeneity across countries and enterprises, though in the aftermath of the Great Crisis, enterprises have relied more heavily on capital markets.

Financialisation rebalanced: Public debt and shadow banking

In contrast to households and non-financial corporations, public debt in core countries grew substantially in the 2010s, with the obvious exception of Germany, as is shown in figure 5.4.

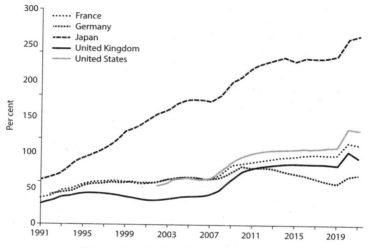

Figure 5.4. Public debt as % of GDP.
Source: Authors' calculations based on IMF fiscal monitor database.

The general trajectory of public debt is remarkably similar across the core countries, except for Germany.[7] More than rising public debt, however, in this period the state began to play an extraordinary role in financial markets through the central bank. The pivotal presence of the state expedited the rebalancing of financialisation as shadow banks took advantage of the new conditions. Growing public debt facilitated the growth of shadow banks.

Reliable figures for shadow banking are hard to obtain, but it has been estimated that at the end of 2019, non-bank financial intermediaries managed assets of around 200 trillion dollars, representing

---

7 Japan is an obvious outlier regarding the size of its public debt, as it has relied increasingly on government borrowing to support aggregate demand since the burst of its own bubble in the late 1980s, which ushered in a long period of weak accumulation. Japan invented quantitative easing policy and initiated the analysis of zombie firms; see R. J. Caballero, T. Hoshi, and A. K. Kashyap (2008) 'Zombie Lending and Depressed Restructuring in Japan', *American Economic Review* 98 (5): 1943–77.

almost half the total stock of financial assets globally.[8] Shadow finance has considerably larger proportions in core economies, though it is far from negligible in peripheral countries, commanding more than half of total financial assets in the former compared with a quarter in the latter.[9]

Moreover, the precise meaning of shadow banking remains unclear. The Financial Stability Board, an international body publishing annual reports on non-bank financial intermediation, defines shadow banking as 'the system of credit intermediation that involves entities and activities outside the regular banking system'.[10] In effect, shadow intermediaries are private enterprises that advance credit through complex chains of securities but without taking deposits that function as money in the normal way of bank deposits. They include a great range of institutions: mutual funds, hedge funds, exchange-traded funds (ETFs), private equity funds, money market mutual funds, and others.[11]

Typically, shadow banks do not face regulations regarding their own capital requirements, nor do they receive deposit guarantees from the state. They also generally lack direct access to credit from the central bank, which is a particularly important factor in times of crisis, when the central bank acts as the lender of last resort.[12] These

---

8 See Financial Stability Board (2020) 'Global Monitoring Report on Non-Bank Financial Intermediation', December, at fsb.org.

9 See, for instance, S. Ghosh, I. Gonzalez del Mazo, and I. Ötker-Robe (2012) 'Chasing the Shadows: How Significant is Shadow Banking in Emerging Markets?' World Bank Economic Premise No. 88, which finds that despite being limited in comparison to advanced countries, the shadow banking sector in emerging markets has expanded quickly, acting as an alternative mechanism for financial flows.

10 See Financial Stability Board (2011) 'Shadow Banking: Scoping the Issues. A Background Note of the Financial Stability Board', April, p. 2, at fsb.org.

11 They could further be made to include finance companies, leasing companies, factoring companies, consumer credit companies, credit insurance companies, financial guarantors, and so on. See A. M. Agresti and R. Brence (2017) 'Statistical Work on Shadow Banking: Development of New Datasets and Indicators for Shadow Banking', Paper presented at the IFC-National Bank of Belgium Workshop on 'Data Needs and Statistics Compilation for Macroprudential Analysis', Brussels, Belgium, at bis.org.

12 For descriptive accounts of shadow banking, see S. Claessens et al. (2012) 'Shadow Banking: Economics and Policy', IMF Staff Discussion Note, December, SDN/12/1; see also S. Claessens and L. Ratnovski (2014) 'What Is Shadow Banking?' IMF Working Paper No. 14-25. For a more detailed analytical description, see P. Mehrling (2011) *The New Lombard Street: How the Fed Became the Dealer of Last Resort*, Princeton University Press: Princeton, NJ.

features give the sector its shadow appellation, but its activities are very disparate and often hardly admit of grouping together. It bears stressing that there is no fundamental opposition between regular banks and shadow banks. On the contrary, commercial and investment banks often create shadow banks as well as actively facilitating their market transactions.[13]

The growth of shadow banking, at the same time as the state assumed a pivotal position in the financial systems of core countries, is likely to have profound implications for capitalist accumulation. The operations of shadow banks differ significantly from those of commercial banks, lending a different outlook to the extraction of financial profit and to class stratification in financialised capitalism. The contrast between the two is important enough to merit an analytical digression in the rest of this chapter from the perspective of Marxist political economy.[14]

Bank capital: A simple summing up

A commercial bank is, in Marx's own terms, a 'bank capital'.[15] Shadow banks are substantially different, although both commercial and shadow banks are broadly similar as financial capitals – that is, capitals guiding the flows of loanable money capital without becoming directly involved in the production of value and surplus value.[16] One way of capturing the key differences between these two types of financial capital is through highly simplified balance sheets, starting with that of a commercial bank (see table 5.1).

---

13 Shadow banking could be considered as an offshoot of regular banking that has facilitated the characteristic shift of the latter toward mediating in open market transactions and providing loans to households; see also P. L. Dos Santos (2013) 'A Cause for Policy Concern: The Expansion of Household Credit in Middle-Income Economies', *International Review of Applied Economics* 27 (3): 316–38.

14 The structural connection between the two forms of financial intermediation is analysed in detail in Z. Pozsar and M. Singh (2011) 'The Nonbank–Bank Nexus and the Shadow Banking System', IMF Working Paper No. 289.

15 This section relies heavily on Marx (1981) [1894] *Capital*, vol. 3, ch. 29. However, the analysis is brought up to date by also drawing on contemporary theory of banking, particularly on the inherently similar post-Keynesian analysis.

16 For the definition of loanable capital and its accumulation, see Lapavitsas (2013) *Profiting without Producing*.

Table 5.1. Commercial bank.

Assets (Uses of funds)	Liabilities (Sources of funds)
Securities	Deposits
Loans	Open market borrowing
Liquidity reserves	Equity capital

A commercial bank is a capitalist enterprise established by investing its own equity capital and aiming to make profits by advancing loanable capital to purchase securities and make loans (including mortgages and consumer loans). The securities purchased are primarily bonds issued by non-financial corporations and the state. To finance its profit-seeking activities, the bank must collect loanable capital from a broad range of sources – that is, it itself must borrow. That means, above all, attracting deposits as well as engaging in open market borrowing. Deposits are highly liquid – indeed, they are the main form of credit money in advanced capitalism – while open market borrowing could also be liquid – in other words, the lender to the bank could be allowed rapidly to withdraw the money advanced.

Consequently, a bank is obliged to keep liquidity reserves, the main form of which is the bank's own deposits held with the central bank. A bank's first port of call for further reserves is the money market, where short-term loanable capital (liquidity) is traded among banks; the trading of short-term loanable capital also involves other enterprises that possess or require liquid assets. If liquidity in the money market were to dry up, banks would be put in an extremely difficult position and their last resort would be to borrow directly from the central bank. This is costly for banks, but also puts them in a privileged position relative to other participants in the money market.

When a bank advances loanable capital to buy securities or make loans, it takes credit risk – that is, the risk that payment of interest and repayment of principal would not proceed according to contract and might even involve borrower default. Therefore, the bank must monitor the enterprises that have received its loans as well as checking the creditworthiness of the securities it buys. The latter is far more impersonal and arms-length than the former, and the difference is vital for the functioning of financial systems.

If the bank loses loanable capital either on securities or loans, it runs the risk of becoming insolvent and going bankrupt. To confront this eventuality, the bank must keep substantial equity capital as a solvency cushion. Other things being equal, banks seek equity capital in open financial markets through the issuing of shares, or via private provision from another bank or corporation. If private sources of equity capital were to dry up, the last recourse of banks would be the public purse, meaning direct injections of tax income from the state. The decades of financialisation have put banks at a unique advantage in this regard compared with other capitalist enterprises.

The privileged position of commercial banks regarding both liquidity and solvency is inextricably linked to deposits acting as the main form of credit money in contemporary capitalism. Commercial banks receive explicit and implicit protection from the state, including guarantees for their deposits. The other side of this coin, however, is that banks must comply with a range of regulations regarding liquidity reserves and equity.

In addition to these basic operations, banks also provide money-related services (money transmission, foreign exchange conversion, etc.).[17] Banks also engage in off-balance-sheet operations, including a broad range of activities associated with financial markets, such as underwriting and broking of securities. The provision of these services could indeed stand as a separate banking business, namely investment banking. Suffice it to mention that investment banks are integral to the operations of financial markets; they typically do not take deposits or make loans, but frequently trade securities on their own account.

Finally, the profits of a commercial bank derive primarily from the difference between the interest received on securities and loans and the interest paid on deposits and open market borrowing. However, banks also earn non-interest profit, for instance from fees and commissions, money-related services, or off-balance-sheet activities. The sum of interest and non-interest profit relative to equity defines the rate of profit of banks, which tends to be equated to the average rate of profit across the economy.

It cannot be overemphasised that banks are capitalist enterprises that seek profits by providing a range of services that are necessary for capitalist accumulation, typically associated with intermediating the flows of loanable capital. The fundamental operating principle of

---

17 Marx calls these 'money-dealing' services; see Marx (1981) [1894] *Capital*, vol. 3, ch. 19.

commercial banks is to advance loanable capital on securities or loans, and subsequently to seek reserves to support the advances already made. For Marxist political economy, banks are active capitalist agents, seeking profits through the placement of loanable capital; they are not merely passive intermediaries that first receive and then distribute spare funds.

Shadow banks as portfolio managers

In contrast to commercial banks, the balance sheet of a shadow bank cannot be easily depicted, since there is minimal uniformity among these institutions. A useful representation would be through the simplified balance sheet of a mutual fund (that also borrows), as is shown in table 5.2. With some mental tweaking, that balance sheet could also serve for a money market mutual fund, an ETF, or even a hedge fund.

Table 5.2. Shadow bank (mutual fund).

Assets (Uses of funds)	Liabilities (Sources of funds)
Debt securities (bonds)	Equity capital (fund shares)
Equity securities (shares)	Open market borrowings
Liquidity reserves	

A shadow bank is a capitalist enterprise established by investing equity capital (that is, issuing fund shares) and aiming to make profits through the purchase of securities. The buyers of fund shares are typically other financial institutions, such as pension funds and insurance companies, which have large pools of household and other savings available for investment. Buyers could also be rich individuals as well as small money owners from the middle class. Buyers could further include other shadow banks investing in each other and thus creating a veritable tangle of property interconnections.

In contrast to a commercial bank, a shadow bank is effectively a portfolio manager – that is, a financial enterprise that advances loanable capital but does not make straightforward loans. The securities it purchases include shares of enterprises (both non-financial and financial) or private and public bonds. Since the shadow bank advances loanable capital through marketable financial instruments, it does not directly monitor those agents who receive it. The relationship between the shadow bank and the recipient is mediated through financial markets and largely involves technical analysis of the securities purchased.

The assets of shadow banks include enormous volumes of enterprise shares, thus entailing complex property relations. At one remove, these relations seem plain: the buyers of fund shares acquire property rights over the shadow bank, but, since the shadow bank regularly buys enterprise shares, said buyers also have indirect property rights over the latter. In effect, the holders of fund shares have property rights over productive resources that are mediated by the shadow bank's portfolio. A moment's reflection indicates, however, that the property relations could be far more complex. The holders of fund shares might well be pension funds, insurance companies, or other intermediaries. Thus, the owner of a pension plan, such as a workers' retirement institution, might have a highly mediated and remote claim to some productive resources through a shadow bank.

In recent years, the shadow layer of the US financial system has become highly concentrated while, at the same time, holding enormous volumes of shares, thus resulting in an unprecedented concentration of property and wealth. During the 2000s and 2010s, the 'Giant Three' among shadow US intermediaries (that is, BlackRock, Vanguard, and State Street Global Advisors) nearly quadrupled their collective ownership of publicly listed companies. The 'Giant Three' have captured the overwhelming bulk of the inflows of loanable capital into the shadow finance sector, and collectively hold an average of roughly a quarter of the voting rights in managing all the enterprises included in the Standard and Poor 500 index.[18] This concentration of property rights is without precedent in the history of capitalism.

In practice, shadow banks are a layer of financial institutions that further separate the sources of loanable money capital from the enterprises that actively create value and surplus value. Both the shadow banks and the original providers of the loanable money capital thereby acquire some of the character of the rentier. They are universal owners in the sense that they hold a fully diversified portfolio stretching over a vast range of enterprises, but appear to play little or no direct role in

---

18 See L. Bebchuk and S. Hirst (2019) 'The Specter of the Giant Three', Boston University Law Review 99: 721–41.

managing the latter.[19] Rather, shadow banks focus on maximising the value of their 'assets under management', thus allowing their own portfolio managers to draw fees.[20]

Shadow bank profits come from dividends on shares and interest on bonds, but crucially also from capital gains on securities. Hence, shadow banks relentlessly seek to expand assets under management and benefit directly from stock market bubbles. In terms of Marxist political economy, their profits are a portion of the annual flow of surplus value but also a part of the money income, the money holdings, and the money capital of all social classes. Shadow bank profits partly reflect financial expropriation in financial markets.

The profits of shadow banks are distributed to the owners of fund shares on a regular basis, paid as dividends per share. The distribution depends on whether shadow banks are 'open-ended' (with an unlimited number of shares) or 'closed-ended' (with a fixed number of shares). A significant portion accrues to shadow bank managers, who typically receive a percentage of the market value of assets under management, irrespective of whether profits have been made in practice. In some shadow banks, such as hedge funds, managers also receive a substantial percentage of the profits. Shadow banking thus offers opportunities for fabulous wealth acquisition to some of its operators.

To finance the growth of their assets and make more profits, shadow banks could potentially issue more fund shares, or perhaps reinvest some of their profits. However, it would make a tremendous difference to their operations if they could also use open market borrowings – that

---

19 See B. Braun (2021) 'American Asset Manager Capitalism as a Corporate Governance Regime', in J. Hacker et al. (eds) *The American Political Economy: Politics, Markets, and Power*, Cambridge University Press: Cambridge, UK, pp. 270–94. If they ever come to acquire such a role, US capitalism will take a dramatically stronger oligarchic outlook, particularly as the concentration of ownership remains on an upward trend. Some leading US lawyers are already talking of the 'Problem of Twelve' – that is, the likelihood that in the near future roughly twelve individuals will have practical power over the majority of US public companies; see J. Coates (2018) 'The Future of Corporate Governance Part I: The Problem of Twelve', Harvard Public Law Working Paper No. 19–07.

20 Minsky's 'money manager capitalism' is clearly relevant in this connection and has frequently been deployed in critical analyses of contemporary developments in finance; see, for instance, L. R. Wray (2011) 'Minsky's Money Manager Capitalism and the Global Financial Crisis', Levy Economics Institute Working Paper No. 661; see also C. J . Whalen (2017) 'Understanding Financialization', Levy Economics Institute Working Paper No. 892.

is, if they became leveraged. Borrowing encourages great variation among shadow banks and boosts speculation, which is typically reflected in different strategies for acquiring securities.

Shadow bank borrowing, speculating, and profit making

Mutual funds are traditionally not leveraged and mostly purchase securities financed by equity capital.[21] In contrast, hedge funds are leveraged and aggressively pick securities that managers consider cheap, essentially betting on capital gains.[22] Index funds, on the other hand, are a type of leveraged mutual fund that tracks a leading stock market index, such as the Standard and Poor 500. In effect, index funds buy assets passively to replicate the movement of an index. After 2007–09, they became the dominant species of shadow banks.[23]

An ETF is a further variation on this theme, but with the crucial difference that its own shares are freely traded in the stock market, thus being subject to potential gyrations of value. ETFs proved instrumental to the collapse of stock markets when Covid-19 struck, as is shown in subsequent chapters. Money market mutual funds, finally, merit separate consideration and are different from other shadow banks, as they operate in the money market.

---

21 Mutual funds typically constrain managers to acquire assets in only a few classes, meeting or exceeding the return on these classes. Based on the allocation made among such assets, it is possible technically to differentiate among the 'styles' of shadow bank managers; see W. Scharpe (1992), 'Asset Allocation: Management Style and Performance Measurement', *Journal of Portfolio Management* 18 (2): 7–19.

22 Hedge funds typically constrain managers to achieve an absolute return target, irrespective of what is happening in the markets. Managers can choose flexibly among asset classes and employ dynamic strategies that include 'short' sales, derivatives, and 'leverage'.

23 Passive surpassed active management of investments in 2019; see J. Fichtner and E. M. Heemskerk (2020) 'The New Permanent Universal Owners: Index Funds, Patient Capital, and the Distinction between Feeble and Forceful Stewardship', *Economy and Society* 49 (4): 493–515. The inevitable result was power acquisition by the index providers, such as S&P Dow Jones indices and FTSE Russell, who choose which companies or countries enter the index, thereby deciding where loanable capital will go. The manipulation of this process is yet another inherently power-related aspect of market-based finance; see J. Petry, J. Fichtner, and E. M. Heemskerk (2019) 'Steering Capital: the Growing Private Authority of Index Providers in the Age of Passive Asset Management', *Review of International Political Economy* 28 (1): 152–76.

Shadow banks acquire leverage in many ways, for instance by obtaining lines of credit from commercial banks, or by buying securities on margin – that is, by putting down a fraction of the security price and paying for the rest with money borrowed from a broker (perhaps a bank). The leveraging practices of shadow banks facilitate speculation and augment their profits, highlighting the drastic transformation of the money market in the years of financialisation.[24]

For when it comes to leveraging, shadow banks have a decisive card at their disposal; namely, they hold an enormous range and volume of securities on the asset side of their balance sheets. Thus, portfolio managers can borrow by 'shorting' securities – that is, by selling securities on condition of repurchasing the same after a short period of time, and using the temporarily sold securities as collateral. This is the characteristic practice of the repo market, briefly discussed in chapter 3, which has become fundamental to the wholesale liquidity money markets of financialised capitalism.[25]

When a shadow bank is leveraged, its portfolio becomes 'long' on the asset side (that is, the shadow bank has purchased securities) and 'short' on the liability side (that is, the shadow bank has temporarily sold securities), while using securities as collateral. The simultaneous holding of 'long' and 'short' positions entails obvious risks for the overall market value of the portfolio of the shadow bank. Consequently, shadow banks typically engage in derivatives trading to cover themselves against risks of price fluctuations, while also keeping liquidity reserves. Moreover, shadow banks, insofar as they allow their shareholders rapidly to cash in their shares, must also hold further liquidity reserves. Therefore, regular access to the money market through repos is a *sine qua non* for shadow banks that aim to expand their assets through leverage.[26]

Market-based finance receives a tremendous boost from the use of securities as collateral to leverage shadow banks. Securitisation accelerates, since, for the mechanisms of shadow banking to work, financial

---

24 See Z. Pozsar (2014) 'Shadow Banking: The Money View', Office of Financial Research Working Paper No. 14 (04) on the crucial role of leveraging within the shadow banking system.

25 See P. Schaffner, A. Ranaldo, and K. Tsatsaronis (2019) 'Euro Repo Market Functioning: Collateral Is King', *BIS Quarterly Review*, December: 95–108.

26 See D. Gabor (2016) 'The (Impossible) Repo Trinity: The Political Economy of Repo Markets', *Review of International Political Economy* 23 (6): 967–1000; see also D. Gabor (2018) 'Goodbye (Chinese) Shadow Banking, Hello Market-Based Finance', *Development and Change* 49 (2): 394–419.

markets must have significant depth in securities available for trading. Ordinary loans, such as mortgages and consumer loans, must be regularly turned into marketable securities to serve as assets and collateral for shadow banks. They are packaged together and sold as new financial assets, deriving their value from the stream of payments to the underlying loans.[27] The loan originator (perhaps a commercial bank) becomes a fee-earning intermediary between the borrower (say, a household) and the asset holder (a shadow bank). The shadow bank is simply a further intermediary relative to the owners of idle money capital. Commercial banks find a new field of profitability in securitisation via fees and commissions as well as by setting up their own shadow banks.

Once securitisation takes hold, the modes of operation of financial institutions, both visible and shadow, come increasingly to rely on obtaining wholesale funding in the money market, as was briefly discussed in chapter 3. To buy securitised assets, shadow banks need a steady supply of wholesale finance obtained by using their assets as collateral.[28] Financial intermediation becomes a process of borrowing short-term by using securities as collateral, while aiming to create and buy still more securities. The scope for pure financial speculation becomes gigantic, since the repo market allows for heavily leveraged transactions, particularly as the same security can be used as collateral in multiple repo transactions by successive borrowers.[29]

A simple way of gaining insight into this transformation is to consider money market mutual funds. The fundamental purpose of the money market is to provide liquidity reserves to regular banks, as was already mentioned in chapter 3. However, the functioning of the money market has greatly expanded in the decades of financialisation. Money market mutual funds are shadow banks operating in the money market by collecting temporarily idle money capital from a broad range of

---

27 See T. Adrian and H. S. Shin (2010) 'The Changing Nature of Financial Intermediation and the Financial Crisis of 2007–2009', *Annual Review of Economics* 2 (1): 603–18.

28 This point has been repeatedly stressed by economists diverging from the mainstream: for instance, Perry Mehrling and Zoltan Pozsar. What matters is not so much the entities but the activities, since regular banks are also engaged in shadow operations. See, for instance, P. Mehrling et al. (2013) 'Bagehot Was a Shadow Banker: Shadow Banking, Central Banking, and the Future of Global Finance', at ssrn.com.

29 See J. Wullweber (2021) 'The Politics of Shadow Money: Security Structures, Money Creation and Unconventional Central Banking', *New Political Economy* 26 (1): 69–85.

institutions, such as large corporations, pension funds, insurance companies, or other shadow banks, subsequently to invest in short-term debt securities, either private or public. Functioning at the heart of the repo market, they effectively coordinate the wholesale funding of other shadow banks.

To deliver this function, the liabilities of money market mutual funds must be considered by their holders to be approximate to regular money in terms of both liquidity and acceptability.[30] A crucial issue in this connection is the pricing of the shares of money market mutual funds, to which the Marxist category of fictitious capital is an indispensable guide.[31]

The share price of a shadow bank is generally based on its net asset value (NAV), which is the difference between the sum of the prices of its assets minus the sum of the prices of its liabilities.[32]

---

30 'Approximating' is the operative word here: there remains a profound difference between actual money deployed as means of payment (and reserves) and the liabilities of shadow banks, be they the shares of money market mutual funds or repos issued by brokers holding public bonds. Advocates of the 'money' approach to shadow banking can be a little too hasty in declaring such liabilities to be 'shadow money'; see, for instance, D. Gabor and J. Vestergaard (2016) 'Towards a Theory of Shadow Money', Institute for New Economic Thinking, Working Paper, April, at ineteconomics.org. The reason is that shadow bank liabilities cannot be used for payment but must first be converted into units of regular money. Pozsar, who has done more than most to establish the 'money' approach, is fully aware of this difficulty, though he seeks to brush it away by claiming that 'these instruments have one common attribute, which is that they promise to trade at par on demand. This makes them money.' See Z. Pozsar (2014) 'Shadow Banking: The Money View', Office of Financial Research, Working Paper No. 4-14, p. 9. Unfortunately, it does not. Money must be able to pay (and form reserves) if it is to function as money. These instruments are, at best, near money – and that holds purely within the financial system. At times of crisis, as in 2007–09 or 2020, their 'moneyness' disappears – that is, precisely when money must emerge as the sole socially acceptable form of value. There is no analogy with bills of exchange, which became the original form of credit money in trade circuits in the nineteenth century, because they were able to pay. To be sure, at times bills failed adequately to deliver the payment function and were eventually overtaken by bank deposits. But there is still no comparison with shadow bank liabilities.

31 See Marx (1981) [1894] *Capital*, vol. 3, ch. 25.

32 In a little more detail, NAV reflects the price at which an open-ended mutual fund sells or purchases its shares at the end of each day. The shares of closed-ended mutual funds, which are not obliged to buy or sell their shares at NAV, could be purchased at a discount (<NAV) or a premium (>NAV) by investors. It follows that closed-ended mutual funds could carry out riskier investments – with higher returns – than open-ended ones.

These prices are fully fictitious capital – that is, sums of money that do not correspond to the actual money invested in the asset, and much less to the value of the capital engaged in production, if the financial asset is a share. They are fictitious because they are essentially estimated by discounting the expected future returns from the asset (including capital gains) using a rate of discount related to market rate of interest. Consequently, these prices reflect the daily gyrations of the financial markets and result in a constantly fluctuating NAV for shadow banks.

The share price of a money market mutual fund would be calculated as its NAV divided by the total number of shares issued by the fund. This is manifestly a fictitious magnitude, a 'shadow price' largely unrelated to the actual flows of loanable capital into the fund's assets and liabilities (and much less to the capital value invested in the activities of the issuers of the securities). Yet this price is of crucial importance in the money market, since, from the perspective of the corporations and other large institutions seeking to invest their temporarily idle capital, it practically stands for a unit of money. Hence, money market mutual funds aim to maintain a NAV per share as close as possible to unity by managing their assets and liabilities as well as by regularly distributing profits to shareholders.

This peculiar price has become a benchmark for the availability of liquidity in the money markets of financialised capitalism. Governments regulate the activities of money market mutual funds, aiming to keep the share price as close as possible to unity. However, speculation made that impossible in the Great Crisis of 2007–09, as several funds had accumulated untrustworthy securitised assets deriving from the housing bubble. The sharpest signal of the emerging gigantic liquidity crisis in 2007–09 was the act of 'breaking the buck' that occurred in the US money market – that is, money market mutual funds becoming unable to honour their liabilities at a rate of one to one with the dollars issued by the Federal Reserve.

In the USA, regulations were brought in by the state in 2016 to allow some flexibility to this price, in the hope of ameliorating the wild panics resulting from 'breaking the buck'. But the turmoil of the 2020s showed that shadow banking speculation could still generate acute liquidity crises pivoting on money market mutual funds. When panic broke out in 2020, it became clear once again that the expansion of shadow banking is conditional on state support.

The rise of shadow banking evidently rests on the new technologies that have spread relentlessly since the 1970s.[33] Portfolio management and the daily calculation of fictitious prices by shadow banks would have been impossible without enormous advances in information and communications technologies as well as artificial intelligence. But the state has also been a crucial actor. For one thing, the spread of securitisation is firmly based on the tremendous expansion of public debt during the last two decades. The benchmark securities in financial markets are public bonds (or publicly guaranteed bonds), both short and long term. Public bonds are the foundation of shadow banking portfolios, while the dominant banks in the securitisation chains are those that undertake the brokering of public debt in the financial markets.

The repo markets also pivot on central banks, which determine the securities acceptable as collateral as well as the price at which these are bought and resold – that is, the implicit rate of interest. Ironically, in practice the central banks of developed countries have become securities dealers of last resort.[34] In that capacity, central banks purchase financial assets to support money markets by providing liquidity and stabilising the price of collateral. Repo markets are the main channel through which central banks provide liquidity in times of crisis and have become an integral part of unconventional monetary policies. Massive purchases of public assets by central banks as part of quantitative easing could, however, also result in shortages of collateral securities in the repo markets.[35]

The enormous growth of shadow finance, especially in the decade after the Great Crisis, has been fully dependent on the state, particularly on the actions of core central banks. The power of central banks to

---

33 It is commonly stated that regulatory changes together with technological development have led to the exponential growth of finance since the 1970s but accelerating in the 1990s and 2000s; see, for instance, D. MacKenzie (2006) *An Engine, Not a Camera: How Financial Models Shape Markets*, MIT Press: Cambridge, MA, and London; see also N. Cerpa Vielma et al. (2019) 'Too Big to Manage: US Megabanks' Competition by Innovation and the Microfoundations of Financialization', *Cambridge Journal of Economics* 43 (4): 1103–21.

34 See Mehrling (2011) *The New Lombard Street*; and (2012) 'Three Principles for Market-Based Credit Regulation', *American Economic Review: Papers & Proceedings* 102 (3): 107–12.

35 See Committee on the Global Financial System (2017) 'Repo Market Functioning', CGFS Papers No. 59, at bis.org.

dominate money markets, furthermore, derives from their command over fiat money. State-guaranteed fiat money is the bedrock of contemporary market-based finance and shadow banking, as well as of financialisation in general.

The Pandemic Crisis provided evidence of the transformation of financialisation since 2007–09 and reaffirmed the extraordinary economic role of the state in the core countries of the world economy. At the same time, it brought to the fore profound differences between core and peripheral states, pointing to increasing divergences in the world economy that are the focus of much of the rest of this book.

6

Core and Peripheral States in the Turmoil of the 2020s

When Covid-19 struck, economic conditions in core countries were already precarious, but the effective cause of the ensuing crisis was the health emergency and the actions taken by states to confront it. Core states implemented measures that crushed aggregate demand and severely disrupted aggregate supply, as was discussed in part I. When the magnitude of the unfolding economic disaster became apparent, core states reacted rapidly to foster recovery through monetary and fiscal policy. They demonstrated colossal power to influence capitalist accumulation by drawing primarily on monopoly control over money as the final means of payment created by the central bank. Intervention by core states on the side of demand, however, exacerbated the deficiency of supply, creating profound instability for financialised capitalism.

States in peripheral countries could not follow the same path. To be sure, peripheral states also command domestic fiat money and can deploy fiscal and monetary policies but are unable to intervene on a scale comparable to core states because, above all, their currencies occupy subordinate positions in the world market. They are also buffeted by forces emanating from the world market that are often triggered by the economic interventions of core states. Divergences between core and periphery became apparent when the pandemic struck and were exacerbated when the Russo-Ukrainian conflict broke out in 2022.

Triggering economic collapse

The first signs of widespread economic turmoil were recorded in the international financial markets in early 2020, and the immediate trigger was the forcible shutting down of entire economic sectors, severely restricting public and private contact among individuals at work and more broadly. The blow to aggregate demand and supply resulted in a synchronised global recession during the first half of 2020. Profound differences rapidly emerged among core and peripheral countries.

Table 6.1 shows that economic activity was already weak in late 2019 but veered sharply toward recession in the first quarter of 2020, followed by an extraordinary global contraction in the second quarter. The retreat of economic activity slowed down in the third quarter of 2020, but output remained far below the previous year's level. The exception was East Asia and the Pacific, where recovery was quick, mainly due to China (and Vietnam): most other countries in the region remained weak.

Table 6.1. Real GDP growth rate, percentage change from the previous year.

	2019	20Q1	20Q2	20Q3	20Q4	2020	21Q1	21Q2	21Q3	21Q4	22Q1
Advanced economies	1.7	-1.1	-11	-3.6	-2.7	-4.6	-0.2	12.6	4.2	4.6	...
United States	2.3	0.3	-9.1	-2.9	-2.3	-3.4	0.5	12.2	4.9	5.5	3.5
Euro area	1.6	-3.3	-14.5	-4.1	-4.3	-6.4	-0.9	14.6	4.1	4.7	5.1
Japan	-0.2	-2.2	-10.1	-5.4	-0.9	-4.6	-1.7	7.4	1.2	0.4	0.5
Developing economies	3.8	-2.4	-6.1	-0.6	2	-1.6	8.5	11.3	5.4	...	...
East Asia and Pacific	5.8	-5.5	1.1	3.4	4.9	1.2	15.3	8.1	4.3	4.1	4.8
Europe and Central Asia	2.7	2.2	-8.8	-1.4	0	-1.9	1.2	13.5	5.6	...	...

Latin America and the Caribbean	0.8	-1	-15.4	-6.9	-2.6	-6.4	-0.1	17.1	-0.1	4	. . .
Middle East and North Africa	0.9	-1	-6.4	-2.6	-2.8	-3.7	-0.9	5.2	6.7	6.2	. . .
South Asia	4.1	2.8	-24.2	-7.2	0.7	-4.5	2.6	19.9	8.2	5.3	. . .
Sub-Saharan Africa	2.6	1.8	-10.1	-4	-1.1	-2	-0.1	11.5	4.3	. . .	. . .

Source: Authors' calculations using data from World Bank Global Economic Prospects June 2021, January 2022, and June 2022.

State-imposed restrictions and lockdowns disrupted interlinked production networks and supply chains, dealing a blow to global manufacturing.[1] The measures dealt an even greater blow to services, particularly transport, travel, tourism, entertainment, restaurants, hotels, and so on. The combined pressure on manufacturing and services led to a collapse of global trade.[2] Trade in services was more severely affected than trade in goods, reflecting the greater impact of state measures on the service sector.

Restrictions and lockdowns also impacted directly on aggregate demand, leading to a decline in consumption.[3] For rich and

1 See B. Javorcik (2020) 'Global Supply Chains Will Not Be the Same in the Post-COVID-19 World', in R. Baldwin and S. Evenett (eds) *COVID-19 and Trade Policy: Why Turning Inward Won't Work*, CEPR Press: VoxEU e-book, pp. 111–16, at cepr.org; S. Miroudot (2020), 'Resilience versus Robustness in Global Value Chains: Some Policy Implications', in Baldwin and Evenett (eds) *COVID-19 and Trade Policy*, pp. 117–30.

2 See United Nations Conference on Trade and Development (UNCTAD) (2020) *Trade and Development Report 2020: From Global Pandemic to Prosperity for All: Avoiding Another Lost Decade*, UNCTAD: Geneva.

3 See IMF (2021) 'World Economic Outlook Update January 2021: Policy Support and Vaccines Expected to Lift Activity', at imf.org.

middle-class households, the decline of consumption led to a rise in savings.[4] But as unemployment rose rapidly and incomes shrank, wide layers of workers faced absolute falls in basic consumption – hunger threatened. Aggregate demand was further reduced as investment collapsed in both core and peripheral countries in the face of extreme uncertainty. The contraction of aggregate demand, however, varied considerably depending on the severity of the restrictions, the mechanisms of economic and welfare support by the state, and the underlying strength of production.[5]

The measures also impacted severely on the financial sector. Stock markets began to fall in February 2020 and the fall took on dramatic dimensions in March for reasons discussed below. At the same time, international portfolio flows to peripheral countries shrank as concern grew regarding the effect of the pandemic on trade and output. A massive flight of capital materialised toward the core, as is shown in chapter 13. A full-blown global financial crisis looked imminent in March 2020.

A series of secondary effects compounded the initial impact of the restrictions and lockdowns. One key factor was the reallocation of aggregate demand toward commodities that could be delivered remotely. Providers of contact-intensive services, such as accommodation, travel, and food and beverages, were devastated, as were countries that specialise in providing these commodities to the world market.[6] In contrast, services requiring limited physical contact, such as telecommunications, information, and programming, benefited enormously. The greatest beneficiaries were the multinational giants of advanced technology, e-commerce, conference service provision, and so on.[7]

4 See M. Dossche, G. Krustev, and S. Zlatanos (2021) 'COVID-19 and the Increase in Household Savings: An Update', in ECB Economic Bulletin, Issue 5/2021, at ecb.europa.eu; J. Franklin et al. (2021) 'Household Debt and Covid', Bank of England Quarterly Bulletin Q2.

5 According to the IMF, in 2020, investment declined by 6.4 per cent in 'Advanced Economies' and 4.5 per cent in 'Developing Economies', although the figure for the latter would jump to 10.6 per cent if China was excluded; see IMF (2021) 'World Economic Outlook Update January 2021', at imf.org.

6 For instance, countries in the Caribbean: see N. Mulder (2020) 'The Impact of the COVID-19 Pandemic on the Tourism Sector in Latin America and the Caribbean, and Options for a Sustainable and Resilient Recovery', Economic Commission for Latin America and the Caribbean International Trade Series No. 157, at cepal.org.

7 See M. Andersson, N. Battistini, and G. Stoevsky (2021) 'Economic Developments and Outlook for Contact-Intensive Services in the Euro Area', ECB Economic Bulletin, Issue 7/2021, at ecb.europa.eu.

A further factor was the escalation of unemployment, particularly in countries that lacked strong labour regulations and failed to prevent mass firings of workers. Severe downward pressure on incomes ensued, impacting heavily on the self-employed as well as on workers in informal sectors, who are particularly prominent in the labour markets of low-income countries.[8] In high-income countries, the layers of informal workers comprise largely women and workers from racial, gender, ethnic, and other groups that typically suffer from systemic oppression. It is not a coincidence that they were most heavily affected by the health emergency.[9] As the pandemic took hold, economic hardship and class prejudice were heightened by police brutality, food scarcity, and work exhaustion.

Lockdowns and restrictions also increased the burden of reproductive labour, which basically refers to unpaid domestic and care work. The onus was made much heavier by the closing down of educational facilities and care facilities for the elderly and for people with mental and other health conditions.[10] Enormous pressures were felt by workers, who had to withstand the lockdown in conditions of overcrowding, without proper access to water or electricity, in the context of high uncertainty and stress, and in many cases deprived of a regular income.[11] Reproductive labour is typically performed by women and migrant workers. Women as doctors, nurses, and care workers were also at the forefront of dealing with the health emergency, facing conditions of overwork and high rates of contagion in jobs that were in some cases already low paid and often informal.[12]

8 See ILO (2020) 'ILO Monitor: Covid-19 and the World of Work', 6th edition, at ilo. org. Covid-19 had deeply unequal consequences both within countries – depending on economic sector – and between countries. Low-skilled and low-paid workers took the worst of the blow; see ILO (2020) 'The Impact of the COVID-19 Pandemic on Jobs and Incomes in G20 Economies', at ilo.org.

9 A. Saad-Filho (2021) *The Age of Crisis: Neoliberalism, the Collapse of Democracy, and the Pandemic*, Palgrave Macmillan: London.

10 S. Stevano et al. (2021) 'Hidden Abodes in Plain Sight: the Social Reproduction of Households and Labor in the COVID-19 Pandemic', *Feminist Economics* 27 (1–2): 271–87.

11 K. Bahn, J. Cohen, and Y. van der Meulen Rodgers (2020) 'A Feminist Perspective on COVID-19 and the Value of Care Work Globally', *Gender, Work and Organization* 27 (5): 656–99.

12 ILO (2020) 'COVID-19 and Care Workers Providing Home or Institution-Based Care', ILO Sectoral Brief; S. Rao et al. (2021) 'Human Mobility, COVID-19, and Policy Responses: The Rights and Claims-Making of Migrant Domestic Workers', *Feminist*

In the suffocating conditions of lockdowns and restrictions, there was also an escalation of gender violence reported in some countries.[13]

The origins, mechanisms, and outcomes of the crisis of 2020 were, thus, very different from those of the Great Crisis of 2007–09. The economic shockwaves emerged primarily in the sphere of trade and production, as states took measures to confront the health emergency, dramatically compressing aggregate demand and disrupting aggregate supply. A gigantic economic crisis started to take shape across the world, particularly as capitalist accumulation was already weak at the core. Moreover, although the crisis did not originate in finance, the financial sector was heavily struck, and the blow threatened to rebound even more destructively onto trade and production.

The financial rout of March 2020

The leading financial markets of the world economy failed to take notice of the initial outbreak of Covid-19 in Wuhan; indeed, they continued to rise, with the US stock market even registering record levels in February 2020.[14] Reality impinged on financial profit making only after the Italian state imposed severe lockdowns across entire regions of Northern Italy. The ground soon began to tremble, and in March 2020 a complete rout took place in the financial markets of core economies.

Faced with extreme uncertainty, shadow banks and other speculators sought to protect their portfolios by rapidly shedding high-risk assets, thus inducing steep price falls in securities. By the end of March, the US stock market had fallen by around 30 per cent from its record high in February. The impact was rapid and dramatic, even

Economics 27 (1–2): 254–70.

13 S. Jaffe (2020) 'Social Reproduction and the Pandemic', with Tithi Bhattacharya, *Dissent Magazine*, at dissentmagazine.org; J. Agüero (2021) 'COVID-19 and the Rise of Intimate Partner Violence', *World Development* 137: 105217; C. Forbes Bright, C. Burton, and M. Kosky (2020) 'Considerations of the Impacts of COVID-19 on Domestic Violence in the United States', *Social Sciences & Humanities Open* 2 (1): 100069.

14 Apart from equity markets in Asia, which saw declines in late January; see Financial Stability Board (2020) 'Holistic Review of the Market Turmoil', 17 December, at fsb.org.

on the financial systems of countries where no cases of the virus had yet been announced. Financial instability spread faster than the virus.

The safest assets in financial markets are government bonds, obviously depending on the perceived solvency of a country, and the leading assets within this category are US Treasury bonds. The yield of the ten-year Treasury bond measures the cost of borrowing by the US government, and the cost falls as the bond price rises. In early March 2020, the yield fell to a historic low of barely above half a percentage point, as panicking holders of the assets of shadow banks rushed to sell their holdings subsequently to buy Treasury bonds. Bizarrely, however, as the financial shock spread, the price of Treasury bonds soon began to fall and the yield to rise. Some financial operators were now selling large volumes of US Treasury bonds amid the unfolding crisis.[15] This peculiar phenomenon casts light on the speculative evolution of finance that took place as shadow banking grew in the 2010s.

Three types of financial assets in the US money market are important in this connection. The first are Treasury bills (TB) – that is, short-term Treasury bonds issued when the government seeks to borrow for immediate liquidity needs. The second are short-term certificates of deposit (CD), which give tradable rights to a deposit with a bank and are issued when the bank seeks to borrow quickly to supplement existing liquidity. The third are commercial paper (CP), which are tradable short-term promises to pay typically issued by large non-financial corporations seeking to cover immediate liquidity needs.[16]

The main financial agents dealing with these assets are regular banks, money market mutual funds, and, most importantly, the central bank. Money market mutual funds, discussed in chapter 5, are the natural

15 See A. Vissing-Jørgensen (2021) 'The Treasury Market in Spring 2020 and the Response of the Federal Reserve', BIS Working Paper No. 966, which discusses the rising yield on US Treasury bonds and finds the liquidity needs of mutual funds particularly important.

16 For descriptions and analysis of the functioning of these assets in recent crises, see Kacperczyk and Schnabl (2010) 'When Safe Proved Risky: Commercial Paper during the Financial Crisis of 2007–2009', *Journal of Economic Perspectives* 24 (1): 29–50; R. G. Anderson and C. S. Gascon (2009) 'The Commercial Paper Market, the Fed, and the 2007–2009 Financial Crisis', *Federal Reserve Bank of St Louis Review* 91 (6): 589–612; P. Cavallino and F. De Fiore (2020) 'Central Banks' Response to Covid-19 in Advanced Economies: Online Appendix', BIS Bulletin 2, at bis.org.

weather vane of financial crises in mature financialised capitalism.[17] As the crisis erupted in 2020, there was a withdrawal of loanable capital from money market mutual funds, strongly indicating that liquidity was becoming short.[18] Faced with the enormous uncertainty created by the health emergency, the large shareholders of the funds were desperate to sell and exit from this supposedly safe investment. In 2007–09, some funds had 'broken the buck', ultimately because they were exposed to worthless securitised assets originating in the real estate bubble. The owners of fund shares in 2020, fully aware of past events, were not going to risk losing their money.

In response, money market mutual funds limited their purchases of CPs and began to sell other assets to shore up their own liquidity. Consequently, the rate of interest began to rise. In these conditions, wholesale funding for shadow banks and for large non-financial corporates began rapidly to disappear. The complex liquidity arrangements of contemporary financialised capitalism proved exceptionally brittle when the pandemic hit. Money market participants, under pressure from scarce liquidity, sought fresh credit lines from their banks, while also selling assets to secure liquidity. Banks also felt the growing liquidity squeeze and started to limit their lending, thus further worsening conditions.

Simply put, in March 2020, there was not a shortage of loanable capital – indeed, there was an abundance of it – but a shortage of money. The liabilities of money market mutual funds no longer passed muster as money among financial agents and large corporations. The money market began to seize up and agents desperately sought a socially acceptable form of value, a reliable form of money.

---

17 A point that is fully appreciated in mainstream economic literature. See, for instance, T. Adrian (2014) 'Financial Stability Policies for Shadow Banking', Federal Reserve Bank of New York Staff Reports No. 664; E. Bengtsson (2013) 'Shadow Banking and Financial Stability: European Money Market Funds in the Global Financial Crisis', *Journal of International Money and Finance* 32: 579–94; E. Eren et al. (2020) 'US Dollar Funding Markets during the Covid-19 Crisis: The Money Market Fund Turmoil', BIS Bulletin 14, at bis.org.

18 See F. Avalos and D. Xia (2021) 'Investor Size, Liquidity and Prime Money Market Fund Stress', *BIS Quarterly Review*, March: 17–29. Similar phenomena were also occurring in the money markets of Europe; see F. Avalos and D. Xia (2021) 'Stress in European Money Market Funds at the Outbreak of the Pandemic', *BIS Quarterly Review*, September: 8–10; see also M. Boucinha et al. (2020) 'Recent Stress in Money Market Funds Has Exposed Potential Risks for the Wider Financial System', *Financial Stability Review*, ECB, May, at ecb.europa.eu.

This is a classic tendency of capitalist crises, analysed many years ago by Marx for the conditions of his time with remarkable prescience.[19] In the mature financialised capitalism of our age, the tendency took the form of seeking credit money privately created by banks that could be ultimately translated into central bank money guaranteed by the state.

The enormous pressures thereby generated were evident in the operations of ETFs, which have grown rapidly since 2007–09. These shadow banks buy securities with the aim of passively tracking a stock market index, and their specific characteristic is that their own shares are also freely traded in the stock market. Two prices are, therefore, key for ETFs: first, their NAV per share, and second, their market price. These two prices are typically close to each other, but in March 2020 the market price fell below the NAV per share. The unfolding crisis had made ETFs illiquid, threatening their existence and forcing them to sell their own assets as fast as possible.

Escalating pressures were also evident for hedge funds, shadow banks that borrow heavily and invest aggressively in securities and derivatives with few regulatory constraints. In the 2010s, hedge funds had found a nicely profitable field in 'basis trade' on Treasury bonds. This is a speculative practice whereby a hedge fund simultaneously sells a spot contract and buys a future contract in Treasury bonds, in the expectation that the gap between the spot and the future price would become larger in the coming period, thus resulting in profits. Unfortunately for hedge funds, the spot price of Treasury bonds began to rise at the first intimation of crisis, thereby bringing massive losses for speculators and forcing them to engage in fire sales of assets urgently to obtain cash.

Thus, amid a gigantic crisis that put a premium on safety, financial operators began to sell US Treasury bonds, supposedly the safest asset in the financial markets, causing prices to fall.[20] It is likely that foreign

---

19 Instances of such analysis are many in Marx's oeuvre. For a remarkably deep and summary statement reflecting the domestic and international institutional conditions of the second half of the nineteenth century, see Marx (1981) [1894] *Capital*, vol. 3, pp. 648–9.

20 See A. Schrimpf, H. S. Shin, and V. Sushko (2020) 'Leverage and Margin Spirals in Fixed Income Markets during the Covid-19 Crisis', BIS Bulletin 2, at bis.org; see also V. Haddad, A. Moreira, and T. Muir (2020) 'When Selling Becomes Viral: Disruptions in Debt Markets in the Covid-19 Crisis and the Fed's Response', NBER Working Paper No. 27168.

financial agents also began to sell US Treasury bonds at the same time for two main reasons: first, foreign government institutions needed US dollars to engage in transactions in the foreign exchange market; second, foreign financial intermediaries also required US dollars to meet their own obligations, which frequently arose from derivatives transactions, including swaps.

A liquidity crunch of epic proportions materialised with astonishing rapidity in March 2020, accompanied by a desperate search for safety and bizarre market fluctuations. The crunch reflected the deep fragility of the financial systems as a result of the growth of shadow banking in the 2010s. Only state intervention could forestall collapse. The reactions of core states revealed the extent to which contemporary market-based financial systems are dependent on the state.

Responding to economic collapse: Monetary policy

Central bank intervention began in late March 2020. In general, the ability of a central bank to intervene in financial markets depends on where the national currency stands in the global hierarchy, as is discussed in the following chapters. The USA and a select group of core countries possess the leading currencies in the world market, thus availing themselves of considerable room for domestic manoeuvre. Above all, the position of the dollar as the main form of world money in contemporary capitalism makes it possible for the Federal Reserve to expand its balance sheet by acquiring public and private securities, while creating immense amounts of essentially fiat money.

Monopoly over fiat money – the final means of payment – proved the foundation of state economic power in financialised capitalism in the crisis of 2020, as it had done in 2007–09. In the Pandemic Crisis, some central banks also engaged in relatively novel forms of intervention, such as direct loans to enterprises or local governments, and even provided credit directly to treasuries. The experience of the Great Crisis and the decade that followed opened new avenues of unconventional monetary policy, and the magnitude of monetary intervention by core states in 2020–21 was unprecedented.

The Federal Reserve intervened, first, through vast repo operations to provide markets with the missing liquidity and, second, through expanding its balance sheet by acquiring huge quantities of public and private securities, thus supplying private financial agents with liquidity, and spurring the further creation of private credit money by banks. In undertaking these actions, the Federal Reserve pushed interest rates toward zero.[21]

In both the crisis of 2007–09 and the pandemic shock, the Federal Reserve acquired primarily Treasury bonds and mortgage-backed securities (MBS) by creating reserves for commercial banks, issuing currency, and augmenting the treasury government account (TGA), from which the US government makes most of its payments. Clearly, the experience of 2007–09 and the decade that followed was rapidly put to use when the pandemic struck. By 2021, the assets of the Federal Reserve were close to 9 trillion US dollars, when the US GDP stood at about 23 trillion.

Moreover, the Federal Reserve introduced a Money Market Mutual Fund Liquidity Facility and a CP Funding Facility in March 2020. The former allowed banks to use money market instruments as collateral for loans from the central bank, and so prevented the fire sale of privately held short-term assets, while shifting the risk onto the public sector. The latter essentially amounted to the Federal Reserve directly buying CP to overcome the logjam in the money market. In short, the Federal Reserve emerged as the pivotal institution of shadow finance, allowing shadow transactions to continue.[22]

Moreover, during March 2020, the Federal Reserve kept announcing that it would commit itself to an ever larger volume of financial asset purchases. On 23 March, it simply removed all ceilings and declared

---

21 For a review of the policy interventions by the Fed in 2020, see: R. H. Clarida, B. Duygan-Bump, and C. Cotti (2021) 'The COVID-19 Crisis and the Federal Reserve's Policy Response', Finance and Economics Discussion Series No. 2021-035, at federalreserve.gov; see also Haddad, Moreira, and Muir (2020) 'When Selling Becomes Viral'; for a discussion of the legal aspects of intervention, see L. Menand (2021) 'The Federal Reserve and the 2020 Economic and Financial Crisis', *Stanford Journal of Law, Business and Finance* 26 (2): 295–361.

22 For more on the Money Market Fund Liquidity Facility and the Commercial Paper Funding Facility see L. Li, Y. Li, M. Machiavelli, and X. Zhou (2021) 'Liquidity Restrictions, Runs and Central Bank Interventions: Evidence from Money Market Funds', in *The Review of Financial Studies* 11(34). For accessible non-academic accounts of the Fed interventions in March 2020, see N. Tankus (2020) 'The Federal Reserve's Coronavirus Crisis Actions, Explained (Part 1)', and (2020) 'The Federal Reserve's Coronavirus Crisis Actions, Explained (Part 2)', at nathantankus.substack.com.

that quantitative easing would vary entirely according to its own discretion. The types of assets purchased were gradually broadened to include Treasury bills, bonds, MBS, investment grade corporate bonds, and even high-yield (also known as junk) bonds directly from primary but also from secondary markets.[23]

In effect, the Federal Reserve created fiat money to acquire a substantial part of the escalating debt of the US government as well as a part of the balance sheet of the private corporate sector of the USA. The central bank emerged as a leviathan astride the US economy, its total assets standing at roughly 40 per cent of US GDP in 2021. In doing so, the Federal Reserve took upon itself some of the risk generated by the private credit decisions of big businesses and financial speculators.

The central banks of other core states followed a similar path. The ECB was slower to respond, but eventually announced the Pandemic Emergency Purchase Programme in March with a ceiling of 750 billion euros which was later increased to 1,850 billion euros. The Bank of England followed suit in March and launched an asset purchasing facility of up to 200 billion GBP, further increasing it later in the year. The Bank of Japan also introduced unlimited quantitative easing. After all, the Japanese central bank had historically initiated quantitative easing to confront the persistent underperformance of the Japanese economy following the bursting of its financial bubble in the 1980s.[24]

Crucially, the public supply of liquidity went together with a cut in short-term interest rates by central banks, which are often referred to as policy rates and act as benchmarks for other rates throughout the credit system. The ostensible aim of lowering policy rates is to encourage lending to private enterprises and individuals by commercial banks, and thus to boost consumption and investment. In practice, the impact of policy rate cuts on investment and profits by industrial capital is modest. Yet the overall impact on accumulation could be substantial, as is shown in the following chapters.

Funded by cheap central bank liquidity, commercial banks greatly

23 For the initial response of the Fed, see the Minutes of the Federal Open Market Committee, 15 March 2020; see also the Minutes of the Federal Open Market Committee, 28–29 April 2020, both at federalreserve.gov.

24 For a detailed account of 'unconventional' monetary policy by the Bank of Japan, see K. Iwata and S. Takenaka (2011) 'Central Bank Balance Sheet Expansion: Japan's Experience', BIS Papers No. 66.

expanded lending to non-financial enterprises, often drawing on explicit government guarantees. The outcome was remarkably rapid growth of the money supply in 2020, notably in the USA. This was a key difference from monetary policies in the Great Crisis, and its impact on the economy was considerable, not least regarding inflation. That aside, abundant provision of credit and money not only averted a global financial crisis but led to a sharp rebound of the stock markets. Toward the end of 2020, financial markets were booming in the USA and other core countries.[25]

Last, but not least, the Federal Reserve once again took decisive steps to defend the role of the dollar as world money, a crucial pillar of US hegemony. A shortage of international liquidity materialised as the health emergency spread, trade was disturbed, and international capital flows dried up. The Federal Reserve stepped in to provide dollar liquidity through swaps with a group of central banks, as it had done in 2008, while also introducing new channels of support, such as repo facilities with foreign monetary authorities.[26]

The import of the international interventions by the Federal Reserve will be considered more fully in chapter 13. It is apparent, however, that as the pandemic shook the global hierarchy of states, the USA showed itself determined to defend the dollar as a key instrument of imperial power. By expanding the international supply of US liquidity, the Federal Reserve reaffirmed its own position as the main pivot of the global financial system.

Recapping, core state intervention in 2020–21 made apparent the extent to which state economic power in financialised capitalism relies on command over domestic money. Monetary authorities proved highly creative when it came to rescuing the status quo and quickly adapted to new conditions. Enormous volumes of money were created to purchase public securities, thus ensuring that the privileged elite that commands financial assets remained liquid and its wealth was protected. Unfortunately for policy makers, it soon became apparent that no

25 See C. P. Chandrasekhar and J. Ghosh (2021) 'A Market Gone Awry', International Development Economics Associates (IDEAS) at networkideas.org.

26 See S. Murau, F. Pape, and T. Pforr (2021) 'The Hierarchy of the Offshore US-Dollar System: On Swap Lines, the FIMA Repo Facility and Special Drawing Rights', GEGI Study, February. See also F. Pape (2020) 'Rethinking Liquidity: A Critical Macro-Finance View', *Finance and Society* 6 (1): 67–75; and D. Gabor (2020) 'Critical Macro-Finance: A Theoretical Lens', *Finance and Society* 6 (1): 45–55.

amount of mere monetary wizardry could restore accumulation since the side of production was profoundly weak, enterprises were closing, and employment was collapsing. Fiscal policy was also necessary.

Responding to economic collapse: Fiscal policy, class divisions, and global hierarchies

In early 2020, even central bankers recognised the limited effectiveness of monetary policy and called openly for a fiscal stimulus to aggregate demand.[27] Core and peripheral states were forced to deploy fiscal policy in extraordinary ways, directly contravening the neoliberal shibboleths of previous decades. Far-reaching Keynesian fiscal levers of boosting aggregate demand were mobilised.

Automatic stabilisers came into play first – that is, fiscal levers that automatically act as countercyclical devices. In an economic crisis, the state normally receives less tax, since household income and enterprise revenue contract, thereby limiting the fall in demand. When the economy recovers, the tax intake rises, and demand growth is kept in check. Similarly, unemployment benefits paid as workers lose their jobs augment aggregate fiscal expenditure even without the state introducing new fiscal measures.

The real difference was made, however, by discretionary fiscal policy. Core countries – and several peripheral ones – put in place measures that completely overshadowed previous fiscal stimuli. Governments paid the wages of workers with the aim of limiting unemployment, thus in effect nationalising the wage bills of a broad swathe of enterprises. Governments also provided support to private businesses by deferring taxes and social security contributions, while offering credit and export guarantees, in practice nationalising the income statements of enterprises.

In a striking move, some governments gave a substantial direct boost to the disposable income of households by making direct cash subventions, a form of pandemic basic income for millions of people in core and peripheral countries. The US government took the lead among core

---

27 This was reported with alacrity in the pages of leading international newspapers; see, for instance, P. Hildebrand (2020) 'Coronavirus: Why Central Bankers Say It Is Time for Fiscal Stimulus', *Financial Times*, 6 March, at ft.com.

countries in these respects, and the sums spent were enormous.[28] Similar policies were also carried out in peripheral countries, such as the Ingreso Familiar de Emergencia (IFE) in Argentina or the Auxílio Emergencial in Brazil.[29]

In 2020–21, nation states demonstrated both the capacity and the will to intervene in the fiscal realm under crisis conditions, despite the dominant neoliberal ideology. While engaging in a torrent of fiscal and monetary measures, however, governments were reluctant to intervene drastically on the side of production, especially by challenging property rights. They were also reluctant to change the balance of power against capital at the workplace. In these critical respects, neoliberalism continued to hold sway.

Moreover, enormous differences rapidly emerged among countries, reflecting national class structures and institutional trajectories, the power of individual states, and the new hierarchies of the world economy. The divisions of core and periphery became sharper as the pandemic struck, and state reactions reflected the underlying unevenness. Further insight into these issues can be gained by more closely considering fiscal policy in 2020–21 and adopting a simplified version of the International Monetary Fund (IMF) classification of fiscal discretionary measures into two broad groups, namely 'above the line' and 'below the line'.[30]

Measures that are above the line include additional government spending (for instance, on health services, unemployment benefits, wage subsidies, and targeted transfers among the population) as well as tax deferrals and forgiveness of obligations. These leave a direct imprint on the government's budget and impose short-term financing requirements, even if tax deferrals do not increase the budget deficit in the long term, since the sums are supposed to be collected in the future.

In contrast, measures that are below the line do not have a budgetary impact in the short term. They include loans and equity injections to

28 See, for instance, White House (2021) 'President Biden Announces American Rescue Plan', at whitehouse.gov.

29 L. Lavinas, L. Bressan, and P. Rubin (2022) 'Brazil: How Covid-Related Relief Policies Inaugurated a New Cycle of Household Indebtedness', Documento de Trabajo CIEPP No. 109.

30 See also D. Kirti et al. (2022) 'Tracking Economic and Financial Policies During COVID-19: An Announcement Level Database', IMF Working Paper No. 22/114.

private enterprises that are in trouble but are still expected to recover. They also include state guarantees to private enterprises, which do not affect the government budget and do not require additional public debt unless they are activated. Such measures could potentially augment the government debt if the enterprise defaulted.

The global fiscal stimulus of 2020 was very large in both of these domains. However, the extent of policy intervention varied greatly across the world depending on the capacities of different states to finance increased fiscal expenditures. To capture these differences, countries could be placed in further groups based on broad criteria, such as income per capita, export diversification, and integration into the global financial system.

The IMF typically identifies three groups, namely advanced economies, emerging market and middle-income economies, and low-income developing countries. For our purposes, the groups could be further simplified into high-income, middle-income, and low-income countries. Note that these distinctions are deployed heuristically, and the groups still exhibit substantial internal heterogeneity. Broadly speaking, high-income countries could be taken as referring to the core, while middle- and low-income countries to the periphery of the world economy.

In 2020–21, high-income countries were able to implement far larger fiscal measures than others. Table 6.2 shows that, on average, they spent roughly 25 per cent of GDP, and the expenditure was divided in broadly equal terms above and below the line.

Table 6.2. Discretionary fiscal response to the pandemic in high-income, middle-income, and low-income countries as % of GDP.

Group of countries	Additional spending and forgone revenue	Equity, loans, and guarantees	Total
High income	12.7	11.3	24.0
Middle income	3.6	2.5	6.1
Low income	1.6	0.2	1.8

Source: Authors' calculations with data from IMF
Fiscal Monitor Update, January 2021;
estimates as of end of December 2020.

However, the averages hide great differences within the group of high-income countries. EU countries increased above-the-line expenditures much less than other countries, and relied heavily on equity injections, loans, and guarantees. The rigid fiscal framework of the EU continued to restrain intervention, even though the EU became considerably laxer than before, as is discussed more fully in chapter 15. EU countries were forced by the restrictive environment of their union to favour below-the-line measures, which were generally less effective. There was much higher above-the-line spending in the USA and the UK than in Germany, France, and Italy. The results were to show in 2021–22, when inflation accelerated.

Nevertheless, differences among high-income countries paled into insignificance when compared with the differences between high-income and middle-income countries. Table 6.2 shows that spending by middle-income countries as a proportion of GDP was on average about a quarter of that of high-income countries. Even large middle-income countries, such as Brazil, did not come close to the levels of developed countries. Moreover, the capacity of middle-income countries to spend below the line was far lower than high-income countries.

Still more striking, however, were the differences between both these groups and low-income countries. Table 6.2 shows that the low-income group spent on average less than 2 per cent of GDP, and the overwhelming bulk of these expenditures were above the line. The weakness of fiscal intervention ensured that the pandemic shock struck developing countries far more severely than the Great Crisis of 2007–09, particularly when China and the Pacific countries are excluded.

The fiscal measures adopted by core countries as well as some middle-income countries ranged widely. Households received cash or in-kind transfers and unemployment benefits. For enterprises, the measures included deferral of taxes and social security payments, tax cuts, accelerated depreciation allowances, loans, guarantees, equity injections, and debt restructuring for enterprises. Employment protection focused on short-term work retention schemes and temporary hiring subsidies. Even the IMF immediately confirmed that the beneficiaries of these measures differed greatly between and among high-income and middle-income countries (data is not available for low-income countries).[31]

In high-income countries, the main beneficiaries were large enterprises, which received roughly a third of the total expenditure, while

---

31 See IMF (2020) Fiscal Monitor, October, at imf.org.

employment and household measures jointly took a little more than another third. Health care received a relatively small part (well below 10 per cent), and the share of public investment was negligible.

In middle-income economies, on the other hand, enterprises received a proportionately smaller share of public expenditure, as did workers, while the share of health care was roughly the same; instead, a substantially larger proportion of fiscal spending went on public investment.[32] The relatively low levels of fiscal expenditure in middle-income and low-income countries, especially in countries that implemented long-lasting and harsh health restrictions, had severe implications for workers. Broad layers of informal workers and day labourers did not obtain even minimal support as their regular sources of income dried up.[33]

Policies to confront the health emergency were marked by a lack of solidarity among countries, as was discussed in chapter 2. This was similarly apparent in the lack of fiscal measures to support poor people across the world. High-income countries refrained from assisting low-income countries; they neglected to institute amelioratory policies like forgiving external debt to increase the fiscal space of debtor governments.[34] Poor people in low-income countries were left to survive by relying mostly on family and communal networks.

It is also notable that in most economies, health spending had a limited share of the fiscal stimulus. In practice, and as the health shock morphed into a full-blown economic crisis, the priorities of the state focused on supporting capitalist accumulation. Nonetheless, the vast fiscal stimulus led to mounting government deficits in 2020. These reached staggering proportions in core countries, especially in view of falling tax income as economic activity collapsed. But deficits were also large in middle-income and low-income countries, as is shown in table 6.3.

---

32 For a preliminary assessment of the effect of Covid-19 on developing countries and the forms of policy intervention, see S. Djankov and U. Panizza (2020) *COVID-19 in Developing Economics*, CEPR Press: VoxEU e-book, at cepr.org.

33 See WIEGO (2021) 'COVID-19 Crisis and the Informal Economy', Women in Informal Employment: Globalizing and Organizing (WIEGO), at wiego.org.

34 C. Laskaridis (2021) 'When Push Came to Shove: COVID-19 and Debt Crises in Low-Income Countries', *Canadian Journal of Development Studies / Revue canadienne d'études du développement* 42 (1–2): 200–20; T. Stubbs et al. (2021) 'Whatever It Takes? The Global Financial Safety Net, Covid-19, and Developing Countries', *World Development* 137: 105171.

The inevitable result was a rapid escalation of public debt across high-, middle-, and low-income countries.[35]

Table 6.3. General government fiscal balance and debt as % of GDP.

	General government fiscal balance		General government debt	
	2019	2020	2019	2020
High income	−3.3	−14.4	105.3	125.5
Middle income	−4.9	−10.7	52.6	62.2
Low income	−4.0	−6.2	43.3	48.8

Source: Authors' calculations with data from
IMF Fiscal Monitor; October 2020.

In 2020 the average level of government indebtedness in high-income countries exceeded 125 per cent of GDP, surpassing the level at the end of the Second World War. Government debt in middle-income countries was considerably lower but still at a historic peak, and public debt in low-income countries was also very high. The vulnerability generated by debt for low-income countries was of a different order from that experienced by richer countries. These increases will eventually have to be confronted, perhaps involving austerity and even a debt crisis for middle- and low-income countries in the time ahead.[36]

Austerity was rapidly and unceremoniously dumped in the face of the pandemic disaster. It cannot be overstressed, however, that even powerful states failed to support the networks of reproductive work that sustain the capitalist economy and proved vital during the pandemic.[37] Workers in the informal sector and day labourers lost their sources of income and had to rely on communal networks for survival, including resorting to foodbanks. Families and communities were pressed to take care of children when schools were closed, as well as looking after the sick and elderly as health facilities collapsed under the strain of the virus.[38]

Across the world, state intervention aimed primarily to support the

35 U. Volz et al. (2021) *Debt Relief for a Green and Inclusive Recovery: Securing Private-Sector Participation and Creating Policy Space for Sustainable Development*, Heinrich-Böll-Stiftung: Berlin, London, and Boston, MA; SOAS, University of London; and Boston University.

36 See D. Munevar (2021) 'A Debt Pandemic: Dynamics and Implications of the Debt Crisis of 2020', Eurodad Briefing Paper, March.

37 See K. Moos (2021) 'Coronavirus Fiscal Policy in the United States: Lessons from Feminist Political Economy', *Feminist Economics* 27 (1–2): 419–35.

38 See Stevano et al. (2021) 'Hidden Abodes in Plain Sight'.

underlying structures of financialised capitalism. States refrained from nationalising strategic sectors of the economy or playing an active role in reorganising production and distribution. They were reluctant to take decisive steps on the side of production even when that was necessary to ameliorate the shortage of essential health equipment. By refusing to intervene on the supply side, core states allowed a strong imbalance with aggregate demand to emerge, which was already visible in 2021. A feeble recovery followed, accompanied by rising inflation, and the outlook for the world economy looked even worse after war broke out in Ukraine in 2022.

7

The Spectre of Inflation

By 2021, core countries had overcome the immediate blow of the pandemic, buttressed by unprecedented state support, and, in early 2022, recovery was on its way, reversing the earlier precipitous contraction of output. Cheap credit allowed the financial sector of the USA to grow rapidly, and asset prices escalated greatly. For a short while, it seemed that all was well, but appearances were misleading.

For one thing, there was pronounced heterogeneity in the recovery across the world, its path depending on the tempo of the health emergency. New variants of Covid-19 continued to emerge that were highly contagious, if less lethal, triggering renewed waves of infection and forcing several states to renew restrictions. Moreover, the likely costs of extraordinary state intervention already weighed heavily upon peripheral countries by 2021. In several middle- and low-income economies, in which state responses had been much weaker than in high-income countries in 2020, state support began to be phased out even before economic activity had fully recovered. The fear of growing debt meant that, once again, poor countries suffered the most.

For another thing, in 2022, the costs of state intervention loomed progressively larger, even in high-income countries. The main culprit was the rapid acceleration of inflation, which delivered a severe blow to the living standards of workers and the middle class as well as threatening the wealth and profits of the financial sector.

The significance of the rise in inflation could not be downplayed. The financialisation of capitalism emerged properly in the 1980s on the back of suppressing the high inflation that had embroiled core countries in the crisis-ridden 1970s. For financial capitals, rapid inflation is a mortal enemy, because it eats into the value of both principal and interest on loans. Suppression of inflation in the 1970s involved severe monetary stringency by central banks, known as the 'Volcker shock' in the USA, dramatically raising the rate of interest and exacerbating deep recessionary tendencies.[1] Throughout the ensuing decades of financialisation, central banks turned the control of inflation into their primary task.

The return of inflation was clearly due to the support of aggregate demand delivered by core states in 2020–21. At a deeper level, however, it reflected the underlying weakness of the supply side and the entrenched malaise of accumulation discussed in previous chapters. In 2020, austerity was jettisoned by core countries faced with the disastrous economic contraction of the pandemic, but since the side of production had remained weak, the outcome was deeply problematic. Rising inflation indicated that the poor performance of capitalist accumulation in core countries after the Great Crisis of 2007–09 was not simply due to persistent austerity compressing aggregate demand. The problem had to do with the underlying weakness of aggregate supply – it was structural and deep.

In the 2010s, core states not only forbore from boosting aggregate demand but, more significantly, proved reluctant to restructure aggregate supply, for the latter would require expanding public investment, rebalancing production domestically and across borders, promoting de-financialisation, and altering property rights over the means of production. It would also require changing the balance of power at the workplace and across society in favour of labour. In short, restructuring the side of supply would potentially entail a systemic retreat of the

---

1 The mainstream bibliography on this issue is extensive. For a historical account of the inflationary pressures leading to the Volcker shock, see A. H. Meltzer (2005) 'Origins of the Great Inflation', *Federal Reserve Bank of St Louis Review* 87 (2), part 2: 145–75. For an assessment of Fed under Volcker and the issue of credibility, see M. Goodfriend and R. G. King (2005) 'The Incredible Volcker Disinflation', *Journal of Monetary Economics* 52: 981–1015. For the changed role of the Fed after the Volcker shock, see I. Morgan (2012) 'Monetary Metamorphosis: The Volcker Fed and Inflation', *Journal of Policy History* 24 (4): 545–71.

dominant capitalist layer. Core states consistently avoided taking such steps and defended oligarchic privileges, thereby entrenching the feebleness of accumulation.

Accelerating inflation put enormous pressure on the living standards of workers and the middle class in the wake of the pandemic shock. The pressure was greatly compounded by the war in Ukraine, with extensive sanctions imposed on Russia by the USA and its European allies, which again disrupted the global networks of energy and food. By 2022, the core of financialised capitalism faced a pronounced disorder touching all aspects of economic, social, and political life, and presenting the capitalist elite with harsh choices.

Igniting inflation

Figure 7.1 traces the changes in the consumer price index in the countries of the Organisation for Economic Co-operation and Development (OECD), the group that contains most core countries of the world economy. The surge of inflation in 2021 and 2022 was manifest, including in the USA.

Rising general price indexes during this period were accompanied by the escalation of the prices of key commodity inputs traded globally. Starting in April 2020 and continuing in 2021, prices increased rapidly

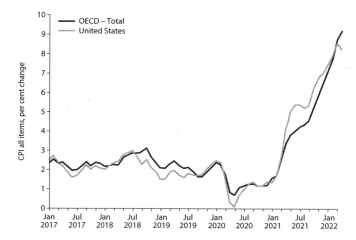

Figure 7.1. Consumer price inflation.
Source: Authors' calculations with OECD data.

for crude oil, copper, nickel, and other minerals, but also for steel.[2] There were inevitable fluctuations in these prices depending on conditions in particular sectors, but when the Ukraine war broke out, prices received a further boost in the first half of 2022. Crucially, for workers and the poor across the world, the price of wheat soared in 2020–21; the price of rice also rose in 2021, after spiking enormously and then subsiding in early 2020. The war in Ukraine worsened conditions by pushing prices up even further in the first half of 2022.[3]

The combined pressure of energy, food, and other price increases on the income of workers and the poor in core countries was huge, as is shown in figure 7.2. In poorer peripheral countries, the rise of foodstuff prices raised the prospect of hunger.

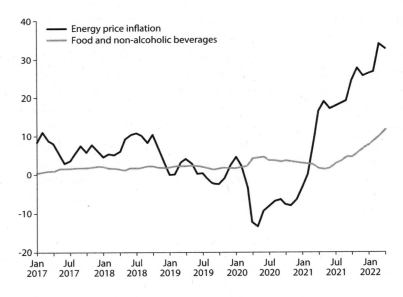

Figure 7.2. Consumer price inflation in energy,
food, and non-alcoholic drinks.
Source: Authors' calculations with OECD data.

2 Price increases followed a short, though significant, downward shock to commodity prices at the very start of the pandemic as aggregate demand and supply took a great blow; see World Bank (2021) 'Causes and Consequences of Metal Price Shocks', Commodity Markets Outlook Special Focus, April.

3 See World Bank (2022) 'The Impact of the War in Ukraine on Commodity Markets', Commodity Markets Outlook Special Focus, April; see also D. Igan et al. (2022) 'Commodity Market Disruptions, Growth and Inflation', BIS Bulletin 54, at bis.org.

Throughout 2021, policy makers in core countries either ignored or dismissed the acceleration of inflation, but in 2022 concern spread, particularly in the USA, where the fiscal boost was substantial.[4] The issue was whether inflation would prove transitory or become entrenched, and the question mattered greatly for policy. The answer depended on what had caused the acceleration of inflation in the first place.

The old Monetarist explanations of inflation, drawing on the Quantity Theory of Money, were quick to stage a return.[5] The Monetarist argument was, as ever, simple: policies to confront the pandemic in 2020–21 led to an extraordinary increase in the money supply and, given the relatively stable velocity of money and the inability of aggregate supply to increase commensurately, the result was inflation. On these grounds, inflation could be expected to continue at high levels for the first half of the 2020s, particularly in the USA.

The Quantity Theory of Money has proven misleading for both theoretical analysis and government policy several times in the history of capitalism. There is no doubt that the money supply in core countries rose dramatically in response to the pandemic shock and certainly in comparison with the Great Crisis of 2007–09. But the simple mechanics of Monetarism offer little in the way of explanation for the surge in inflation after 2021.

A point of vital importance is that inflation is a blanket term that could obfuscate price movements as much as revealing underlying tendencies. The aggregate price level is calculated across several

---

4 The public debate took place mostly in the pages of newspapers, blogs, and – inevitably – Twitter, and was conducted primarily among the conservative neo-Keynesian guard that dominates contemporary mainstream economics. The side that rang the alarm bell included O. Blanchard and L. Summers among its members, while the side that downplayed the risks counted P. Krugman and J. Stiglitz. For an early snapshot of the debate, see J.-P. Landau (2021) 'Inflation and the Biden Stimulus', VoxEU, CEPR at cepr.org/voxeu. Throughout 2021, the Federal Reserve and the Biden administration were broadly on the side of the 'downplayers', but by the middle of 2022 things had changed and there was global concern regarding the persistence of inflation. The White House apparently considered inflation its 'top domestic priority', as reported by *The Washington Post* on 18 June 2022. Concern was also evident among the economists of the multilateral international organisations: see, for instance, R. Aggarwal and M. Kimbal (2022) 'Will Inflation Remain High?', *Finance & Development* 59 (2): 24–7, at imf.org.

5 See J. Castañeda and T. Congdon (2020) 'Inflation: The Next Threat?' Institute of Economic Affairs, Briefing No. 7, at iea.org.uk.

economic sectors, often masking great differences in the behaviour of the price of output in one sector compared with another. The rate of inflation is supposed to capture the common elements in price increases (or decreases) observed across economic sectors. But these common elements are notoriously difficult to isolate empirically, and they are practically impossible to connect to increases (or decreases) in the money supply.

The fundamental reason for these well-known difficulties is that in every period, the price of the output in each sector is determined by qualitatively different factors, reflecting real resource adjustments. These can vary widely and include the patterns of weather in agriculture, the introduction of new technology in manufacturing, the existence of adequate shipping capacity for minerals, the impact of monopolistic arrangements by oil producers, the changes in seasonal or other demand for certain commodities, and so on. The more closely one examines the price behaviour of the output of a sector, the clearer it becomes that price fluctuations result primarily from real, not monetary, factors which are usually specific to the sector and hard to generalise.

Radical monetary theory has drawn attention to these characteristics of inflation for a long time, and its position has been frequently confirmed by empirical research.[6] Thus, for the USA in 2021, mainstream economic research showed that when inflation is generally low, the fluctuations of aggregate price indices are determined primarily by sector-specific forces.[7] The common elements that presumably drive inflation are generally weak. Upward movements of prices tend to be the result of adjustments in real resources within sectors, a feature that is particularly prominent across the service sector.

That is not to say that monetary factors could not generate rapid inflation, and even hyperinflation, as is argued in chapter 8. Indeed, in advanced capitalism, in which the final means of payment is effectively

---

6 This crucial point regarding inflation was established in the nineteenth century by Thomas Tooke of the Banking School in his classic *History of Prices*. Tooke lacked the notion of the price level, as was common among political economists at the time, but was able to show through empirical analysis that the observed price fluctuations in key markets were typically due to real factors. There is little doubt that this was also Marx's fundamental view. For further detail on Tooke's arguments in this connection, see A. Arnon (1991) *Thomas Tooke: Pioneer of Monetary Theory*, University of Michigan Press: Ann Arbor, MI.

7 C. Borio et al. (2021) 'Inflation, Relative Prices and Monetary Policy: Flexibility Born Out of Success', *BIS Quarterly Review*, September: 15–29.

fiat money created by the central bank, monetary authorities could potentially induce substantial fluctuations in the price level. The extraordinary increases in the money supply in the USA and other core countries in 2020–21 were certainly related to the burgeoning of aggregate demand. The real issue, however, was the inability of aggregate supply to respond commensurately, and in this regard the Quantity Theory of Money has little to offer.

For radical political economy, the roots of rising inflation in the early 2020s are to be found in the interaction of aggregate demand and supply, together with the operations of the financial system, along lines that are discussed in chapter 8.[8] Inflation in the 2020s was spurred by the boost to aggregate demand, particularly as the expansionary policies of core states were compounded by the lifting of Covid-19 restrictions in 2021, which facilitated the recovery of private expenditure. It appears, furthermore, that growing demand was allocated toward goods rather than services, since the networks of the latter took the strongest blow from the pandemic, as was discussed in earlier chapters.

Rising inflation primarily reflected the inability of aggregate supply adequately to respond to recovering demand. In part, this was due to the disturbance of production networks across the world, the fragility of which is discussed in chapter 12, with respect especially to the internationalisation of productive capital under the auspices of huge multinational enterprises. It was also due to the deep – and related – malaise of the production side in core countries manifested in poor profitability, low productivity growth, and the prevalence of zombie firms, as was discussed in chapter 4.

It should further be noted that rising inflation in peripheral countries reflected primarily the soaring prices of key commodities, including fossil fuels. In the main, inflation in these countries was not due to government policy supporting aggregate demand, since the latter was not remotely on a par with that of the core countries, as was shown in

---

8 The neo-Keynesian establishment of mainstream economics was certainly aware of these relations, as could be seen in the increasingly urgent debates in 2022; see, for instance, D. Reifschneider and D. Wilcox (2022) 'The Case for a Cautiously Optimistic Outlook for US Inflation', Policy Brief No. 22-3, March, Pietersen Institute for International Economics (PIIE), at piie.com; see also O. Blanchard (2022) 'Why I Worry about Inflation, Interest Rates, and Unemployment', Debating Inflation and What the Fed Should Do, PIIE Series, at piie.com. The point is, however, that focusing on the underlying weakness of production would raise awkward problems for the mainstream.

chapter 6. Rather, inflation in peripheral countries was mostly associated with the mechanisms of production across the world economy in conjunction with global finance. Fundamental to it was the disturbance to global production networks as states imposed severe restrictions on work, travel, and trade, thus also increasing transport costs.[9] Global supply processes were further disrupted by severe sectoral disparities, as digital services and industrial activities recovered quickly but other services (entertainment, restaurants, hotels, and others) lagged behind.[10]

The trajectory of inflation in core countries for the rest of the 2020s is likely to hinge on the conduct of labour markets and the corresponding path of wages. In political economy terms, the path will depend on the struggle over the distribution of value, output, and income between capital and labour. In principle, a rise in prices could amount to a loss of real income for workers appropriated as profit by capitalists. But it could also result in a loss of profits for capitalists if workers' income kept pace with inflation and prices were administratively controlled. This is what is at stake when mainstream economists engage in debates on whether the expectations of inflation already are or will become 'de-anchored'.[11] Inflationary conditions reflect the level of organisation and the confidence of workers as well as the growth of labour productivity.

To be a little more specific, if workers lost out in the conflict over distribution, their real income would fall, and the loss would directly correspond to a transfer of income to capitalist profits, as is discussed

9 B. Javorcik (2020) 'Global Supply Chains Will Not Be the Same in the Post-COVID- 19 World', in Baldwin and Evenett (eds) *COVID-19 and Trade Policy*, pp. 111–16; S. Miroudot (2020), 'Resilience versus Robustness in Global Value Chains: Some Policy Implications', in Baldwin and Evenett (eds) *COVID-19 and Trade Policy*, pp. 117–30.

10 M. Andersson, N. Battistini, and G. Stoevsky (2021) 'Economic Developments and Outlook for Contact-Intensive Services in the Euro Area', ECB Economic Bulletin, Issue 7/2021, at ecb.europa.eu.

11 Economists have long been concerned about the possibility of inflation expectations becoming 'de-anchored'; for a formal model analysis, see L. Gobbi, R. Mazzocchi, and R. Tamborini (2019) 'Monetary Policy, De-Anchoring of Inflation Expectations, and the "New Normal" ', *Journal of Macroeconomics* 61: 103070. For the USA, P. Dash, A. K. Rohit, and A. Devaguptapu (2020) 'Assessing the (De-)Anchoring of Households' Long-Term Inflation Expectations in the US', *Journal of Macroeconomics* 63: 103183, claimed that household inflation expectations have been 'de-anchored' since the 1990s. For the Eurozone, D. Nautz, L. Pagenhardt, and T. Strohsal (2017) 'The (De-) Anchoring of Inflation Expectations: New Evidence from the Euro Area', *The North American Journal of Economics and Finance* 40: 103–15, argued that expectations have become de-anchored since 2011.

below in relation to Keynes's original analysis of inflation. It is notable that even in countries where employment recovered more strongly after the pandemic, as in the USA and the UK, nominal wages have failed to keep pace with inflation.[12] Profits were the direct beneficiary of escalating inflation in the early 2020s.

If, on the other hand, nominal wages matched the rise in prices, the outcome for inflation would depend on the response of enterprises, especially of the large monopolists within the global networks of production. Inflation could potentially be absorbed as a loss of profits, and that would be the socially rational thing to do, since it was not caused by rising wage costs in the first place. But that is highly unlikely to happen without administrative controls on prices imposed on enterprises by the state. The spontaneous reaction of enterprises would be to raise output prices seeking to maintain the same level of profits. Capitalists acting by themselves would pass the burden onto workers and appropriate a part of workers' income as profits.

The underlying weakness of aggregate supply, together with the distributional struggle between labour and capital, are the factors that determine inflation.[13] Wages are a passive element in this process, as workers attempt to maintain living standards. The active element is profits as capitalists pass cost increases onto output prices to sustain profits, and potentially to obtain the income loss of workers as additional profits. To prevent that outcome and protect workers' income, it would be necessary to impose administrative controls on prices and wages.

The distributional struggle of the early 2020s is a test of the current strength of labour. The rise of financialised capitalism during the last four decades – accompanied by the relocation of industrial capital across borders – dealt a major blow to workers' ability to organise in high-income countries.[14] Relocation went together with a global wave of labour market reforms that worsened the conditions of labour,

12 See K. Forster van Aerssen et al. (2021) 'The US and UK Labour Markets in the Post-Pandemic Recovery', ECB Economic Bulletin 8/2021; S. Howard, R. Rich, and J. Tracy (2022) 'Real Wages Grew During Two Years of COVID-19 after Controlling for Workforce Composition', Federal Reserve Bank of Dallas Economics, at dallasfed.org.

13 Goodhart and Pradhan argue that such a process is already underway because the great surge in globally available labour power witnessed over the last three decades is coming to an end; see C. Goodhart and M. Pradhan (2020) *The Great Demographic Reversal: Ageing Societies, Waning Inequality, and an Inflation Revival*, Palgrave Macmillan: London.

14 See, for instance, W. Milberg and D. Winkler (2013) *Outsourcing Economics: Global Value Chains in Capitalist Development*, Cambridge University Press: Cambridge, UK.

including sustained attacks on trade union organisation and the gross weakening of public welfare provision. Formerly thriving industrial areas experienced surges of unemployment, which often had an impact on workers along racial and ethnic lines, as manufacturing was relocated to East Asia, East Europe, Mexico, and elsewhere to take advantage of cheaper wages and looser labour and environmental regulations.[15]

The trajectory of labour markets during the last four decades was thus very different from what one might expect from a historical analysis of capitalism. Far from the formal practices of wage labour in core countries acting as a benchmark for peripheral countries as industrial capitalism took root, the opposite has occurred. Labour markets in high-income countries have acquired a distinct resemblance to labour markets in low-income countries, which have long been characterised by precarious, temporary, and informal employment.[16] The consequences have included stagnation of real wages, increases in inequality, and a decline in labour's share in national income, as was shown in earlier chapters.[17] Technological advances related to digitalisation and platform work have further intensified the growth of precarious employment, as is discussed in chapter 12.[18]

When the pandemic struck in 2020, the growth of unemployment was relatively modest in countries that had strong labour protection measures in place. There were also pronounced differences between the experiences of informal and formal workers, since the latter were often shielded from unemployment and their incomes were protected.[19] But

15 See G. Starosta (2016) 'Revisiting the New International Division of Labour Thesis', in G. Charnock and G. Starosta (eds) *The New International Division of Labour*, Palgrave Macmillan: London, pp. 79–103.

16 See J. Greenstein (2020) 'The Precariat Class Structure and Income Inequality among US Workers: 1980–2018', *Review of Radical Political Economics* 52 (3): 447–69; see also ILO (2016) 'Non-Standard Employment around the World: Understanding Challenges, Shaping Prospects', at ilo.org; for a broader discussion of precarious labour, see G. Standing (2011) *The Precariat: The New Dangerous Class*, Bloomsbury Academic: London.

17 See A. Benanav (2020) *Automation and the Future of Work*, Verso: London and New York; see also B. Milanović (2016) *Global Inequality: A New Approach for the Age of Globalization*, The Belknap Press of Harvard University Press: Cambridge, MA.

18 See C. Muntaner (2018) 'Digital Platforms, Gig Economy, Precarious Employment, and the Invisible Hand of Social Class', *International Journal of Health Services* 48 (4): 597–600.

19 See, ILO (2020) 'ILO Monitor: Covid-19 and the World of Work', 3rd edition, at ilo.org.

working hours in 2021 remained significantly below pre-pandemic levels, and across the world economy there were great volumes of under-utilised wage labour, especially among low-wage earners and the young (women in particular).[20] In high-income countries, there were significant levels of underutilised labour in 2022.[21] Since substantial numbers of workers still lay outside the process of value creation, aggregate supply did not recover strongly and workers lacked power relative to capital.

The distributional struggle between capital and labour and the resulting trajectory of inflation are issues of prime importance as the implications of the Pandemic Crisis continue to emerge. If high inflation became entrenched, it would deliver a body blow to financialised capitalism.[22] To consider this issue in further detail, it is important briefly to revisit Keynes's analysis, especially his celebrated pamphlet *How to Pay for the War*, written soon after the outbreak of the Second World War. The discussion of Keynes's pamphlet, however, would be far from adequate without also calling upon Marx.

Keynes on inflation covering the resource costs of state expenditure

The problem that concerned Keynes in 1940 was covering the huge military costs of the unfolding world conflict. How would the vast resources that the British government had begun to direct toward military production be obtained?

Keynes noted that the supply side of the British economy could not possibly meet the requirements of both war production and peacetime

---

20 See ILO (2021) 'ILO Monitor: Covid-19 and the World of Work', 8th edition, at ilo.org.

21 The point held even in view of econometric attempts to show that the US labour market was in practice far more tight than official figures of employment suggested; see A. Domash and L. H. Summers (2022) 'How Tight Are US Labour Markets?' NBER Working Paper No. 29739. Even if these calculations were right, there were still millions of workers available for hiring, and that is without even mentioning the poor quality of the jobs created.

22 Already in 2022 there were voices claiming that entrenchment was well underway in the USA and that a policy response similar to the 'Volcker shock' was required: see M. A. Bolhuis, J. N. L. Cramer, and L. H. Summers (2022) 'Comparing Past and Present Inflation', NBER, Working Paper No. 30116. Others appeared more sanguine, but their deep concern could not be disguised: see J. B. DeLong (2022) 'America's Macroeconomic Outlook', Project Syndicate, at project-syndicate.org.

consumption.[23] Consequently, private consumption would have to be reduced to release resources for war. But a decline in private consumption would never take place through a rise in voluntary saving that would somehow occur spontaneously.[24] How, then, could the problem be solved?

Keynes further noted that the required resources could not be obtained in full by taxing the wealthier strata of society – the rich and the middle class – as the sums simply did not add up. Taxes could be a means of obtaining extra resources, as could voluntary saving, but they would not be enough by themselves, and certainly not if they were exclusively imposed on the wealthy.[25] Moreover, only a part of the required resources could be obtained by borrowing from the capitalist class and the rich, with the additional drawback that these social strata would acquire further claims on the national debt, thus altering the distribution of income in their favour after the war.

For Keynes, it followed that the bulk of the required resources would have to be released by reducing the consumption of workers and others on modest incomes. This was hard enough to achieve, but would become even more complex as government military spending would inevitably boost aggregate demand, leading to full employment. Workers would have considerable disposable income and would seek to increase consumption. An imbalance of aggregate demand and supply would result, and thus the prospect of inflation would arise.

Keynes acknowledged that inflation could potentially be an answer for how to pay for the war. Since an established system of wage indexation did not exist in Britain, the nominal income of workers would hopelessly chase after the rising prices of goods, and workers' consumption would fall in real terms. In effect, inflation would operate as a tax on workers – a 'forced saving', in the sense that workers would claim less of the national output – releasing resources for the war effort. At the same time, the rise in prices would favour the profits of capitalists, which might be partly taxed but would still leave net gains for the capitalist class. Inflation would transfer income from workers to capitalists, severely worsening inequality. For these

---

23 See J. M. Keynes (1940) *How to Pay for the War*, Macmillan: London, ch. 1.
24 Ibid., p. 9.
25 Ibid., ch. 4.

reasons, Keynes was opposed to funding the war by generating inflation.[26]

It should be stressed that Keynes's arguments did not stop Britain from adopting precisely the 'forced saving' method in India, which was, at the time, still a British colony.[27] Faced with the threat of Japanese invasion and heavily constrained by the expenses of war in Europe and Africa, Britain opted for inflation to cover the costs of re-arming the Asian subcontinent. As inflation accelerated, the purchasing power of vast swathes of the poorest peasants in West Bengal was destroyed. 'Forced saving' to meet war expenditures in India took the form of a famine that killed three million people, while capitalist profiteers were enriched. Keynes and other British liberals obviously did not advocate this outcome, but nor did they actively oppose it. Imperial considerations held sway.

The disaster of India aside, for Keynes, the preferred method of paying for the war was through a national plan to create 'forced saving' directly. The plan did not include heavy reliance on a system of rationing and price fixing, both of which seemed problematic to Keynes.[28] Rather, his aim was administratively to defer a part of workers' income by placing it in personal deposits that would be kept in special national accounts.[29] There would also be increased taxation of other income, including that of capitalists, but the main release of resources would be through the planned deferment of workers' income, thus avoiding the boost to aggregate demand that would lead to inflation and the inevitable swelling of capitalist profits.

Keynes's plan would still increase the national debt, but workers would also have a strong claim on the augmented debt of the state and would be able to draw down the accumulated funds after the war. The best time to allow for such withdrawals would be at the onset of the first post-war slump – that is, as soon as aggregate demand fell below aggregate supply.

---

26 Keynes's analysis had a sustained influence on the theory of war finance; see, for instance, L. Ohanian (1997) 'The Macroeconomic Effects of War Finance in the United States: World War II and the Korean War', *American Economic Review* 87 (1): 23–40; see also V. Barnett (2009) 'Keynes and the Non-Neutrality of Russian War Finance during World War One', *Europe–Asia Studies* 61 (5): 797–812.

27 For an exemplary analysis of Keynes's plan and the disastrous implications of British imperial policy, see U. Patnaik (2018), 'Profit Inflation, Keynes and the Holocaust in Bengal, 1943–44', *Economic and Political Weekly* 53 (42): 20.

28 See Keynes (1940) *How to Pay for the War*, ch. 8.

29 Ibid., ch. 2.

Not surprisingly, the labour movement in Britain opposed Keynes's plan because of its calculated contractionary effect on workers' income.[30] In the event, the plan was not adopted by the British government, and the war was financed through higher taxation, higher domestic borrowing, rationing, and borrowing heavily from abroad – particularly from the USA. The exercise was mostly of theoretical value.

Confronting the costs of state intervention in the 2020s

Keynes's *How to Pay for the War* became a point of reference in UK public debate as soon the health emergency occurred in early 2020.[31] The crisis, after all, bore a resemblance to war, with curfews and restrictions, extraordinary government intervention in economic and social life, and a vast escalation of public debt.

But the pandemic was not a war, and its social conditions were very different from those that concerned Keynes. Even if it was catalysed by the state, the economic turmoil remained a recognisable crisis of financialised capitalism, reflecting the sustained loss of dynamism by capitalist accumulation in core countries. In dealing with the economic shock, powerful states emerged as arbiters of the direction of capitalist accumulation amid intensified global competition, including an intensified struggle for hegemony.

To add another layer of complexity, unlike a war, the pandemic shock initially depressed aggregate demand and disrupted aggregate supply, leading to rapid increases in unemployment and severe underutilisation of resources. Several governments were faced with falling consumption and rising saving by workers and other strata, while enterprises postponed investment. Without the extraordinary fiscal and monetary boost of 2020–21, unemployment and underutilised resources would have reached unprecedented levels.

30 See R. Toye (1999) 'Keynes, the Labour Movement and "How to Pay for the War"', *Twentieth Century British History* 10 (3): 255–81; for a political rejection of Keynes's plan from the left, see I. Deutscher (1940) 'Starve for Victory! Compulsory Saving or Compulsory Inflation', *Workers Fight*, at marxists.org.

31 See, for instance, R. Skidelsky (2020) 'Lessons from Keynes in the Age of Coronavirus', *Prospect*, 19 March, at prospectmagazine.co.uk; see also A. Bollard (2020) 'How to Pay for Coronavirus: Lessons from Previous Wars', *Forum Hōtoke Royal Society Te Apārangi*, at royalsociety.org.nz; and I. Goldin (2021) 'How the Pandemic Could Save Us', VoxEU, CEPR, 20 June at cepr.org/voxeu.

The response of core governments did, however, result in a problem similar to that faced by Keynes. For, in substance, Keynes believed that the aggregate supply of peacetime goods when full-scale war broke out in 1939–40 would be unable to meet growing aggregate demand as full employment was reached by expanding military production. A boost to aggregate demand in the Great Depression of the 1930s, on the other hand, would not have led to inflation, since there was extensive under-used productive capacity that would have generated extra output.[32] Keynes's war problem reappeared in core countries in 2022, even though overt war conditions were absent, except in Ukraine.

Aggregate supply proved unable to meet the boost delivered to aggregate demand by governments in 2020–21, especially in the USA. The discrepancy became even greater as living conditions were steadily normalised, and workers and other strata found themselves in possession of savings accumulated during the period of severe restrictions. The difference with Keynes's time was, needless to say, that the inability of supply to respond was due to the underlying malaise of financialised capitalism. Marxist analysis of the weaknesses of capitalist accumulation is highly relevant in this respect, as well as offering insight into the resource costs of state interventions in the pandemic.

As was shown in the preceding chapters, the resources committed to confront the turmoil related in part to fiscal expenditures on unemployment benefits, family support, direct subventions of household income as subsidies, and the payment of wages from the public purse to restrain unemployment. Even more prominently, they related to fiscal spending to cover enterprise losses as well as providing tax relief, credit guarantees, and so on. Resource costs also arose due to monetary policy, including the massive provision of liquidity by central banks, the lowering of interest rates close to zero, and the expansion of private credit and money supply. These costs were largely indirect and barely recognised in public debate, as is shown in the next chapter.

Boosting aggregate demand through fiscal policy amounts to the government facilitating or generating claims on resources belonging to others; hence, the government must provide an equivalent to the resource owners. Since the governments of core states do not produce marketable resources (nationalised industries aside), they must obtain the equivalent through other methods. There are obviously three

---

32 Keynes (1940) *How to Pay for the War*, p. 4.

fundamental options: to tax, to borrow, or to create fiat money. Keynes discussed the first two options in his pamphlet but left the third out of his account. The third option is, however, crucially important to contemporary capitalism, as will be shown in the following chapter.

Taxation is the traditional method of obtaining requisite resources and, from the perspective of workers and the poor, the resource costs of the turmoil of the 2020s ought to be met at least in part through a progressive tax reform. The decades of neoliberalism were marked by tax breaks for enterprises and the rich, which were frequently matched by austerity for the rest of society. Taxing the income and wealth of the rich as well as the profits of corporations could support future fiscal expenditures as well as having beneficial redistributive effects. After all, expansionary monetary policy in 2020–21 brought great increases in financial asset prices, while corporate profits were boosted by the real-location of demand and government support. There is certainly scope for increased taxation of corporate profits and financial wealth.

The ruling elites of core countries would undoubtedly oppose significant increases in their own taxation seeking to impose the burden on workers and other social strata. It is also likely that they would support a steady return to austerity, reducing welfare and other expenditures, and shifting the costs further onto the rest of society. The ruling elites of peripheral countries are likely to make similar choices, exacerbated by the fear of external dependence.[33]

However, austerity and taxes on workers and the poor entail severe political risks, which have become especially acute after decades of neoliberal policies. It is possible, therefore, that core countries would tackle the costs of intervention by tolerating high public borrowing, depending on the specific conditions of each country. But the risks of increased borrowing are also substantial. Rising public debt typically alters the distribution of income in favour of the rich, who acquire additional claims on future national output. More acutely, it raises the issue of sustainability – that is, of the ability of the state to make payments on its debt according to contract, particularly when debt is owed abroad.

Governments borrowing primarily in their own currency could continue to service a high debt for significant lengths of time, if the

---

33 I. Ortiz and M. Cummins (2021) 'Global Austerity Alert: Looming Budget Cuts in 2021–25 and Alternative Pathways', IPD, GSJ, ITUC, PSI, AWC, BWP, and TNW Working Paper.

country had an adequate tax base and could eventually obtain the resources to make the requisite payments. The distributional effects would be negative, as the beneficiaries would be the holders of national debt, but the political risks of austerity would be avoided. Time would also be gained, perhaps allowing more intensive production of output ahead and thus covering the repayment of debt.

If, however, a government borrowed in a foreign currency, or even in the domestic currency but from foreign lenders, meeting the resource costs of the turmoil through debt would assume an entirely different character. Regular payments on the debt would ultimately rest on the ability of the country to ensure inflows of the necessary foreign currency, or alternatively to ensure that foreigners would somehow continue to hold debt denominated in its own currency. The economic implications would be profound, as is discussed in part III, which touches directly upon the issue of the hierarchy of currencies in the world economy and thus on imperialism and hegemony.

There is, furthermore, a particular difficulty for core countries in this connection, which applies above all to the USA. The US dollar stands at the top of the hierarchy and functions as world money. Consequently, the USA issues the most important public debt in the world, even if it is denominated in its own domestic currency.[34] For the US ruling elite, the volume and creditworthiness of its public debt are matters of paramount importance in sustaining the dollar as world money. There is a balance of fear in this respect, whereby the international holders of dollars – typically in the form of US public debt instruments – rely on the continuing global acceptability of the dollar, while the US government relies on the international acceptability of its debt to guarantee the world role of the dollar. Ballooning US public debt could potentially destabilise this delicate balance, undermining the value of dollar reserves.

34 At the end of 2019, about 60 per cent of US public debt was in domestic hands, while 40 per cent was in the hands of foreigners. Of the domestic holdings, 13 per cent belonged to the Federal Reserve, forming a very distinctive part of public debt, which, moreover, increased substantially as the pandemic struck. The rest of the domestic holdings were mostly in the hands of financial institutions: mutual funds, financial intermediaries, pension funds, and so on. Of the foreign holdings of US public debt, moreover, 7 per cent was in Japanese and 7 per cent in Chinese hands. The great bulk of foreign holdings belonged to public financial institutions (central banks) and acted as liquidity reserves. See Congressional Budget Office (2020) 'Federal Debt: A Primer', Congress of the United States, March, at CBO.gov.

There are, in short, no easy options for ruling elites across the world in confronting the resource costs of the Pandemic Crisis of the early 2020s. Is it possible, then, to meet these costs through inflation, the very policy that Keynes rejected? There is no doubt that persistent and high inflation would be the death knell of financialisation, destroying the value of loanable capital. It would thus be unacceptable to the ruling elite of core countries as a method of dealing with the resource costs of the turmoil. If rapid inflation became a realistic threat, the monetary authorities of core countries would draw on the accumulated experience of the last forty years and seek to suppress it by hiking interest rates and imposing austerity.

By June 2022, the Federal Reserve had begun significantly to increase interest rates, signalling the likely path of policy in the period ahead. The trouble is that a repeat of the 'Volcker shock' would be a very different affair in the 2020s. In the intervening decades, the world economy has become awash with private and public debt, the bitter fruit of financialisation in both core and periphery.[35] Escalating interest rates would not only bring recession and further losses for workers but also major debt crises across the world, particularly among peripheral countries that are already exposed to high public debt, as was shown in previous chapters. Moreover, the precipitous fall in asset prices that would result from escalating interest rates would also entail substantial losses of wealth for the ruling elite.

In sum, the pandemic shock, coming hard on the heels of a decade of weak accumulation, has resulted in exceptionally hard choices for the ruling blocs in both core and peripheral countries. In this light, the next chapter considers more closely the extraordinary role of central banks and the prospect of meeting resource costs through the issuance of state-based fiat money.

---

35 For an estimate of total debt levels in 2021, see V. Gaspar, P. Medas, and R. Perrelli (2021) 'Global Debt Reaches a Record $226 Trillion', 15 December, at blogs.imf.org.

8

The Monetary Power of Core States and Its Limits

Since the Great Crisis of 2007–09, core states have demonstrated enormous economic power, including the ability to engage in unprecedented fiscal and monetary policy. Their power derives, in large measure, from command over the final means of payment. In this respect, core states contrast sharply with peripheral states, which also exercise substantial domestic command over the final means of payment, but whose domestic monies are ranked low in the global hierarchy of currencies. There is also a sharp contrast with the Chinese state, which, in addition to commanding the final means of payment, derives economic power from direct possession over the means of production.

The bulk of the money of contemporary capitalist economies is created by private commercial banks as they engage in lending operations: it is private credit money. Yet, private credit money rests on the money issued by the central bank – that is, on public credit money with a distinct aspect of fiat deriving from the will of the state, which acts as the final means of payment. Command over this peculiar form of money is a founding stone of financialised capitalism and an indispensable lever of social and political power. It is also a means of differentiating among states in the world economy: a lever of imperial power for some and a cause of subordination for others.

Central banks issuing the final means of payment have emerged as the leading economic institutions of core countries in financialised capitalism. The ascendancy of central banks occurred while core states divested themselves of productive resources through privatisation, often based on neoliberal perceptions regarding the putative superiority of markets. And yet the path followed by core states regarding money – a pivotal commodity in a capitalist economy – has been the exact opposite of neoliberal ideology. Far from applying competitive market principles, core states strengthened the monopoly power of the central bank over the final means of payment, acting as guarantors of 'moneyness'.

Contemporary fiat money issued by central banks merits closer attention, including its potential deployment to achieve a range of broader economic objectives, as is characteristically advocated by Modern Monetary Theory (MMT), a prominent current of radical opponents of capitalism. The rest of this chapter analyses the monetary power of core states in the current turmoil from the perspective of Marxist political economy.

The peculiar fiat money of financialised capitalism: A summing up

The development of capitalism since the beginning of the twentieth century has been marked by the domestic ascendancy of central bank money. Its rise is closely related to the retreat of commodity money (gold) as domestic money but also as means of international payments and reserve formation in the world economy, replaced by the US dollar, as is discussed in part III of this book.[1]

Contemporary central bank money is qualitatively different from simple forms of fiat money issued directly by the state to meet current expenditures.[2] Simple fiat money typically comprises paper notes printed by, for instance, a state ministry and given obligatory circulation to, say, pay the salaries of state employees, fund public procurement, or receive taxes. These forms of fiat money have been known since the early days of classical political economy and derive their 'moneyness' from the power of the state, which allows them to act as symbols of

---

1 The historical literature is substantial, including notably B. J. Eichengreen (1996) *Globalizing Capital: A History of the International Monetary System*, Princeton University Press: Princeton, NJ; and M. De Cecco (1984) *The International Gold Standard: Money and Empire*, St Martin's Press: New York.

2 See Lapavitsas (2013) *Profiting without Producing*, ch. 4, which provides the basis for much of the theoretical analysis in this and the following sections, together with M. Itoh and C. Lapavitsas (1999) *Political Economy of Money and Finance*, Palgrave Macmillan: London.

commodity money. Crucially, the creation and circulation of such money does not rely on private banks, or indeed on any banks at all.

The money issued by the central banks of contemporary capitalist states is qualitatively different; indeed, it is a peculiar hybrid. The final means of payment is created as a liability of the central bank on its balance sheet, backed by financial assets that include public and private securities. It derives its 'moneyness' partly from the state but also from the credit operations of the central bank in the financial system and, above all, in the money market.

The process of creating such money resembles the generation of credit money by private banks. Simply put, the central bank issues its own liabilities to acquire securities issued by the state and private corporations. When central bank assets mature and are paid off by their issuers, the liabilities of the central bank tend to shrink, other things being equal.[3]

Nonetheless, central bank money also has an unmistakable fiat character deriving largely from the guarantee (implicit or explicit) of its 'moneyness' by the state. The guarantee takes a practical, material form through the public securities held by the central bank as its own assets. The fiat character is further strengthened by the state removing all formal obligations to convert such money into a commodity with produced value. The holder of a unit of central bank money could only demand formal conversion into another unit of central bank money. At the same time, central bank money is typically capable of settling commercial and other obligations.

Private bank money compared with central bank money

The peculiarity of central bank money as a hybrid incorporating aspects of both fiat and credit money can be demonstrated by comparing its

---

3 That is, the Law of Reflux as a characteristic feature of credit money, proposed in the nineteenth century by the Banking School, and broadly accepted by Marx, continues to hold. However, the form that the Reflux takes in twenty-first century capitalism is very different from that of the nineteenth century, since financial systems have been greatly transformed. The primary business of banks is no longer the discounting bills exchange to support the needs of industry for working capital. Banking in mature financialised capitalism involves trading in securities to extract speculative profits, as was discussed in previous chapters, and the implications for the operations of central banks are profound.

creation to that of private credit money by a commercial bank. The analysis would be greatly facilitated by deploying some fundamental categories of Marxist political economy, while referring directly to the simplified balance sheet of a commercial bank in chapter 5.

Consider first a commercial bank that makes a loan or purchases a security by opening a deposit, thereby initially making available to the borrower or the security seller the bank's own (private) credit. Crucially, the bank assumes that it could command sufficient loanable capital to back up the deposit. To that purpose, the bank either already possesses the necessary loanable capital as reserves or expects to acquire it by borrowing fresh reserves, typically in the money market.[4] In either case, the reserves must be readily convertible into central bank money, since the deposit that the private bank has just created is convertible into such money. For, once the deposit holder starts to make payments, the bank must have access to central bank money to honour these payments.

Two vital conclusions follow for a private commercial bank making loans or purchasing securities. First, it must anticipate (and ensure access to) the flow of loanable capital available as reserves in the money market. Second, it must also anticipate the payment of interest and principal on its loans and securities, thus ensuring the return and expansion of the loanable capital it has advanced. The former is vital to the liquidity and the latter to the solvency of a private bank.

---

4 This is the typical banking process assumed to underpin the creation of credit money by radical monetary theory. Within post-Keynesian theory, for instance, two main strands stand out, namely horizontalism and structuralism. Horizontalism fundamentally claims that the supply of bank reserves is perfectly elastic at the interest rate set by the central bank. This view is associated primarily with Basil Moore. See, for instance, in B. J. Moore (1978) 'A Post Keynesian Approach to Monetary Theory', *Challenge* 21 (4): 44–52; (1983) 'Unpacking the Post Keynesian Black Box: Bank Lending and Money Supply', *Journal of Post Keynesian Economics* 5 (4): 537–56; (1988) *Horizontalists and Verticalists: The Macroeconomics of Credit Money*, Cambridge University Press: Cambridge, UK; and (1988) 'The Endogenous Money Supply', *Journal of Post Keynesian Economics* 10 (3): 372–85. Structuralism is more diffuse and basically claims that the supply of bank reserves is not perfectly elastic but could be manipulated by the central bank. See, for instance, R. Pollin (1991) 'Two Theories of Money Supply Endogeneity: Some Empirical Evidence', *Journal of Post Keynesian Economics* 13 (3): 366–96; L. R. Wray (1990) *Money and Credit in Capitalist Economies: The Endogenous Money Approach*, Edward Elgar: Aldershot; and T. I. Palley (1996) 'Accommodationism versus Structuralism: Time for an Accommodation', *Journal of Post Keynesian Economics* 18 (4): 585–94. For recent attempts to synthesise the two approaches, see M. Deleidi (2020) 'Post-Keynesian Endogenous Money Theory: Horizontalists, Structuralists and the Paradox of Illiquidity', *Metroeconomica* 71: 156–75.

The flow of loanable capital available as reserves in the money market and the flow of repayments on loans and securities have very different determinants. The former comprises money capital (and other sums of money) that has become idle for short periods of time across the sphere of circulation and is available for trading in the money market, along the lines discussed in chapters 5 and 6. The latter amounts to flows of surplus value (or other money profits) deriving from the completion of capital-ist projects (and other transactions). Yet, both types of flows are inte-grally related to each other on the balance sheet of a commercial bank, since prompt payments on loans and securities are vital to securing the liquidity necessary for further expansion of the asset side. Private banks constantly walk this tightrope as they seek profits.

Consider now a central bank that purchases securities or makes loans by creating fresh liabilities on its balance sheet. At one remove, there is an entirely formal difference with a private bank, since central bank liabilities are mostly held by private banks, or even directly by the state. Moreover, the corporeal forms of central bank liabilities include depos-its (held by private banks) that are book entries or electronic records, but also banknotes held mostly by the public (typically a privilege of the central bank granted by the state). The two forms are qualitatively the same as banking categories and together comprise central bank money, but the balance between them varies according to a country's historical and institutional features.[5]

At a further remove, however, there exists a qualitative difference between central and private banks regarding the mobilisation of loanable capital underlying the transaction. In advancing a loan or buying a secu-rity, the central bank initially makes its own credit available to the

---

5 See Lapavitsas (2013) *Profiting without Producing*, ch. 4. The Bank of Japan, for instance, issues a greater proportion of banknotes than other central banks. More complexly, the Federal Reserve allows the US Treasury to hold an account directly (which has ballooned in the Pandemic Crisis), in sharp contrast to, say, the relationship between the ECB and the member states of the EMU. For a historical analysis of the role of cash across countries and social structures, see K. S. Rogoff (2017) *The Curse of Cash: How Large-Denomination Bills Aid Crime and Tax Evasion and Constrain Monetary Policy*, Princeton University Press: Princeton, NJ. An excellent institutional account of the process of money creation and the role of commercial as well as central banks can be found in M. McLeay, A. Radia, and R. Thomas (2014) 'Money in the Modern Economy: An Introduction', Bank of England Quarterly Bulletin Q1: 4–13, deploying simplified T-accounts to show the stylised liabilities of central banks, namely currency in circulation and reserves.

counterparty in the standard manner of a bank, but its credit is public and normally stands for the highest grade of credit in a country. At the same time, its liabilities are the final means of payment by dint of the state. Consequently, unlike private banks, the central bank does not need to hold or obtain liquidity reserves to support its banking operations. On the contrary, its liabilities are directly and immediately liquid, since they are fiat money, and could be freely used by the counterparties (typically private banks) to make payments. Thus, the natural environment for the operations of the central bank is the money market, which it dominates.

To trade in the money market, however, the central bank must command loanable capital, as is also the case for private banks and other agents. The nature of this loanable capital is easier to grasp by considering the repayments made on the central bank's securities and loans. Since a large proportion of these are public, the central bank expects the regular receipt of a share of the tax revenues of the state in the form of interest and repayment of principal. Insofar as the securities it holds are private, the central bank expects a regular flow of repayments out of the profits of a wide range of enterprises.

In effect, the central bank makes an advance of its own credit by anticipating tax receipts and private enterprise profits, thereby transforming a part of the latter into the loanable capital with which it operates. It could also directly collect the loanable capital of others by selling or issuing securities in the open markets. On this basis, the central bank could make a regular profit, particularly as its liabilities typically cost it nothing, or very little. This is the contemporary form of seigniorage – that is, of the charge imposed by the state for assigning its imprimatur to money.[6] Unlike private banks, however, the driving motive of the central bank is not profit making, but the design and implementation of monetary policy and the management of fiat money.

If repayments on central bank assets were disrupted or altogether cancelled, loanable capital would be destroyed, and the central bank would make losses which, since it is a public institution, would ultimately be imposed on society. However, given its privileged position in the financial system, the central bank has considerable leeway in dealing with losses, even allowing its own capital to become negative, without preventing its functioning, or inducing bankruptcy. Losses could be

---

6 See McLeay, Radia, and Thomas (2014) 'Money in the Modern Economy', p. 10, n. 7, for a brief operational definition of seigniorage.

covered gradually by accumulating returns on other assets – that is, from future seigniorage. Losses could also be covered by recapitalising the central bank out of the tax revenue of the state.

Consequently, large-scale central bank purchases of public securities by creating fiat money constitute a highly peculiar process. The central bank makes a loan to the state, receives interest and principal payments out of tax revenue, and makes payments to the state out of its profits. Simultaneously, it transforms a part of the state's tax receipts into loanable capital. Essentially, the state makes an advance payment to itself out of the tax revenue it expects to receive in the future, transforming part of it into loanable capital.

This is a circuitous operation that could, potentially, be extended without formal limit. If tax receipts did not materialise as planned, the state could simply issue fresh securities, which the central bank would acquire by creating fresh fiat money, out of which the state could make payments on its maturing securities. The result would be rising public debt, growing liabilities of the central bank, and postponement of the return of the loanable capital to the central bank. If tax returns failed to materialise altogether, the central bank would take a loss, but that would not immediately affect its operations and could be covered out of future seigniorage.

It is also apparent that the state could potentially deploy this circuitous operation to finance its fiscal deficits. The practice of monetising deficits in core countries would face no internal limits, since the liabilities and the assets of the central bank would move jointly. The public debt would expand, but a significant proportion of it would be held by the central bank – that is, by another branch of the state. The limits to this practice would be external, i.e., they would derive from the impact on the general conditions of capitalist accumulation.

One obvious external limit would be the risk of inflation, a point that casts further light on the discussion of inflation in chapter 7. The public securities obtained by the central bank could be purchased from commercial banks or other private owners in the secondary markets – that is, in open financial markets for already existing public securities. In that case, the purchases would increase the reserves of private banks held at the central bank, thus allowing for an increase in the overall supply of private credit money.

Alternatively, the public securities could be bought directly by the central bank from the government in the primary markets – that is, in open financial markets for newly issued securities. In such cases, the reserves of private banks would begin to increase only after the government started spending the proceeds from the sale of securities, thus making payments to enterprises and others who would eventually channel the funds to banks after further transactions. The result, however, would again be to allow for a potential increase in the supply of private credit money.

Nonetheless, there would not be a direct connection between such increases in the money supply and the rate of inflation. Much would depend on the further operations of the financial system, and they would be directly related to the rate of interest. After all, central bank money is created through credit operations and is, thus, integrally linked to the rate of interest, as is shown in the following section. Central banks set the benchmark rate of interest for the domestic credit system, and in the decades of financialisation they have acquired unprecedented control over interest rates.

Capitalism with near-zero interest rates

Intervention by the central banks of core states in 2007–09 and 2020 drove interest rates to extremely low levels, and the trading of liquidity in the money markets became entirely dependent on the massive provision of fresh central bank liabilities. The existence of near-zero rates of interest managed by a public agent residing at the heart of the credit system is an extraordinary development in the history of capitalism, with significant resource implications.[7]

The ECB and the Bank of Japan even adopted negative interest rates – that is, they began to charge commercial banks interest on their reserves. Negative interest rates are equivalent to a tax on commercial banks for holding reserves, and result in a downward shift in market interest rates and compression of commercial bank profitability. The

---

7 The mainstream literature on this issue is particularly concerned with the effectiveness of monetary policy when the rate of interest is very low; see, for instance, C. Borio and L. Gambacorta (2017) 'Monetary Policy and Bank Lending in a Low Interest Rate Environment: Diminishing Effectiveness?' *Journal of Macroeconomics* 54 (B): 217–31; M. T. Kiley and J. M. Roberts (2017) 'Monetary Policy in a Low Interest Rate World', *Brookings Papers on Economic Activity* 48 (1): 317–96; and C. Borio and B. Hofmann (2017) 'Is Monetary Policy Less Effective when Interest Rates Are Persistently Low?' BIS Working Paper No. 628. The implications for resource allocation are at least as important, however.

aim was to force banks to reduce the volume of reserves and thus to increase lending.[8]

As the pandemic unfolded, furthermore, the state took further steps to ensure that banks would lend strongly to the private sector. Thus, banks were banned from paying dividends and, crucially, public guarantees were offered on new loans, effectively protecting banks by socialising possible losses.[9] The result was an extraordinarily rapid rise of the supply of private credit money in the USA and other core states, as was discussed in the previous chapter.[10]

It is important to stress that few of these unconventional monetary policies by core central banks are to be found among peripheral countries. Neither the power of core states deriving from their command over fiat money nor their ability to manipulate interest rates are replicated across vast swathes of peripheral countries. The financial systems of the latter also depend on the state, but a peripheral state's ability to intervene is severely circumscribed by the subordinate position of its currency in the international financial system, as is shown in part III.

The rate of interest is a fundamental price in this connection, and its behaviour characterises the outlook of the financial system. For Marxist political economy, the rate of interest has no 'natural' level, nor does it reflect any fundamental relationship of production and circulation. It is a pure – if peculiar – price resulting from the interplay of demand and supply of loanable capital in the financial markets.[11] Since it does not

---

8 For a review of negative interest rates in Japan and Europe, as well as their effects on monetary policy transmission mechanisms and banks, see S. Angrick and N. Nemoto (2017) 'Central Banking Below Zero: The Implementation of Negative Interest Rates in Europe and Japan', *Asia Europe Journal* 15: 417–43; N. Yoshino, F. Taghizadeh-Hesary, and H. Miyamoto (2017) 'The Effectiveness of the Negative Interest Rate Policy in Japan', *Credit and Capital Markets* 50 (2): 189–212.

9 See C. Borio (2020) 'The Prudential Response to the Covid-19 Crisis', speech given at the Annual General Meeting of the Bank for International Settlements, Basel, 30 June, at bis.org.

10 The exceptionally fast growth rate of the money supply (M2) in the USA and Eurozone is shown in L. Bê Duc et al. (2022) 'The Increase in the Money Supply during the Covid Crisis: Analysis and Implications', *Bulletin de la Banque de France* 239: Article 2, January–February. They estimate 12 per cent growth rate of the money supply in the Eurozone in 2020 (compared with 5 per cent in 2019) and 25 per cent growth rate in the USA (compared with 5 per cent in 2019).

11 See, for instance, T. Evans (2004) 'Marxian and Post-Keynesian Theories of Finance and the Business Cycle', *Capital & Class* 28 (2): 47–100; see also L. Harris (1976) 'On Interest, Credit and Capital', *Economy and Society* 5 (2): 145–77; Lapavitsas (2013) *Profiting without Producing*, pp. 116–17; and N. Aguila and J. Graña (2020) 'The

reflect deep material processes of the capitalist economy, the rate of interest could potentially be driven to zero without bringing capitalist accumulation to a halt. The fall of interest to zero would indicate that the holders of loanable capital are unable to draw a part of the produced surplus value directly through lending.

There is no analogy between the rate of interest and the rate of profit in this regard.[12] The rate of profit reflects key dimensions of capitalist production, including the division of capital into fixed and variable components, the standard of living of workers, the length of the working day, the intensity of labour, and the turnover rate of capital. If the rate of profit fell and remained at zero, capitalist accumulation would stop. The rate of interest bears no relationship of this kind with capitalist accumulation, and yet it remains a key price. If it was driven toward zero through state action, capitalist accumulation would continue, but there would also be perverse results with significant resource implications.

For one thing, the rate of interest is a factor in the investment decisions of functioning capitalists. Capital tends to flow among sectors of production as capitalists compare returns, generally moving from low to high return sectors, and thereby equalising the average rate of profit. The operative return for capitalists in this regard is the rate of profit of enterprise – that is, the rate of profit accruing net of interest relative to the capitalist's own equity. Other things being equal, a fall in the rate of interest would raise the rate of profit of enterprise across the economy. Mainstream economic theory typically concludes that a fall in the rate of interest would consequently increase investment and be beneficial to accumulation. There is, however, little empirical confirmation of

---

Influence of the Interest Rate in Capitalist Competition: Capital Differentiation and Structural Change', *Bulletin of Political Economy* 14 (2): 153–77.

12 See Itoh and Lapavitsas (1999) *Political Economy of Money and Finance*, ch. 3, where it is shown that the two magnitudes are determined at different levels of abstraction. There is an apparent tension in Marx's own writings in this connection, since, on the one hand, Marx claimed that there is no 'natural' rate of interest but, on the other, he clearly thought that the rate of profit of banks is equalised with the average rate of profit. Anwar Shaikh has stressed the importance of this tension and proposed a way of resolving the issue by relating the rate of interest to the rate of profit through competition; see, for instance, A. Shaikh (2016) *Capitalism*, Oxford University Press: New York, pp. 476–9. But the issue of the qualitative difference between interest and profit remains.

investment responding positively to low interest rates.[13] Things are rather more complicated.

Capital does not flow from low to high return sectors directly and immediately. Analogously, capitalists do not regularly abandon the sector they are already operating in to move to another, nor is it common to operate simultaneously in several sectors, continually shifting among them according to profitability. Rather, the movement of capital among sectors is highly mediated and occurs via the financial system as temporary surpluses of idle funds are mobilised to meet demand for investment capital.

The equalisation of the rate of profit consequently occurs through flows of loanable capital traded by financial intermediaries or directly in financial markets. A crucial function of the financial system in a capitalist economy is to enable the equalisation of the rate of profit, and the rate of interest as the price of loanable capital is pivotal to that process. Therefore, the resource implications of driving the rate of interest toward zero are significant.

For financial intermediaries, a drop in the rate of interest typically represents a fall in profits from handling loanable capital that belongs to others. As was discussed in chapter 5, the profits of commercial banks depend heavily on the spread between the interest rate received on loans and the interest rate paid on deposits and other liabilities. If the rate of interest fell across the economy, the spread would tend to narrow, and bank profits would tend to decline. At the same time, a fall in the rate of interest would normally boost the price of financial assets, and thus a bank could make capital gains on the assets it holds.

With lower interest rates, banks would be encouraged to trade financial assets partly to seek capital gains and partly to obtain fees and commissions from facilitating trading by others. Broadly similar considerations hold for shadow banks, or the owners of loanable capital operating directly in financial markets. When the rate of interest is driven toward zero, speculative activity is encouraged, as borrowed money becomes practically free, thereby potentially leading to a financial bubble. For non-financial capitalists, on the other hand, a fall in the rate of interest would raise the

13 See, for instance, F. Petri (1997) 'On Aggregate Investment as a Function of the Interest Rate', Universita Di Siena Working Paper No. 217; see also K. Lane and T. Rosewall (2015) 'Firms' Investment Decisions and Interest Rates', Reserve Bank of Australia Bulletin, June: 1–7; and S. A. Sharpe and G. Suarez (2014) 'The Insensitivity of Investment to Interest Rates: Evidence from a Survey of CFOs', Federal Reserve Board Finance and Economics Discussion Series No. 2.

rate of profit of enterprise and encourage enterprises to seek further funds by borrowing in financial markets or from banks.

However, the decision of a non-financial capitalist to invest depends on far more than the rate of interest. Lowering the rate of interest does not eliminate the imponderables of investment. If, for instance, aggregate demand was weak and productivity was not rising, the field of profitability in production would be constrained. In that context, even if interest rates were close to zero, the decision by a non-financial capitalist need not be to increase investment. A more attractive choice might be to hold substantial reserves of liquid financial assets with a view to future use. Such behaviour has marked the financialisation of capitalism in core economies in recent decades.[14]

For the state, finally, the resource implications of driving interest rates toward zero are profound. Since the state is a major borrower, the servicing costs of public debt would decline. By the same token, the proportion of tax revenue that would be received as interest by the holders of public securities would fall. The implications could be severe for financial intermediaries holding substantial volumes of public debt, such as pension funds and insurance companies. The proportion of national income directed toward pensioners and holders of insurance policies would tend to fall. On the other hand, as the rate of interest falls, the price of public securities tends to rise, and financial asset holders would make capital gains.

In sum, if interest rates fell precipitously, both financial intermediaries and owners of loanable capital would face a severe squeeze on returns from regular lending. They would be encouraged to seek profits from capital gains in financial transactions as well as obtaining fees and

---

14 See, for instance, S. P. Kothari, J. W. Lewellen, and J. B. Warner (2014) 'The Behavior of Aggregate Corporate Investment', Simon Business School Working Paper No. FR 14-18, Tuck School of Business Working Paper No. 2511268, MIT Sloan Research Paper No. 5112-14, which finds that US corporate investments between 1952 and 2010 were driven primarily by profitability and seem uncorrelated with interest rate changes. See also Sharpe and Suarez (2014) 'The Insensitivity of Investment to Interest Rates', which uses a survey to determine that firms are unresponsive to interest rates when it comes to investment plans. On the impact of financialisation on investment by non-financial corporations, see O. Orhangazi (2008) 'Financialisation and Capital Accumulation in the Non-Financial Corporate Sector: A Theoretical and Empirical Investigation on the US Economy: 1973–2003', *Cambridge Journal of Economics* 32 (6): 863–86; and L. E. Davis (2018) 'Financialization and the Non-Financial Corporation: An Investigation of Firm-Level Investment Behavior in the United States', *Metroeconomica* 69 (1): 270–307.

commissions from trading. When rates are driven toward zero, the search for financial returns can become frantic and speculative pressures may increase. The allocative function of the financial system across the sectors of the capitalist economy would be profoundly disturbed and profit rate equalisation would be disrupted.

The light cast by these developments on financialised capitalism is harsh, as is discussed in further detail in subsequent chapters. It is imperative to state again, however, that what holds for core countries does not hold for peripheral countries. The dollar stands at the top of the currency hierarchy and is typically used as the unit of account, means of payment, and means of reserve formation across the world market. Several other currencies stand high in the hierarchy and compete against the dollar, including the euro, the yen, the Swiss franc, and so on. The currencies of peripheral countries stand lower, reflecting their subordinate position globally. What holds for the Federal Reserve does not hold for the central banks of a huge raft of peripheral countries. This is a critical point when considering MMT and its claims regarding the monetary power of states in contemporary capitalism.

The impact and relevance of MMT

During the 2010s, MMT gained considerable prominence in public discourse, above all in the USA, by claiming that a sovereign government could implement fiscal policies that would take the economy to full employment by issuing currency.[15] The flagship proposal of MMT is the *job guarantee*, which amounts to deploying fiscal policy to generate the possibility of public employment for anyone who wants to work at a minimum living wage with health care and other benefits (such as childcare). Presumably, the job guarantee would ensure full employment and a high and stable level of aggregate demand.[16]

---

15 This section draws heavily on C. Lapavitsas and N. Aguila (2020) 'Modern Monetary Theory on Money, Sovereignty, and Policy: A Marxist Critique with Reference to the Eurozone and Greece', *The Japanese Political Economy* 46 (4): 300–26.

16 See S. T. Fullwiler (2007) Macroeconomic Stabilization through an Employer of Last Resort', *Journal of Economic Issues* 41 (1): 93–134; see also W. F. Mitchell (1998) 'The Buffer Stock Employment Model and the Path to Full Employment', *Journal of Economic Issues* 32 (2): 547–55; see also L. R. Wray et al. (2018) 'Guaranteed Jobs through a Public Service Employment Program', Levy Economics Institute, Economics Policy Note Archive No. 18-2.

The claims of MMT rest on notions explored in the previous sections, namely that a central bank could issue its own currency or purchase government securities to finance fiscal spending without internal limits.[17] Moreover, the advocates of MMT argue that coordination between the central bank and the government could determine the interest rate charged on public debt. Since a government could always pay debt denominated in domestic currency by issuing fresh money, there are no potential problems regarding debt sustainability.

For MMT, consequently, policy makers need not focus on the size of fiscal deficits, but rather on the rate of inflation. As long as output remained below the level of full employment, there would be scope for the state to spend without fearing the acceleration of inflation.[18] It follows that the true limit of fiscal policy is not given by a financial constraint on the government budget, but by a real constraint – that is, the available resources in the economy.

Even more strikingly, for MMT, taxation is not required to finance additional spending by the government. Money is taken to be simply a unit of account arbitrarily chosen by the state and created by the central bank. Taxation is a means of destroying money created by the central bank, since it takes such money out of circulation. Taxation is also a means of generating demand among the public for money created by the state, since tax must be paid in the chosen unit of account.[19] Taxation could also discourage 'bad' behaviour or be deployed for politically desired redistributive reasons, and to dampen aggregate demand to reduce inflation. But there is no need for taxes to cover the costs of fiscal expenditure.

The combined weight of these proposals has given MMT considerable public prominence, especially among radical critics of capitalism in the USA. The notion that the state can create money *ex nihilo* to command real resources naturally leads to the conclusion that the state

17 See S. Bell (2000) 'Do Taxes and Bonds Finance Spending?' *Journal of Economic Issues* 34 (3): 603–20; S. T. Fullwiler (2006) 'Setting Interest Rates in the Modern Money Era', *Journal of Post Keynesian Economics* 28 (3): 495–525.

18 See P. R. Tcherneva (2007) 'Chartalism and the Tax-Driven Approach to Money', in P. Arestis and M. Sawyer (eds) *A Handbook of Alternative Monetary Economics*, Edward Elgar: Aldershot, ch. 5.

19 See P. R. Tcherneva (2007) 'Chartalism and the Tax-Driven Approach to Money'; see also L. R. Wray (2010) 'Money', Levy Economics Institute Working Paper No. 647; see also L. R. Wray (2015) 'Tax Policy for Sovereign Nations', in *Modern Money Theory*, 2nd edition, Palgrave Macmillan: London, pp. 137–57.

could alter the distribution of income without the political and social inconvenience of removing income from the rich, or another social layer. The state could simply create money to buy output from one social group to give to another, thus avoiding the distributional conflicts inherent to imposing taxes.

When the pandemic struck, core states adopted policies seemingly consonant with MMT prescriptions. Governments significantly increased fiscal deficits, which were partly financed by the central bank through purchases of public securities, while interest rates were pushed toward zero, or even became negative. However, there is little evidence that the fiscal and monetary policies of core states were in practice informed by MMT. Increasing fiscal expenditure in a crisis, potentially even financed through money creation by the central bank, is a government policy that has often been deployed throughout the history of capitalism. To be sure, its magnitude and forms in the 2020s were unprecedented, but that has to do with the underlying transformation of financialised capitalism. The crisis was not an 'MMT moment', although the actions of core governments were reminiscent of MMT proposals.

In view of the analysis in this book, three aspects of MMT proposals merit further attention. First, MMT underestimates the risk of financial asset speculation inherent to expansionary monetary policy. MMT writers usually ignore the broader consequences of low interest rates for the economy, other than the impact on public debt sustainability.[20] Low interest rates for long periods of time boost financial asset speculation and could lead to financial bubbles. If the speculative tendencies of finance were to be confronted when interest rates were lowered, there would have to be profound structural change, including of shadow banking.

The same fundamental problem is also present when the consequences of US monetary policy are considered from the perspective of other countries. Low interest rates in the USA could encourage capitalists to search for speculative yield by engaging in capital flows to peripheral countries, with dramatic consequences for financial stability. Similarly, increases in interest rates in the USA could trigger 'flights to quality' and induce debt crises in peripheral countries. In short, the

---

20 This is 'the mystery of the missing Minsky', as Epstein aptly called it in G. A. Epstein (2019) 'The Mystery of the Missing Minsky: Financial Instability as a Constraint on MMT Macroeconomic Policy', in G. A. Epstein (2019) *What's Wrong with Modern Money Theory?*, Palgrave Macmillan: London, pp. 65–75.

repercussions of monetary expansion and fluctuating interest rates in the USA extend far beyond its borders and matter greatly to analysing the outcomes of monetary policy across the world.

Second, and related to the first, probably the most frequent criticism of MMT by heterodox economists is that it pays insufficient attention to the monetary realities of peripheral countries.[21] The core problem in this regard is that MMT views and treats monetary sovereignty as essentially a policy choice for a country: a poor country could achieve similar sovereignty in the monetary domain to the USA.[22] But this perspective is deeply misleading in the world market.

It will be shown in part III that monetary sovereignty is inextricably linked to the ability of a state to acquire and hold world money required for international commodity transactions, transfers of value, and settlement of obligations across the world. Sovereignty depends on the mode of integration of a country in the world market, which corresponds to a hierarchically structured global monetary system. Peripheral countries lack monetary sovereignty not because of policy choices, but due to their subordinate position in the international hierarchy. In short, the possession of monetary sovereignty by the USA is the other side of the coin to the lack of monetary sovereignty experienced by poorer countries.

The subordinate position of peripheral countries is reflected in the policies of their central banks regarding reserves of world money. International reserves are required to purchase essential means of domestic production and consumption as well as to settle existing financial commitments. To this purpose, central banks must constantly balance their liabilities relative to their international reserves.

More concretely, if the central bank of a peripheral country were to

---

21 See B. Bonizzi, A. Kaltenbrunner, and J. Powell (2019) 'Subordinate Financialization in Emerging Capitalist Economies', Greenwich Papers in Political Economy No. GPERC69; D. Prates (2020) 'Beyond Modern Money Theory: A Post-Keynesian Approach to the Currency Hierarchy, Monetary Sovereignty, and Policy Space', *Review of Keynesian Economics* 8: 494–511; E. Pérez Caldentey and M. Vernengo (2019) 'The Historical Evolution of Monetary Policy in Latin America', in S. Battilossi, Y. Cassis, and K. Yago (eds) *Handbook of the History of Money and Currency*, Springer: Berlin, pp. 1–28.

22 See P. R. Tcherneva (2016) 'Money, Power, and Monetary Regimes', Levy Economics Institute Working Paper No. 861; see also E. Tymoigne (2020) 'Monetary Sovereignty: Nature, Implementation, and Implications', *Public Budgeting & Finance* 40 (3): 49–71; and L. R. Wray (2019) 'MMT and Two Paths to Big Deficits', *Challenge* 62 (6): 398–415.

issue local currency to push its economy toward full employment, it would soon come up against an external constraint.[23] The exchange rate of the domestic currency would tend to fall, with significant implications for the income of workers, the ability of enterprises to obtain inputs abroad, and the servicing of public debt. It is not accidental that the fiscal response of peripheral countries in the 2020s was far more modest than in core countries, as was shown in chapter 5. An internationally subordinate position is a major constraint on fiscal and monetary policy.

Third, and perhaps most significant, MMT largely ignores the importance of transformative interventions by governments on the side of aggregate supply and focuses primarily on aggregate demand. MMT proposals aim at changing the distribution of income without fundamentally changing the structure of production. Radical change could presumably be achieved by pumping aggregate demand through the creation of money to deliver the job guarantee.

For Marxist political economy, this is a narrow approach to radical policy, particularly as it downplays the inherent unity of production, circulation, and distribution in a capitalist economy. It is impossible radically to change distribution without also radically altering production and circulation, including the realm of finance. The job guarantee of the MMT is certainly concerned with broader issues but assumes that these could be tackled through aggregate demand policies.

Aggregate demand policies are certainly important, but profound change is inconceivable without focusing on production, including the extraordinary concentration of property rights. Redistributive taxation and drastic change of property rights in favour of workers and the poor are vital to confronting the subordination of human need in favour of profit. The answer to the disasters of capitalism is a democratically organised and coordinated economy based on socialist property relations, not more kindly versions of capitalism. The scope for such a transformation is further explored in part III by considering the formation of core and periphery and the intensification of hegemonic contests in the world economy as financialised capitalism has continued to unravel.

---

23 See N. S. Sylla (2020) 'What Does MMT Have to Offer Developing Nations?', *Brave New Europe*, 27 February, at braveneweurope.com, which uses some MMT concepts to trace the colonial functioning of taxes and money as well as radically to rethink real and monetary constraints to economic sovereignty in Africa.

PART III

States and Capitals in the World Economy

In the early 2020s, the state, long a vital prop of capitalist accumulation, emerged as a true pillar of contemporary capitalism. Individual states, nonetheless, responded to the pandemic in greatly varying ways, as was discussed in chapter 2. Once vaccines had become the main prophylactic choice, the vaccination of peripheral populations lay at the mercy of the large pharmaceutical oligopolies that dominated the world market. Moreover, peripheral countries were unable fully to adopt the economic policies of core countries, or even at all. At the same time, several countries outside the core, particularly China, demonstrated considerable capacity to confront the health emergency independently as well as dealing with the ensuing economic convulsions. Divergence ruled the roost.

The variable responses reflected differences in institutions, political traditions, historical development, and thus, ultimately, in domestic class structures. Yet deeper factors were also at play. The Pandemic Crisis cast fresh light on the balance between core and periphery, and the relations of hegemony and imperialism in the world economy. After four decades of neoliberal ascendancy and three decades of sole US hegemony, a new global configuration of power began to emerge.

Divisions between core and periphery and the struggle for global hegemony are far from novel phenomena in the world economy.[1] Capitalist production, trade, and finance tend to create a single world market, entailing a global division of labour that gives rise to mutual dependence among countries. At the same time, these economic processes continually redefine hegemony and imperialism across the world.

The decades of neoliberalism and unchallenged US hegemony since the early 1990s have been shaped by an extraordinary combination of internationalised productive capital and globally active financial capital. It is shown in the following chapters that fundamental to contemporary imperialism are giant multinationals, originating primarily in core countries, which dictate international production and trade by forming global networks. They have a symbiotic relationship with international finance, which is commanded by giant commercial banks and shadow banks. Neither the multinationals nor the international financial intermediaries dominate each other, but jointly determine the world division of labour, thus shaping the contours of hegemony.

Global in scope and insatiable in its appetite for profit, this pairing of capitals moulds economic, political, and social life across the world. In doing so, it constantly refashions divisions between core and periphery, assigning fresh content to the notions of imperialism and hegemony. Unprecedented social and political turbulence has followed, raising even the spectre of a catastrophic world war.

It is a myth of the period of the triumphant ascent of globalisation – notably the 1990s – that nationality and the state no longer matter to internationally active capital. The dominant forms of private capital rely on both core and peripheral states to navigate the legal, institutional, and monetary framework of the world economy. Internationally active enterprises – non-financial and financial – necessarily develop relations with several states in different jurisdictions as they engage in producing, trading, borrowing, and lending across borders. Core states are actively

---

1 Analysis of state power in domestic financialisation in the preceding chapters rested tacitly on the profound reflections of Antonio Gramsci regarding the hegemonic 'apparatuses' of the bourgeoisie and hegemonic class positions; see, for instance, the penetrating discussion of P. Thomas (2009) *The Gramscian Moment: Philosophy, Hegemony and Marxism*, Brill: Leiden and Boston, MA; see also P. Sotiris (2018) 'Gramsci and the Challenges for the Left: The Historical Bloc as a Strategic Concept', *Science & Society* 82(1): 94–119. This chapter and the next, however, deal with imperialism and hegemony among states, particularly in the wake of the Pandemic Crisis. The notion of hegemony in this context refers to the power of each capitalist class in the world economy, rather than in the domestic context.

involved in shaping the framework of the world economy in the interests of giant multinationals and global financial intermediaries. They compete for power against each other, often privileging the enterprises that originate in their territories.

The USA, as the hegemonic state, is still the decisive actor in constructing the scaffolding of the world economy, drawing on command over world money and enormous military power. It dominates other core powers and confronts new challengers that have emerged as the underlying balance of productive, trading, and financial relations has continued to shift. US hegemonic interventions are critically important to the global presence of US multinationals and financial intermediaries, while also setting the parameters for other globally active enterprises.

Since the early 1990s, the USA's sole hegemony has rested on its internationalised productive capital and global financial capital, alongside its conscious construction of an institutional, political, and military framework to facilitate the global spread of these capitals. Unfortunately for the USA, the more that it pursued this endeavour, the more it undermined its hegemony, including the economic underpinnings of its pre-eminence. China has emerged as the leading contestant among the powers that challenge US power. The early 2020s lifted the curtain on a period of intensified hegemonic contests, complete with military rearmament, geostrategic tensions, and war.

Imperialist and hegemonic contests that are integral to global capitalism call for close analysis. The preceding chapters focused on domestic accumulation, the *modus operandi* of financialised capitalism, and the indispensable role of the state. The rest of this book turns to the international conduct of the belligerent pair of capitals that is continually reshaping the world economy. The struggle for social transformation in the interests of workers and the poor, and the prospect of peaceful and equitable international relations, call for clear perspectives on what lies ahead.

9

The Changing Forms of Imperialism

Empire and capitalist imperialism

Empires long predate the emergence of capitalism and its world market. Examples abound – ancient China could be considered an early empire, while the Achaemenids of Persia formed a vast empire in the sixth century BCE, followed by Alexander of Macedon in the fourth century BCE. Rome remains a historical benchmark for European expansionism and has bequeathed the characteristic terms of imperial rule to several European languages. Empires would look even more varied if other political formations were also considered, from the Mongols to Mali, the Incas, and so on.

It follows immediately that there can be no transhistorical definition of imperialism. The historical commonalities that potentially exist among empires, such as the exploitation of the dominated, or the cultural and linguistic supremacy of a hegemonic group, are not sufficient for a theoretical understanding of imperialism, especially one that casts light on modern expansionism.[1] Analysis of successive capitalist

---

1 The historical succession of imperial formations has led to theories of the rise and fall of empires, including that of imperial overstretch; see, for instance, P. Kennedy (1987) *The Rise and Fall of the Great Powers: Economic Change and Military Conflict from 1500 to 2000*, Vintage: New York. Such theories cast limited light on capitalist imperialism *per se*, but might offer insight into the self-perception of the hegemonic power, particularly if the latter is worried about loss of vigour. This is an age-old phenomenon. In the later stages of the Ottoman Empire, for instance, the *Muqaddimah*

empires, furthermore, requires a historically concrete approach that is able to fix the meaning of imperialism in terms of political economy, while allowing for variation in both form and content.

The global European ascendancy that commenced at about the time of Columbus's journey to the Americas and closed with the First World War was incontrovertibly aggressive and empire-creating. Once mercantile capitalism had properly stirred in the sixteenth century, economic, military, cultural, and political expansion became the aim of the major European powers. The aggressive, exploitative, and oppressive nature of early European expansionism is not in dispute. The Portuguese and Spanish empires rested on the forcible acquisition of other people's productive assets, including systematic enslavement, while British imperial power relied on slavery well into the nineteenth century. Robbing others of their wealth and enslaving millions lay at the foundations of European ascendancy, and would have been impossible without naked military power, especially of the seaborne variety.

And yet, there is a wide gap between early European imperialist practices and policies and, say, the Treaty of Balta Limani, imposed upon a weakened Ottoman Empire by British naval power in 1838. The treaty determined import and export duties, forcibly opening the domestic Ottoman market in favour of British textiles and other capitalistically produced commodities. The leading imperial power certainly sought to trade profitably, while constraining the options of the subordinate power through the vast disparity in military capability. As it forced open the Ottoman economy, however, Britain exacerbated already existing tendencies of capitalist transformation that eventually engulfed Ottoman society and its constituent peoples.[2]

Compelling the Ottomans to submit in this manner was far from an isolated incident. At precisely the same time, Britain obliged China to

---

of Ibn Khaldun, a fourteenth-century theory of the cyclical succession of sovereign imperial powers, moulded the thinking of a ruling elite battered by the onslaught of Western European imperialism; see S. Ilicak (2011) 'A Radical Rethinking of Empire: Ottoman State and Society during the Greek War of Independence, 1821–1826', PhD Thesis, Harvard University, Graduate School of Arts and Sciences.

2 The literature on this issue is broad; see, very selectively, Ş. Pamuk (1987) *The Ottoman Empire and European Capitalism, 1820–1913: Trade, Investment and Production*, Cambridge University Press: New York; E. Frangakis-Syrett (2015) *Implementation of the 1838 Anglo-Turkish Convention on Izmir's Trade: European and Minority Merchants*, New Perspectives on Turkey, vol. 7, Special Issue on 'The 1838 Convention and Its Impact', pp. 91–112.

open to trade through the First Opium War, resulting in the Treaty of Nanjing in 1842. But that subordinate power was neither as submissive nor as receptive of domestic capitalist transformation as the Ottoman Empire.[3] The Second Opium War in the 1850s brought still more European imperial powers (and the USA) into the fray, the British and the French even burning the Summer Palace of the Son of Heaven, no doubt to expedite the path of China to progress and prosperity. Japan was similarly cowed into opening its economy to trade, famously in 1853 by Commodore Perry's 'Black Ships' entering Edo Bay while flying the flag of the USA, but in truth by the threat of British gunboats that had already shown what they could do in China.

European imperial expansion had assumed a novel quality by the mid-nineteenth century. It would change again rather dramatically by the century's end, as European powers acquired endless tracts of formal colonies across the world.[4] The change was evident in India, the jewel in the crown of the British Empire, which had long been run as a commercial enterprise by the British East India Company. In the late nineteenth century, the diktat of the British state became ever more naked and direct, while India was openly treated as a colony.

Much of South America was also effectively dominated by British power, which paid little heed to the Monroe Doctrine of 1823 that had valiantly attempted to preserve the Western hemisphere for US interests. The new imperialism was at its most unbridled in Africa, with nearly the entire continent divided by European powers into colonies in the notorious 'Scramble for Africa' after the 1880s.[5] Even Belgium managed to acquire an enormous colony in the Congo, King Leopold excelling in brutality and rapacity. A true era of capitalist imperialism and colonialism had begun, which calls for fuller theoretical analysis.

---

3 For the difference between Ottoman and Chinese reactions to British imperialism, see R. Kasaba (1993) 'Treaties and Friendships: British Imperialism, the Ottoman Empire, and China in the Nineteenth Century', *Journal of World History* 4 (2): 215–41.

4 The shift was succinctly captured by Eric Hobsbawm in his historical overview of late European expansionism; see E. Hobsbawm (1989) *The Age of Empire: 1875–1914*, Vintage: New York.

5 A brief but path-breaking Marxist analysis of this process was advanced by W. Rodney (1970) 'The Imperialist Partition of Africa', *Monthly Review* 21 (11): 103–14.

The domestic roots and the world
domain of capitalist imperialism

The changed character of imperial expansion was rooted in the transformation of European capitalism in the nineteenth century, during which the domestic economies of imperial powers became thoroughly capitalist. To be sure, early European mercantile imperialism was motivated by the search for commercial profits. The profits of global traders were augmented by the lack of mutual knowledge among the societies that were connected through trade as well as by direct expropriation of resources through regular resort to violence. And yet, the search for profits was not rooted in capitalist imperatives in production in the domestic European economies. Above all, it was not based on a relentless drive to achieve cost efficiency in production and to beat others in price through productivity gains.[6]

This point is of paramount importance, for precisely these factors had come to characterise the British economy by the mid-nineteenth century. By the 1840s and 1850s, British domestic production had become capitalist for all intents and purposes, which also lent to British imperial expansion a characteristically capitalist character. Even more crucial for our purposes is that by the 1890s the domestic functioning of capitalist economies in Europe had changed significantly since the 1850s. The classic colonial, aggressive, and arrogant outlook of European imperialism in the late nineteenth and early twentieth centuries was integrally related to this change.

The dominance of capitalist relations in domestic production in Britain and other European countries underpinned the emergence of a true world market in the nineteenth century. Long-distance commerce in previous periods was certainly capitalist in outlook, but mere international trading does not amount to a capitalist world market. For that to emerge, much more is required than the plain sum of international transactions by merchants, financiers, and others. The world market is a separate and distinct order of economic activity, incorporating states as well as private enterprises, and functioning differently from the domestic market. The differences are pronounced with respect to the

---

6 As was powerfully argued by E. Meiksins Wood (2003) *Empire of Capital*, Verso: London. Her stress on the domestic transformation of imperialist powers must, however, be supplemented by an analysis of the world market.

equalisation of returns to capital, the role of money, and the formation of prices and exchange rates.

Capitalist imperialism proper emerged in the nineteenth century as the domestic and the international orders of economic activity became intrinsically linked, gradually resulting in a world economy. The form and content of imperialism reflected the character of capitalist accumulation in the imperial countries, including the dominant industries, the mode of enterprise organisation, the specific relations between production and finance, and so on. At all times, however, capitalist imperialism retained a primordial streak of violence and rapaciousness, always alert to opportunities for the forcible expropriation of the resources of others.[7]

As the sphere of production became capitalist in Britain and other parts of Europe with the expansion of the domest industrial sector, the nascent world market began to present a historically novel division between core and periphery.[8] The division emerged partly because industrial capitalism unleashed the domestic productive forces of core countries in a historically unprecedented way. But it also resulted from the forcible integration of peripheral countries into the world market, allowing for the systematic appropriation of resources by the core, which frequently proved catastrophic for the productive forces of the periphery.

A characteristic example is the previously mentioned Treaty of Balta Limani. Its provisions devastated the domestic Ottoman economy, especially the textile industry, a sector of long historical standing that was highly developed and fully capable of meeting local needs. Ottoman commercial textile production was pulverised by Manchester, taking forty years to re-emerge modestly on an industrial capitalist basis. Deindustrialisation firmly consigned the dominated Ottoman economy to the periphery, even as domestic capitalist production began to take

---

7 David Harvey calls it 'accumulation by dispossession' in a related context, although primitive accumulation has nothing to do with it; see, for instance, D. Harvey (2004) 'The "New" Imperialism: Accumulation by Dispossession', *Socialist Register* 40: 63–87.

8 Pomeranz has shown that even in the late eighteenth century there was very little to differentiate the overall economic performance of Western Europe from other parts of the world, including the Yangzi Delta in China and South Asia. It is very difficult to think of Western Europe up to that time as being the core and the rest of the world as being the periphery, with everything this implies for livelihoods and relative state power. Western Europe truly thrust ahead in the nineteenth century with the advent of capitalist industrialisation; see K. Pomeranz (2000) *The Great Divergence: China, Europe, and the Modern World Economy*, Princeton University Press: Princeton, NJ, and Oxford.

root in the Empire.[9] Ottoman domestic agriculture was also transformed, shifting toward production of grains for export to the world
market, led by large estates that had a commercial outlook but did not
systematically practise capitalist agriculture. The political subjection of
the Ottomans to European imperialism led to economic retrogression
that lasted for decades.

Nonetheless, the emerging relationship between core and periphery
proved inherently fluid, variable, and complex. Japan, after its forcible
opening, succeeded in marshalling its resources to create a dynamic
capitalist economy based on domestic accumulation. It soon emerged as
an imperialist power, capable of colonising Taiwan in the 1890s as well
as defeating a Russian navy in 1905, a feat unimaginable for an Asian
country at the time. Barely four decades intervened between Japan's
humiliation by Perry's 'Black Ships' and its becoming an imperialist
force contesting European powers in Asia. Imperialist rivalries went
through successive paroxysms in Europe and Asia at the turn of the
twentieth century, rapidly shifting the boundaries between core and
periphery. That is the context in which the Marxist analysis of imperialism took shape.

Classical Marxist theory of imperialism

The distinguishing feature of the classical Marxist theory of imperialism
is that it connects the form and content of imperialism to the underlying
economic interests of capital.[10] Marxist theory seeks to go deeper than
the mere geopolitical and military dimensions of imperialism, identifying the economic channels of domination in the world economy. This is
its greatest strength and provides the basis for the approach to

---

9 This process has been thoroughly analysed by D. Quataert (1993) *Ottoman
Manufacturing in the Age of the Industrial Revolution*, Cambridge University Press:
Cambridge, UK. See also Ş. Pamuk and O. Williamson (2011) 'Ottoman
De-Industrialization, 1800–1913: Assessing the Magnitude, Impact, and Response',
Economic History Review 64 (S1): 159–84. For the emergence of industrial textile
capitalism in the Ottoman context, see C. Lapavitsas and P. Cakiroglu (2019) *Capitalism
in the Ottoman Balkans: Industrialisation and Modernity in Macedonia*, IB Tauris:
London.

10 Brewer's work remains the most comprehensive survey of relevant literature to
this day; see A. Brewer (1980) *Marxist Theories of Imperialism: A Critical Survey*,
Routledge and Kegan Paul: London.

contemporary imperialism in the rest of this book. But it could also prove a weakness by encouraging crass materialism.

For, to seek the economic underpinnings of imperialism is not to interpret imperialist rivalries as resulting directly and immediately from enterprise profits, or from the extraction of surplus from dominated countries. Economic interests are certainly fundamental to imperialist contests, but their impact is mediated by layers of political, institutional, ideological, and other factors. Fully aware of the complexity of these relations, classical Marxists sought the tap root of imperialism in the molecular economic structures of capitalism rather than in mere calculations of profit and loss from imperial escapades. That is, theoretical analysis had to go beyond the sordid motives of the policies of imperialist conquest by identifying the production relations that underpinned these policies.

For classical Marxism, imperialism in the early twentieth century resulted ultimately from the transformation of productive and financial capital that had taken place during the preceding decades in core countries, and thus in the world economy. The production relations that emerged as capitalism matured were embodied in monopolistic concentrations of capital in core economies. At the root of imperialism lay exploitation deriving from a particular configuration of productive and financial capitals with a highly distinctive conduct. The aggressive, colonial, and militaristic behaviour of the imperialists was further shaped by non-economic factors, typically relating to state power. Oppression of entire nations and bellicose hegemonic contests were integral parts of capitalist imperialism.

The intellectual breakthrough in this respect was made by Rudolf Hilferding in the early 1900s. For Hilferding, imperialism resulted from economic channels of domination comprising monopolistic enterprises and large banks, and the associated international flows of capital. The driving force of imperialism was to be found in the concentration of capital affording monopoly power to both non-financial enterprises and banks, the fusion of which resulted in 'finance capital', with banks in the dominant role.[11] This form of capital pursued territorial exclusivity for its commodity output and actively sought protective tariffs.

Nikolai Bukharin, who took his cue from Hilferding, offered further

---

11 Hilferding's *Finance Capital* owes its name precisely to the increased 'dependence of industry upon the banks' and to the concentration of money capital in the hands of 'nonproductive classes'; R. Hilferding (1981 [1910]) *Finance Capital: A Study of the Latest Phase of Capitalist Development*, Routledge and Kegan Paul: London and Boston, MA, p. 224.

insight.[12] For Bukharin, as monopolies grew and dominated the domestic economy, overproduction and falling profitability became more prominent. The result was the export of capital toward geographical areas that could ensure higher profitability. Capital was exported abroad, exploitation also occurred globally, and differences between relations of production from country to country became more blurred. At the same time, national economies protected domestic monopolistic concentrations by erecting tariff barriers against foreign monopolists.

In short, two economic tendencies stood out in the account of imperialism by Hilferding and Bukharin. First, non-financial enterprises coupled with banks formed monopolies dominating domestic production and turning into 'ephors' of imperialism. Second, capital flows across borders became a tool of monopolistic profit extraction but also reflected a deep asymmetry in the world economy between core and periphery. These fundamental economic features of imperialism were succinctly outlined by Lenin: 'Typical of the old capitalism, when free competition held undivided sway, was the export of *goods*. Typical of the latest stage of capitalism, when monopolies rule, is the export of *capital*.'[13]

On these grounds, Lenin put forth the canonical Marxist definition of imperialism (and associated colonialism) as a particular stage – a period – in the historical development of capitalism.[14] The stage of imperialism commenced in the late nineteenth century, as the monopolisation of non-financial enterprises and banks permeated the domestic economy. The world was territorially divided among imperialist countries, in effect creating a small capitalist core and a vast periphery where capitalist relations were far weaker.

For Lenin, international flows of capital helped align – at least in part – the interests of ruling layers in both dominant and dominated countries. A 'rentier' layer at the core provided loanable capital, while a

---

12 See, for instance, N. Bukharin (1929 [1917]) *Imperialism and World Economy*, Martin Lawrence: London, ch. 7. Bukharin's analysis of the domestic and the world market overemphasised the integral connections between the two realms, while postulating profit rate equalisation. Bukharin also overstressed the organising role of cartels in the domestic economy to the extent of eliminating the intrinsic instability of capitalist production; ibid., ch. 13.

13 V. Lenin (1999 [1916]) *Imperialism: The Highest Stage of Capitalism*, Resistance Books: Sydney, p. 70.

14 Lenin also drew explicitly on Hobson's non-Marxist analysis of imperialism. Hobson clearly associated imperialism with investment abroad and the search for higher profits; see J. A. Hobson (1902) *Imperialism: A Study*, Part I, James Pott: New York.

domestic bourgeoisie in the periphery operated in cahoots with the foreign 'rentiers'. Imperialism gave rise to multiple forms of exploitation, including the double exploitation of workers in the periphery by both the local and the imperial bourgeoisie. This form of cross-border exploitation corresponded to the putative emergence of a thin layer of 'labour aristocracy' in core countries which benefited from flows of profits from the periphery.

It is important to note that Rosa Luxemburg took a different path, stressing the insufficiency of effective demand in mature capitalist countries as domestic monopolisation proceeded. The solution to the problem of selling the output of capitalist production lay with sources of demand outside the capitalist domain, thus leading to the export of capital and the rise of imperialism dominating the non-capitalist areas of the world.[15] Even for Luxemburg, however, capital exports played a critical role, originating in core countries and subsequently flowing back with exploitative returns from peripheral countries. Loans were a tool used by imperialism to constrain 'young capitalist states' to a subordinate position vis-à-vis the advanced industrial countries.[16] To a lesser extent, a similar argument can also be found in Kautsky, although he mostly stressed the drive to command agricultural land in the periphery to support the expansion of industry at the expense of agriculture in imperialist countries. Kautsky was also quick to realise that imperial power had an impact on the institutions regulating the world economy.[17]

In sum, for Hilferding, Bukharin, Luxemburg, and Lenin, the state and monopoly capital were indissoluble partners in the imperialist era. Political life in core countries was dominated by the interests of big banks and large enterprises. Countries that joined the core relatively late, such as Germany and Japan, had to surmount the problem of a world already divided territorially by the incumbent imperialist powers. Militarism and the redrawing of imperial borders became exigent issues for the ascending capitalist elites.[18] War followed.

---

15 See R. Luxemburg (2003 [1913]) *The Accumulation of Capital*, Routledge: London, ch. 26.

16 Ibid., p. 401.

17 See K. Kautsky (1970) 'Ultra-Imperialism', *New Left Review* 59 (1): 41–6.

18 In sharp contrast, Kautsky claimed that there could be intra-imperialist cooperation, leading to 'cartelisation of foreign policy' and peaceful development in a stage of 'Ultra-Imperialism'; ibid., p. 46. He even conjectured the 'consolidation of the

What remains of classical Marxism on imperialism?

Classical Marxism is an indispensable guide to analysing contemporary imperialism and hegemony, but more than a century later, the molecular structures of capital and the corresponding outlook of the world economy are distinctly different.

For one thing, the notion of 'labour aristocracy' has little persuasiveness in a world of rampant neoliberalism, with precarious employment and tremendous inequality within core countries. For another, the great bulk of capital exports take place among core countries, as is shown in subsequent chapters. The leading exporters are simultaneously the leading importers of loanable capital, including the hegemonic USA. During the last two decades, furthermore, the export of capital among peripheral countries has assumed substantial dimensions. Further still, although the concentration of capital has been relentless and gigantic monopolistic enterprises dominate production and trade across the world economy, banks do not tend to amalgamate with industrial capital, nor do they dictate terms to giant monopolies.

The deeper significance of the concept of financialisation for the analysis of imperialism emerges at this juncture. The cornerstone of the classical Marxist analysis of imperialism was the peculiar amalgamation of industrial and banking capital – 'finance capital' – that could be considered the first historical bout of financialisation. Contemporary imperialism emanates from a very different combination of productive and financial capital, which is also the foundation of the financialisation of the last four decades.

The conduct of monopolistic non-financial enterprises is a pillar of contemporary financialisation but must be approached with caution. It is misleading, for instance, to think of the giant monopolies as constantly choosing between the sphere of production and the sphere of finance while seeking profits. There is no systematic evidence that the profits of non-financial enterprises are significantly skewed toward financial activities, even if financial skills and activities have grown among

---

capitalist nation-states into a super-national state'; see S. K. Holloway (1983) 'Relations among Core Capitalist States: The Kautsky–Lenin Debate Reconsidered', *Canadian Journal of Political Science* 16 (2): 321–33, at p. 323. Lenin, as is well known, forcefully rejected this view; see, for instance, the preface he wrote for Bukharin's book.

industrial and commercial enterprises.[19] It is, moreover, analytically false to postulate that profitability in finance could somehow be systematically higher than profitability in production – competition tends to equalise rates of return among sectors.

Financialisation is not about non-financial enterprises becoming banks or shadow banks. Rather, its distinguishing features are to be found in the sources of investment funds and the distribution of profits. The crucial issue in this respect is the capacity of giant enterprises to finance investment from profits and sales revenue, particularly from temporarily idle funds, as revenues flow into their coffers. In recent decades, such funds have become enormous, allowing non-financial enterprises to be major participants in the repo and other markets for short-term loanable capital.[20]

In sum, contemporary financialisation is characterised by greater independence of non-financial enterprises from financial intermediaries, together with the acquisition of substantial financial skills by the former. At the same time, financialisation has had an impact on the internal governance of giant monopolistic enterprises, assigning greater weight to financial instruments of command, while systematically channelling profits to shareholders via financial mechanisms.[21] These developments are the counterpart to the transformed banks and the ascendant shadow banks that dominate global finance, which were analysed in earlier chapters. They are underscored by the systemic shift toward market-based finance in core countries, indeed across the world economy.

Giant financialising enterprises, together with transformed financial institutions, drive contemporary imperialism. This relentlessly aggressive set of capitals has a global appetite and does not seek territorial

---

19 See J. Rabinovich (2019) 'The Financialization of the Non-Financial Corporation: A Critique to the *Financial Turn of Accumulation* Hypothesis', *Metroeconomica* 70 (4): 738–75. See also T. Auvray and J. Rabinovich (2019) 'The Financialisation–Offshoring Nexus and the Capital Accumulation of US Non-Financial Firms', *Cambridge Journal of Economics* 43 (5): 1183–218.

20 See Lapavitsas (2013) *Profiting without Producing*, chs 5 and 6. On the formation of idle money capital, see C. Lapavitsas (2000) 'On Marx's Analysis of Money Hoarding in the Turnover of Capital', *Review of Political Economy* 12 (2): 219–35.

21 A path-breaking analysis of this process was put forth by W. Lazonick and M. O'Sullivan (2000) 'Maximizing Shareholder Value: A New Ideology for Corporate Governance', *Economy and Society* 29 (1): 13–35. For further discussion, see also W. Lazonick (2013) 'The Financialization of the US Corporation: What Has Been Lost, and How It Can Be Regained', *The Seattle University Law Review* 36 (20): 857–909.

exclusivity, despite having national origins. Rather, it requires rules of investing, producing, trading, lending, and money transferring that could facilitate profit extraction across the world. It seeks an overall framework for the world market that would be advantageous to its own interests.

It cannot be overstressed, however, that striving for a global framework conducive to capitalist profits does not amount to a common purpose among internationally active capitals. There is no transnational capitalist class in the world economy. Core countries are dominated by capitalist elites that command giant non-financial and financial enterprises, relying on monetary and fiscal policy, especially to confront the recurring crises of financialised capitalism, as was shown in the earlier parts of this book.[22] The elites continually contest the framework of the world market, resulting in relations of hierarchy and hegemony among core countries. For others in the periphery, subordination ensues.

The hegemonic USA has played a decisive role in shaping the rules of global investing, trading, and transferring money – in the interests primarily of its own multinational enterprises and internationally active financial capital. Crucial in this regard is the role of world money, an aspect of the world market that had a minor presence in classical Marxist analysis but is fundamental to contemporary imperialism. The hegemon has safeguarded the dollar as world money first and foremost to favour the interests of its own domestic ruling bloc, while succouring its clients and others according to its imperial calculations.

It should also be stressed that nothing in this alignment of capitals and states implies that it would be impossible for the world market to fragment, even if the underlying interests of the dominant forms of capital were determinedly global. There is no inescapable economic

---

22 However, there is no 'organised capitalism', contrary to what both Bukharin and Hilferding expected. For Bukharin ((1929 [1917]) *Imperialism and World Economy*, ch. 13), the coalescence of monopolies and the state effectively neutralised the organising role of the market in the domestic economy, leading to 'state' capitalism and preparing the way for socialism as capitalism matured. A similar undertow is present in Hilferding's classic work, including the notion that a 'general cartel' could dominate the economy; see, for instance, Hilferding (1981) [1910] *Finance Capital*, ch. 21. Indeed, in the 1920s, Hilferding postulated the emergence of 'organised capitalism' based on the state, monopolies, and organised labour, which had, apparently, overcome internal crises; see W. Smaldone (1988) 'Rudolf Hilferding and the Theoretical Foundations of German Social Democracy', *Central European History* 21 (3): 267–99. In the era of ascendant neoliberalism, the notion of 'organised capitalism' has little explanatory power.

necessity that would prevent the breaking up of global capitalist connections. The contest for hegemony is as old as capitalist expansionism and could impose severe constraints on the functioning of private capital. The US hegemon took dramatic actions in the Russo-Ukrainian conflict that broke established global mechanisms, including freezing the central bank reserves of opposing states and even confiscating the private property of globally active capitalists based in Russia.

In sum, contemporary imperialism rests on the symbiotic pair of internationally active financialising monopolies and globally functioning financial capitals, which is distinct from the 'finance capital' of classical Marxism. Its singular character derives to a large extent from the operations of global financial markets, and further insight into it can be gained by briefly considering the ascendancy of market-based finance.

Market-based finance in the ascendant

It was shown in part II that during the last four decades there has been a historic shift away from bank-based and toward market-based finance. This system-wide aspect of financialisation holds even in countries in which financial systems remain primarily bank-based. It is rooted in the conduct of non-financial enterprises and has involved a transformation of relations among financial intermediaries, financial markets, and the state. In this respect, it is characteristic of contemporary imperialism.

The distinction between market-based and bank-based financial systems is of long standing in economic theory, and its implications for the development of capitalism have been much debated.[23] The contemporary debate originates in the seminal contribution of Alexander Gerschenkron in the 1960s, who claimed that financial systems based on banks rather than stock markets offer important advantages to late developers seeking to join the world market.[24] Above all, according to Gerschenkron, banks were able to mobilise funds across the economy to finance investment by non-financial enterprises on a long-term basis.

---

23 For a standard mainstream discussion, see F. Allen and D. Gale (2000) *Comparing Financial Systems*, MIT Press: Cambridge, MA. For recent evidence of the continuing debate, see José L. García-Ruiz and M. Vasta (2021) 'Financing Firms: Beyond the Dichotomy between Banks and Markets', *Business History* 63 (6): 877–91.

24 A. Gerschenkron (1962) *Economic Backwardness in Historical Perspective*, Belknap Press of Harvard University Press: Cambridge, MA.

The developmental implications of Gerschenkron's thesis were ultimately the reason for the lasting influence of his work in the decades
after the Second World War.[25]

In truth, however, the distinction has deeper theoretical antecedents
than Gerschenkron, most prominently in Hilferding's work.[26]
Gerschenkron was fully aware of Hilferding's arguments and analysis.[27]
His focus on late development and the potential advantages offered by
banking is of a piece with Hilferding's attention to the success of
Germany as a late developer.[28] After all, Hilferding's concept of 'finance
capital' pivoted on the provision of long-term loans by big banks to large
enterprises for fixed investment. These long-lasting (and rolled-over)
loans resembled equity in the enterprises, and hence banks developed
long-term relationships with their borrowers. Banks became directly
involved in enterprise monitoring and governance, including through
participation in the board of directors, and thus took the upper hand in
the decision making of non-financial enterprises.

Nonetheless, for Hilferding, the units of 'finance capital' remained
heavily involved in stock market operations. They took advantage of
opportunities for 'founder's profit' – that is, financial profit deriving
from the difference between the stock price and the actual value invested
in an enterprise when an initial public offering is made in the stock
market. In brief, the financial intermediaries that Hilferding had in
mind when he proposed the notion of 'finance capital' were banks that
lent on a long-term basis to enterprises, while also transacting in the

25 It is evident, for instance, in the seminal work by Alfred Chandler: A. D. Chandler
(1990) *Scale and Scope: The Dynamic of Industrial Capitalism*, Harvard University Press:
Cambridge, MA. But it is also in the background of M. Aoki and H. Patrick (1994) *The
Japanese Main Bank System: Its Relevance for Developing and Transforming Economies*,
Oxford University Press: Oxford; in the very influential work P. Hall and D. Soskice
(2001) 'An Introduction to Varieties of Capitalism', in P. Hall and D. Soskice (eds)
Varieties of Capitalism: The Institutional Foundations of Comparative Advantage, Oxford
University Press: Oxford, pp. 1–68; and in the related work B. Amable (2003) *The
Diversity of Modern Capitalism*, Oxford University Press: Oxford.

26 For Hilferding's views on banking and stock markets in relation to the history of
economic thought, see C. Lapavitsas (2004) 'Hilferding's Theory of Banking in the Light
of Steuart and Smith', *Research in Political Economy* 21: 161–80.

27 See M. van der Linden (2012) Gerschenkron's Secret: A Research Note, *Critique:
Journal of Socialist Theory* 40 (4): 553–62.

28 As well as being reminiscent of Trotsky's classic formulation of 'uneven and
combined' development, as van der Linden (ibid.) rightly pointed out; see L. Trotsky
(1977 [1930]) *The History of the Russian Revolution*, Pluto Press: London, pp. 26–7.

stock market. They were 'universal banks' in the German (and Austrian) mould.

More recent historical research has shown that the actual practices of banks in Germany, Japan, and the USA in the early stages of capitalist development were not that dissimilar from each other. It is also far from certain that banks have historically complied with Gerschenkron's view as levers of early capitalist industrialisation.[29] What is beyond dispute, however, is that the wave of financialisation since the late 1970s has strengthened market-based finance even in countries that have long been the paragons of bank-based systems, such as Germany and Japan.

Hilferding's analysis of enterprises, banks, and stock markets offers strong guidelines for comprehending these developments, even if present day mechanisms, institutions, and processes are vastly different. What matters are not formal differences between financial systems as capitalism matures but relations among financial institutions and productive capitalists that emanate from the investment requirements of non-financial enterprises and shape enterprise governance. These relations pivot on the characteristics of loanable money capital, the inherently fluid, flexible, and peculiar commodity traded in capitalist financial systems, which earns the rate of interest rather than the rate of profit.[30]

The foundations of contemporary imperialism are to be found in the interactions between non-financial and financial enterprises, though not in the form that prevailed in Hilferding's time. To be more specific, banks are capitalist businesses that specialise in trading loanable capital – collecting it, on-lending it, and anticipating its return. When banks systematically engage in long-term lending, they create close relations with industrial and other enterprises, thus exposing themselves to great risks, for in doing so, they lock the loanable capital of others (the providers of loanable capital) into risky long-term assets. If a commercial bank went down this path while at the same time maintaining highly liquid

29 For the USA, see N. Lamoreaux (1994) *Insider Lending: Banks, Personal Connections, and Economic Development in Industrial New England*, Cambridge University Press: Cambridge, UK; for Germany, see C. Fohlin (2007) *Finance Capitalism and Germany's Rise to Industrial Power*, Cambridge University Press: Cambridge, UK; for Japan, see Y. Suzuki (1987) *The Japanese Financial System*, Clarendon Press: Oxford, and N. Tamaki (1995) *Japanese Banking: A History,1859–1959*, Cambridge University Press: Cambridge, UK.

30 For a fuller discussion of these issues from a Marxist standpoint, see Itoh and Lapavitsas (1999) *Political Economy of Money and Finance*, chs 4 and 5.

liabilities, it would run the risk of becoming illiquid and insolvent in short order. Long-term lending by banks must rest on stable and secure liabilities.

Stock and other financial markets, on the other hand, preserve the fluidity and flexibility of loanable capital by allowing for the regular sale and resale of financial assets. It follows that a productive enterprise obtaining loanable capital via this means would soon come under the cosh of stock market volatility. Changes in financial asset prices would impact directly on enterprise functioning, while its time horizons would narrow, since it would have to defend its stock price. The fluidity and flexibility of loanable capital would be preserved, but at the cost of short-term constraints on decision making by the productive enterprise. There would also be a proliferation of speculative opportunities offered by transacting in financial assets.[31]

These contrasting influences have repeatedly appeared in capitalist accumulation during the last two centuries, placing their mark on imperialism, though their specific form has changed over time. As the world market matured in the nineteenth and twentieth centuries, financial systems came to reflect the specific features of productive accumulation in particular countries, while also being shaped by historically contingent factors, including, above all, the actions of the state.

Bank-based systems have long relied on state support. To engage in long-term lending, commercial banks have typically received protection of their liabilities from the state, varying from guarantees of deposits to preferential funding of banks, to controls over interest rates, and so on. At the same time, market-based systems have also relied on the state. Trading loanable money capital in open markets requires establishing and protecting property rights, ensuring the free flow of information across the economy, and enforcing contracts. These factors depend critically on the regulatory and legal framework of finance created by the state.

For these reasons, the regulatory role of the state has been vital to determining the character of the financial system throughout the history of capitalism. Thus, the German and the Japanese financial systems moved characteristically in a bank-based direction after the First World

---

31 There is extensive and long-standing empirical substantiation of these claims in heterodox economics, including for developing countries; see, for instance, A. Singh (1997) 'Financial Liberalisation, Stockmarkets and Economic Development', *Economic Journal* 107 (442): 771–82.

War and even more so during the first decades after the Second World War, due to state intervention. The aim of policy was to facilitate the flows of loanable capital to enterprises via banks rather than the stock market.[32]

The shift toward market-based finance in the decades of financialisation has also relied on state policy, particularly on regulations that systematically transform idle money across society into loanable money capital. Since the 1970s, in the USA alone, pension systems and the mechanisms of housing provision have channelled the savings of millions of people toward stock markets. The most important factor allowing the US state to shape the character of the financial system and to promote the global turn toward market-based finance has been command over the dollar. The peculiar fiat money created by the Federal Reserve acts as world money, affording enormous power to the USA and buttressing the global shift toward market-based finance.

Summing up, the classical Marxist analysis of imperialism has limited explanatory power over contemporary phenomena, not least as the institutional framework of global finance and the mechanisms of world money have changed profoundly. However, the underlying approach of classical Marxism, which locates the roots of imperialism in the accumulation of capital, remains valid. In this light, the following chapters consider more closely the interaction of domestic accumulation with global economic activity, paying particular attention to the role of money domestically and internationally.

32 See S. Vitols (2001) 'The Origins of Bank-Based and Market-Based Financial Systems: Germany, Japan, and the United States', Economic Change and Employment Discussion Papers No. FS I 01-302, WZB Berlin Social Science Center. For Japan in particular, see M. Okuno-Fujiwara and T. Okazaki (1999) *The Japanese Economic System and Its Historical Origins*, Oxford University Press: Oxford.

10

Money, Hegemony, and Imperialism

Hegemonic imperial power and world economy

The advance of the modern era in Europe was accompanied by the growth of international trade among European countries but also with Asia, Africa, and North and South America, much of the latter based on slavery. Expanding international trade inevitably meant growing monetary circulation and complex finance. And yet, as was discussed in the previous chapter, the practices of trade and finance in the era of mercantile capitalism were not sufficient to constitute a world market as a separate and distinct order of capitalist activity, for they occurred among economies that were not themselves permeated by the capitalist mode of production.[1]

Growing international trade and finance also ushered in various degrees of violence – occasionally taking genocidal forms – as well as the ruthless extraction of surpluses through naked state power. Trade brought war and war furthered trade. 'Warmaking, extraction, and capital accumulation', Charles Tilly succinctly noted, 'interacted to shape

---

1 For a penetrating analysis of this point and a critique of approaches that fail to take it into account, see U. Patnaik (1982), '"Neo-Marxian" Theories of Capitalism and Underdevelopment: Towards a Critique', *Social Scientist* 10 (11): 3–32.

European statemaking'.[2] The advance of the modern era was marked by continuous contests for hegemonic dominance that were directly related to the emerging commercial and financial mechanisms across the world.

For Giovanni Arrighi, in particular, the last four centuries have witnessed repeated phases of financial domination, heralding the eventual decline of the hegemonic power, a process that Arrighi named 'hegemonic transition'.[3] Thus, Genoa was replaced by Amsterdam, which was replaced by Great Britain, which gave its place to the USA. Hegemonic crises that were often – but not inevitably – accompanied by major wars led to the reorganisation of world affairs and the displacement of the powerful and affluent hegemon.

British hegemony in the nineteenth century was, nevertheless, of a qualitatively different type to preceding forms of hegemonic domination. By the mid-century, a world market had emerged that was integrally linked to domestic British capitalist accumulation through flows of commodity and money capital, and potentially even of productive capital. The rhythms of British industrial capitalism were intertwined with the fluctuations of international value flows, resulting in the characteristic periodic crises of the early and middle nineteenth century.[4] At that time, London enjoyed global power and control incomparably greater than that of Amsterdam in the heyday of seventeenth-century mercantile capitalism.

The power of Britain rested on domestic industrial profits founded on capitalist production, mostly of textiles, coal, and iron. Domestic profits allowed a small island off the coast of Europe to acquire a Royal Navy without equal in the nineteenth century. To that purpose, it was also

---

2 Charles Tilly (1982) 'War Making and State Making as Organized Crime', University of Michigan Center for Research on Social Organization (CRSO) Working Paper No. 256, p. 3.

3 Giovanni Arrighi and Beverly J. Silver (2001) 'Capitalism and World (Dis)order', *Review of International Studies* 27: 257–9, at p. 261. The argument *in extenso* can be found in Arrighi (1994) *The Long Twentieth Century: Money, Power and the Origins of our Times.*

4 The historical literature on this issue is extensive and often from impeccably mainstream sources; see, for instance, R. C. O. Matthews (1954) 'The Trade Cycle in Britain, 1790–1850', *Oxford Economic Papers* 6 (1): 1–32. A classic economic history account is P. Deane and W. A. Cole (1967) *British Economic Growth, 1688–1959: Trends and Structure*, 2nd edition, Cambridge University Press: Cambridge, UK.

necessary to rely on the 'fiscal state' – that is, on the British state's newly developed ability to regularly tax income as well as borrow in the structured financial markets that had become an integral part of domestic private capitalist accumulation.[5]

Systematic taxation and public borrowing further meant that the British state, which previously had not even pretended to involve the mass of the population in its affairs, explicitly sought to secure social support, or, in modern parlance, broad legitimacy. Prominent taxpayers acquired rights to proclaim on state expenses and increasingly participated in affairs of state. Representation in parliament became a political goal which promised eventually to turn subjects into citizens. Property was the Lydian stone of participation in the emerging sophisticated bourgeois polity, and if that worked against the propertyless, so much the worse for them.

The tacit support mechanism of Pax Britannica was, however, the gold standard.[6] As the capitalist world market expanded, the functioning of world money – above all, in hoarding value and settling obligations – became the cornerstone of market operations. The primary form taken by money in delivering its functions in the world market was gold, and the British pound sterling acted as the gateway to gold for both enterprises and states. The ability of gold to act as world money in the nineteenth century relied heavily on the global discounting of bills of exchange in the City of London. In turn, possessing the most advanced and effective financial system in the world allowed London swiftly to mobilise the armies and navies that secured its empire. The period of the

5 See D. Stasavage (2003) *Public Debt and the Birth of the Democratic State: France and Great Britain, 1688–1789*, Cambridge University Press: Cambridge, UK; the standard reference is P. G. M. Dickson (1967) *The Financial Revolution in England: A Study in the Development of Public Credit, 1688–1756*, Macmillan: London.

6 A penetrating historical account of the deployment of the gold standard to support British imperial power can be found in M. De Cecco (1975) *Money and Empire: The International Gold Standard, 1890–1914*, Rowman and Littlefield: Totowa, NJ. For a mainstream summary of the functioning of the gold standard in a wide-ranging collection of relevant texts, see B. Eichengreen and M. Flandreau (1997) 'Editor's Introduction', in B. Eichengreen and M. Flandreau (eds) *The Gold Standard in Theory and History*, 2nd edition, Routledge: London, pp. 1–21. For further mainstream discussions, see also M. Bordo and A. J. Schwartz (eds) (1984) *A Retrospective on the Classical Gold Standard, 1821–1931*, University of Chicago Press: Chicago. For a brief Marxist discussion, see R. Vasudevan (2007) 'From the Gold Standard to the Floating Dollar Standard: An Appraisal in the Light of Marx's Theory of Money', *Review of Radical Political Economics* 41 (4): 473–91.

most aggressive imperialist expansion of European powers at the end of the nineteenth century was also the peak of the gold standard.

Capitalist hegemony and imperialism are integrally linked to world money, for this function of money spans the intersection of domestic accumulation with the world market, and more broadly with the world economy. To be sure, the domestic and the international realms of capitalist economic activity interact in several ways, including flows of commodities, finance, and productive capital. But the most critical interaction lies in the monetary field, where the state is inevitably present, creating a natural abode for imperial power. A brief theoretical discussion of this issue in the following sections can cast further light on contemporary imperialism and hegemony.

The domestic and international orders of capitalist accumulation

For Marxist political economy, the world market is a distinct order within the capitalist mode of production. As was argued in chapter 9, the world market comes into being when domestic production is dominated by capitalist relations, gradually giving rise to a world economy with a corresponding division of labour and a hierarchical separation into core and periphery. The critical point in this respect is that the world market is qualitatively different from the domestic market even though they are organically linked to each other.

When capitalist enterprises dominate the domestic sphere of production, economic activity is based on the reallocation of resources in search of profits according to price signals from the domestic market. The economy becomes integrated, since both means of production and labour power are systematically redistributed among economic sectors, tending to equalise profit rates.[7] A domestic capitalist order emerges, with a homogeneous market coordinating the transfer of resources.

In the domestic market, money acts as the quasi-automatic organiser of resource transfers via a complex array of functions: measure of value,

---

7 As had already been made abundantly clear by Adam Smith in several places in his foundational work on political economy: see A. Smith (1904 [1776]) *An Inquiry into the Nature and Causes of the Wealth of Nations*, Book I, edited by E. Cannan, Methuen: London, ch. X.

means of circulation, means of payment, and means of hoarding. The full functioning of domestic money is in turn based on a multilayered structure of domestic institutions – economic, legal, social, and political. The ultimate social foundation of the full domestic functioning of money is the commodification of labour power, creating entire fields of consumer goods that sustain workers through purchases in open markets. The labour market is the bedrock of the domestic capitalist order, and it relies fully on the general organising function of money.

The international order is related to the domestic order but remains separate from it. In the international realm, there is no continuous real-location of the means of production and labour power as in the domestic realm. To participate in international production and trade, capitalist enterprises must normally possess higher levels of internal organisation, technology, and management skills. The search for profits is then guided by price signals emanating not only from the domestic economy but also from the international order, with transactors placed across borders. Political economy was quick to see that under these conditions, there would not be a systematic tendency to equalise profit rates through trade across borders.[8]

The crucial analytical point is that the world economy is not simply a larger version of the domestic economy. It is a distinct terrain, the heterogeneity of which contrasts sharply with domestic homogeneity. By analogy, the world market is not organised through an international equivalent of domestic money – indeed, no such thing exists. Rather, the world market is based on world money, which has a limited but still crucial set of functions including, above all, its roles as means of payment and means of hoarding (reserve).[9] Without the paying function of

---

8 As was demonstrated by David Ricardo with his customary brilliance in chapter 7 of the *Principles*; see D. Ricardo (1951) [1817] *On the Principles of Political Economy and Taxation*, vol. 1 of P. Sraffa and M. Dobb (eds) *The Works and Correspondence of David Ricardo*, Cambridge University Press: Cambridge, UK. Foreign trade could, of course, raise the domestic rate of profit by lowering the cost of inputs and especially the cost of the wage basket. Direct investment by individual capitals abroad could similarly allow the extraction of exceptional ('super') profits.

9 This point would not have been acceptable to Ricardo, for whom the Quantity Theory of Money held both domestically and internationally, with money acting as global organiser of trade through flows across borders. It is, nonetheless, a view characteristic of late Mercantilism, reflected above all in the works of Sir James Steuart, which greatly influenced Marx. For Marx, the Quantity Theory of Money is invalid at both the world and the domestic level. This is the foundation of his analysis of world money and of the implicit hierarchy of currencies in the world market; see C. Lapavitsas

world money, it would be impossible to maintain clearing and settlement operations internationally, and global trading and finance would grind to a halt. The functioning of world money in turn relies on several international institutions, whose construction is necessarily intertwined with hegemony.

Turbulence regularly emerges where the domestic and international realms come into contact, particularly as the price signals of the domestic market could potentially contradict those of the world market. The crucial point in this connection is that when the domestic price level changes at a rate that is different from that of another country (or a group of other countries), there is no automatic economic mechanism through which the two sets of prices could be spontaneously made to cohere with each other.[10] The resolution often involves economic turbulence, non-economic forces, and even imperial power.

To be more specific, if aggregate prices in the domestic and the international realms are significantly out of kilter with each other, the re-establishment of balance is never a smooth process.[11] On the

---

(1996) 'The Classical Adjustment Mechanism of International Balances: Marx's Critique', *Contributions to Political Economy* 15: 63–79.

10 The nearest thing to a theory of automatic adjustment in contemporary economic theory is the 'Monetary Approach to the Balance of Payments', or International Monetarism; see H. G. Johnson (1972) 'The Monetary Approach to Balance-of-Payments Theory', *Journal of Financial and Quantitative Analysis* 7 (2): 1555–72. This theory has notoriously weak empirical foundations but remains instrumental to the approach of multilateral institutions, such as the International Monetary Fund. In effect, it is the Quantity Theory of Money in global garb. Classical political economy originally formulated it as the price-level-specie-flow mechanism of Hume; see D. Hume (1985 [1752]) *Of the Balance of Trade*, in *Essays Literary, Moral, and Political*, Part II, E. F. Miller (ed.), Liberty Classics: Indianapolis, IN, Essay V. Hume's theory was given definitive form by Ricardo based on the labour theory of value and supplemented with the theory of comparative advantage; see, respectively, D. Ricardo (1951) [1810] *The High Price of Bullion*, vol. 3 of *The Works and Correspondence of David Ricardo*; and D. Ricardo (1951) [1817] *On the Principles of Political Economy and Taxation*, vol. 1 of *The Works and Correspondence of David Ricardo*, ch. 7. Marxist economics has always rejected both the domestic and the international versions of the Quantity Theory of Money.

11 It is important to note in this connection that Ricardo's international Quantity Theory of Money was an integral part of his theory of comparative advantage in international trade. For Ricardo, countries specialised in trade according to international price movements induced by adjustments in the quantity of money. From the perspective of Marxist political economy, there is no such monetary mechanism, and the theory of comparative advantage does not hold; see A. Shaikh (1999) 'Real Exchange Rates and the International Mobility of Capital', Levy Economics Institute Working Paper No. 265;

contrary, adjustment tends to be forceful, and often involves violent ruptures of economic activity, including foreign exchange crises, that eventually must be confronted through political decisions. In an exchange rate crisis, trade across borders is disrupted and the organising role of domestic money is severely disturbed, as often domestic recession emerges, followed by unemployment and loss of productive capacity. On such occasions, the role of world money is decisive and dominates the functioning of domestic money.

The resolution of international crises normally requires the intervention of non-market authorities to ensure access to world money. Commanding world money becomes a pressing issue for both core and peripheral countries to enable international payments and the settlement of international obligations. The hegemonic state plays a decisive role in this respect, setting the conditions for accessing world money. Political power is projected, and the sovereignty of countries that are short of world money is directly challenged.[12]

It is surprising that the classical Marxist debates on imperialism paid relatively little attention to this aspect of hegemonic capitalist power, whose extraordinary importance, particularly in the twentieth century, is beyond dispute. Hegemony and imperialism persist in the interstices

---

see also A. Shaikh (1984) 'The Laws of International Exchange', in E. Nell (ed.) *Growth, Profits and Property: Essays in the Revival of Political Economy*, Cambridge University Press: Cambridge, UK, ch. 13. The rebalancing of the domestic and the international realms does not take place through the adjustment of relative prices as money flows internationally. Rather, it involves debt accumulation and the violent elimination of value through crises in which world money plays a determining role; see Lapavitsas (1996) 'The Classical Adjustment Mechanism of International Balances'.

12 A recent example would be helpful in this connection. After the establishment of the euro in the late 1990s, the domestic price level of Greece rose faster than the domestic price level of Germany. Greek international competitiveness fell, resulting in substantial current account deficits and overburdening the Greek national debt. But there was nothing automatic about addressing the imbalance. Instead, German imperial power compelled the Greek state to accept a course of action that shifted the inevitable costs of adjustment onto Greek society. For further discussion, see H. Flassbeck and C. Lapavitsas (2015) *Against the Troika: Crisis and Austerity in the Eurozone*, Verso: London and New York. A further example in a different but related context is the conversion of the East German Mark into the West German Deutsche Mark in 1990. The West German state imposed its will irrespective of market rates. For the conflicting opinions within the West German government as well as the West and East German central banks, see Rolf Hasse (1993) 'German–German Monetary Union: Main Options, Costs and Repercussions', in A. Ghanie Ghaussy and Wolf Schäfer (eds) *The Economics of German Unification*, Routledge: London, New York, p. 28.

of the world economy where the domestic meets the international order, their interaction pivoting on world money. Fundamental to this is the role of the state, which differs greatly in the two realms, as is shown in the following sections.

The state in the domestic order: Homogenising money

Capitalist states comprise a multitude of mechanisms and institutions, including those of the military, domestic security, justice, political representation, welfare, and potentially education, health, and so on. It is almost superfluous to point out that the particulars of these institutions, including their structures and functions, vary substantially among states, reflecting the class dynamics of each country.[13] State institutions shape history and politics and are in turn shaped by historical and political events, constantly evolving through broader interactions with other states.

There is no analogy between the conduct of states (domestically and internationally) and the conduct of private enterprises, as that of the latter is based on a profit-maximising calculus. National states comprise bureaucracies with their own rules and practices, which are qualitatively distinct from the managerial bureaucracies of large enterprises. Capitalist states must certainly account for monetary income, expenditure, and debt, and might well be sites of monetary corruption, but their conduct is guided by calculations of power and shaped by ideology.

In core countries, the state's power of compulsion and influence over economic and social affairs is several orders of magnitude greater than

---

13 There is an enormous literature on these issues which is not directly relevant for our purposes. The approach adopted in this book draws heavily on the analysis of Nicos Poulantzas, especially in his last work; see N. Poulantzas (1978) *State, Power, Socialism*, New Left Books: London. Poulantzas moved away from mechanical interpretations of the state as a tool of the capitalist class and grasped the state as a condensation of class relations, intervening in multiple ways to sustain capitalist social reproduction; see also N. Poulantzas (1979) *Classes in Contemporary Capitalism*, Verso: London. The mechanisms and institutions of state are, consequently, a field of class conflict, and this is a crucial insight in analysing state economic and other policies. Lest it be misunderstood, Poulantzas was prone to the abstract formalism of the French Althusserianism of his time, as Ralph Miliband pointed out in their debate in the 1960s and 1970s. Nonetheless, Miliband's own Anglo-Saxon predilection for empirical substantiation of the class nature of capitalist state mechanisms (evident in R. Miliband (1969) *The State in Capitalist Society*, Weidenfeld & Nicolson: London) is not nearly as far removed from Poulantzas as the tone of their famous debate would imply.

that of even the strongest private actors. For this reason, state mechanisms and institutions always form a contested terrain among domestic social classes, even if the state as a collective entity is dominated by the capitalist class. The elites that govern contemporary capitalism gauge the requirements to secure their privileged position through access to state mechanisms, irrespective of their private political and financial power base. It is not an accident that in the great capital cities of core countries there are massive concentrations of political lobbyists, all attempting to obtain political advantages for their corporate and private clients.

The mechanisms and institutions of the state have been critical to the homogenisation of the domestic market since the early beginnings of the capitalist mode of production. State interventions include the quotidian technology of commercial transactions, such as weights and measures. They extend to the legal structures supporting the domestic market, such as the law of contract, the law of tort, the law of establishment of enterprises, and the licensing of commercial transactions. Not least, core states also reinforce a multitude of market-related bodies regulating commercial and productive practice, frequently with the full backing of the law.

Above all, core states ensure the reproduction and allocation of labour power through legal, cultural, and welfare measures. There is nothing natural or spontaneous about creating and sustaining a working class, and the process always involves degrees of violence, including compulsion to ensure worker discipline. States are fully present while the capitalist mode of production is continually legitimated in the minds of citizens through ideology and everyday practice. Without constant recourse to state mechanisms, including pure force, capitalism would not be the social and economic reality, and even the mental horizon, of working people.[14]

---

14 The debate between Poulantzas and Miliband opened a path for analysing these complex domestic interventions by the state. Unfortunately, the subsequent intellectual ascendancy of Michel Foucault, with his focus on biopolitics and governmentality, in practice hindered the development of Marxist analyses of the state precisely as neoliberalism took sway; see M. Foucault (2007) *Security, Territory, Population: Lectures at the Collège de France (1977–1978)*, Palgrave: New York. A recent exception that is important for this book is L. Panitch and S. Gindin (2012) *The Making of Global Capitalism: The Political Economy of American Empire*, Verso: London and New York. Following Poulantzas and Miliband, they consider the state as a relatively autonomous actor that also reflects domestic class struggles. Neoliberal ideology and policy from this

In this regard, the most characteristic economic act of capitalist states is to develop the institutions that back domestic money. Creating a national currency is a vital component of national sovereignty. As was discussed in part II, in contemporary capitalism such money takes a fiat form that is linked to the central bank and provides the basis of monetary and fiscal policy. The power of core states to create vast quantities of fiat money in recent years reflects the homogeneity of the domestic market as well as the control that the state can exercise over it. But it has not eliminated the tensions generated by decades of neoliberalism and financialisation.

It is crucial to stress, furthermore, that the state is neither omniscient nor omnipotent. State policies can be based on faulty theory, or may serve particular interests, thus exacerbating the intrinsic instability of capitalist accumulation. The enormous bubble of the 2000s that ended with the Great Crisis of 2007–09 was, for instance, also sustained by the faulty economic analysis of the 'Great Moderation'.[15] Moreover, state intervention to confront the crisis of 2007–09 failed to assuage the deep malaise of financialised accumulation in core countries.

The state in the international order: Hegemonic power and world money

State action in the international realm differs from state interventions in the domestic economy in most respects. For one thing, states act as independent economic agents in the world market, transacting with each other as well as with private enterprises. They buy and occasionally

---

perspective is a means of establishing US hegemony across the world. What is relatively absent from their analysis is an exposition of the organic links between the state and domestic accumulation. These links – discussed in detail in part II of this book in relation to contemporary capitalism – are historically specific and vary with the material characteristics of accumulation. The deepest roots of imperialism are to be found in that connection.

15 Faulty policies that hinder capitalist interests and even accumulation itself have been a frequent feature of state interventions ever since the first eighteenth-century financial experiments in France and Britain. The classic instance was provided by Britain initiating theory-based monetary policy as the country approached the peak of its imperial power. The Bank Act of 1844 ushered in systematic economic intervention, with disastrous results. The Act was subjected to a devastating critique by Marx for its theoretical obtuseness; see, for instance, Marx (1981) [1894] *Capital*, vol. 3, ch. 34.

sell commodities, borrow, and lend money capital, advance subsidies, and provide financial aid to other states or private enterprises. But the calculus of state actions in the world market is chiefly based on power and ideology, not profit making. Non-economic relations are pre-eminent, including prestige, trust and mistrust, hostility and alliances, religious and ideological antagonisms, war, and peace. National sovereignty is continually contested and re-established on the interstate terrain.

The world market is, thus, profoundly different from the domestic market with regard to the motivation and conduct of its participants, and not merely in terms of price formation and profit rate equalisation. It is inherently subject to interstate contests and lacks the functional equivalent of the sovereign state, which stabilises domestic economic, social, and political tensions. Imperialist states rise above the rest by being able to influence the world market to suit the interests of particular blocs of capitalists. The hegemonic state stands apart from other imperialist states due to its power to mould the institutions of the world market and materially alter its functioning.

Hegemonic power in the world economy is a special and acute instance of imperialist power. It takes multiple forms, such as determining the rules of accounting for private enterprises in the world market, manipulating tariff and non-tariff barriers to trade, dictating the legal framework for tackling commercial disputes (extraterritoriality included), setting the governing law for international debt, shaping international investment treaties, and so on. By far the most privileged terrain for the exercise of hegemonic power is, however, that of world money. The hegemon possesses a singular ability to influence the functioning of world money through a range of institutions, practices, and mechanisms.

British imperialism in the nineteenth century offers evidence regarding the practices, the institutions, and the learning processes through which a hegemonic power exercises influence on world money. The British ruling class was gradually able to manage the gold standard, but such knowledge came neither easily nor smoothly. During the first half of the nineteenth century, there were fierce debates on monetary policy, including in particular the Bullion and the Banking-Currency Controversies, which focused on the causes of international drains of gold from the Bank of England and sought appropriate methods for protecting the Bank's hoard. The debates culminated in the Bank Act of

1844, the provisions of which – essentially, rigid quantitative control of the liabilities of the Bank of England – were effectively a failure.

Success came in the second half of the century, although not through theoretical innovations or intellectual breakthroughs. Rather, as the world market matured in practice, there was gradual institutional development which facilitated the functioning of gold as world money. Above all, the City of London emerged as the leading financial market in the world and consequently the provision of credit necessary for international commercial transactions – whether involving British enterprises or not – came to rely heavily on British credit mechanisms. Core and peripheral countries had to comply with the institutional framework established in the City of London to obtain credit in sterling. Access to gold typically required access to the domestic money of Britain and the financial mechanisms that supported it.

Toward the end of the nineteenth century, the British ruling bloc learnt to manage the mechanisms of providing world money without attempting to impose quantitative controls on the balance sheet of the Bank of England.[16] Instead, the Bank became adept at manipulating the bank rate charged in the money market, thus attracting loanable capital from across the world. Thereby the Bank could keep a modest hoard of gold, minimising the costs to Britain from holding value in idle form. As is often – and rightly – said, the British Empire was run on a shoestring.

The ability of the Bank of England to manipulate the bank rate relied primarily on the regular and substantial availability of loanable capital across the world, which rested on the steady formation of a mature world economy. Still, it would have been impossible to support the gold standard without the British colonies, particularly India. Colonial domination of the Asian subcontinent led to the exploitation of Indian producers on a mass scale, transferring to London vast surpluses. Ruthless colonial extraction was frequently disguised through the tax and spend mechanisms of the fiscal administration of the Indian Raj.[17] There is no doubt that Indian surpluses buttressed the hoard of the Bank of England and were indispensable to the pound sterling operating as the global gateway to gold.

16 The classic statement of growing confidence and maturity was made by W. Bagehot (1873) *Lombard Street: A Description of the Money Market*, Henry S. King & Co.: London.

17 See U. Patnaik and P. Patnaik (2021) 'The Drain of Wealth: Colonialism before the First World War', *Monthly Review* 72 (8).

The hegemonic power afforded to Britain through its control over world money was confirmed by the essential failure of the Latin Monetary Union in the second half of the nineteenth century.[18] An alliance of European powers including France (but not Germany) attempted to establish an alternative form of world money that combined gold and silver. The attempt fell prey to the incessant fluctuations of the exchange value of the two metals, which disrupted the determination of prices and the value of past obligations. The mature world market would not tolerate two metals acting simultaneously as the measure of value, and gold was firmly fixed as the global universal equivalent.

The final ascent of gold, however, also implied severe constraints for the British hegemon. Gold is a commodity and its functioning as world money is related to its own value content. Gold as global reserve of value or as international means of payment depends on its intrinsic value (abstract labour), which is inseparable from its physical form, and lies manifestly beyond the control of the state. British credit mechanisms could provide considerable flexibility to the mechanisms settling transactions across the world, but gold also had to be physically present. The corporeality of world money was a constraint that the British state could not overcome.

Despite the constraints of intrinsic value, the gold standard was a pillar of British imperialism, and its ultimate guarantee lay in the British gunboats that were permanently to hand to compel foreign debtors and others to comply with formal payment obligations. The waning of British hegemony was surely due to the country's inability to ensure pre-eminence in the new industrial fields that dictated the character of productive accumulation toward the end of the nineteenth century. But its death knell sounded in 1914, when the hegemon was compelled, effectively, to sideline the gold standard to protect the gold hoard and face the demands of war.

It cannot be overstressed that there was no gradual process through which one form of world money was substituted for another in the early twentieth century. When reviewing the historical trajectory of world money for analytical purposes, it is vital to be alert to discontinuities as well as continuities. The demise of gold as dominant world money was neither natural nor inevitable. The gold standard was in practice suspended

18 See L. Einaudi (2000) 'From the Franc to the "Europe": The Attempted Transformation of the Latin Monetary Union into a European Monetary Union, 1865–1873', *Economic History Review* 53 (2): 284–308; for further historical detail, see also L. Einaudi (2001) *Money and Politics: European Monetary Unification and the International Gold Standard (1865–1873)*, Oxford University Press: Oxford.

through the political choices of the hegemonic state (and it main contestants) in 1914, representing a major historical discontinuity in the development of capitalism.

During the enormous turbulence that marked the interwar years, attempts were made to reinstate new versions of the gold standard, but it proved impossible in the conditions bequeathed by the First World War. British economic and financial power had declined precipitously during the war, and the ruling bloc had to admit defeat in 1931, when the Great Depression of the 1930s wrought disaster across international banking. The decline of British hegemony was in line with the broader retreat of European powers, as Germany lay prostrate through war and reparations, France lacked the economic strength to dominate the world market, Austro-Hungary disintegrated, and Russia adopted a socialist regime after 1917. The First World War represented the collective suicide of European imperialists as rulers of the world.

The USA was in the ascendant as the leading site of capitalist accumulation after the First World War, and by the 1920s New York had already begun to replace London as the world centre of financial transactions. Yet, there was no US hegemony in the interwar years. The period was an interregnum marked by enormous crises, the fragmentation of finance across the world, and the inability to generate a reliable form of world money. Monopolies continued to dominate domestic accumulation in the leading countries, and formal empires survived the turmoil, but in the 1930s the world market fragmented beyond easy repair, as did global finance.

During the 1930s, the domestic money of core countries was largely inconvertible into gold and increasingly managed by state mechanisms. Moreover, in Nazi Germany, the state took a far more interventionist role in domestic accumulation, in cahoots with big business, through investment in public construction and massive rearmament, while also engaging in extensive privatisations.[19] In the Soviet Union, meanwhile, state-led industrialisation made enormous leaps throughout the 1930s. Even in the USA, the state assumed an active interventionist role through the New Deal to confront the disasters of the Depression.

The management of money took fuller form after the Second World

---

19 See Adam Tooze (2007) *The Wages of Destruction: The Making and Breaking of the Nazi Economy*, Penguin: London; Germà Bel (2006) 'The Coining of "Privatization" and Germany's National Socialist Party', *Journal of Economic Perspectives* 20 (3): 187–94; Germà Bel (2009) 'From Public to Private: Privatization in 1920's Fascist Italy', European University Institute (EUI) Working Paper No. RSCAS 2009/46.

War, as US hegemony emerged properly through paths discussed further in the following chapter, and the world market was reconstituted. But the foundations of US hegemonic power were very different from the classical imperialist era, resting on giant multinational enterprises that gradually began to employ armies of industrial workers across the globe and interacted with finance under substantial state regulation and control. US hegemony drew its strength from the internal combustion engine, the production of machine tools and electrical appliances, and the use of oil for energy. Its main contestant was the Soviet Union, and the contest required a network of military bases and interventionist political mechanisms across the West and its former colonies.

Crucial to our purposes is that the USA relied heavily on the role of the dollar as world money under the Bretton Woods system, which provided for a degree of convertibility into gold, as is briefly discussed in the next chapter. Moreover, the dramatic shift toward sole US hegemony that occurred in 1989–91, as the Soviet Union collapsed, was accompanied by even greater dependence of US hegemony on the dollar. The rise of the USA to sole hegemony was preceded by the collapse of Bretton Woods in 1971–73, after which the dollar became a form of world money that was entirely inconvertible into gold, and financialisation gradually took hold of core economies.

The interregnum that commenced with the Great Crisis of 2007–09, marked by the Pandemic Crisis and the Russo-Ukrainian War, has witnessed the end of sole US hegemony. The currently unfolding hegemonic contest is moulded by advanced electronics, telecommunications, digital technologies, and artificial intelligence. It pivots on the aggressive coupling of internationalised productive capital together with global finance, as is discussed in subsequent chapters. The main contestants are the USA and China, and the battle will also involve the power to determine contemporary world money.

To analyse the emerging contest, however, it is necessary to consider more closely the trajectory of US hegemonic power, including its role in creating the institutional framework of world money and overseeing its functioning through economic means. The hegemon must possess sufficient political and military clout to ensure acceptance of preferred monetary practices across the world economy. The following chapters examine the extraordinary power of the USA, and the challenges it faces, in these respects.

11

Core and Periphery under US Hegemony

Capitalist hegemonic contests are inseparable from the interaction between the domestic and the international orders of accumulation. The aim of capitalist producers is not to satisfy social needs but to generate profits and augment the capital invested. Individual capitalist enterprises constantly attempt to increase the scale of output and expand to new geographical areas, eventually forming the world market. Capitalist production is inherently an international process, and capitalist relations of production incessantly strive to expand their ambit.[1]

Summarily put, the capitalist mode of production is domestic in form but international in essence.[2] The individual countries that form the components of the world economy participate in the world market stretching across national borders, and the place of an individual country in the international division of labour is fundamental to analysing the modalities and performance of its domestic economy. At the same time, hierarchy is integral to the world economy and the lines are perpetually redrawn between core and periphery. Peripheral countries

---

1 J. Iñigo Carrera (2013) *El capital: razón histórica, sujeto revolucionario y conciencia*, Imago Mundi: Buenos Aires; A. Fitzsimons and G. Starosta (2018) 'Global Capital, Uneven Development and National Difference: Critical Reflections on the Specificity of Accumulation in Latin America', *Capital and Class* 42 (1): 109–32.

2 Carrera (2013) *El capital*; G. Caligaris (2016) 'The Global Accumulation of Capital and Ground-Rent in "Resource Rich" Countries', in G. Charnock and G. Starosta (eds) *The New International Division of Labour*, Palgrave Macmillan: London, pp. 55–77; G. Starosta (2016) 'Revisiting the New International Division of Labour Thesis', in Charnock and Starosta (eds) *The New International Division of Labour*, pp. 79–103.

are integrated in a subordinate manner, but subordination takes historically specific forms, as does its opposite, hegemony.

Capitalist expansion in the nineteenth century was mostly based on
trade and finance and occurred through a historical process of blood
and fire which gave birth to the political forms of colonialism. A global
division of labour emerged as the world economy took shape, comprising a largely European core and a vast swathe of peripheral countries.
The core appropriated peripheral natural resources, exploited peripheral labour power, extracted wealth through public and private debt
repayment, and, on occasion, enslaved huge numbers of people.

In sharp contrast to previous periods, US hegemony has been marked
by sustained internationalisation of capitalist production – not merely,
or mostly, of trade and finance – particularly during the decades of
neoliberal ascendancy. The current hegemonic contest is inextricably
linked to this development of international capitalist accumulation
together with the global spread of finance and the transformation of
world money. The conditions for the internationalisation of production
are, however, highly demanding compared with those for the internationalisation of trade and finance, as is shown in the rest of this book.
These conditions, together with global finance, have shaped contemporary imperialist and hegemonic struggles.

An economic contest for hegemony bereft of ideology

The trajectory of imperialism in the twentieth century largely coincided
with the USA's path to hegemony. It is not true that US capitalism has
been historically averse to imperialism, despite the frequently vocifer-
ous attacks on European imperialism within US polity.[3] In the 1850s,
the USA was an aggressive participant in the forcible opening of Japan

3 See Robert J. McMahon (2001) 'The Republic as Empire: American Foreign Policy
in the "American Century" ', in Harvard Sitkoff (ed.) *Perspectives on Modern America:
Making Sense of the Twentieth Century*, Oxford University Press: Oxford and New York,
pp. 80–100; see also Amy Kaplan and Donald Pearce (eds) (1993) *Cultures of United
States Imperialism*, Duke University Press: Durham, NC, and London. For a broad
coverage of imperialist and anti-imperialist ideologies in the formation of the US nation,
see Mary Ann Heiss (2002) 'The Evolution of the Imperial Idea and US National Identity',
Diplomatic History 26 (4): 511–40. For the persistent reluctance of US intellectuals to
accept the notion of a US empire, see Robert J. McMahon (2001) 'Cultures of Empire',
The Journal of American History 88 (3): 888–92.

and China to international trade; in the 1890s, Hawaii was effectively colonised by the USA; above all, the Spanish–American War of 1898 bequeathed several colonies to the USA, including the Philippines and Cuba, securing for the USA the status of a great power.[4] Nevertheless, US hegemony in the twentieth century signalled a dramatic shift away from the colonial imperialism of the nineteenth century.

The ascent of the USA to a hegemonic position rested on the strength of its domestic accumulation, including production and trade, the forms of labour, and the organisational technologies of large multinational enterprises that corralled productive capital. Instead of seeking colonial exclusionary zones, the USA continually reshaped the framework of the world economy, operating through international multilateral coalitions and institutions created by itself and primarily benefiting its own ruling power bloc.[5] Furthermore, the USA built an 'ideological empire', seeking 'to transform the world into its own image and likeness'.[6]

US imperialism differed substantially from its European predecessors, resting on non-colonial forms of division between core and periphery in the world economy. Capitalist expansion after the Second World War continued to rely on trade and finance but also drew systematically on the spreading of production across borders led by multinational enterprises. Core countries played a dominant role in the international flows of commodity, loanable, and productive capital, with the US hegemon in pivot position. The new forms of imperialism and hegemonic power also rested on command by the USA over world money. Peripheral countries were placed in subordinate positions depending on the global flows of capital, access to world money, and their domestic conditions.

However, the defining feature of US hegemony from the end of the Second World War to 1991 was that the main rival of the USA, the Soviet

---

4 Conservative political theorists calmly accept these plain historical facts; see, for instance, J. Mearsheimer (2001) *The Tragedy of Great Power Politics*, W.W. Norton & Company: New York and London, p. 6.

5 These institutions allowed the USA to act as both a 'system maker' and a 'privilege taker' in the world economy. For a discussion of these terms, see Michael Mastanduno (2009) 'System Maker and Privilege Taker: US Power and the International Political Economy', *World Politics* 61 (1): 121–54; Doug Stokes (2018) 'Trump, American Hegemony and the Future of the Liberal International Order', *International Affairs* 94 (1): 133–50.

6 E. Hobsbawm (1999) 'First World and Third World after the Cold War', *CEPAL Review* 67: 7–14.

Union, had a different form of social organisation and did not compete directly for a commanding place in the global flows of productive, commodity, and financial capital. The hegemonic contest in the four decades after the Second World War was military, political, and ideological, but not economic.

In contrast, the decades since 1991 have been marked by the rise of independent centres of industrial capitalist accumulation beyond the historical core countries, above all in China and other parts of Asia. This seismic shift is related to the technological revolution during this period and the concomitant internationalisation of production overseen by multinational enterprises.[7] It is also related to the global spread of finance, the advance of financialisation in core countries, and the emergence of subordinate forms of financialisation in peripheral countries. All these developments are intrinsically connected to the role of the dollar as global reserve currency.

Contemporary divisions between core and periphery have emerged as capitalism has penetrated every corner of the globe. There are no significant geographical, social, or economic areas across the world that escape domination by capitalist relations. The concept of periphery no longer refers to parts of the world economy in which capitalism has made limited inroads and whose ruling elites could be motivated by non-capitalist notions. Peripheries in contemporary capitalism comprise countries that find themselves in a subordinate position relative to the core but are no less capitalist for that reason.

The Pandemic Crisis left no doubt in this respect, as the trajectories of individual countries varied according to the commodities supplied to the world market, the form of insertion in the global chains of production, and the nature of exposure to international finance.[8] Domestic fiscal and monetary policies were crucial to increasing divergence, as was shown in part II, depending on each country's form of integration into the world economy as well as the lockdown policies implemented during the pandemic.

---

7 For a Marxist perspective on enterprise management and organisation as parts of technological development, see D. Harvey (2017) *Marx, Capital, and the Madness of Economic Reason*, Oxford University Press: Oxford, pp. 94ff.

8 See, for instance, B. Tröster and K. Küblböck (2020) 'Unprecedented but not Unpredictable: Effects of the COVID-19 Crisis on Commodity-Dependent Countries', *The European Journal of Development Research* 32: 1430–49. See also T. Franz (2021) 'Spatial Fixes and Switching Crises in the Times of COVID-19: Implications for Commodity-Producing Economies in Latin America', *Canadian Journal of Development Studies* 42 (1–2): 109–21.

The current hegemonic contest reflects growing divergence within the world economy but is largely devoid of ideological content. Western liberal oligarchies are bereft of political ideas capable of mobilising large numbers of people. The attempts by the US ruling bloc to present its hegemonic struggle with China and its military contest with Russia as a defence of democracy versus authoritarianism smack of ideological desperation. The Chinese and Russian polities, on the other hand, appear to be domestically secure but are lacking in ideological allure across the world.

In striking contrast to the period prior to 1991, the current contest is purely about power and economic advantage within the existing capital-ist relations of hierarchy, exploitation, and exclusion. It is a throwback to the imperialist wrangles preceding the First World War, and for that reason it is extremely dangerous and entirely cynical. Fundamental to it is the ideological impasse that has emerged since the disorderly retreat of socialist politics in core capitalist countries, the collapse of the Eastern Bloc, and the intellectual exhaustion of Western liberal democracies. The underlying factors can be gauged by considering the evolution of US hegemony in further detail.

The first phase of US hegemony

The first phase of US hegemony was shaped by the Second World War and lasted until the collapse of the Soviet Bloc. Soviet troops experienced the heaviest fighting, but the USA emerged as the pre-eminent military power, controlling the seaways, possessing the atom bomb, and wielding enor-mous economic power. In 1945, it commanded almost half the global manufacturing capacity and most of the world's gold reserves.

Until the middle of the 1970s, the hegemon relied on the preponder-ant weight of its domestic accumulation. During the three remarkable decades of the long post-war boom, the US economy was driven by production for mass consumption (automobiles, electrical appliances, furniture, food, and so on) and the corresponding mass production of investment goods.[9] Mass consumption was based on rising real wages,

---

9 The literature on the long boom following the Second World War is very extensive; see S. Marglin and J. Schor (eds) (1990) *The Golden Age of Capitalism: Reinterpreting the Postwar Experience*, Oxford University Press: Oxford and New York.

extended presence of the state in social provision, moderate volumes of household credit, and steady increases in labour productivity as new technologies were introduced. A further fundamental feature of the period was the permanent militarisation of the USA, requiring vast military expenditures on an annual basis. A military–industrial complex emerged at the heart of US domestic accumulation, sustained by enormous public expenditures.[10]

During that exceptional period, the analytical foundations of imperialism laid by classical Marxists had to be reconsidered. Domestic accumulation in the USA was dominated by oligopolistic behemoths, which also ruled the world market until challengers emerged in the 1960s, most of which were German and Japanese industrial competitors. At the same time the US financial sector was placed under a battery of domestic and international controls. US commercial banks were, for years, laden with public debt acquired during the war and operated under strict regulations on interest rates and flows of credit. Moreover, the export of private loanable capital was limited, while the export of productive capital, which began to assume substantial dimensions in the 1960s, occurred primarily among core countries and not from core to periphery.

Although US capitalism drew substantially on private sources of dynamism, the state was important to its functioning, first and foremost in terms of military expenditure. State purchases of arms and other goods and services created a vast network of public procurement that indirectly supported the large enterprises dominating the US economy, particularly the enormous military–industrial complex. The economic power of the US state was also apparent in both fiscal and monetary policies and backed by regulation of the monetary sphere.

The characteristic institutions of Pax Americana were built by drawing on these domestic foundations. It was, ostensibly, a framework of international cooperation through multilateral institutions, open markets, security cooperation arrangements, and political leadership by the USA and its allies allegedly to promote democracy and freedom.[11]

---

10 Discussed mostly by sociologists following the path-breaking analysis of C. Wright Mills (1956) *The Power Elite*, Oxford University Press: New York.

11 Mainstream references in this spirit are legion; see, for instance, D. Deudney and G. J. Ikenberry (1999) 'The Nature and Sources of Liberal International Order', *Review of International Studies* 25: 179–96; see also G. J. Ikenberry (2012) *Liberal Leviathan: The Origins, Crisis, and Transformation of the American World Order*, Princeton University Press: Princeton, NJ.

In practice, much of the periphery was consigned to local ruling elites that sought unhindered profits, pursued vigorous anticommunism, suppressed democratic rights, and accommodated US policy goals. Assorted military and civilian autocrats, coup plotters, corrupt racists, and even genocidal dictators received the blessing of the hegemon.

The main economic institutions constructed by the USA included the General Agreement on Tariffs and Trade (GATT), established in 1947, and the World Bank and the International Monetary Fund (IMF), created as part of the Bretton Woods Agreement in 1944. Their synergies set the ground for the functioning of the dollar as world money.[12] Voting rights in the IMF and the World Bank depended on the amounts of capital subscribed by the participants to these institutions, thus providing the USA with effective control.[13] The main military support of Pax Americana, finally, was the North Atlantic Treaty Organization, the premier military force in the world.

The Bretton Woods Agreement fixed exchange rates by establishing the formal convertibility of the dollar into gold at 35 US dollars per troy ounce among central banks. A hierarchy of currencies was established in practice: the dollar at the apex, the currencies of other industrial countries next, and the currencies of poor countries further down. US hegemony over the world market through the dollar functioning as world money was incomparably more institutional and formal than the British gold standard. The fiction of formal equality among countries in international institutions masked the reality of hugely unequal power and economic prospects.

The GATT substantially reduced tariffs and other barriers to trade, although the USA also tolerated state support for nascent industries in both Europe and Japan. This trade strategy reflected the relatively low reliance of the US economy on imports, its hegemony resting primarily on domestic production.[14] At the same time, the USA sought to create new markets for its dominant manufacturing industry.[15] It also promoted

---

12 See A. H. Meltzer (1991) 'U.S. Policy in the Bretton Woods Era', *Federal Reserve Bank of St. Louis Review*, May/June: 53–83.

13 See M. Wan (2016) 'The AIIB versus the World Bank and the ADB', in M. Wan (2017) *The Asian Infrastructure Investment Bank: The Construction of Power and the Struggle for the East Asian International Order*, Palgrave Macmillan: New York.

14 B. J. Silver and G. Arrighi (2003) 'Polanyi's "Double Movement": The Belle Époques of British and US Hegemony Compared', *Politics & Society* 31: 325–55, p. 339.

15 See I. Wallerstein (2006) 'The Curve of American Power', *New Left Review* 40: July/August.

foreign direct investment by its multinational enterprises, infiltrating fast-growing areas, particularly in Western Europe.

The internationalisation of productive capital dominated by large monopolistic enterprises – a hallmark of contemporary capitalism – has its roots in the first decades after the Second World War. Its specific character and the implications for the internal organisation of the multinational giants that dominate the world market today are considered in chapter 12. The difference between the first and the second period of US hegemony in this regard lies in the qualitative transformation of the internationalisation of productive capital together with the enormous revival of loanable capital flows.

US hegemony in the heyday of Pax Americana from the 1950s to the 1970s was marked by a disjuncture between its economic, political, and military aspects, already noted in the previous section. The political and military contestant was the Soviet Union, whose economy functioned on non-capitalist principles and was never a competitor to the USA in the world market. Faced with powerful labour movements associated with socialist and communist parties, the core capitalist powers submitted to the hegemonic role of the USA. The periphery of the world economy, meanwhile, comprised a vast array of countries that freed themselves from the formal shackles of the old European empires.

The hegemony of the USA since the Second World War has been seen through many prisms. Charles Kindleberger, for instance, articulated the US self-image, painting a rosy picture of a benevolent country that suffered net losses from exercising hegemony, while merely attempting to pacify economic rivalries and promote world prosperity.[16] Kindleberger turned a blind eye to the ruthless application of political and military power throughout the decades of American hegemony. Robert Gilpin, on the other hand, portrayed the USA as a coercive bully, using military and economic force to recoup the costs of hegemony from other countries.[17] But the use of

---

16 See C. P. Kindleberger (2013) *The World in Depression: 1929–1939*, University of California Press: Berkeley, p. 304

17 See R. Gilpin (1981) *War and Change in World Politics*, Cambridge University Press: Cambridge, UK. For an analysis of US foreign policy as a prime mover in the 'century of war', see G. Kolko (1994) *Century of War: Politics, Conflict, and Society since 1914*, The New Press: New York; G. Kolko (2004) *Another Century of War?*, 2nd edition, The New Press: New York.

coercive force by the USA was not supportive of its power in the longer term.[18]

The first period of US hegemony came to an end with the collapse of the Eastern Bloc in the late 1980s and early 1990s, allowing the USA to emerge as the sole military and political hegemon.[19] By that time, however, the characteristic features of capitalist accumulation and the world economy had already been substantially altered. The turning point in accumulation, marked by falling profitability and signalling the end to the long post-war boom, came with the global economic crisis of 1973–74. The economic foundations of the first period of US hegemony were shaken long before the demise of the Soviet Union.

The manufacturing industries of Germany and Japan emerged as successful competitors of the USA in the world market by the mid-1960s, and the rate of profit of US manufacturers collapsed in the years before 1973.[20] Inflation accelerated as the hegemon became heavily involved in the Vietnam War and its fiscal expenditures ballooned. The US current account began to register deficits, while the capital account showed significant net outflows as private US enterprises invested abroad. European countries acquired large dollar claims, which bore heavily on the gold reserve of the USA. These combined pressures led to the end of Bretton Woods in 1971–73 and the USA suspending convertibility into gold and allowing the dollar to depreciate substantially. As the era of financialisation dawned, the US currency became an inconvertible means of hoard formation and payments across the world market, providing a fluctuating standard of value in the world market.

The political nadir of the first period of US hegemony came a little later. The debacle of US military power in the Vietnam War was accompanied by the victories of anti-imperialist struggles in much of Africa as well as the Soviet army's intervention in Afghanistan. Domestic social unrest with strong racial dimensions in the late 1960s and 1970s deepened the sense of crisis for US hegemony. Meanwhile, the economic

---

18 It is well understood that coercion can lead to growing hostility, ultimately undermining the legitimacy of the hegemon; see Clark (2007) *Legitimacy in International Society*; Silver and Arrighi (2003) 'Polanyi's "Double Movement"'.

19 See E. Todd (2004) *La chute finale: Essais sur la décomposition de la sphère Soviétique*, Robert Laffont: Paris.

20 See R. Brenner (2006) *The Economics of Global Turbulence: The Advanced Capitalist Economies from Long Boom to Long Downturn, 1945-2005*, Verso: London, p. 41.

malaise of accumulation in the 1970s also engulfed the other core countries of the world economy facing similar problems of low profitability.[21] With global capitalism seemingly facing a lethal threat, anti-capitalist movements spread, and euphoric young radicals challenged
political and cultural norms.

Things took a rather unexpected turn, however, and a period of
unbridled capitalist profit making and labour retreat was to follow,
guided by renewed US hegemony. The reaction of the USA power nexus
to the blows of the 1970s was fierce, including aggressive foreign interventions, deploying fresh ideological weapons, and redirecting domestic economic policies to alter the social balance in favour of capital.
Neoliberalism was a critically important response to the decline of US
hegemony in the 1970s. Taxes were cut for high-income earners, finance
was further liberalised, and virtually unrestricted freedom of action for
capitalist enterprises was guaranteed.[22] Keynesianism was abandoned
and capitalist profit making was left unrestrained.[23]

As the political and military contest between the USA and the Soviet
Union headed toward resolution in the 1980s, profound changes took
place in the economic foundations of hegemony. Financialisation gathered speed, while the globalisation of commercial, financial, and productive capital proceeded apace, with huge multinationals dominating
commodity flows in the world market. The technological base of production also shifted toward information technology, telecommunications,
and advanced electronics.

After 1991, US hegemony entered its second phase. Actively reshaping the framework of the world market, the hegemon took particular
care to protect the role of the dollar as world money and facilitate the
global spread of productive and financial capital. The unleashing of
capitalism across the globe, however, had unexpected results. While
core and periphery were placed on a different footing, China emerged as
a major economic competitor. Its economic, technological, political,
and military ascendancy was systematically underestimated by the
ruling elite of the USA, and the hegemonic challenge emerged clearly in
the 2010s.

---

21 Ibid., p. 137.

22 The literature on these issues is enormous; a clear account can be found in Silver
and Arrighi (2003) 'Polanyi's "Double Movement"'.

23 For a concise summing up, see A. Glyn (2007) *Capitalism Unleashed: Finance,
Globalization, and Welfare*, Oxford University Press: Oxford.

The second phase: Hegemonic power undermines itself

Throughout the 1990s and 2000s, the USA exercised sole hegemony, with unmatched political and military power, while engaging in several wars to entrench its dominance. Neoliberalism, globalisation, and financialisation placed their stamp on the world economy. The Great Crisis of 2007–09 signalled both the end of the golden era of financialisation and the beginning of the end of the second phase of US hegemony. The spread of productive capital across the world and the emergence of independent centres of industrial accumulation, together with the international expansion of financial capital, gradually altered the global balance of power, putting hegemony on a new footing.

During the second period, the USA further reshaped the global economic order by imposing neoliberal policy precepts and transforming a range of global institutions in line with the underlying changes in capitalist accumulation. For one thing, in 1995, the GATT morphed into the World Trade Organization (WTO), its membership widening across the world. The WTO developed rules and enforcement mechanisms to set the framework for trade in goods and services but also for intellectual property rights and investment. It proved instrumental to facilitating the crossing of borders by productive capital that created global chains pivoting on huge multinational enterprises.

The USA also built an institutional and legal framework of trade and investment for the world economy without relinquishing its power to alter international economic arrangements in ways favourable to its own giant multinational corporations. The hegemon remained the global leader in foreign direct investment (FDI) flows, both inward and outward, as is shown in chapter 13. Through inward flows of FDI it signalled its position as the guarantor of capitalist order across the world, while through outward flows it commanded productive capacity in other countries and thus access to future sources of innovation and revenue streams.[24]

The dollar proved an even more vital pillar of US hegemony after 1991. Its role as world money allowed the USA to run enormous current account deficits without immediate concern about foreign exchange reserves. Throughout this period, the Federal Reserve has been the

24 See S. Strange (1988) *States and Markets*, Pinter: London.

ultimate supplier of dollars to the world economy, thus exercising a determining influence on global borrowing costs. The global role of the dollar shielded the USA from capital flight in periods of global economic turbulence.

US hegemony in its second phase was codified in the Washington Consensus, imposing an agenda of neoliberal reforms on peripheral countries.[25] The World Bank and the IMF were instrumental to spreading neoliberalism and enforcing the Washington Consensus through loan provision, imposing conditionalities on domestic policies, and forcing openness to trade and capital flows. The soft disciplining power of the multilateral organisations together with the intellectual capture of the ruling elites across a range of developing countries – often trained at US universities – proved effective in entrenching US dominance.

Nonetheless, the second period of US hegemony was marked by pronounced monetary turbulence in the world market as well as weaker accumulation in both core and periphery. Countries with hierarchically low currencies were obliged to hold huge reserves of US dollars to be able to participate in the world market, as is further shown in chapter 13. Flexible exchange rates and deregulated capital flows spurred repeated crises across the world market, particularly as domestic credit expansion often went together with enlarged capital inflows. Such crises occurred frequently among developing countries, but none was as dramatic as the Great Crisis of 2007–09 that struck primarily the hegemon.

The beginning of the second period of US hegemony was also the context in which the European Economic and Monetary Union (EMU) finally took shape. The leading powers of the EU aimed to stabilise exchange rates and create a currency capable of competing with the dollar as world money. The institutions of the EMU generated a form of money that was presumably domestic, while simultaneously acting as an international means of payment among member states, and potentially challenging the dollar internationally. In practice, the monetary union acted as a lever of German hegemony in Europe, creating a peculiar form of localised Pax Germanica with several new peripheries attached to it. The hegemonic position of Germany, crucial to Europe, remains subordinate to the USA in global terms. The highly

---

25 See B. Fine, C. Lapavitsas, and J. Pincus (eds) (2001) *Development Policy in the Twenty-First Century: Beyond the Post-Washington Consensus*, Routledge: London.

peculiar features of German hegemony in Europe are examined in chapter 15.

China joined the WTO in 2001 following negotiations that had lasted for more than a decade. The US hegemon appeared to be drawing China firmly into the neoliberal order and perhaps also encouraging domestic political change. But the outcome was not what the USA had expected. By 2008 China was the leading exporter in the world economy; indeed, by the end of the 2010s its share of global exports of goods was roughly double that of the USA. As the pandemic unfolded in 2020, the country registered enormous exports in the low-technology sector of textiles, while having a strong presence in the medium-technology sector of electrical machinery and an even stronger presence in the high-technology sectors of office machinery and telecommunications equipment.[26]

In the 2010s, US hegemony came under sustained pressure, including from Russia, which possesses a vast nuclear arsenal and has developed significant industrial capacity in advanced military production, as well as in steel, energy, and other fields, becoming apparent in the course of the Russo-Ukrainian War in 2022. The true challenge is, however, posed by China. International political and military competition interlocks with commodity and productive capital flows in the world market commanded by huge enterprises. China has enormous strengths in these fields, but remains unable to compete with the USA in terms of finance and world money, as is shown in chapter 14. Finally, the contest between the USA and China will also depend on developments in the constantly shifting periphery of the world economy.

Capitalism is a global system and the hegemonic shifts in the world economy are inseparable from the development of the periphery. To pursue the analysis further in the following chapters, it is important briefly to sketch the intellectual trajectory of debates on core and periphery in the world economy following the classical Marxist analysis of imperialism.

26 See A. Nicita and C. Razo (2021) 'China: The Rise of a Trade Titan', April, UNCTAD, at unctad.org.

Structuralist and dependency theories of core and periphery

Theoretical concern with US hegemony has naturally been stronger in Latin America, the oldest periphery of the USA, which has long been subordinated both economically and politically. The theory of Structuralism first emerged in the late 1930s, as Raúl Prebisch began to analyse the relations between the USA as the core and Latin America as the periphery of the world economy. Analysis took more radical forms through Dependency theory and the work of Latin American Marxists, underlining the asymmetric structures of production and the hierarchical domination of the periphery by the core. For the Structuralists, peripheral countries could evade subordination by industrialising, while the radical theorists saw in the asymmetry of core and periphery an inherent feature of international capitalism.

The chief contribution of Prebisch and his school was to emphasise the economic imbalances, reflected in current account deficits and surpluses, that were created by the division of labour in the world economy. The industrialised core relied on raw materials and food produced by the periphery, thereby creating a world economy with the core in hegemonic position.[27] Peripheral countries were marked by high income elasticity of imports for manufactured goods, while the price elasticity of agricultural goods was low, and agriculture was dominated by large estates.

According to this approach, as time passed, the net barter terms of trade could be expected to move against peripheral countries.[28] Moreover, when conditions were favourable for peripheral countries and domestic income increased, imports would surge, resulting in growing current account deficits. The subordinate position of the periphery would thus translate into a pressing need to possess dollars as the global means of payment.

To close the external gap, Structuralists advocated industrialisation

---

27 For brief summaries, see J. L. Love (1980) 'Raul Prebisch and the Origins of the Doctrine of Unequal Exchange', *Latin American Research Review* 15 (3): 45–72; A. R. Puntigliano and Ö. Appelqvist (2011) 'Prebisch and Myrdal: Development Economics in the Core and on the Periphery', *Journal of Global History* 6 (1): 29–52.

28 This is the well-known Prebisch–Singer thesis in development economics; see R. Prebisch (1950) 'The Economic Development of Latin America and Its Principal Problems', UN ECLA: New York; also published in *Economic Bulletin for Latin America* 7 (1): 1–22; H. Singer (1950) 'The Distribution of Gains Between Investing and Borrowing Countries', *The American Economic Review* 40 (2), Papers and Proceedings of the Sixty-Second Annual Meeting of the American Economic Association: 473–85.

and a policy of 'inward' development, mainly through import substitution. The aim was to alter the structure of peripheral economies through controls on trade, limiting their tendency to import. The focus of industrialisation was on 'light' industry to cover domestic needs, thus favouring imports of investment goods. The domestic financial system would also have to be mobilised for this objective, to apply controls on interest rates and credit flows. It was evident, nonetheless, that investment would still have to exceed domestic saving levels and the capacity of domestic finance. To close the internal gap, liquid capital would have to come from abroad.[29] This could involve flows of private capital, but given the regulations of the Bretton Woods system, it also meant official aid or similar sources closely associated with US power.

Control over world money and the flows of finance were integral elements of both US hegemony and core–periphery divisions in the heyday of Pax Americana. For the Structuralists, equally important was the role of large enterprises, the multinational or transnational corporations. Their presence had grown substantially in the years following the Second World War, and the steady internationalisation of production at the time reinforced the core–periphery division. Multinational enterprises acted as the private 'muscles' of hegemony by allocating resources and technology, thus entrenching the gap between core and periphery.

Dependency theory, on the other hand, stressed the dependence of peripheral development on the core. Take, for instance, the notion of 'associated-dependent development' proposed by Fernando Henrique Cardoso and Enzo Faletto: dependent development for the periphery was due to the interaction of internal and external forces. Even where industrialisation occurred, it was concentrated in a few sectors serving the needs of the capitalist core and reflecting the interests of the domestic bourgeoisie.[30] The interests of the domestic bourgeoisie, together with the 'dominant international classes', determined

---

29 Eventually giving rise to two-gap models of development mostly associated with H. Chenery; see H. B. Chenery and M. Bruno (1962) 'Development Alternatives in an Open Economy: The Case of Israel', *Economic Journal* 72 (285): 79–103. For an enlightening discussion, see L. Taylor (1994) 'Gap Models', *Journal of Development Economics* 45 (1): 17–34.

30 See F. H. Cardoso (1973) 'Associated-Dependent Development: Theoretical and Practical Implications', in A. Stepan (ed.) *Authoritarian Brazil: Origins, Policy, and Future*, Yale University Press: New Haven, pp. 149–72; See also F. H. Cardoso and E. Faletto (1979) *Dependency and Development in Latin America*, University of California Press: Berkeley, CA.

dependency and shaped national and international class conflict mediated by the state.

The 'internalisation of external interests' became crucial to the analysis of US hegemony in the immediate post-war decades.[31] Multinational enterprises operated as 'ephors of dependency', replacing the earlier direct imperialist actions of core states.[32] For Cardoso, 'dependency, monopoly capitalism and development are not contradictory terms: there occurs a kind of dependent capitalist development in the sectors of the third world integrated into the new forms of monopolistic expansion'.[33]

There is an obvious affinity between Dependency theory and the Marxist tradition of the *Monthly Review* developed by Paul Baran in the 1950s, stressing the role of large monopolistic enterprises in sustaining US imperialism. In Baran's work, there are three main means of dependency: aid relationships, foreign investment (capital flows), and trade. In his words, the main task of imperialism at that time was 'to prevent, or, if that is impossible, to slow down and to control the economic development of underdeveloped countries'.[34] There are also clear links – as well as differences – with Dependency theory, particularly the work of Andre Gunder Frank, Arghiri Emmanuel, Samir Amin, and Immanuel Wallerstein, all of whom were associated to a variable degree with Marxism.[35]

Frank coined the term 'development of underdevelopment' – that is, underdevelopment due to capitalist expansion as multinational corporations took advantage of governments creating global institutions advantageous to core countries.[36] Frank further claimed that the rulers

---

31 See, for example, G. M. Grossman and E. Helpman (1994) 'Protection for Sale', *The American Economic Review* 84 (4): 833–50; J. E. Alt et al. (1996) 'The Political Economy of International Trade', *Comparative Political Studies* 29 (6): 689–717.

32 O. Sunkel (1973) 'Transnational Capitalism and National Disintegration in Latin America', *Social and Economic Issues* 22 (1): 132–76; O. Sunkel, (1973) *Past, Present, and Future of the Process of Latin-American Underdevelopment*, Center for Afro-Asian Research of the Hungarian Academy of Science: Budapest.

33 F. H. Cardoso (1972) 'Dependency and Development in Latin America', *New Left Review* 74 (1): 83–95.

34 P. A. Baran (1957) *The Political Economy of Growth*, Monthly Review Press: New York, p. 340.

35 For a recent discussion of the continuing relevance of the dependency approach, see I. H. Kvangraven (2021) 'Beyond the Stereotype: Restating the Relevance of the Dependency Research Programme', *Development and Change* 52(1): 76–112.

36 A. G. Frank (1966) 'The Development of Underdevelopment', *Monthly Review* 18

of peripheral countries were the agents of multinational corporations – a 'lumpen-bourgeoisie'.[37] Peripheral ruling elites exploited people in their own country as well as facilitating further exploitation by the bourgeoisie of the core. Moreover, they embodied the spirit of dependency, helping to subject peripheral countries to the power of the imperialist core.

Emmanuel, on the other hand, attempted to trace the economic processes through which the core exploited the periphery by focusing on the world market. His objective was to prove that 'unequal exchange' took place between core and periphery, causing a surplus flow from the latter to the former.[38] This putative mechanism was essentially an adaptation of Marx's analysis of the equalisation of profit rates across domestic sectors with different organic compositions of capital. As is well known, in the domestic economy, sectors that are labour intensive transfer surplus value to sectors that are capital intensive.

In this spirit, Emmanuel claimed that the world market is characterised by free trade and free movement of capital, while real wage levels differ structurally, and are dramatically lower in peripheral countries. The result is the entry of foreign capital which takes advantage of low wages, selling the output produced at lower prices but still ensuring higher profits than in advanced countries. This form of 'unequal exchange' was for Emmanuel the presumed source of capitalist superprofits. This theory overlooked the qualitative differences between the domestic and the international orders of capitalist accumulation, discussed in the previous chapter. It is deeply problematic to attempt to analyse foreign trade and investment by deploying Marx's schema of domestic profit-rate equalisation.

Amin adopted Emmanuel's theory of 'unequal exchange' and gave it

---

(4): 17–31; A. G. Frank (1978) 'Development of Underdevelopment or Underdevelopment of Development in China', *Modern China* 4 (3): 341–50; A. G. Frank (1998) *ReORIENT: Global Economy in the Asian Stage*, University of California Press: Berkeley, CA; Wallerstein (2004) *World-Systems Analysis*.

37 A. G. Frank (1972) *Lumpenbourgeoisie: Lumpendevelopment. Dependence, Class, and Politics in Latin America*, Monthly Review Press: New York and London.

38 See A. Emmanuel (1972) *Unequal Exchange: A Study in the Imperialism of Trade*, Monthly Review Press: New York. The implications for political activity were obviously dramatic, since the working class of core countries would be a beneficiary, and thus a sharp debate ensued; see A. Emmanuel and C. Bettelheim (1970) 'International Solidarity of Workers: Two Views: The Delusions of Internationalism; Economic Inequality Between Nations and International Solidarity', *Monthly Review* 22 (2): 13–24.

a still broader remit. Amin postulated an asymmetric core–periphery paradigm, in which peripheral accumulation was based on production for export, while core accumulation was 'self-centred' and based on the internal market.[39] They were, presumably, two sides of the same coin in a neo-imperialist and neo-colonialist international structure, in which domination was established without directly controlled investment or political intervention.[40]

Wallerstein, finally, established the theoretical tradition of World-Systems analysis, postulating a world economy that has presumably existed for five centuries and seeking to explain its trajectory.[41] He aimed to show that the dominant capitalist class of the core countries exploited not only the working class but the entire 'world system'. The economics of 'unequal exchange' were not a major concern of Wallerstein, since he focused primarily on the role of the state and monopolies. The backbone of hegemony were monopolistic enterprises patronised by strong states.[42]

Wallerstein eventually proposed a taxonomy of countries within the world system marked by different levels of dependency.[43] According to this perspective, the hegemon of the advanced world system relies on the power of monopolies rather than on direct intervention, while other states take intermediate positions. Instead of the plain core–periphery distinction, Wallerstein put forth the notion of a 'semi-periphery' that is crucial for the reproduction of the hierarchical system because it provides political support for the hegemon. The room for manoeuvre

---

39 S. Amin (1974) *Accumulation on a World Scale: A Critique of the Theory of Underdevelopment*, Monthly Review Press: New York; S. Amin (1974) 'Accumulation and Development: A Theoretical Model', *Review of African Political Economy* 1 (1): 9–26.

40 Amin (1974) *Accumulation on a World Scale*, p. 22.

41 Special reference ought to be made in this connection to Giovanni Arrighi, who drew on Wallerstein's analysis, but even more strongly on the monumental historical work of Fernand Braudel, to produce a theory of financialisation as the 'autumn' of the hegemon in the world economy. As was already mentioned, Arrighi considered this 'autumn' the interregnum during which a new hegemonic power emerges. See F. Braudel (1982) *Civilization and Capitalism, 15th–18th Century*, 1st US edition, 3 vols, Harper & Row: New York; Arrighi (1994) *The Long Twentieth Century*; and G. Arrighi (2007) *Adam Smith in Beijing: Lineages of the Twenty-First Century*, Verso: London.

42 Wallerstein (2004) *World-Systems Analysis*, p. 28.

43 I. Wallerstein (2002) [1979] *The Capitalist World-Economy: Essays*, repr., transferred to digital print, Studies in Modern Capitalism, Cambridge University Press: Cambridge, UK.

available to 'semi-peripheral' states could also allow for successful capitalist development to occur.[44] However, overall change in the world system had, apparently, remained limited from the late 1930s until the 1980s.[45]

Characterising contemporary imperialism

Theories of core and periphery, despite generating several penetrating insights and widespread influence, have attracted sustained criticism. Dependency theory, in particular, was criticised by Latin American Marxists for several reasons.[46] For one thing, it is hard to justify the theoretical counterposing of 'dependent' and 'autonomous' countries, since trade is a reciprocal act: the buyer and the seller are mutually dependent on one another. As supporters of Dependency theory recognise, capitalist accumulation in the core is also 'dependent' on the exploitation of the periphery. The capitalist world economy is global, and each national space of capitalist accumulation ought to be analysed as a component part of that unity. Subordination exists and is constantly recreated, but that is not the same as the 'dependency' of some countries on the 'autonomy' of others.

For another, Dependency theorists struggled to provide a theoretically and empirically coherent explanation of the economic mechanisms through which resources are drained from the periphery. Perhaps the

44 C. Chase-Dunn (1988) 'Comparing World-Systems: Toward a Theory of Semiperipheral Development', *Comparative Civilisations Review* 19 (19): 29–66.

45 G. Arrighi and J. Drangel (1986) 'The Stratification of the World-Economy: An Exploration of the Semiperipheral Zone', *Review (Fernand Braudel Center)* 10 (1): 9–74; G. Arrighi (2002) 'Global Capitalism and the Persistence of the North-South Divide', *Science & Society* 65 (4): 469–76.

46 See, for instance, F. Lastra (2014) '¿Superexplotación o venta de la fuerza de trabajo por debajo de su valor? Un análisis en relación al caso argentino', *Razón y Revolución* 27: 43–58 ; F. Lastra (2018) 'La teoría marxista de la dependencia y el planteo de la unidad mundial. Contribución a un debate en construcción', *Cuadernos de Economía Crítica* 4 (8): 129–151 ; J. I. Carrera (2008) 'La unidad mundial de la acumulación de capital en su forma nacional históricamente dominante en América Latina. Crítica de las teorías del desarrollo, de la dependencia y del imperialismo', Sociedad Latinoamericana de Economía Política y Pensamiento Crítico (SEPLA); J. I. Carrera (2018) 'Precios, productividad y renta de la tierra agraria: Ni 'términos de intercambio deteriorados', ni "intercambio desigual"', *Realidad Económica* 47 (317): 41–78.

most popular accounts were 'unequal exchange' and the 'super-exploita-tion of the labour power', but neither is theoretically persuasive.[47] Latin American Marxists stressed that, in practice, substantial inward flows of value took place in Latin America in the form of ground rent through the export of agricultural commodities as well as through foreign debt, both of which subsequently led to further outflows.

Dependency theories were also challenged by the rise of powerful centres of industrial accumulation in what used to be considered periph-eral regions or countries, such as Taiwan and South Korea, in the 1970s and after. Equally significant was the sharp turn in the balance of power against labour within core countries, resulting in intensified inequality and precariousness of employment. The retreat of labour in core coun-tries followed the internationalisation of productive capital that strengthened the bargaining power of corporate enterprises. Finally, the financialisation of the world economy during the last four decades has posed evident analytical problems for Dependency theory, at the very least in terms of the structure of core economies.[48]

For a time, interest in theories of imperialism and dependency declined precipitously in core countries, and even the terms fell out of favour. The 1990s, in particular, were a decade of obsessive concern with the notion of globalisation that would, presumably, eliminate old divi-sions, making the nation state obsolescent. US State Department offi-cials declared the *end of history* conjointly with left-wing intellectuals who envisaged an all-encompassing empire confronted by spontaneous and multivalent multitudes.[49] The cacophony of globalisation silenced

---

47 For a devastating Marxist critique of the economics of 'unequal exchange', see K. Bharadwaj (1984) 'A Note on Emmanuel's "Unusual Exchange" ', *Economic and Political Weekly* 19 (30): PE81–PE87. Nonetheless, the lure of this problematic idea remains powerful, since it appears to offer a 'hard' economic explanation for the surplus transfers from the dominated periphery to the dominant core. It lies, for instance, at the core of Smith's argument that 'super-exploitation' is the characteristic feature of contemporary imperialism; see J. C. Smith (2016) *Imperialism in the Twenty-First Century: Globalization, Super-Exploitation, and Capitalism's Final Crisis*, Monthly Review Press: New York. For a more recent example, see G. Carchedi and M. Roberts (2021) 'The Economics of Modern Imperialism', *Historical Materialism* 29 (4): 23–69.

48 Attempts have recently been made to update dependency theories to account for the financialisation of the periphery. See N. Reis and F. A. de Oliveira (2021) 'Peripheral Financialization and the Transformation of Dependency: A View from Latin America', *Review of International Political Economy* 30 (2): 511–34. It is more instructive, however, to adopt the financial subordination approach summed up in chapter 13.

49 F. Fukuyama (1989) 'The End of History?', *The National Interest* 16: 3–18. A

realist voices arguing that state antagonisms would continue to evolve along the same lines as before, not to mention historical sociologists who insisted wryly that what had crashed in 1989–92 was liberalism and not socialism.[50] Thirty years later, it is certain that hegemony has not disappeared, and imperialism remains rampant, as more recent Marxist work has claimed.[51]

The nature of contemporary imperialism and hegemony after decades of neoliberalism nonetheless calls for closer investigation. Classical Marxist theory remains a reliable guide, and there are valid insights from the theories summed up in the preceding sections. The crucial point is that core and periphery today refer to countries that are capitalist and fully integrated into the global division of labour. The ruling blocs of peripheral countries are not only component parts of the global circuits of capital but also capable of generating surpluses for themselves through international transactions.

This is not to deny the existence of subordination, which frequently takes forms such as an unbearable debt burden, dependence on foreign financial institutions, supplying cheap labour power to global production chains dominated by multinationals, and lacking sovereignty in implementing fiscal and monetary policy. Imperialism continues to involve appropriation of resources from the periphery by the core through the power of non-financial enterprises conjoined with financial capital and backed by states. But in a fully capitalist world, the

---

prime example on the left is M. Hardt and A. Negri (2000) *Empire*, Harvard University Press: Cambridge, MA, which proved an enormous publishing success despite its lack of clarity on exactly what 'Empire' is. See also M. Hardt and A. Negri (2004) *Multitude: War and Democracy in the Age of Empire*, Penguin Books: Harmondsworth.

50 For instance, Mearsheimer (2001) *The Tragedy of Great Power Politics*; see I. Wallerstein (1992) 'The Collapse of Liberalism', *The Socialist Register* 28: 96–110.

51 David Harvey, for one, claiming that contemporary imperialism facilitates 'accumulation by dispossession' – that is, the direct expropriation of resources and value from peripheral parts of the world economy; see D. Harvey (2003) *The New Imperialism*, Verso: London. Also notable is the work of Utsa Patnaik and Prabhat Patnaik, who have essentially revived Rosa Luxemburg's theory of imperialism in conjunction with Keynes's theory of 'forced saving' and inflation, discussed in chapter 6 of this book. Summarily put, 'tropical' countries produce agricultural goods that are essential to core countries but have a sharply rising supply curve and could thus spur inflation. Control over the flows of such goods from periphery to core is a defining feature of imperialism; see U. Patnaik and P. Patnaik (2017) *A Theory of Imperialism*, Columbia University Press: New York; see also U. Patnaik and P. Patnaik (2021) *Capital and Imperialism*, Monthly Review Press: New York.

relationship of domestic ruling elites to the hegemonic power is complex and contradictory.

Contemporary imperialism is rooted in the pairing of international-ised productive capital, operating under the auspices of giant multinational enterprises, with global financial capital led by giant commercial and shadow banks. US hegemony in its second phase is inseparable from the globalising thrust of these aggressive types of capital. Cross-border flows of productive, commodity, and loanable capital are integral to imperial power, while resting critically on the role of the dollar as world money. The strategic use of the dollar by the US ruling bloc during the last three decades is indisputable.

The following chapters consider more closely the internationalisation of productive capital and the characteristics of loanable capital flows, especially since the start of the new millennium. Varied and complex issues arise in relation to the unfolding hegemonic contest between the USA and rising powers but also regarding the construction of an alternative to capitalism.

12

The Internationalisation of Productive Capital

Global and fragile production networks

Production for the contemporary world market tends to be fragmented into relatively small tasks that are coordinated and integrated globally through international networks dominated by multinational enterprises. Commercial transactions occurring within and among the networks of global production determine the bulk of international trade.[1] The Pandemic Crisis underscored the extent to which the global division of labour hinges on these networks.

The centrality of production networks to the world economy, and the fragility thereby entailed, became apparent in the so-called 'great trade collapse' during the 2007–09 crisis.[2] A nearly synchronised contraction in international trade took place, with major consequences for individual countries, the collapse of trade being particularly evident in the markets for investment and intermediate goods. Similar phenomena were also observed during the slowdown of international trade in the 2010s.[3]

---

1 Seventy per cent of international trade involves exchanges of raw materials, intermediate goods, services for business and capital goods; see OECD (2020) 'COVID-19 and Global Value Chains: Policy Options to Build More Resilient Production Networks', *OECD Policy Responses to Coronavirus (COVID-19)*, 3 June.

2 M. Ferrantino and D. Taglioni (2014) 'Global Value Chains in the Current Slowdown', VoxEU, CEPR, 6 April, at cepr.org/voxeu.

3 Since the 2010s there has been some decline in fragmentation of production across borders, and thus in international trade; see OECD (2020) 'COVID-19 and Global Value Chains'. Dani Rodrik, writing before the pandemic, pointed to the lessening

Commodities that involved relatively complex production processes proved more sensitive to global downturns than simpler commodities.

The turmoil of the 2020s further highlighted the interdependence and fragility of national economies due to global production networks.[4] More specifically, the critical importance of China in manufacturing and trade across the world economy through such networks became palpably obvious. In early 2020, the spectre of profound instability arose as the outbreak of Covid-19 led to lockdowns in China disrupting the supply of vital manufactured commodities worldwide.[5] Since global production networks rely on regular, stable, and timely logistics, as soon as restrictions and lockdowns interrupted transport, suppliers were forced to close or limit production.[6] The impact of the shock was magnified by the concurrent collapse of demand and further exacerbated by losses in employment and income as well as by the heavy blow of the restrictions on services.

The economic impact of Covid-19, nonetheless, varied across countries and sectors depending on the degree of fragmentation of production, the position of individual enterprises in global production chains, the intensity of physical human contact in the production process, and the extent of introduction of digital technologies that could replace physical interactions.[7] The severity of quarantine measures imposed by governments domestically and at international borders was also critically important.

Still, there is no doubt that the pandemic shock was felt more strongly

of the fragmentation of production, arguing that the trend – including for trade and global demand – did not seem transitory, except in Asia; see Dani Rodrik (2018) 'New Technologies, Global Value Chains, and Developing Economies', NBER Working Paper No. 25164.

4 OECD (2018) 'Multinational Enterprises in the Global Economy: Heavily Debated but Hardly Measured', OECD Policy Note, May 2018.

5 See, for instance, OECD (2020) 'COVID-19 and Global Value Chains'; X. Fu (2020) 'Digital Transformation of Global Value Chains and Sustainable Post-Pandemic Recovery', *Transnational Corporations Journal* 27 (2): 157–66.

6 International flows of goods and services dropped by 5.6 per cent after the pandemic broke out in 2020, but in the second half of the year they rebounded; see UNCTAD (2021) *Trade and Development Report*, UNCTAD: Geneva. Although it is difficult to measure it accurately, the trade collapse during the Covid-19 crisis could be larger than the collapse during the Great Crisis due to supply chain disruptions; see R. Baldwin (2020) 'The Greater Trade Collapse of 2020: Learnings from the 2008–09 Great Trade Collapse', VoxEU, CEPR, 7 April at cepr.org/voxeu.

7 See Fu (2020) 'Digital Transformation of Global Value Chains'.

by contact-intensive services than manufacturing. Financial services and some parts of retail trade were less severely affected, since they could be moved online. Peripheral countries took a harsher blow because labour-intensive manufacturing and contact-intensive services are typically prominent in their economies, often constituting large parts of the informal sector. It is also relevant that the disruption of global networks persisted even after the worst of the health emergency had passed.[8] Production networks did not return to their previous state in 2021, despite the mild recovery following the boost to aggregate demand by core countries. The war in Ukraine in 2022 also disrupted global production once severe sanctions were imposed on Russia by the USA and its allies.

The disruption of production networks in the 2020s had deep and profoundly asymmetric effects on core and peripheral countries, as was discussed in part II. It exacerbated the weakness of aggregate supply but also cast light on relations of hierarchy in the world economy and the subordinate position of peripheral countries in the global division of labour. Specifying the character of contemporary imperialism calls for closer examination of the networks of internationalised production.

The internationalisation of productive capital

From the perspective of Marxist political economy, the functioning of global production networks could be elucidated by reference to the well-known formulation of the circuit of industrial capital. The capital of an enterprise takes three forms – money (i.e. money invested, M, and money revenue from the sale of output, M'), commodity (i.e. means of production and workers hired, C, and final output for sale, C'), and

---

8 The debate regarding the possible directions and the (re)organisation of global production chains/networks to enhance their resilience is not an issue for this chapter. See, for instance, Sébastien Miroudot (2020) 'Reshaping the Policy Debate on the Implications of COVID-19 for Global Supply Chains', *Journal of International Business Policy* 3: 430–42; Marc Bacchetta et al. (2021) 'COVID-19 and Global Value Chains: A Discussion of Arguments on Value Chain Organization and the Role of the WTO', Economic Research and Statistics Division Staff Working Papers No. 20213; James X. Zhan (2021) 'GVC Transformation and a New Investment Landscape in the 2020s: Driving Forces, Directions, and a Forward-Looking Research and Policy Agenda', *Journal of International Business Policy* 4: 206–20.

productive (i.e. productive capacity in place, P, which includes labour power):[9]

$$M - C \ldots P \ldots C' - M'$$

The three forms follow each other sequentially in circuit time but coexist in real time as money holdings, inventory stocks of inputs and output, and productive capacity (including labour power), as is apparent from even a cursory glance at the accounts of an industrial enterprise, whose assets would typically include money, inventories, and plant and equipment.[10]

The crucial point for our purposes is that productive capital has far more rigid social requirements than the other two, including ready availability of appropriate wage labour, regular access to raw materials through a range of markets, a sustained supply of energy, access to pertinent technologies of production, and a stable market for the disposal of final output. Meeting these requirements systematically in the domestic economy involves profound social transformations as well as the active intervention of the state in whose jurisdiction the productive capacity is established.

The money and commodity forms of industrial capital, on the other hand, are more fluid and fungible. Their requirements are far less demanding, comprising mostly a legal framework that could be promptly enforced, as well as several well-established social conventions of transacting in commodities and money lending, including, above all, conventions relating to paying for purchases and settling credit obligations.

Indeed, the money and commodity forms could potentially emerge as independent capitalist activities even if production was not organised

---

9 For perhaps the clearest presentation of the fundamental forms of capital in its circuit, when it is treated as a circular flow of value, see B. Fine (1975) *Marx's Capital*, Macmillan Education: Houndmills.

10 Since the circular motion of industrial capital is in principle continuous, each form could also be taken as defining a distinct circuit, namely the circuit of money capital, the circuit of commodity capital, and the circuit of productive capital. In part, these are simply conventional elaborations of the overall circular motion of capital reflecting an arbitrary starting point – money, commodity, or productive capacity. But it is apparent that each distinct circuit also reflects important dimensions of industrial capitalism. The circuit of money capital is the general form of the industrial circuit when the capitalist mode of production dominates the economy.

along capitalist lines. Complex forms of banking and merchanting have existed for centuries and arguably since deep antiquity precisely because their social prerequisites are less demanding. If a significant part of the social output was directed to market, particularly over long distances, a realm of money-based transactions would emerge that could potentially allow the two forms of capital to take root and seek profits, irrespective of how production was organised. In contrast, the form of productive capital is properly established only when industrial capital begins to dominate the domestic economy, a slow and complex process, as was discussed in chapters 9 and 10.

Moreover, and even more pertinent for our purposes, the money and commodity forms continue to provide scope for independent capitalist profit making even after the full establishment of the capitalist mode of production. Fluidity and fungibility as well as fewer social prerequisites are the bedrock of the proliferation of merchant capital and various types of financial enterprises in advanced capitalism. For Marx, once the capitalist mode of production was properly established, the distinctive circuits of the types of capital that avoid entering production derived from the functional forms taken by industrial capital in the sphere of circulation.[11] They were subordinated to the circuit of industrial capital, which was rooted in production and dictated social reproduction.

This conclusion by Marx remains pivotal to the analysis of mature capitalism. However, the classical Marxist theory of imperialism – and the contemporary analysis of financialisation, summed up in the preceding chapters of this book – foregrounded significant changes in the development of capitalism since the time when Marx produced his theoretical work. In particular, the links between the circuits of industrial and financial enterprises were closely analysed by classical Marxists, for whom bank capital was even capable of dominating industrial capital, thus creating the novel form of 'finance capital'. For contemporary industrial enterprises, the circuits of productive capital are still the decisive part of their operations, but the conditions of production are profoundly altered.

To be more specific, and as was previously stated, capital in all its

---

11 Marx made this point frequently throughout his writings, but perhaps nowhere more clearly than in Volume 2 of *Capital*; see K. Marx (1978) [1885] *Capital*, vol. 2, Penguin Classics: London, pt. 1, ch. 1.

forms is inherently international in its outlook. However, for productive capital, given its social prerequisites, there are formidable difficulties in transcending borders and internationalising its activities, even when it dominates the domestic economy. It is one thing for an industrial enterprise to sell commodities abroad, or even to borrow and lend across borders, and quite another to set up productive capacity in another country or to integrate domestic with foreign productive circuits of capital. Analogously, it is one thing for a financial intermediary to lend to borrowers abroad, or for a merchant to sell commodities in the world market, and quite another for an industrial enterprise to produce across borders.

The feasibility of internationalising productive capital depends, first, on the technical characteristics of the production process, including its physical and technological aspects, in conjunction with the types of the means of transport. It also depends on the availability of appropriate labour power abroad as well as the proximity of the markets for the final output. While some forms of capitalist production – for instance, mining – have successfully crossed borders since the early days of capitalism, the core of manufacturing started to become significantly internationalised only as capitalism matured in the twentieth century.[12]

Beyond the technical features of production, the internationalisation of productive capital also depends on the forms of organisation of production, including, above all, the coordination of what is fundamentally a process of cooperative labour. Marx called this type of coordination the 'labour of superintendence' undertaken by the capitalist.[13] The forms taken by 'superintendence' are closely related to property rights over the means of production and the final output, as well as to the specific features of wage labour. This point matters greatly for analysing contemporary internationalised production and comparing with past periods.

The labour of superintendence has varied considerably throughout the history of capitalism. The earliest forms of capitalist production, for instance, occurred through the 'putting out' system, particularly in

12 The slow pace of the internationalisation of productive capital has long been appreciated in Marxist political economy; see, for instance, B. Fine and L. Harris (1979) *Rereading Capital*, Macmillan: London, pt. 2.

13 See K. Marx (1976) [1867] *Capital*, vol. 1, Penguin Classics: London, ch. 13.

textiles, whereby a merchant would coordinate production by providing raw materials to formally independent artisans. In effect, the merchant would operate an elementary system of subcontracting or outsourcing of the component parts of textile production.[14] A complex articulated productive circuit would be created in which the aggregate productive capital would be broken into several components independently owned by the artisan operators but coordinated by the merchant-capitalist. Production would normally be localised, drawing heavily on the institutional mechanisms of domestic power for social and political stability.

In sharp contrast, as capitalist relations came to dominate the domestic economy in the nineteenth century, production tended to occur in factories directly owned and controlled by capitalists, and the labour of superintendence changed drastically. The prime example was Britain, and the transformation went together with new technologies of production, as in textiles and metal working. Factory production depended critically on abundant supplies of energy through coal, which was also produced capitalistically in deep mines.[15] The transformation further relied on the homogenisation of the domestic economy through the actions of the state. Needless to say, factory production also characterised the twentieth century in the sectors of chemicals, steel, and food, followed by automobiles, electrical appliances, and other household goods, all produced in giant industrial complexes.

The internationalisation of productive capital in the nineteenth and early twentieth centuries occurred only in a few sectors, and typically in extractive activities, including metal mining and oil.[16] It is important to note in this connection that the bulk of the international flows of productive capital during the period of classical imperialism were

14 The putting-out system was discussed extensively by Marx, ibid., pp. 943–1084. Historians have long known that 'cottage industries' were critical to the emergence of capitalism. Indeed, the putting-out system is a persistent form of organisation of textile capitalism even in contemporary capitalism; see, for instance, A. Littlefield and L. T. Reynolds (1990) 'The Putting-Out System: Transitional Form or Recurrent Feature of Capitalist Production?' *The Social Science Journal* 27 (4): 359–72.

15 These points are well understood in institutional economics; see, for instance, A. Leijonhufvud (1986) 'Capitalism and the Factory System', in R. N. Langlois (ed.) *Economics as a Process: Essays in the New Institutional Economics*, Cambridge University Press: New York, pp. 203–23.

16 G. Jones (2004) *Multinationals and Global Capitalism: From the Nineteenth to the Twenty First Century*, Oxford University Press: Oxford, ch. 9.

primarily from core to periphery.[17] Extractive industries afford immediate scope for internationalisation, since the source of the output is often located abroad; manufacturing activities, however, such as textiles, food, steel, and chemicals, are far more demanding. If such productive capital is to become genuinely international, competitive advantages must exist abroad, including command over a disciplined and cheap labour force as well as a secure legal and institutional framework for investment and profit taking. There is nothing automatic about the emergence of such favourable conditions for productive capital.

Capitalist production began to assume a stronger international form in manufacturing only after the Second World War, dominated mainly by multinational corporations originating in the USA. By the 1960s, US-based and other multinational corporations had already started to coordinate manufacturing production through affiliates across the world. Much of the expansion of internationalised manufacturing occurred among core countries, with the flows of capital taking place primarily from the USA to Europe.[18] The internationalisation of production during that period led to early forms of international production networks, as can be seen, for instance, in the emergence of North American production chains in automobile production in the 1960s.

More important for our purposes, however, are the developments that have occurred primarily in the past couple of decades. During this period, which also witnessed the expansion of financialisation globally, the world economy was permeated by worldwide production networks or, as they are widely referred to in the literature, 'global value chains' or 'global production networks'.[19] US

---

17 The quality of the data is not high, but historical work broadly corroborates this point; see E. Graham (1995) 'Foreign Direct Investment in the World Economy', IMF Working Papers No. 059.

18 G. Jones (2004) *Multinationals and Global Capitalism*, chs 2 and 4.

19 The transformation of production processes and the associated trade linkages have attracted attention from various disciplines in the past couple of decades. There is a vast theoretical and empirical literature on 'global value chains' and on 'global production networks' (and earlier, on 'global commodity chains'), much of which is not directly relevant to our purposes. Throughout this chapter, references will be made as necessary. It should be noted that despite the differences between the initial studies, the underlying approaches have converged over the last decade. For the pioneering work on global value chains, see G. Gereffi (1994) 'The Organization of Buyer-Driven Global Commodity Chains: How U.S. Retailers Shape Overseas Production Networks', in G. Gereffi and M. Korzeniewicz (eds) *Commodity Chains and Global Capitalism*, Praeger: Westport, pp. 95–122; G. Gereffi and M. Korzeniewicz

multinational corporations have played a leading role in this transformation.

The shift in the strategies of US corporations was spurred by intensified price competition and slowly rising product prices domestically, thus encouraging manufacturing giants to focus on lowering costs.[20] Multinationals began to construct global production networks by connecting suppliers through contractual means, steadily reducing their reliance on vertically organised structures comprising parent enterprises with domestic and foreign affiliates.[21] As production became increasingly fragmented and relocated across borders, the coordination of complex production processes gradually moved away from direct property rights toward other methods discussed in the following section. Multinational enterprises remained paramount to the proliferating networks, impacting heavily on relations of hierarchy and power across the world economy.

Multinational corporations and global production networks

The motivations for industrial capital to expand productive capacity beyond national borders are many and varied, including lowering wage and other production costs, reaching remote markets, obtaining

(eds) (1994) *Commodity Chains and Global Capitalism*; G. Gereffi (1999) 'International Trade and Industrial Upgrading in the Apparel Commodity Chain', *Journal of International Economics* 48 (1): 37–70. On global production networks, see J. Henderson et al. (2002) 'Global Production Networks and the Analysis of Economic Development', *Review of International Political Economy* 9 (3): 436–64; N. M. Coe and H. W. Yeung (2015) *Global Production Networks: Theorizing Economic Development in an Interconnected World*, Oxford University Press: Oxford. For a general account of the literature and discussion, see Coe and Yeung (2015) *Global Production Networks*, ch. 1; Gary Gereffi (2018) *Global Value Chains and Development: Redefining the Contours of 21st Century Capitalism*, Cambridge University Press: Cambridge, UK, ch. 1; N. M. Coe and H. W. Yeung (2019) 'Global Production Networks: Mapping Recent Conceptual Developments', *Journal of Economic Geography* 19 (4): 775–80.

20 W. Milberg (2008) 'Shifting Sources and Uses of Profits: Sustaining US Financialization with Global Value Chains', *Economy and Society* 37 (3): 420–51; W. Milberg and D. Winkler (2010) 'Financialisation and the Dynamics of Offshoring in the USA', *Cambridge Journal of Economics* 34 (2): 275–93.

21 In the 1990s, for instance, US multinationals with a historic global presence, such as Ford, General Motors, and International Business Machines (IBM), discarded entire divisions that previously belonged to internal vertical structures and created separate entities. Increasingly, the multinationals started sourcing the inputs through independent suppliers as well as affiliates around the world.

essential skills and resources, pursuing greater flexibility in production, and reducing risks by diversifying the location of production.[22] The driving force in all instances is the search for higher profits.

However, the obstacles are also formidable, such as coping with differences in legal systems (including property rights), managing customary practices in national labour markets and among local capitalists, and accessing the domestic and international financial system. The largest global corporations, other things equal, are better placed to confront these difficulties.[23] Needless to say, the liberalisation of international trade and finance has been critical to multinationals expanding productive activities abroad.

A multinational enterprise could engage in production across borders in different ways. It could, for instance, undertake direct investment abroad, either by buying existing productive capacity outright, or by creating fresh capacity from scratch. In this case, the property rights would reside with the multinational, and the organisation of production would mainly have a vertical hierarchy comprising affiliates along with some independent suppliers. With reference to the circuit of productive capital, the multinational would be directly augmenting its existing circuit either through productive investment across borders or via the acquisition and integration of the circuit of an already existing enterprise abroad. The circulation of output among the vertically integrated components would appear as international trade, but it would in practice be internal to the structure.

Alternatively, a multinational could engage in 'outsourcing', or manufacturing by contract. Production would also be located 'offshore' through a strategic alliance or a contractual relationship with independent enterprises abroad, but without holding property rights in the productive capacity of the latter. The overall circuit of productive capital would again be enlarged, but not through investment or acquisition. Rather, the original circuit of the multinational would be articulated with the circuits of independent enterprises via contract. In this case

---

22 Milberg and Winkler (2010) 'Financialisation and the Dynamics of Offshoring in the USA'.

23 The *Frontline Report* of the International Trade Union Confederation (ITUC) for 2016 points out that the largest multinationals gravitate toward countries with low labour costs, aiming to construct supply chains; the result is intensive exploitation of the workers in the supplier enterprises, along with tax avoidance by multinationals; see ITUC (2016) *Frontline Report – Scandal: Inside the Global Supply Chains of 50 Top Companies*, ITUC: Brussels.

too, the output of the individual circuits would be formally traded among the allied enterprises, appearing as a part of global commerce, but would in practice be transacted within the network.

Summarily put, a production network combines the circuits of a multinational with those of independent enterprises, or of its own affiliates, and perhaps the combined circuits could even be integrated with that of another multinational. In effect, an articulated and expanded productive circuit is created in which the overall productive capital is fragmented into discrete components that are formally independent and located across several borders. Thus, even if a subcontracted enterprise remained rooted in the national economy, the articulated productive circuit in which it participated would be international. The internationalisation of productive capital would occur without necessarily shifting the production process across borders.

Constructing an articulated circuit evidently requires coordinating production and circulation across several individual circuits. The task typically falls on the multinational enterprise that assumes the role of 'lead firm', setting the terms of productive, commercial, and financial linkages.[24] Even when organisation is primarily based on contracts rather than equity relationships, multinationals engage in vital control and coordination functions, resulting in the establishment of hierarchy and power relations within networks.[25]

A glimpse of the complexity of the task for the lead multinational could be gained by noting that the profitability of each of the smaller productive circuits depends on turnover time, which is in turn the sum of production time and circulation time in buying inputs and selling output: the lower the turnover time, the higher the rate of profit.[26] For

---

24 L. Kano, E. W. K. Tsang, and H. W. Yeung (2020) 'Global Value Chains: A Review of the Multi-Disciplinary Literature', *Journal of International Business Studies* 51: 577–622.

25 The coordination and controlling role exercised by multinationals can have different forms, which are analysed under a number of typologies of governance. For the debate, see, for instance, G. Gereffi, J. Humphrey, and T. Sturgeon (2005) 'The Governance of Global Value Chains', *Review of International Political Economy* 12 (1): 78–104; C. Rikap (2021) *Capitalism, Power and Innovation: Intellectual Monopoly Capitalism Uncovered*, Routledge: London and New York.

26 For analysis of turnover time and other technical aspects of the circuit, see D. Foley (1982) 'Realization and Accumulation in a Marxian Model of the Circuit of Capital', *Journal of Economic Theory* 28: 300–19; see also D. Foley (1986) *Understanding Capital: Marx's Economic Theory*, Harvard University Press: Cambridge, MA.

the network as a whole, consequently, it would be paramount for the lead multinational to articulate several component circuits with the aim of minimising the overall turnover time, thus raising profitability across the network. The inventories of finished output as well as the delivery schedules of participating enterprises would have to be managed to keep turnover times (and inventory costs) to a minimum. It is immediately apparent that the fragility of articulated global networks derives in part from the tendency to minimise overall turnover time.

Lead multinationals act as part producers, part coordinators, and part controllers of networks. They integrate geographically dispersed affiliates, strategic partners, specialised suppliers, and customers into complex structures. They initiate new products and spur the movement of resources and information across networks, depending on the relative advantages of different countries and regions. They also organise the flows of intermediary goods, services, and final products, have an impact on the employment of labour, command the transfer of technology, manage the accrual of profits, and manipulate the payment of tax on a global scale.

Indeed, if lead multinationals are purely commercial enterprises, they need not even take part in production directly but could simply undertake the coordinating role from the standpoint of the seller of output. It would even be possible for multinationals to reduce the volume of their own investment, since a range of production tasks including services would be subcontracted to other enterprises within the chain.

The lead multinational's choice of partners at home and abroad depends on the specific character of production, the preservation of a technological cutting edge, the costs of supervising the production process, the trading and shipping expenses, and the availability of financial mechanisms to sustain the flow of capital within the articulated circuit.[27] As well as taking advantage

27 See, for instance, OECD (2018) 'International Trade and Investment: Two Sides of the Same Coin?' OECD Policy Note, May; OECD (2018) 'Multinational Enterprises in the Global Economy'; C. Fengru and L. Guitang (2019) *Global Value Chains and Production Networks*, Academic Press: London. Foreign direct investment (FDI) can be 'vertical', whereby a multinational enterprise fragments the production process to achieve cost benefits in different countries, or 'horizontal', whereby the multinational replicates the productive process in different countries aiming, for instance, to gain broader market access. The bulk of FDI in peripheral countries tends to be 'horizontal'. Nonetheless, the distinction between horizontal and vertical strategies is not clear across all instances.

of lower wages abroad, multinationals could reduce operating and inventory costs for themselves, while transferring risks and costs onto subcontractors within the network. Outsourcing and offshoring generate cost advantages that could help multinationals focus on their core business.

In this respect, the impact of global networks on the provision of services is particularly important. There is a broad range of services that are integral to the process of production, including product design, telecommunications, and transport of inputs and finished goods as well as complementary services, such as finance, accounting, management of labour, marketing, advertising, and so on.[28] Furthermore, constructing global production networks would be impossible without major advances in the provision of services in, above all, transport and information and communication technologies.

The size and scope of service production in relation to manufacturing have increased and become more visible in recent years.[29] While some service activities are undertaken by manufacturing firms as a part of production, manufacturing-related services are also increasingly provided by independent firms. Moreover, as global production networks have proliferated, the provision of services has fragmented across borders, augmenting the volume of services already produced and hence leading to separate profit-generating capital circuits.[30]

---

28 Keeping some services activities within the multinational, particularly when they are complementary with the core strategic functions of the firm, like research and development or IT, has an economic rationale. See S. Miroudot and C. Cadestin (2017) 'Services in Global Value Chains: Trade Patterns and Gains from Specialisation', OECD Trade Policy Papers No. 208.

29 This transformation is often called the 'servicification' of manufacturing, whereby the manufacturing sector becomes increasingly reliant on obtaining services as inputs to in-house activities within manufacturing enterprises, or as outputs that are bundled together with goods. The latter is also called 'servitisation' in the literature – that is, combining the sale of goods with services such as installation, maintenance, and repair, as well as financial processes. See, for instance, Miroudot and Cadestin (2017) 'Services in Global Value Chains'; S. Miroudot (2019) 'Services and Manufacturing in Global Value Chains: Is the Distinction Obsolete?' Asian Development Bank Institute Working Paper No. 927; National Board of Trade (2016), *Report: The Servicification of EU Manufacturing: Building Competitiveness in the Internal Market*, National Board of Trade Sweden: Stockholm.

30 Services are not only inputs or specific products bundled together with goods, but also the output of particular production chains, and there is also a fragmentation and internationalisation of the production of services; K. D. Backer and S. Miroudot (2013) 'Mapping Global Value Chains', OECD Trade Policy Papers No. 159; Miroudot (2019) 'Services and Manufacturing in Global Value Chains'.

The ostensible growth of the service sector is in large part the outcome of the expansion and fragmentation of manufacturing across borders.[31] The circuits of capital that have thereby emerged lie formally within the service sector but are in practice components of manufacturing and industry. The introduction of digital technologies has delivered an additional boost to the internationalisation of services both in volume and content, as is discussed further below.[32]

Finally, the growth of global production networks has taken place while financialisation has been advancing and portfolio finance has spread to peripheral countries.[33] The coincidence is far from accidental, as the financialisation of giant enterprises is an integral part of the internationalisation of production. Financialisation has, in turn, bolstered the engagement of multinationals in offshore production through global production networks.[34]

Crucially, financialisation has provided several instruments for governing production networks. Lead multinationals deploy financial mechanisms of control by setting the terms of commercial credit, making it easier to obtain liquidity, enabling the use of financial techniques of risk management, and facilitating access to world money. Furthermore, financial techniques are used to create debt obligations that bind independent suppliers to the network. Moreover, transferring parts of the fragmented production process onto independent suppliers has created further scope for returning profits to shareholders through dividend payments and share repurchases.[35] It is highly relevant that

---

31 Miroudot and Cadestin (2017) 'Services in Global Value Chains'.

32 In addition to provision of various novel services, digital technologies drive the 'unbundling' of services, making them more 'tradeable' and thus supporting more complex networks of services; UNCTAD (2019) *Digital Economy Report. Value Creation and Capture: Implications for Developing Countries*, UNCTAD: Geneva.

33 The literature on the financialisation and global production networks/chains relationship is still underdeveloped, however. See Milberg (2008) 'Shifting Sources and Uses of Profits'; Milberg and Winkler (2010) 'Financialisation and the Dynamics of Offshoring in the USA'; Tristan Auvray and Joel Rabinovich (2019) 'The Financialisation: Offshoring Nexus and the Capital Accumulation of US Non-Financial Firms', *Cambridge Journal of Economics* 43 (5): 1183–218.

34 Milberg (2008) 'Shifting Sources and Uses of Profits'.

35 Milberg and Winkler argue that financialisation reduces the 'dynamic gains' from offshoring which could be achieved by reinvesting profits in productive assets that raise productivity, growth, employment, and income; see Milberg and Winkler (2010) 'Financialisation and the Dynamics of Offshoring in the USA'; see also Milberg (2008) 'Shifting Sources and Uses of Profits'.

multinationals can deploy a range of financial skills to transfer profits within the network, such as transfer pricing, charges for intangible assets, and internal debt and interest payments.[36]

The internationalisation of productive capital and the global spread of finance have moved together during the last several decades. Lead multinationals are typically adept at obtaining finance from international financial institutions as well as holding liquid funds in secure financial assets. Internationally producing industrial enterprises and globally active financial institutions are driven by different concerns but exist symbiotically. Neither requires territorial exclusivity, whether through colonies, annexation, or the creation of separate trading blocs, and both take the entire world economy as their natural terrain. The ascendancy of this pair of capitals has relied on US hegemony dictating the legal, institutional, financial, and monetary framework of the world economy with the aim of facilitating profit making, always within a hierarchy of core and peripheral countries.

Integrating into the world economy through production networks

Global production networks have changed the mode of integration of individual countries in the world economy. Particularly for peripheral countries, networks entail far more complex processes of integration than simply producing labour-intensive commodities or receiving capital flows from core countries.[37] The fragmentation of production into

36 T. Torslov, L. Wier, and G. Zuchman (2020) 'The Missing Profits of Nations', NBER Working Paper No. 24701.

37 Although the interconnectedness of production across the world is widely accepted, its empirical representation appears to be more complicated due to various measurement problems and lack of data. Since the 2010s there have been a number of studies, particularly by UNCTAD, OECD and WTO, aiming to create consistent and comprehensive databases; see M. K. Lenzen, et al. (2012) 'Mapping the Structure of World Economy', *Environmental Science and Technology*, 46 (15), 8374–81; Pascal Lamy (2013) 'Global Value Chains, Interdependence, and the Future of Trade', VoxEU, CEPR, 18 December at cepr.org/voxeu; C. Cadestin et al. (2018) 'Multinational Enterprises and Global Value Chains: New Insights on the Trade-Investment Nexus', OECD Science, Technology and Industry Working Papers No. 05, Paris; C. Cadestin et al. (2018) 'Multinational Enterprises and Global Value Chains: The OECD Analytical AMNE Database', OECD Trade Policy Papers No. 211. For a discussion of data issues, see for instance, S. Inomata (2017) 'Analytical Frameworks for Global Value Chains: An

several articulated components characterised by cross-national transfers of tasks has assigned fresh content to the division of labour between
core and periphery in which giant multinational enterprises play a decisive role.[38]

For peripheral countries, participation in global production networks
is often claimed to be a new path toward development and growth.[39]
According to this perception, enterprises in peripheral countries, if they
have sufficient specialisation and productivity, could become competitive in delivering specific tasks within a network without possessing the
capacity to produce the entire final good or service.[40] Therefore, peripheral country enterprises could participate in high-technology production processes even when the technological infrastructure is not very
advanced across the economy. Participating in a global production
network would presumably further upgrade productive capabilities,
thus boosting growth and development, still without needing to master
all the stages of the production process.[41]

Overview', *Global Value Chain Development Report*, WTO: Geneva; Kano, Tsang, and
Yeung (2020) 'Global Value Chains'. In this book, the changing nature of international
production is analysed from a political economy perspective without going into
measurement and data issues.

38 The integration of peripheral countries into the world economy under the new
international settings has been a central issue of concern for multilateral organisations
since the 2010s. See, for instance, the UNCTAD *2013 World Investment Report*, a
document of considerable importance for analysing internationalised production in
peripheral countries. For the earlier approaches to the issue, see OECD (2013)
Interconnected Economies: Benefiting from Global Value Chains, OECD: Paris; UNCTAD
(2013) *World Investment Report: Global Value Chains, Investment and Trade for
Development*, UNCTAD: Geneva.

39. See OECD (2013) *Interconnected Economies: Benefiting from Global Value Chains*;
UNCTAD (2013) *World Investment Report*; Gereffi (1999) 'International Trade and
Industrial Upgrading in the Apparel Commodity Chain'; R. Baldwin (2012) 'Global
Supply Chains: Why They Emerged, Why They Matter, and Where They Are Going',
Centre for Economic Policy Research (CEPR) Discussion Paper No. 9103; Fu (2020)
'Digital Transformation of Global Value Chains'; L. Chen (2021) 'Digital Asia: Facing
Challenges from GVCs Digitalisation, US–China Decoupling, and the COVID-19
Pandemic', Economic Research Institute for ASEAN and East Asia (ERIA) Policy Brief,
No. 05.

40 V. Kummritz, D. Taglioni, and D. Winkler (2017) 'Economic Upgrading through
Global Value Chain Participation: Which Policies Increase the Value Added Gains?',
World Bank Policy Research Working Paper No. 8007; Rodrik (2018) 'New Technologies,
Global Value Chains, and Developing Economies'.

41 World Bank (2020) *World Development Report 2020: Trading for Development in
the Age of Global Value Chains*, World Bank: Washington, DC.

In practice, nothing guarantees such an outcome. Global production networks entail significant power asymmetries, as the control function is typically exercised by multinationals based in core countries.[42] Lead multinationals largely determine the conduct of networks and do not willingly share advantages with others. They deploy complex global strategies to ensure their dominant position, including constant relocation of parts of their production process, together with a variety of financial techniques. Peripheral countries are often treated as vast repositories of cheap labour to undertake mechanical and mundane tasks.

Playing the leading role within a network gives considerable power to shape profit margins across the articulated individual circuits. The lead multinational focuses on tasks that are considered strategic and carry high profit margins, such as product development and design, trans-divisional research, technological development, marketing, distribution, and business intelligence.[43] Activities with a lower value content are left to other participants in the network. Hierarchical structures emerge, and enterprises from peripheral countries find themselves in subordinate positions, trapped in the labour-intensive, low-technology, and generally simpler production tasks of a fragmented production process, often operating with lower rates of profit.[44]

After determining the quality and other standards of the product, lead multinationals could potentially allow contracted enterprises, including those from peripheral countries, to decide how and where to produce. Even critically important functions, such as the design of the final product, could also on occasion be assigned to enterprises from peripheral countries. In all instances, however, lead multinationals seek overall control of the production network and dictate profit rates by, above all, manipulating technology and intellectual property rights. Enterprises from peripheral countries confront major difficulties in

42 Developing countries do not comprise a single bloc, and participation in global production networks have had varying implications for them. In this connection, multinational enterprises from some Asian countries have succeeded in creating their own networks.

43 Gereffi, Humphrey, and Sturgeon (2005) 'The Governance of Global Value Chains'; J. Lee and G. Gereffi (2015) 'Global Value Chains, Rising Power Firms and Economic and Social Upgrading', *Critical Perspectives on International Business* 11 (3/4): 319–39.

44 The implications of new digital technologies for the participation of developing countries in global production networks are considered below.

enhancing technological capabilities and raising the sophistication of their production process.

Nonetheless, the spread of production networks has transformed the way in which individual countries participate in the international division of labour. Initially, the integration of developing countries was driven by the inclusion of local producers into global production networks led by multinationals from the core. As production internationalised, enormous concentrations of capital emerged outside core countries, primarily in East Asia, with considerable capacity to compete in the world market.[45] Locally based multinationals, including in China, have made their presence increasingly felt in the world economy. The shift in the centre of gravity of global capitalist production has occurred in part due to global networks, but it would have been impossible without the active mobilisation of national resources and the continuing and pervasive role of the state.

China is the obvious, and leading, instance of the emergence of independent capitalist production in peripheral countries through the active intervention of the state, as is shown in chapter 14. Its joining the WTO in 2001 was an important event in this regard. At the time, the hegemonic USA treated China as a subordinate entrant into the world economy, a vast pool of cheap wage labour, and a potential market for US output. The misperception was historic. China has emerged as the main contestant for hegemony and faces the entrenched hostility of the USA. The contest will be shaped by the industries that will determine the character of internationalised production in the coming period.

Digital technologies will be crucial in this regard, and US multinationals have increasingly felt the pressure of competition in this field, particularly as Chinese enterprises have moved aggressively in 5G infrastructure and e-commerce, while attempting to catch up in artificial intelligence, big data management, cloud computing, and so on. The Chinese state has actively promoted the development of these technologies, while effectively barring the entry of foreign digital giants into China's domestic market.[46] Similarly, the USA has increasingly taken measures to restrict foreign – mainly Chinese – data-driven companies

45 Gereffi and Fernandez-Stark argue that the primary forces in global production and trade are emerging economies: G. Gereffi and K. Fernandez-Stark (2016) *Global Value Chain Analysis: A Primer*, Duke University, Center on Globalization, Governance and Competitiveness: Durham, NC.

46 Chen (2021) 'Digital Asia'.

from entering its market and to control data outflows.[47] A closer look at digitalisation, even if brief, could thus shed further light on the unfolding internationalisation of productive capital.

The digital transformation of production and power within the networks

The introduction of digital technologies is part and parcel of the intrinsic tendency of capitalist enterprises under competitive pressure to automate production, aiming to increase the rate of profit. Digital tools and digitally operated processes could potentially raise the productivity of labour in a particular sector, thus lowering unit costs. Digital technologies utilise flows of information on a vast scale to enable automated but flexible responses of production in manufacturing, agriculture, and services.

The automation of production is far from a new trend in mature capitalism, but digitalisation has given it entirely new dimensions. For one thing, digitalisation connects production stages via a digital thread allowing activities to be accomplished online or through remote control of the workplace. For another, its implications for production networks and production in general are much broader and deeper than plain automation. Digital technologies, including artificial intelligence, big data analytics, robotics, cloud computing, blockchain technologies, three-dimensional printing, 5G telecommunications, the Internet of Things, and other internet-based services, have significant implications for economies and societies, even if it is difficult to measure their impact accurately.[48]

Digital technologies have become integral to the functioning of the world economy in shipping, transport, retail, distribution, finance, and manufacturing. They have impacted on global production networks by altering the fragmentation and geographical location of tasks, the organisation of production, and the hierarchical relations within

---

47 UNCTAD (2021) *Digital Economy Report: Cross-Border Data Flows and Development: For Whom the Data Flow*, UNCTAD: Geneva.

48 Measurement difficulties stem from defining the content of the digital economy as well as obtaining reliable statistics. For a discussion of some of these issues, see, for instance, UNCTAD (2019) *Digital Economy Report: Value Creation and Capture*.

networks.[49] The articulated circuits of global production networks are bound together and controlled through a digital thread of data collection and analysis, making the geographical anchoring of productive capital even less relevant.

At the same time, there has been a great expansion of the services that could be produced and traded digitally, allowing global production networks to obtain services from enterprises (or individuals) across the world. The digital transformation has further accelerated the production of services associated with manufacturing, thus contributing to the growth of trade in services.[50]

Digitalisation has, thus, created additional scope for enterprises from peripheral countries to participate in global production networks without needing to undertake the entire production process. It has further spurred the outsourcing and offshoring of a range of services, lowering the barriers to entry for enterprises (and even for individuals) in the periphery.

However, for digital technologies to work, it is imperative to obtain massive amounts of data across all spheres of life – economic and social. Accessing data and transforming it into digital intelligence is increasingly essential to the competitiveness of enterprises, allowing them to target demand, coordinate activities, and tailor production to markets.[51] In this connection, the emergence of 'digital platforms' has been of critical importance.

Digital data largely arises from the footprint of personal, social, and corporate activities occurring on digital platforms that provide infrastructure and intermediation functions. Digital platforms monitor and collect huge amounts of such data, which they subsequently commercialise, thus accruing profits as well as political and social power. In instances in which local knowledge might create an advantage, locally rooted digital platforms emerge, offering services tailored to local users. Most of the time, however, the dominance of global digital platforms

---

49 Despite an expanding literature on global value chains and global production networks, the theoretical analysis of the impact of digital transformation on global production chains/networks is less well-established; see, for instance, C. Foster and M. Graham (2017) 'Reconsidering the Role of Digital in Global Production Networks', *Global Networks* 17 (1): 68–88.

50 Rodrik (2018) 'New Technologies, Global Value Chains, and Developing Economies'.

51 UNCTAD (2019) *Digital Economy Report: Value Creation and Capture*; UNCTAD (2021) *Digital Economy Report: Cross-Border Data Flows and Development*.

and the control over data by a few large enterprises tend to intensify divergences among countries.[52]

Lead multinationals are in command of digital tools and engage in data collection and analysis that helps them coordinate production networks. Moreover, participating in digitalised production networks necessitates specific skills and adequate digital infrastructure. For peripheral countries that are not able to obtain the required technologies, digitalisation results in divergence from the core.[53] Control of technology resides with multinational enterprises originating in core countries, and most peripheral countries are remote from innovation centres.[54]

Digitalisation has also altered the labour process drastically, including the required skills of workers. Digitalised production generally calls for fewer workers and is less contact intensive, even making the physical presence of the worker at the place of employment redundant.[55] It could also potentially change the composition of employment, since it impacts most heavily on work involving routine cognitive tasks, for instance accounting, administration, and office employment, but also on manual work in agriculture, construction, operating machinery and plant, and elsewhere.

One likely result is the decline in employment of relatively unskilled labour in manufacturing, and perhaps in some services.[56] The impact of

52 UNCTAD (2021) *Digital Economy Report: Cross-Border Data Flows and Development*; Rikap (2021) *Capitalism, Power and Innovation*.

53 Fu (2020) 'Digital Transformation of Global Value Chains'.

54 It should be underlined that the economic geography of digital transformation does not point to a typical divide between core and periphery. In terms of capacity to engage in and benefit from the data-driven digital economy, two countries are prominent: the USA and China. Together they command the spreading of call centres, the extent of adaptation to 5G, the funding of artificial intelligence start-ups, the proliferation of researchers into artificial intelligence, the production of patents into blockchain technology, and almost 90 per cent of the market capitalisation of the largest digital platforms. See UNCTAD (2019) *Digital Economy Report: Value Creation and Capture*; UNCTAD (2021) *Digital Economy Report: Cross-Border Data Flows and Development*.

55 See C. B. Frey and M. Osborne (2015) *Technology at Work: The Future of Innovation and Employment*, Citi GPS: Global Perspectives & Solutions. See also C. Degryse (2016) 'Digitalisation of the Economy and Its Impact on Labour Markets', European Trade Union Institute (ETUI) Working Papers, No. 2016.02.

56 Rodrik (2018) 'New Technologies, Global Value Chains, and Developing Economies'. Increased used of digital technologies could lead to significant job losses as labour is replaced by automation and artificial intelligence. See, for instance, UNCTAD

digitalisation on the productivity of labour, on the other hand, depends on the nature of the productive task and would vary across industrial and service sectors.[57]

The concentration of investment and labour skills required to pursue the technological advance of digitalisation has facilitated the meteoric rise of a handful of enterprises, so-called 'Big Tech', that dominate the sector and lead the transformation process. Big Tech primarily includes giant US-based multinationals – for instance, Alphabet (Google), Apple, Amazon, Meta (Facebook), and Microsoft – and their Chinese counterparts – such as Alibaba and Tencent. They operate in a range of digital fields, each striving for dominance in its core area of business.[58]

Differences aside, Big Tech enterprises form the 'infrastructural core' of the digital transformation that is currently under way, thereby controlling and restricting access to digitalisation.[59] These enterprises have risen to an extraordinarily powerful position, colonising the professional, personal, and even public spheres of contemporary capitalism during the last couple of decades.[60] They possess enormous technological, financial, and market power, and control flows of information and communication in economic and social domains on a global scale.

The giants dominate the process of digitalisation, with thousands of digital platforms revolving around them. Digital platforms created by, or based on, Big Tech generate a vast range of digital interactions, providing transport and holiday services, making payments, offering entertainment, delivering education, and so on. These services have negligible direct costs for users but allow providers to collect huge amounts of data. The data is subsequently analysed and parcelled into lots, thereby becoming a peculiar commodity, sold to advertisers, banks,

---

(2019) *Digital Economy Report: Value Creation and Capture*.

57 Rodrik (2018) 'New Technologies, Global Value Chains, and Developing Economies'.

58 Amazon, Alibaba, Facebook, and Tencent were not even among the top 100 companies in 2009. To consolidate their competitive positions, Big Tech companies have been taking steps including acquiring competitors, or potential competitors, as well as expanding into complementary products and services; see, for instance, UNCTAD (2019) *Digital Economy Report: Value Creation and Capture*.

59 J. Dijck, T. Poell, and M. Waal (2018) *The Platform Society: Public Values in a Connective World*, Oxford University Press: Oxford, p. 12.

60 Hendrikse et al. call this tendency of Big Tech to dominate almost every aspect of socio-technical domain the 'big techification of everything'. See R. Hendrikse et al. (2022) 'The Big Techification of Everything', *Science as Culture* 31 (1): 59–71.

and other enterprises. Profits aside, the collection and processing of data affords enormous power with direct implications for political processes.

The potential for social surveillance but also for control of labour in the workplace offered by big data is without historical precedent, and Big Tech enterprises were among the first to demonstrate that potential on their own labour force. They monitor the speed and capabilities of workers in the physical workplace or even through remote working, and use electronic communication remorselessly to intensify labour. Digital technology developed and mobilised by Big Tech poses a direct threat to the rights of workers and their ability to organise. It is common for workers' representatives to be excluded from the decision-making process of implementing digital tools. In platforms it is particularly difficult to attain effective forms of workers' organisation, given the supposedly transitory, fragmented, and often isolated nature of the activities.

The result of the expansion of platforms around Big Tech has been the rapid growth of highly precarious employment, characteristic of digitalisation in general, which is typically called the 'gig economy'. This is short-hand for the spread of service activities relying on digital technology to mobilise workers on the basis of extraordinarily flexible, insecure, and variable employment. Platform jobs can be very diverse, including routine and non-routine activities and involving simple as well as complex labour.

All platform jobs, however, tend to reduce workers' bargaining power compared with more conventional jobs of a similar type. Platforms transfer much of the risk of market fluctuations onto workers through extraordinarily flexible terms of employment. The result is the intensification of exploitation and precariousness of work.

At the same time, Big Tech enterprises exemplify the financialisation trend of multinational corporations.[61] They use their extraordinary profits to invest in financial assets, deploy financial techniques to control production networks, and mobilise enormous accumulations of liquidity to consolidate their monopoly power. The Great Crisis of 2007–09 accelerated the trend toward consolidation in the digital field, and the Big Tech enterprises uncompromisingly expanded their acquisitions by targeting

---

61 Despite the differences, Big Tech enterprises deploy several common methods and strategies for financial and other procedures. This commonality is known as the 'Big Tech model'. See R. Fernandez et al. (2020) *Engineering Digital Monopolies: The Financialisation of Big Tech*, Stichting Onderzoek Multinationale Ondernemingen (SOMO): Amsterdam.

potential rivals and enterprises in complementary areas, even in completely unrelated ventures.[62]

In sum, digitalisation has further enhanced the power of the huge multinationals that direct internationalised production, offering additional levers to control global production networks. It has also led to the emergence of gigantic monopolistic enterprises with a global presence that dominate the sector. Its rapid growth casts a sharp light on the aggressive internationalised productive capital lying at the roots of contemporary imperialism. But contemporary imperialism is also inextricably linked to finance. The next chapter turns to these financial underpinnings by examining global capital flows and their transformation during the last four decades.

---

62 For instance, Google's investments in self-driving cars, or the consumer Internet of Things, to extract data.

13

Finance and Contemporary Imperialism

Global capital flows

Financial capital is intrinsically international, as indeed are all forms of capital, and it has historically operated across borders long before industrial capital. It would be a mistake, therefore, to consider international capital flows, and the associated relations of exploitation and power, solely in terms of core and periphery. For several decades, cross-border capital flows have taken place primarily among core countries, even if, in recent years, a growing proportion were directed from core to periphery – and a significant part from periphery to periphery. The financial underpinnings of contemporary imperialism ought to be considered in this light.

In the period of classical imperialism, financial profits would often be channelled directly from peripheral countries to the core. After the Second World War, however, the absence of colonial relations meant that the transfer of monetary value and the projection of hegemonic power through finance took masked forms. International capital flows have played a complex role in this respect, particularly since the collapse of the Bretton Woods system in the 1970s.

Three main types of capital flows are important for the analysis in this chapter, namely FDI, portfolio, and banking flows; portfolio flows further consist of equity and debt flows. The three basic types differ with respect to leading agents, purpose, and risk profile. Moreover, the scope of each flow has been subject to significant changes over time.[1]

To give a little more detail, FDI comprises substantial and long-term investments by a financial capitalist, or an enterprise, that take place in an existing enterprise, or *ab ovo*, in a different country. Portfolio flows, on the other hand, are purchases of private and public financial assets by foreign buyers. If the assets were shares in an enterprise, the difference between a portfolio purchase and FDI would simply be that the former did not reach the legal threshold of share ownership required to be classified as FDI (usually 10 per cent of total voting power).

Portfolio flows are more prominent in core countries, although they have become increasingly important in peripheral countries. In general, portfolio flows can be very large and extremely volatile, spurred by interest rate differentials and exchange rate movements, which are often influenced by the monetary policy choices of respective governments.[2] Finally, banking flows – sometimes called 'other' flows in financial statistics – are similar to portfolio flows, but the credit provider is a bank. It is clear, in view of the analysis in part II, that banking flows normally exhibit lower volatility than portfolio flows.

During the decades of financialisation, there occurred a global expansion of financial networks together with the steady ascent of market-based finance, resulting in what might be called international portfolio finance. Currently, global capital flows result largely from the microeconomic decisions of financial enterprises, including banks, that manage vast portfolios. The portfolio decisions of these private lenders are strongly speculative and influenced by the monetary policies of core countries; above all, by interest rates and the provision of credit by central banks. These characteristics of global flows became particularly prominent during the ascendancy of shadow banking that was discussed in part II.

Financial enterprises engaging in international portfolio finance do not seek to create exclusive zones of operation. On the contrary, they are keen to secure global reach, but always within an institutional framework guaranteeing the ability to move loanable capital fluidly across borders

---

1 For a thorough discussion of the technical aspects of flow measurement, see R. Koepke and S. Paetzold (2020) 'Capital Flow Data – A Guide for Empirical Analysis and Real-Time Tracking', IMF Working Paper No. 171.

2 See C. Alcidi (2020) 'Analysis of Developments in EU Capital Flows in the Global Context. Increasing uncertainty in the wake of the COVID-19 pandemic', European Commission, at op.europa.eu.

and to transfer financial profits. Fundamental to their global reach is access to world money, ensuring the preservation of value in the money form and enabling international payments, particularly in times of crisis.

Core countries, led by the hegemon, shape the institutional framework required for the global operations of financial enterprises. They are the leading suppliers and recipients of global capital flows, while also setting the legal and practical terms on which flows occur and by which financial profits are extracted. For peripheral countries, on the other hand, participating in international capital flows entails their subordinate integration into global financial networks and their dependence on world money. Core countries, led by the hegemonic USA, dictate the terms of subordinate integration, with exploitative and destructive results for workers and entire countries.

Moreover, during the last two decades, forms of subordinate financialisation have emerged in several middle-income countries across the world economy. Domestic financial sectors have expanded, further complicating the integration of domestic accumulation in peripheral countries with the world economy. The extraction of financial profits and the transfer of money value have become far more complex than in previous historical periods.

The USA draws immense power from global portfolio finance. Its dominance derives in part from active participation in international capital flows as the largest provider and the largest recipient of flows globally. It also derives from control over the contemporary world money – the fiat dollar of the Federal Reserve. Further to pursue these points, the next section outlines the distinctive transformation of international finance in the decades of neoliberalism.

The rise of international portfolio finance

It was shown in part II that a hallmark of domestic financialisation in core countries is portfolio management, with the attendant trading of securities and securitisation of regular loans, aiming for speculative capital gains and high returns; this has signalled the ascendancy of market-based finance. Portfolio considerations also currently dominate global capital flows driven by internationally active financial enterprises. The international flows of private loanable capital have come to depend on the global availability of credit, ultimately linked to the monetary policies of core countries – above all, the hegemonic USA.

For Marxist political economy, the rise of portfolio finance, both domestically and internationally, has roots in the circuit of industrial capital. As it goes through its circuit, industrial capital generates variable quantities of temporarily idle money that are potentially loanable capital, depending on the stage of the circuit that is traversed at every time. Naturally, when industrial capital undertakes production internationally, some of the temporarily idle funds will be generated across borders.[3]

In this light, the point of departure for the analysis of global portfolio finance is the circular motion of capitalist accumulation, both domestically and across borders, resulting in temporarily idle sums of money often owned by multinational enterprises. The financial system transforms such idle money into loanable money capital, seeking returns both domestically and internationally.

The ways in which this transformation takes place and the financial operations to which it gives rise vary according to historically specific factors, including the role of the state. Both the forms and the volumes of cross-border flows of loanable capital depend on the institutional and legal framework of the world market, and include bank lending, official aid, securities purchases, public loans, trade credit finance, and so on.

The early beginnings of international portfolio finance – backed by the dollar as world money – could be placed in the 1960s with the establishment of the 'Eurodollar' markets that existed beyond the control of US authorities, opening the way toward financial liberalisation both domestically and internationally. The collapse of the Bretton Woods system in 1971–3 ushered in floating exchange rates, and international financial liberalisation accelerated rapidly to the point of becoming policy 'orthodoxy'.[4]

Before the end of Bretton Woods, capital flows among core countries

3 See D. Harvey (2006) *The Limits to Capital*, Verso: London and New York; M. Itoh (1988) *The Basic Theory of Capitalism: The Forms and Substance of the Capitalist Economy*, Macmillan Press: London; Itoh and Lapavitsas (1999) *Political Economy of Money and Finance*.

4 There is a vast literature on these topics, but for a concise and informative introduction to the consequences of the move to floating exchange rates and the growth of the Eurodollar markets in the context of financialisation, see G. Epstein (2005) 'Introduction: Financialization and the World Economy', in G. Epstein (ed.) *Financialization and the World Economy*, Edward Elgar: Cheltenham, pp. 3–16; see also E. Dickens (2005) 'The Eurodollar Market and the New Era of Global Financialization', in Epstein (ed.) *Financialization and the World Economy*, pp. 210–19; for a recent discussion, see B. Braun, A. Krampf, and S. Murau (2021) 'Financial Globalization as Positive Integration: Monetary Technocrats and the Eurodollar Market in the 1970s', *Review of International Political Economy* 28 (4): 794–819.

were mostly private, occurring via the profit-making decisions of commercial banks. Core-to-core flows, moreover, were relatively limited in size and subject to controls and regulations. Flows from core to periphery, on the other hand, as well as being limited and subject to controls and regulations, included a substantial official component (aid) and typically resulted in the accumulation of sovereign debt by peripheral countries. Whether private or official, the macroeconomic function of capital flowing from core to periphery, broadly speaking, was to provide funding for investment and to cover deficits in the current accounts. During that time, the theory and practice of 'development finance' began to take shape, some elements of which were briefly considered in chapter 11 in the context of US hegemony.

After the collapse of Bretton Woods and the steady lifting of controls as financial liberalisation gathered momentum, private flows escalated toward both core and periphery, becoming increasingly short-term and focusing on the balance of return and risk for the suppliers of funds.[5] Meanwhile, official flows from core to periphery became far less significant. Put plainly, financial relations between core and periphery shifted toward portfolio finance.

Since the end of Bretton Woods, international capital flows have occurred mostly between core countries, although core-to-periphery and even periphery-to-periphery flows have also acquired substantial dimensions, as is shown in subsequent sections of this chapter. In more recent times, there has been a shift in the composition of capital flows away from banking and toward portfolio debt, affording great power to institutions managing international portfolios, including shadow banks. These changes are in line with the development of financialised capitalism in core countries and the entrenchment of market-based finance.

Private cross-border flows currently pivot on the perceptions of risk and return among internationally active financial enterprises managing their portfolios. These perceptions partly reflect macroeconomic variables, such

---

5 For broad historical accounts, see B. Eichengreen (2010) *Global Imbalances and the Lessons of Bretton Wood*, MIT Press: Cambridge, MA; and M. D. Bordo and B. Eichengreen (eds) (2007) *A Retrospective on the Bretton Woods System: Lessons for International Monetary Reform*, University of Chicago Press: Chicago, IL. For a historical account of the role of European banks after Bretton Woods, see C. E. Altamura (2016) *European Banks and the Rise of International Finance: The Post-Bretton Woods Era*, Routledge: London; see also M. De Cecco (2002) 'Capital Controls in the Bretton Woods and post-Bretton Woods International Financial System', *Jahrbuch Für Wirtschaftsgeschichte/Economic History Yearbook* 43 (1): 65–80.

as the state of the recipient's current account and growth prospects, as well as the stability of the domestic financial system and the legal provisions for transferring money value out of a country. More prominently, however, they reflect interest rate differentials and the expectations of exchange rate movements within narrow time horizons, both of which are directly affected by monetary policy, particularly by core central banks.

The direction of private cross-border flows is of considerable importance in this connection. It is typically assumed in economic theory that if liquid money capital was easily available and rates of return declined in the domestic economy, financial enterprises would seek profits across borders. It follows that there would be capital flows among core countries as well as from core to periphery. It cannot be overemphasised, however, that there are moments in the overall trajectory of global accumulation when sizeable capital flows occur from periphery to core, represented by so-called 'flights to quality' and perhaps even leaving debt crises behind.[6]

Moreover, during the last two decades there have been massive capital flows from periphery to core reflecting current account surpluses among peripheral countries as well as an enormous accumulation of world money by peripheral countries in the form of reserves. Reverse capital flows from periphery to core are a characteristic feature of contemporary imperialism and impose a heavy burden on the periphery, acting as a form of tribute paid to core countries. However, whether it flows from core to periphery or vice versa, internationally active loanable capital is a systemic lever that transmits pressures from the global to the national spaces of capital accumulation.[7]

In sum, international portfolio finance has little to do with development requirements across the world and is driven by short-term calculations of capital gains, interest, and speculative profit. Flows from core to periphery increasingly respond to the decisions of asset managers seeking to speculate on exchange rates and interest rate differentials, rather than provide long-term credit for development. This is a source of substantial instability, as portfolio flows are volatile and often unrelated to domestic economic conditions, leading to waves of sharp inflows followed by sudden outflows.

---

6 H. Cleaver (1989) 'Close the IMF, Abolish Debt and End Development: A Class Analysis of the International Debt Crisis', *Capital & Class* 13 (3): 17–50.

7 I. Alami (2019) 'Post-Crisis Capital Controls in Developing and Emerging Countries: Regaining Policy Space? A Historical Materialist Engagement', *Review of Radical Political Economics* 51 (4): 629–49.

The impact on peripheral countries is direct and deep: it is one thing to cope with flows of official funding, such as aid, that are presumably directed toward development needs, and quite another to deal with floods of loanable capital funnelled by banks, shadow banks, and other financial enterprises and seeking short-term and speculative returns.

Confronted with these forces, peripheral countries face unrelenting pressures to implement domestic policies favourable to international portfolio managers. They are typically forced to pursue financial liberalisation by opening the capital (or financial) account of the balance of payments – that is, removing controls on capital flows.[8] They are also compelled to adopt exchange rate policies compatible with the interests of international financiers that are often inimical to the domestic economy. Not least, peripheral countries are under pressure to accumulate enormous reserves of world money to face up to the violent fluctuations of global flows.

In these complex ways peripheral countries are relegated to subordinate positions and are even forced to absorb the risks of private enterprises transacting in international loanable capital.[9] A closer theoretical look at financial subordination is thus instructive at this point.

Financial liberalisation, subordinate integration, and subordinate or dependent financialisation of peripheral countries

Mainstream economic analysis of international financial liberalisation has always had a strongly prescriptive component. Freeing the financial account of the balance of payments and opening the domestic economy to international capital flows would presumably contribute to a better development performance. In theory, a peripheral country could deepen its domestic financial markets through an inflow of foreign savings; the entry of foreign banks and other financial institutions would help develop domestic financial infrastructure.[10]

---

8 See Lapavitsas (2013) *Profiting without Producing.*

9 For Daniela Gabor, the state removes risks from private financiers – it is the 'derisking state', embedded in an emerging development finance framework called the 'Wall Street Consensus'; see D. Gabor (2021) 'The Wall Street Consensus', *Development and Change* 42 (3): 429–59.

10 For typical examples of this mainstream perspective, see, selectively, D. J. Mathieson and L. Rojas-Suarez (1992) 'Liberalization of the Capital Account: Experiences and Issues', IMF Working Paper No. 46; B. Eichengreen et al. (1998) 'Hedge Funds and Financial Market Dynamics', IMF Occasional Paper No. 166; M. A. Kose et

Reality proved quite different, however, as the growth outcomes of financial liberalisation and deregulated cross-border capital flows were poor, while vulnerability and crises proliferated. Portfolio finance and the attendant vast expansion of global liquidity have entailed profound changes in the operations of both non-financial corporations and banks in peripheral countries.[11] The result was to intensify the subordinate integration of peripheral countries into the world economy.

Fundamental to the subordinate position of peripheral countries is the conduct of domestic non-financial corporations, which often participate in global production networks and are component parts of the global division of labour, as was discussed in chapter 12. Peripheral non-financial enterprises have acquired substantial capacity to participate in financial operations in domestic and international financial markets.[12] The role of international banks and institutional lenders is

al. (2006) 'How Does Financial Globalization Affect Risk-Sharing? Patterns and Channels', IMF 7th Jacques Polak Annual Research Conference Paper; P. B. Henry (2007) 'Capital Account Liberalization: Theory, Evidence, and Speculation', *Journal of Economic Literature* 45 (4): 887–935; A. Kose et al. (2011) 'Threshold in the process of international financial integration, *Journal of International Money and Finance* 30 (1): 147–79; for sustained critical evaluations of liberalised capital flows, see J. P. Painceira (2012) 'Developing Countries in the Era of Financialisation: From Deficit Accumulation to Reserve Accumulation', in C. Lapavitsas (ed.) *Financialization in Crisis*, Brill: Leiden, pp. 185–215; D. Rodrik and A. Subramanian (2009) 'Why Did Financial Globalization Disappoint?' *IMF Staff Papers*, 56 (1): 112–38; E. Stockhammer (2010) 'Financialization and the Global Economy', PERI Working Papers No. 240; B. Bonizzi (2013) 'Financialization in Developing and Emerging Countries' *International Journal of Political Economy* 42 (4): 83–107; and J. Garcia-Arias (2015) 'International Financialisation and the Systemic Approach to International Financing for Development', *Global Policy* 6 (1): 24–33.

11 Analysis in this section and the next draws heavily on C. Lapavitsas and A. Soydan (2022) 'Financialisation in Developing Countries: Approaches, Concepts, and Metrics', *International Review of Applied Economics* 36 (3): 424–47.

12 See, very selectively, F. Demir (2009) 'Financialization and Manufacturing Firm Profitability under Uncertainty and Macroeconomic Volatility: Evidence from an Emerging Market', *Review of Development Economics* 13 (4): 592–609; F. Demir (2009) 'Financial Liberalization, Private Investment and Portfolio Choice: Financialization of Real Sectors in Emerging Markets', *Journal of Development Economics* 88 (2): 314–24; F. Demir (2007) 'The Rise of Rentier Capitalism and the Financialization of Real Sectors in Developing Countries', *Review of Radical Political Economics* 39 (3): 351–59; and E. Karwowski (2018) 'Corporate Financialization in South Africa: From Investment Strike to House Bubble', *Competition & Change* 22 (4): 413–16; E. Karwowski (2012) 'Financial Operations of South African Listed Firms: Growth and Financial Stability in an Emerging Market Setting', 3rd Biannual IESE conference, Maputo, Mozambique, September.

vital in this connection, through debt intermediation and equity financing.[13]

It is shown in the following sections that even FDI is partly unrelated to productive capital, or to the transfer of industrial and technical capabilities to peripheral countries.[14] Equally important are changes in the mode of operation of domestic banks, which are borrowing more heavily abroad and becoming exposed to international financial markets.

It is important to stress, nonetheless, that qualitative differences remain between core and peripheral countries in all these regards. Only the largest non-financial enterprises in peripheral countries are systematically able to use market-based finance, and even then more modestly than their counterparts in core countries.[15] The majority still rely on retained earnings, funds from parent enterprises or affiliates, and credits from the banking system; by this token, peripheral countries are still largely bank-based.[16] Financial subordination in this context manifests itself as intensified economic vulnerability and loss of policy space for governments, due in large part to the volatility of international capital flows.[17]

13 See, again selectively, M. Farhi and R. A. Zanchetta Borghi (2009) 'Operations with Financial Derivatives of Corporations from Emerging Economies', Estudos Avançados 23 (66): 169–88; H. Cho (2010) South Korea's Experience with Banking Sector Liberalisation; Correa and Vidal (2012) 'Financialization and Global Financial Crisis in Latin American Countries'; and J. Tyson and T. McKinley (2014) 'Financialization and the Developing World: Mapping the Issues', FESSUD Working Paper Series, No. 38.

14 See Garcia-Arias (2015) 'International Financialisation and the Systemic Approach to International Financing for Development'.

15 See, for instance, L. Rethel (2010) 'Financialisation and the Malaysian Political Economy', Globalizations 7 (4): 489–506; J. Powell (2013) 'Subordinate Financialisation: A Study of Mexico and its Non-financial Corporations', unpublished PhD Thesis SOAS; A. Bowman (2018) 'Financialization and the Extractive Industries: The Case of South Africa Platinum Mining', Competition & Change 22 (4): 388–412.

16 This point is amply documented in the literature. See, for instance, N. Levy-Orlik (2012) 'Financial Markets in Developing Countries', in J. Toporowski and J. Mitchell (eds) Handbook of Critical Issues in Finance, Edward Elgar: Cheltenham, UK, pp. 113–20; G. Isaacs (2015) 'The Commodification, Commercialisation and Financialisation of Low-Cost Housing in South Africa', FESSUD Working Papers Series, No. 142; G. Isaacs and A. Kaltenbrunner (2018) 'Financialization and Liberalization: South Africa's New Forms of External Vulnerability', Competition & Change 22 (4): 437–63; and Gezici et al. (2019) 'Determinants of Investment in Turkey: A Firm-Level Investigation', Emerging Markets Finance and Trade 55 (6): 1405–16.

17 See, selectively, Stockhammer (2010) 'Financialization and the Global Economy'; Y. Akyüz (2014) 'Internationalization of Finance and Changing Vulnerabilities in Emerging and Developing Economies', UNCTAD Discussion

Non-financial corporations in peripheral countries have historically tended to borrow from domestic banks, while also holding
public debt securities that offer low risk and liquidity.[18] As international portfolio finance spread its tentacles, large non-financial
corporations have tended to accumulate foreign-denominated
debt, resulting in mismatches of currency and maturities between
the asset and the liability sides of their balance sheets. These
mismatches could contribute to sudden stops of capital flows and
exacerbate foreign exchange crises. Even when peripheral enterprises are able to borrow internationally in their own currency, the
mismatches do not disappear but are simply transferred onto the
balance sheet of the lender, thus remaining a source of instability
for a peripheral country.[19]

The impact is magnified by the macroeconomic implications of free
cross-border flows, which, as was already noted, tend to be short-term
and volatile. The risks that emerge for the economies of peripheral

Papers, No. 03; Y. Akyüz (2017) 'Global Economic Landscape and Prospects', paper
presented at South Centre Conference, 13 February, Geneva; J. Tyson and T. W. te
Velde (2014) 'Post-Crisis Trends in Private Capital Flows to Developing Countries',
Overseas Development Institute, Briefing/Policy Papers, 7 August, at odi.org; J. Tyson
and T. McKinley (2014) 'Financialization and the Developing World: Mapping the
Issues'. The seminal mainstream paper by H. Rey (2013) 'Dilemma Not Trilemma: The
Global Financial Cycle and Monetary Policy Independence', paper presented at the
25th Federal Reserve Bank of Kansas City Symposium (Jackson Hole Symposium),
21–23 August, Wyoming, postulates the existence of global financial cycles marked by
commonalities in the fluctuations of asset prices, gross capital flows, and leverage.
These cycles reflect international financial integration and are ultimately related to the
US monetary policy.

18 The relevant literature is large. See, indicatively, I. Erturk (2003) 'Governance or
Financialisation: The Turkish Case', *Competition & Change* 7 (4): 185–204; Demir (2009)
'Financialization and Manufacturing Firm Profitability under Uncertainty and
Macroeconomic Volatility: Evidence from an Emerging Market'; Demir (2009) 'Financial
Liberalization, Private Investment and Portfolio Choice: Financialization of Real Sectors in
Emerging Markets'; E. Araujo et al. (2012) 'Financialization against Industrialization: A
Regulationist Approach of the Brazilian Paradox', *Revue de La Régulation. Capitalisme,
Institutions, Pouvoirs* 11 (1); and A. Cibils and C. Allami (2013) 'Financialisation vs.
Development Finance: The Case of the Post-crisis Argentine Banking System', *Revue de
La Regulation: Capitalisme, Institutions, Pouvoirs* 13 (1). J. Becker (2016) 'Financialisation,
Industry and Dependency in Turkey', *Journal für Entwicklungspolitik* 32 (1/2): 84–113
calls this feature of financialisation of peripheral countries 'state-centred' and claims
that it has a detrimental impact on public capacity and productive investment.

19 See B. Hoffman et al. (2020) 'Emerging Market Economy Exchange Rates and
Local Currency Bond Markets amid the Covid-19 Pandemic', BIS Bulletin 5, at bis.org.

countries are gigantic, since liquidity could suddenly disappear if capital flows dried up or were reversed. To confront these risks, peripheral countries are obliged to hold vast reserves of dollars as world money, a policy that is very costly and amounts to a transfer of resources primarily to the USA, as is shown in subsequent sections.[20]

Costs aside, the holding of vast reserves also has major implications for the conduct of non-financial corporations in peripheral countries. The existence of the national reserve cushion allows enterprises, on the one hand, to borrow abroad and, on the other, to avoid investing the funds productively in the domestic economy. Instead, they are able to speculate on the difference between the domestic and the foreign yield of financial assets, especially in connection with expected changes in the exchange rate. The so-called 'carry trade' involves borrowing abroad to make domestic financial investments, thus earning profits from the interest rate spread and from any upward bias in the exchange rate.[21]

Such financial speculation is exacerbated by the monetary policies of peripheral countries, which are often compelled to adopt inflation targeting that typically requires high domestic interest rates.[22] The

---

20 For a recent discussion, see J. P. Painceira (2021) *Financialisation in Emerging Economies: Changes in Central Banking*, Routledge: London and New York.

21 See, for instance, Demir (2009) 'Financialization and Manufacturing Firm Profitability under Uncertainty and Macroeconomic Volatility: Evidence from an Emerging Market'; Demir (2009) 'Financial Liberalization, Private Investment and Portfolio Choice: Financialization of Real Sectors in Emerging Markets'; J. Becker et al. (2010) 'Peripheral Financialization and Vulnerability to Crisis: A Regulationist Perspective', *Competition & Change* 14 (3–4): 225–47; J. P. Painceira (2011) 'Central Banking in Middle Income Countries in the Course of Financialisation: A Study with Special Reference to Brazil and Korea', unpublished PhD dissertation, SOAS, University of London; and O. Orhangazi and G. Ozgur, (2015) 'Capital Flows, Finance-Led Growth and Fragility in the Age of Global Liquidity and Quantitative Easing: The Case of Turkey', PERI Working Paper Series No. 397.

22 For technical discussions of inflation targeting in developing countries and its relation to exchange rates, see J. Aizenman, M. Hutchison, and I. Noy (2011) 'Inflation Targeting and Real Exchange Rates in Emerging Markets', *World Development* 39 (5): 712–24. See further G. Epstein (2008) 'An Employment Targeting Framework for Central Bank Policy in South Africa', *International Review of Applied Economics* 22 (2): 243–58, which analyses real interest rates to target low inflation which translate into lower economic growth. Portfolio rebalancing and rising capital inflows as a result of inflation targeting lead to appreciation of the exchange rate, thus hurting exports (and promoting imports); see L. M. Galindo and J. Ros (2008) 'Alternatives to Inflation Targeting in Mexico', *International Review of Applied Economics* 22 (2): 201–14.

foreign providers of liquid capital are thereby protected, but the result is sustained overvaluation of the exchange rate, and thus an even more pressing need to hold large international currency reserves. Domestic capitalists can engage in financial speculation, while the scope for independent domestic monetary policy becomes practically non-existent. The implications for growth and domestic incomes are uniformly negative.[23]

In broad terms, the opportunities for such speculation arise because exchange rates, interest rates, financial asset prices, and real estate prices across the world economy increasingly depend on cross-border capital flows, and thus on the portfolio considerations of international financial enterprises.[24] The result is co-movement of financial prices across peripheral countries, intensifying financial subordination and economic vulnerability.[25] The most important factor in this respect is the monetary policy of the USA, the hegemonic power.

Mainstream economic theory commonly describes this relationship as the 'global financial cycle'. Broadly speaking, the term describes a high degree of international co-movement of (risky) asset prices, capital flows, credit availability, and other financial factors.[26] The common

23 For an extensive review of inflation targeting and its consequences in peripheral countries, see P. R. Agénor and L. A. Pereira da Silva (2019) *Integrated Inflation Targeting: Another Perspective from the Developing World*, BIS: Basel.

24 See A. Kaltenbrunner and J. P. Painceira (2015) 'Developing Countries' Changing Nature of Financial Integration and New Forms of External Vulnerability: The Brazilian Experience', *Cambridge Journal of Economics* 39 (5): 1281–306; A. Kaltenbrunner and J. P. Painceira (2018) 'Subordinated Financial Integration and Financialisation in Emerging Capitalist Economies: The Brazilian Experience', *New Political Economy* 23 (3): 290–313; Isaacs and Kaltenbrunner (2018) 'Financialization and Liberalization: South Africa's New Forms of External Vulnerability'.

25 The literature on this is wide; see, selectively, A. Kaltenbrunner (2010) 'International Financialization and Depreciation: The Brazilian Real in the International Financial Crisis', *Competition & Change* 14 (3–4): 296–323; Correa and Vidal (2012) 'Financialization and Global Financial Crisis in Latin American Countries'; Akyüz (2014) 'Internationalization of Finance and Changing Vulnerabilities in Emerging and Developing Economies'; Isaacs (2015) 'The Commodification, Commercialisation and Financialisation of Low-Cost Housing in South Africa'; and Isaacs and Kaltenbrunner (2018) 'Financialization and Liberalization: South Africa's New Forms of External Vulnerability'.

26 See Rey (2013) 'Dilemma not Trilemma'. For further analysis, see S. Miranda-Agrippino and H. Rey (2015) 'World Asset Markets and the Global Financial Cycle', NBER Working Paper No. 21722. For recent elaborations, see: B. Scheubel, L. Stracca, and C. Tille (2019) 'Taming the Global Financial Cycle: What Role for the Global Financial Safety Net?' *Journal of International Money and Finance* 94: 160–82; and M. M.

point of reference of the co-movements of prices is the Federal Reserve.[27] When the hegemonic central bank relaxes domestic monetary policy, global liquidity becomes abundantly available and private financial institutions across the world can more easily create credit, thus pushing financial asset prices up. Cross-border flows are boosted as portfolio managers seek high returns abroad, thus making financial expansion more likely in peripheral countries. The outcomes for growth and income are typically negative.

The 1990s and much of the 2000s in core countries were termed the Great Moderation, as was mentioned in earlier chapters. From a global perspective, however, this period, far from being a time of moderation, represented unprecedented instability and crises, even if these were frequently confined to peripheral countries. Indeed, the liberalisation of international finance has witnessed more financial crises than the period of the gold standard and classical imperialism.[28]

The coexistence of financial crises in the periphery and the 'Great Moderation' at the core reflects the profound asymmetric effect of cross-border capital flows. When peripheral countries find themselves mired in financial crises, core countries might even benefit as loanable capital withdraws in search of security. In contrast, when the core is in crisis, there are major spillover effects on the periphery through capital flows, as was shown in part II and is further discussed in the rest of this chapter. Financial subordination is costly.

Furthermore, since the early 2000s, and as international portfolio finance firmly dominated cross-border flows, several middle-income countries entered the path of financialisation, the most prominent aspect of which is rapid growth of the financial sector relative to the rest of the economy. In core countries, the emergence of financialisation is heavily associated with internal causes, and also depends on the social and political framework of laws, rules, and state policies.[29] In peripheral

Habib and F. Venditti (2019) 'The Global Capital Flows Cycle: Structural Drivers and Transmission Channels', ECB Working Paper No. 2280.

27 See Miranda-Agrippino and Rey (2021) 'World Asset Markets and the Global Financial Cycle'.

28 See M. D. Bordo and B. Eichengreen (2002) 'Crises Now and Then: What Lessons from the Last Era of Financial Globalization', NBER Working Paper No. 8716.

29 C. Lapavitsas and J. Powell (2013) 'Financialisation Varied: A Comparative Analysis of Advanced Economies', Cambridge Journal of Regions, Economy and Society 6 (3): 369–79 put forth the term 'financialisation varied' to underline substantial differences of financialisation across core countries. 'Variegated financialisation' was

countries, financialisation is primarily related to external causes,
particularly the liberalisation of the financial account of the balance of
payments augmenting cross-border flows, and the entry of foreign
banks.

Financialisation in peripheral countries presents phenomena similar but also different to that in core countries, taking a subordinate or
dependent form that still reflects the domestic peculiarities of individual peripheral countries. Its emergence is closely related to cross-
border capital flows and leads to further subordination. The entry of
foreign banks in peripheral financial systems is also important in this
respect because it introduces the practices of financialisation from
core countries, including lending to households. Domestic banks soon
begin to compete in this profitable field by acquiring the requisite
skills. Substantial expansion of credit to households follows, typically
as consumer loans, including credit from banks, but also mortgage
debt.[30]

---

proposed to indicate the pervasive but diverse forms of financialisation in Europe. A.
Brown et al., (2015) 'The Nature and Variegation of Financialisation: A Cross-country
Comparison', FESSUD Working Paper Series, No. 127; A. Brown et al. (2017) 'The
Extent and Variegation of Financialisation in Europe: A Preliminary Analysis', *Revista
de Economia Mundial* 46: 49–69; and Karwowski et al. (2017) 'Financialization:
Dimensions and Determinants. A Cross-country Study', Kingston University
Economics Discussion Papers No. 01, discussed variegated financialisation by
empirically analysing a group of core countries. K. P. Lai and J. A. Daniels (2017)
'Financialization of Singaporean Banks and the Production of Variegated Financial
Capitalism', in B. Christophers, A. Leyshon, and G. Mann (eds) *Money and Finance
after the Crisis: Critical Thinking for Uncertain Times*, Chichester: Wiley-Blackwell, pp.
217–44, used the term to discuss peripheral countries, and the case of Singapore in
particular.

30 See, selectively, C. Lapavitsas and P. L. Dos Santos (2008) 'Globalization and
Contemporary Banking: On the Impact of New Technology', *Contributions to Political
Economy* 27 (1): 31–56; Farhi and Zanchetta Borghi (2009) 'Operations with Financial
Derivatives of Corporations from Emerging Economies'; P. L. Dos Santos (2011) 'A
Policy Wrapped in "Analysis": The World Bank's Case for Foreign Banks', in K. Bayliss,
B. Fine, and E. van Waeyenberge (eds) *The Political Economy of Development: The World
Bank, Neoliberalism and Development Research*, London: Pluto Press, pp. 188–214; Dos
Santos (2013) 'A Cause for Policy Concern: The Expansion of Household Credit in
Middle-Income Economies'; Correa and Vidal (2012) 'Financialization and Global
Financial Crisis in Latin American Countries'; E. Karacimen (2014) 'Financialization in
Turkey: The Case of Consumer Debt', *Journal of Balkan and Near Eastern Studies* 16 (2):
161–80. Note that despite the strong growth of household debt, the proportion to GDP
in peripheral countries remains far below that in core countries, even though in some
peripheral countries there are high levels of mortgage debt associated with rising prices
of housing and real estate, mostly with reference to higher income groups. See H. Cho

The emergence of financialisation in the periphery of the world economy has given rise to a broad theoretical and empirical literature, in which two theoretical currents stand out: first, the approach of subordinate financialisation, drawing heavily on Marxist political economy, with post-Keynesian insights; second, the approach of dependent (or peripheral) financialisation, based on the Regulationist school, with Marxist and post-Keynesian influences.[31]

For both approaches, financialisation in peripheral countries is derivative from financialisation in core countries, reflecting hierarchical relations in the world economy and the prior financialisation of core countries. Both approaches, furthermore, stress the importance of liberalised capital flows, reserve accumulation, and the entry of foreign financial institutions into peripheral countries.

The dependent financialisation approach draws on the analysis of the Regulation school and identifies financialisation in the periphery as a new type of dependency.[32] Regulation theory analyses financialisation at the core as due to a shift from the Fordist to the finance-led accumulation regime of capitalism, eventually resulting in a transition from peripheral Fordism to peripheral financialisation.[33]

(2010) *South Korea's Experience with Banking Sector Liberalisation*; Ashman et al. (2011) 'The Crisis in South Africa: Neoliberalism, Financialization and Uneven and Combined Development', *Socialist Register* 47: 174–95; Isaacs (2015) 'The Commodification, Commercialisation and Financialisation of Low-Cost Housing in South Africa'; C. Choi (2018) 'Subordinate Financialization and Financial Subsumption in South Korea', *Regional Studies* 54 (2): 209–18; Karwowski (2018) 'Corporate Financialization in South Africa'.

31 See, for instance, B. Bonizzi (2013) 'Financialization in Developing and Emerging Countries', *International Journal of Political Economy* 42 (4): 83–107, for an early and broad evaluation of theoretical and empirical work. E. Karwowski and E. Stockhammer (2017) 'Financialisation in Emerging Economies: A Systematic Overview and Comparison with Anglo-Saxon Economies', *Economic and Political Studies* 5 (1): 60–86 offer an assessment of several empirical studies. A. Kaltenbrunner and E. Karacimen (2016) 'The Contested Nature of Financialization', in T. Subasat (ed.) *The Great Financial Meltdown: Systemic, Conjunctural or Policy-Created?*, Cheltenham: Edward Elgar, pp. 287–304, review studies of financialisation of the non-financial corporate sector.

32 See Becker et al. (2010) 'Peripheral Financialization and Vulnerability to Crisis: A Regulationist Perspective'; J. Becker and J. Jager (2012) 'Integration in Crisis: A Regulationist Perspective on the Interaction of European Varieties of Capitalism', *Competition & Change* 16 (3): 169–87; Becker and Weissenbacher (2015) 'Changing Development Models: Dependency School Meets Regulation Theory'.

33 For the proposed regime shift, see, for instance, Boyer (2000) 'Is a Finance-Led Growth Regime a Viable Alternative to Fordism? A Preliminary Analysis', *Economy and Society* 29 (1): 111–45.

The subordinate financialisation approach, on the other hand, is associated with the Marxist framework of financialisation, as was discussed in earlier chapters. According to this approach, financialisation in the periphery exhibits some of the fundamental tendencies observed in the core, but assumes a subordinate form shaped by imperial relations. Vital to this are global capital flows and the dominant role of world money, with the resulting hierarchy of currencies in the world market.

The trajectory and composition of capital flows since the early 2000s

In view of these theoretical considerations and further to pursue the financial underpinnings of contemporary imperialism, it is instructive empirically to consider the trajectory of international capital flows in recent years.

As was mentioned in the preceding sections, following the collapse of Bretton Woods in 1971–3, global capital flows began to rise rapidly. The flows of capital from core to periphery soon created great accumulations of short-term debt by sovereign borrowers as well as currency mismatches between borrower assets (in domestic currency) and borrower liabilities (in foreign currency), culminating in successive financial crises.[34]

The heaviest borrowing in the early years was in Latin America, led by core banks, and the 1980s was a 'lost decade' of crisis for Latin America. In the 1990s, on the other hand, the leading recipients of capital flows were in East and South-East Asia and Russia.[35] That wave of

---

34 For more on the effects of global financialised capitalism on the global south up until the Great Crisis, see BIS (2009) 'Capital Flows and Emerging Market Economies', CGFS Papers No. 33.

35 The classic early analysis from a critical perspective on the rise of financial instability due to liberalisation is by C. Diaz-Alejandro (1985) 'Good-Bye Financial Repression, Hello Financial Crash', *Journal of Development Economics* 19: 1–24. For a mainstream study of both the Latin American and the East Asian crises, see G. L. Kaminsky and C. M. Reinhart (1998) 'Financial Crises in Asia and Latin America: Then and Now', *The American Economic Review* 88 (2): 444–8; on the Latin American crises of the 1980s, see F. Mishkin (1999) 'Lessons from the Tequila Crisis', *Journal of Banking and Finance* 23: 1521–33; see also G. Bird and A. Milne (1999) 'Miracle to Meltdown: A Pathology of the East Asian Financial

lending was also led by core banks and ended with an enormous crisis, marked by several sovereign defaults, lasting broadly from 1997 to 2001. The damage to peripheral countries was enormous, but the banks of the core also took losses.[36]

Following the crisis of 1997–2001, global portfolio finance properly took off, ushering in novel developments in the subordination of peripheral countries. Figures 13.1 to 13.9 sum up the key characteristics of global flows during this period. The first four figures capture outflows and inflows of capital relating to banks and portfolio holders but without considering FDI, which is discussed in the subsequent sections. The data for outflows refers to gross advances of capital by domestic to foreign agents across the countries in the sample, and vice versa for inflows.

To be more precise, the data captures the gross cross-border outflows and inflows for the agents of each country and sums these up across the countries in each group. To facilitate analysis, the agents were grouped into banks (deposit-taking institutions), non-banks (the rest of the private sector, including shadow banks), and the public sector (mostly governments and central banks).[37] The figures are in billions of current

---

Crisis', *Third World Quarterly*, 20 (2): 421–37; N. Roubini, G. Corsetti, and P. Besant (1998) 'What Caused the Asian Currency and Financial Crisis?' Bank of Italy Economic Working Paper No. 343; and S. Radelet and J. Sachs (1998) 'The East Asian Financial Crisis: Diagnosis, Remedies, Prospects', *Brooking Papers on Economic Activity* 29: 1–90.

36 In the mainstream literature, there are three generations of currency and by extension financial crisis models. The first generation focuses on the link between domestic fiscal policies and pegged exchange rates, as, for instance, in the Mexican crisis of 1982; the second generation hinges on the idea of 'self-fulfilling' expectations by financial operators, i.e. on speculative attacks on pegged exchange rates irrespective of domestic policies as, for instance, the exit of the UK from the exchange rate mechanism of the EU in 1992; the third generation turns more fully to the impact of financial liberalisation on the balance sheets and the practices of financial institutions as, for instance, in the extended crisis of 1997–2001. The third-generation models are evidently concerned with the implications of international portfolio finance. For a summary, see S. Claessens and M. A. Kose (2013) 'Financial Crises Explanations, Types, and Implications', IMF Working Paper No. 28.

37 The dataset used for figures 13.1 to 13.4 is collated and constructed by BIS (Working Papers No. 760), and consists of data from the IMF (Balance of Payments and International Investment Position), Locational Bank Statistics and Consolidated Bank Statistics from BIS (available at bis.org), The International Debt Securities Statistics (also from BIS), Quarterly External Debt Statistics (from IMF and World Bank, available at worldbank.org), and finally the Debt Reporting System data from World Bank (available

US dollars and are added up for each group.

Core countries are those selected in the early chapters of this book, i.e. the USA, UK, Japan, Germany, and France. Selecting peripheral countries, on the other hand, is much more complex and arbitrary. The group chosen comprises Brazil, Russia, India, China, and Turkey – unless otherwise stated – because it contains some of the largest peripheral countries with a strong presence in global markets, which are also prominent in the unfolding hegemonic contest.[38] Financial relations within and between these two groups are likely to be important in the years ahead as well as casting light on the direction of global finance.

Figures 13.1 and 13.2 show the gross flows of capital for the core countries selected here, and several conclusions are apparent through mere visual inspection.

Both figures show that there was an extraordinary escalation of cross-border bank flows within core countries during the bubble of the 2000s. Non-bank cross-border flows also increased substantially during this period, but the bulk of lending was done by banks (also borrowing heavily abroad). Bank inflows and outflows collapsed after the Great Crisis of 2007–09 and barely recovered toward the end of the 2010s – core banks took a severe hit after the bubble of the 2000s. The pace of debt outflows during the 2010s was dictated by portfolio flows (included in non-bank flows). Finally, the public debt of core countries, funded from abroad, increased heavily in the years immediately after the Great Crisis.

In all these respects, the figures are consistent with the analysis in the earlier chapters, pointing to the weakness of core banks after the burst of the bubble of the 2010s, the rise of shadow finance, and the escalation of public debt. Financialised capitalism took a major blow in the Great Crisis and was significantly rebalanced not only domestically but also with respect to the international flows of debt. Although it is not shown in the figures, the USA received significant debt inflows during

---

at worldbank.org). The foundation of the dataset is the Balance of Payments data – the other datasets are incorporated to fill gaps. The dataset used for figures 13.5 to 13.9 is the World Development Indicators, published by the World Bank.

38 In effect, these are the so-called BRICS countries but with Turkey instead of South Africa. Apart from hosting some of the most dynamic centres of capitalist accumulation in the world economy, they obviously contain the main challengers to US hegemony.

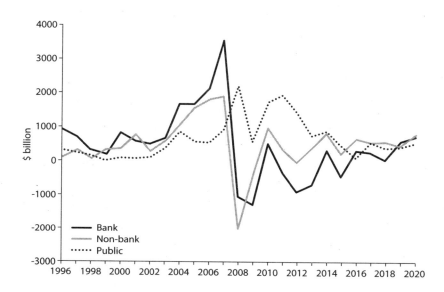

Figure 13.1. Capital inflows, core countries; current US $, bn.

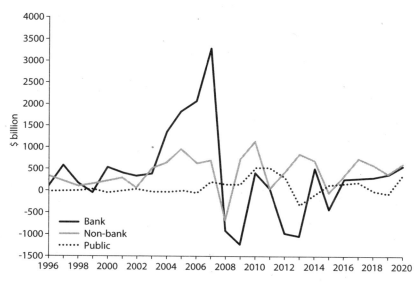

Figure 13.2. Capital outflows, core countries, current US $, bn.

the Great Crisis as international lenders sought the security of the dollar as
world money by largely buying US Treasury bonds.[39] In contrast, the
Eurozone experienced net outflows of capital and greater instability than
the USA.[40]

Consider now figures 13.3 and 13.4, which show capital flows relating
to the group of peripheral countries chosen along similar lines to the
core countries in figures 13.1 and 13.2. Several points are clear and in
line with the earlier analysis.

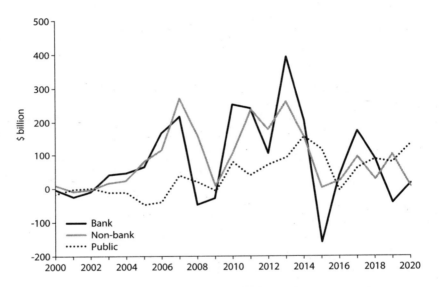

Figure 13.3. Capital inflows, peripheral countries, US $, bn.

The great bulk of international debt flows during the last two decades
took place among core countries.[41] Peripheral countries also experienced a surge of both inflows and outflows of capital in the 2000s,
coming to a sudden stop with the Great Crisis of 2007–09. Following the

39 For more on the composition and size of inflows to the US during the Great
Crisis, see C. Bertaut and L. Pounder (2009) 'The Financial Crisis and U.S. Cross-Border
Financial Flows', Federal Reserve Bulletin, 95.

40 See M. Fratscher (2012) 'Capital Flows, Push Versus Pull Factors and the Global
Financial Crisis', Journal of International Economics 88 (2): 341–56.

41 This point is well established in mainstream literature; see, for instance, G. M.
Milesi-Ferretti, C. Tille, G. I. P. Ottaviano and M. O. Ravn (2011) 'The Great
Retrenchment: International Capital Flows During the Global Financial Crisis', Economic
Policy 26 (66): 287–342.

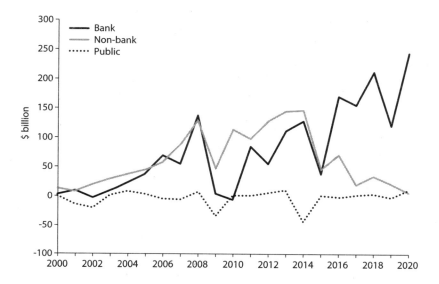

Figure 13.4. Capital outflows, peripheral countries, US $, bn.

shock of the Great Crisis, flows to and from peripheral countries recovered more strongly than for core countries. In particular, banks and non-bank holders of capital from the core sought profitable outlets in peripheral countries, but these flows weakened toward the end of the 2010s.[42]

The data that truly stands out after the Great Crisis of 2007–09, however, relates to capital flows across borders by peripheral banks, which increased greatly in the second half of the 2010s. Much of this increase originated from Chinese banks. Recent estimates – tackling data reporting gaps – suggest that Chinese financial institutions account for one quarter of all bank lending to all other countries in the periphery.[43] In effect, in the 2010s China emerged as the largest provider of cross-border debt to peripheral countries – and the banks providing the loans were publicly owned.

Consider now the inflows and outflows of FDI for both core and peripheral countries in figures 13.5, 13.6, 13.7, and 13.8.

---

42 The inclusion of China in the group, which is necessary in view of the still-peripheral character of Chinese capitalism outlined in chapter 13, obviously complicates the picture. But it does not alter the fundamental pattern.

43 S. Horn, C. Reinhart and C. Trebesch (2019) 'China's Overseas Lending', NBER Working Paper No. 26050 suggests that 50 per cent of China's lending to other peripheral countries might not be reported either to the IMF or to the World Bank.

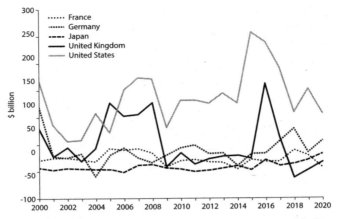

Figure 13.5. FDI inflows, core countries, current US $, bn.

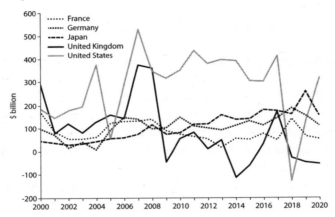

Figure 13.6. FDI outflows, core countries, current US $, bn.

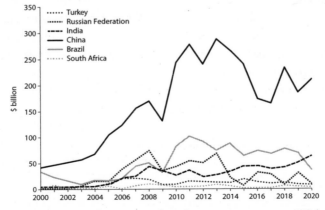

Figure 13.7. FDI inflows, peripheral countries, current US $, bn.

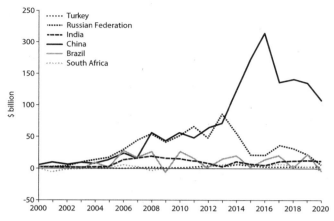

Figure 13.8. FDI outflows, peripheral countries, current US $, bn.

Three important points follow from these figures. First, heavy FDI flows took place among core countries in both directions, reflecting in part the continuing internationalisation of productive capital within the core. The hegemonic USA is simultaneously the largest recipient and the largest provider of FDI across the world economy. Second, FDI flows proved generally more durable than portfolio flows following the Great Crisis of 2007–09. Third, China stands out among peripheral countries as the leading recipient of FDI, and since the crisis of 2007–09 it has also been a major supplier of FDI. The Russian Federation was also a significant recipient and supplier of FDI until 2014, when the sanctions imposed on it by the USA and its allies following the first outbreak of hostilities in Ukraine led to a severe contraction of flows.

It cannot be overemphasised that FDI is frequently mobilised for purposes of tax avoidance. This phenomenon, known as 'phantom FDI', typically relates to flows of capital into an enterprise officially appearing as productive investment but, in practice, reflecting the channelling of money capital into a subsidiary as a way of avoiding tax. It has been estimated that phantom FDI accounts for nearly 40 per cent of all FDI, and the culprits are largely multinational enterprises.[44] Luxembourg and the Netherlands are champions of this practice, receiving enormous volumes of fugitive capital.[45]

44 See BIS (2021) 'Changing Patterns of Capital Flows', CGFS Papers No. 66.
45 See J. Damgaard T. Elkjaer and N. Johannesen (2019) 'The Rise of Phantom Investments', *Finance & Development* 56 (3): 11–13, at imf.org.

In sum, loanable capital flows from core to periphery rebounded after the Great Crisis of 2007–09, driven by banks, shadow banks, and public financial institutions. There was also a sharp increase in debt incurred by governments in peripheral countries, which is evident in the loanable capital inflows in figure 13.3.[46] The rebound of cross-border flows weakened significantly in the second half of the decade, but the substantial weight of portfolio flows indicated a continuing shift toward market-based finance.[47]

These patterns are fully consistent with the transformation of financialisation in core countries and the advance of subordinate financialisation in middle-income countries. The power of the managers of mutual funds, hedge funds, and the like has been in the ascendant even in peripheral countries. Exchange-traded funds (ETFs), for instance, have played an important role in cross-border flows from core to peripheral countries.[48] The growing importance of ETFs went together with that of the enterprises that form the stock market indices on the basis of which the funds engage in asset purchases. In effect, the various methodologies of forming international financial indices determine which countries and corporations are considered 'investment worthy'.[49] The flows of private capital to peripheral countries (but also among the core) have come to depend on the murky and arcane procedures through which some private businesses decide which enterprises are to be included in stock market indices.[50]

The dollar as lever of imperial power: Reserve accumulation

World money is essential to the functioning of the world market, as was discussed in Chapter 10, and serves 'as the universal means of payment,

46 See S. Avdjiev, B. Hardy, S. Kalemli-Özcan, and L. Servén (2018) 'Gross Capital Flows by Banks, Corporates and Sovereigns', BIS Working Paper No. 760.

47 See BIS (2021) 'Changing Patterns of Capital Flows', CGFS Papers No. 66.

48 For discussion and evidence, see N. Converse, E. Levy-Yeyati, and T. Williams (2020) 'How ETFs amplify the global financial cycle in emerging markets', International Finance Discussion Papers No. 1268, at federalreserve.gov.

49 See J. Petry, J. Fichtner, and E. Heemskerk (2021) 'Steering Capital: The Growing Private Authority of Index Providers in the Age of Passive Asset Management', Review of International Political Economy 28 (1): 152–76.

50 See B. Scheubel, L. Stracca, and C. Casanova (2021) 'Old Risks in New Clothes: The Changing Nature of Capital Flows', in VoxEU, CEPR at cepr.org/voxeu on the difference between banks and non-bank financial institution lending. The latter tend to behave more pro-cyclically than banks.

as the universal means of purchase, and as the absolute social materialisation of wealth as such.'[51] Its contemporary form is primarily the US dollar, while other national currencies are ranked according to an implicit hierarchy based on their ability to deliver the functions of world money.[52]

The growth of debt and FDI flows since the early 2000s has gone together with an enormous escalation of reserve holdings of world money, shown in figure 13.9 for four of the peripheral countries in our sample. The holding of vast reserves – mostly denominated in dollars – is directly related to the advance of international portfolio finance and reflects US imperial power.

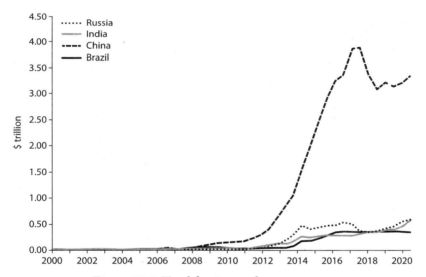

Figure 13.9. Total foreign exchange reserves
(including gold), current US $, tr.
Source: World Bank Development indicators

51 See Marx (1976) [1885] *Capital*, vol. 1, p. 242.

52 See Lapavitsas (2013) *Profiting Without Producing*; and Powell (2013) 'Subordinate Financialisation: A Study of Mexico and its Non-Financial Corporations', for Marxist treatments of currency hierarchy. See also Kaltenbrunner (2010) 'International Financialization and Depreciation'; P. G. Bortz and A. Kaltenbrunner (2018) 'The International Dimension of Financialization in Developing and Emerging Economies', in *Development and Change* 49 (2): 375–93; and Kaltenbrunner and Painceira (2018) 'Subordinated Financial Integration and Financialisation in Emerging Capitalist Economies' for further analysis along broadly post-Keynesian lines.

The pressure to accumulate reserves derives primarily from the risks associated with short-term cross-border capital flows. Even if individual countries managed to borrow internationally in their own currency, they would still be open to the adverse implications of volatile capital flows and associated exchange rate movements. Reserves could help stabilise exchange rates, thus providing some protection to domestic exporters. Reserves could also create an anticipatory preventative cushion at times when liquidity became inaccessible in international markets – for instance, due to sudden capital flight.

Two individual countries truly stand out in these respects: China and Japan. For core countries in Europe, the creation of the euro has dramatically altered the operational framework regarding reserves, as is discussed in detail in chapter 15. For the purposes of the present chapter, reserve accumulation by peripheral countries, including China, has escalated without precedent as international portfolio finance has expanded its presence.

The composition of reserves, shown in figure 13.10, reflects the global hierarchy of currencies.[53] Thus, in the early 2020s, total reserves comprised mostly holdings of the US dollar – nearly 60 per cent of the whole.

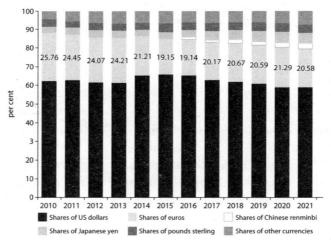

Figure 13.10. Currency composition of
official foreign exchange reserves.
Source: IMF Currency Composition of Official
Foreign Exchange Reserves (COFER)

53 The data for figure 13.10 is drawn from the Currency Composition of Official Foreign Exchange Reserves (COFER), International Financial Statistics (IFS) published by the IMF.

The mild decline of the share of the dollar in total reserves in the second half of the 2010s resulted from greater competition for the function of world money among several lesser currencies, such as the Japanese yen and the Chinese renminbi. Such competition occurs effectively at the margin and reflects the search for greater flexibility in preserving value reliably among internationally active capitals as US hegemony has come under pressure.[54]

It is notable that no single major rival to the dollar has yet emerged, particularly as the euro has failed to become a significant threat in more than two decades, as is clear from figure 13.10, for reasons that are discussed in chapter 15. Even though its role as reserve currency received a boost in the 2010s, the Chinese renminbi remains a very minor participant, with less than 3 per cent of the total of reserves. As long as China retains tight public control over the financial account of the balance of payments, and thus applies controls over international portfolio finance, it is highly unlikely that the renminbi will become a reliable abode of value for global finance. At the same time, China is by far the largest holder of dollars as world money.

Reserves of world money entail substantial costs for the economies of the holders.[55] To obtain dollar reserves, the buyer advances liquid funds to the USA typically in exchange for public financial assets that are presumably safe and could be easily sold again. In effect, core countries, such as Japan, rising industrial powers, such as China, great fossil fuel producers, such as Saudi Arabia and Russia, but also a broad range of the global poor, lend money capital to the USA to accumulate dollar reserves. In 2014, at the peak of its reserve formation, China's purchases of US Treasury bonds reached 10 per cent of US GDP.[56]

Since they are held as foreign public financial assets, reserves earn little interest compared with the high interest paid on domestic financial assets by peripheral countries. Furthermore, countries with currencies toward the bottom of the hierarchy pay higher interest rates in international markets as well as providing lenders with larger dividends

54 For a recent empirical study of the changing currency hierarchy, see S. Arslanalp, B. Eichengreen, and C. Simpson-Bell (2022) 'The Stealth Erosion of Dollar Dominance: Active Diversifiers and the Rise of Nontraditional Reserve Currencies', IMF Working Paper No. 58.

55 See D. Rodrik (2006) 'The Social Cost of Foreign Exchange Reserves', *International Economic Journal* 20 (3): 253–66, where an original contribution to this debate is made.

56 See Horn, Reinhart, and Trebesch (2019) 'China's Overseas Lending'.

and capital gains to offset heightened risk perceptions.[57] Reserve accumulation amounts to paying a hidden tribute to the hegemon.

Reserves declined soon after the Great Crisis, including for China. This development was partly due to the decline in revenues by oil exporters as the price of oil weakened in the 2010s. Mostly, however, it was due to China, which attenuated its reserve holding in the 2010s while allowing a significant outflow of banking capital, as is implicit in figure 13.4. Reserves, however, increased again toward the end of the decade and in the 2020s as concerns about financial stability grew.

The pandemic capital flow panic

Enormously expensive as they are for peripheral countries, reserves were to demonstrate their importance when the pandemic struck. Throughout the 2010s, the boost to finance delivered by monetary policies in core countries induced sustained growth of stock markets, especially in the USA, as was discussed in part II. By 2018, it was clear that stock market rises bore no relation to the underlying performance of accumulation, and there were widespread expectations of a new financial crisis and a recession.[58] The parallel expansion of cross-border capital flows to peripheral countries, shown in figure 13.5, also created highly unstable conditions internationally. The ground was set for the huge shock of the pandemic.

In March 2020, global finance witnessed the largest capital flight on record. Portfolio outflows from peripheral countries were about fifty percentage points larger in volume than those during the Great Crisis a little over a decade earlier.[59] Panicking holders of risky financial assets – often synonymous with peripheral country debt instruments – sold and sought safety in the core, primarily the USA. While the crisis of

---

57 On this issue see, selectively, L. M. Paulani (2010) 'Brazil in the Crisis of the Finance-Led Regime of Accumulation', *Review of Radical Political Economics* 42: 3; Isaacs and Kaltenbrunner (2018) 'Financialization and Liberalization'; Kaltenbrunner and Painceira (2015) 'Developing Countries' Changing Nature of Financial Integration and New Forms of External Vulnerability'; and Kaltenbrunner and Painceira (2018) 'Subordinated Financial Integration and Financialisation in Emerging Capitalist Economies'.

58 See, for instance, H. Böhme (2018) 'Will 2019 Be the Year of the Crash?', *Deutsche Welle*, 25 December, at dw.com.

59 See F. E. Martin et al. (2020) 'Capital Flows During the Pandemic: Lessons for a More Resilient International Financial Architecture', Bank of England, Financial Stability Paper No. 45.

2007–09 mainly hit banks and their cross-border flows, the enormous shock of 2020 involved portfolio holders, reflecting the diminished role of banks in the previous decade.

The blows on peripheral countries came from several directions. As loanable capital holders fled to the USA, the dollar rose, putting downward pressure on peripheral country exchange rates as well as constraining domestic financial systems that had dollar-denominated liabilities.[60] The cost of dollar liabilities also increased as major international banks faced rising funding costs in the US money markets and charged higher rates to peripheral banks.[61] Peripheral countries experienced portfolio outflows and loss of reserves on a huge scale.[62] Figure 13.11 shows the magnitude of the outflows.

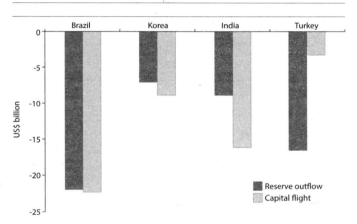

Figure 13.11. Capital outflows, March 2020.
Source: The dataset used is the OECD Monthly Capital Flow Dataset and is mainly based on data reported by central banks.[63] The data comes specifically from the Bank of Korea, Reserve Bank of India, Central Bank of the Republic of Turkey, and Banco Central do Brazil.

---

60 See E. Eren, A. Schrimpf, and V. Sushko (2020) 'US Dollar Funding Markets During the Covid-19 Crisis – The International Dimension', BIS Bulletin No. 15, at bis. org.

61 See Martin et al. (2020) 'Capital Flows During the Pandemic'.

62 See P. Hördahl and I. Shim (2020) 'EME Bond Portfolio Flows and Long-Term Interest Rates During the Covid-19 Pandemic', BIS Bulletin No. 18, at bis.org.

63 A. de Crescenzio and E. Lepers (2021) 'Extreme Capital Flow Episodes from the Global Financial Crisis to COVID-19: An Exploration with Monthly Data', OECD Working Papers on International Investment No. 05.

To make matters worse, the risky assets sold by shadow banks were often bonds denominated in the domestic currency of peripheral countries. This became a negative feedback loop, whereby weakening local currencies caused losses for foreign investors, leading to sales of local-currency-denominated assets, and thus putting further pressure on exchange rates.[64] The balance sheets of peripheral enterprises also worsened as dollar-denominated debt became more difficult to bear.

At the same time, core countries witnessed sizeable capital inflows into banks, associated with currency swap lines provided by the Federal Reserve, which are discussed in the following section.[65] The central bank of the hegemon provided access to the desperately coveted dollar, acting as a lever of economic policy but also of political power. The allies of the USA were first in line.

When the crisis hit in March 2020, broad swathes of peripheral countries that lacked the privilege of hegemonic favour faced dollar shortages and capital flight. They had to rely on the financial resources provided by the IMF.[66] Peripheral countries also engaged in foreign exchange interventions, such as selling their US dollar reserves, to confront the capital flight.[67] The pressure abated only after the USA and other core countries had dramatically loosened their monetary policies. There was no doubt regarding who controlled the mechanisms of stability and who determined the rules of global financial interaction in the last instance.

Exercising imperial power: Dollar swap lines

It is a rule of contemporary international portfolio finance that if a country has high volumes of exposure to globally active US financial institutions and strong trade bonds with the US economy, it is more likely to obtain access to dollars via swap lines.[68] An unspoken but

---

64 See Martin et al. (2020) 'Capital Flows During the Pandemic'.

65 See Crescenzio and Lepers (2021) 'Extreme Capital Flow Episodes from the Global Financial Crisis to COVID-19'.

66 See the footnotes to IMF (2022) 'COVID-19 Financial Assistance and Debt Service Relief', March, at imf.org.

67 See Martin et al. (2020) 'Capital Flows During the Pandemic'.

68 For empirical work on this, see J. Aizenman, H. Ito and G. K. Pasricha (2022) 'Central Bank Swap Arrangements in the COVID-19 Crisis', *Journal of International Money and Finance* April, 122: 102555.

equally important factor is that the country should also be a political ally of the USA and ready to support the hegemon's military interventions across the world. The swap lines provided by the Federal Reserve in 2007–09 applied to countries that effectively comprised the top tier of the currency hierarchy – standing just below the dollar.[69] In March 2020, the Fed extended swap lines to a further range of central banks, though these were limited in volume.

Swap lines among central banks – primarily those with the Federal Reserve – alleviated dollar-funding stresses among core countries and in effect helped stabilise the outflows of capital from periphery to core. They are a vital support instrument for the aggressive financial enterprises that dominate international portfolio finance and strive for global reach. In this respect, they are also a plain manifestation of imperial power.

Swap lines are reciprocal payment arrangements between central banks: one central bank agrees temporarily to swap parts of its balance sheet with that of another, with the obligation to reverse the swap after a given time. The central bank of a country short of dollars, for instance, would obtain an account with the Federal Reserve, while the latter would receive an account denominated in the currency of the other country and held at its central bank for a period of time. When the swap is reversed – at the same exchange rate – interest is paid to the Federal Reserve.

Core central banks also offer swaps in other currencies, including the euro, the Japanese yen, the pound sterling, and the Swiss franc.[70] The spread of bilateral swaps is one factor accounting for the rising share of the smaller leading currencies in the global reserves of world money, as is shown in the rest of this section. Standing swap arrangements – particularly those that involve the Federal Reserve – aim to provide liquidity to stabilise exchange rates and financial markets. In moments of crisis, swap lines allow the US Federal Reserve to function as an international lender of last resort, providing global markets with world money and thereby protecting financial agents from destabilising

---

69 See P. Mehrling (2015) 'Elasticity and Discipline in the Global Swap Network', Institute for New Economic Thinking Working Papers No. 27.

70 For a recent review of the network of bilateral swap lines, see M. Perks, Y. Rao, and K. Tokuoka (2021) 'Evolution of Bilateral Swap Lines', IMF Working Papers No. 210. For the Eurozone in particular, see, for instance, S. Albrizio et al. (2021) 'ECB Euro Liquidity Lines', Banco d'Espana Working Paper No. 2125.

losses.[71] It is a backstop that supplies bridging liquidity until private
financial enterprises can resume trading.[72]

Central banks making loans of world money to each other in times of
international turmoil is an old practice that goes back to at least the
crises of the early nineteenth century. The aim was to make the reserves
of another central bank available to the central bank of a country facing
an outflow of gold, thus stabilising the exchange rate and dealing with
financial panic. Until the collapse of the Bretton Woods system, swap
lines retained their character as tools for exchange rate management.
The ascendancy of international portfolio finance and particularly the
rise of shadow finance during the last two decades has brought major
changes to the deployment of swap lines.

Since the Great Crisis of 2007–09, swap lines have acted as instruments of intervention in international money markets, including in the
enormous Eurodollar market that lies beyond the regulatory jurisdiction of the US government. Swap lines enable the Federal Reserve to
influence interest rates abroad, but still in line with domestic US monetary policy. The US central bank is, thus, capable of easing the funding
requirements of banks and shadow banks, which also engage in swaps
among themselves as they manage their private portfolios.[73] The Federal
Reserve acts as the swap agent of last resort, facilitating the speculative
activities of international financial enterprises.[74]

The entanglement of swap lines, international money markets in
dollars, and global financial markets highlights the interconnection
between the domestic and international orders of capitalist accumulation with respect to finance. It also demonstrates the hybridity between
private financial market agents and public authorities that continually

71 The role of emergency US dollar swap lines in the early days of the pandemic
shock was analysed by N. Cetorelli, L. S. Goldberg, and F. Ravazzolo (2020) 'How Fed
Swap Lines Supported the US Corporate Credit Market Amid COVID-19 Strains'
Federal Reserve Bank of New York Liberty Street Economics, No. 20200612, showing
that the provision of swap facilities primarily covered the funding needs of banks. See
also M. Choi et al. (2022) 'The Fed's Central Bank Swap Lines and Fima Repo Facility',
Economic Policy Review 28 (1): 93–113.

72 See P. Mehrling (2014) 'Why Central Banking Should Be Re-Imagined', BIS
Working Paper No. 79.

73 See I. Aldasoro et al. (2020) 'Central Bank Swap Lines and Cross-Border Bank
Flows', BIS Bulletin No. 34, at bis.org.

74 For a study of the effectiveness of the Federal Reserve as an international lender
of last resort, see S. Bahaj and R. Reis (2021) 'Central Bank Swap Lines: Evidence on the
Effects of the Lender of Last Resort', Review of Economic Studies 89 (4): 1654–93.

create those links.[75] Swap lines are essential to the USA projecting its hegemonic power over both core and peripheral countries in the realm of global finance.

Beyond swap lines, the US ruling bloc has repeatedly used access to the dollar as world money for strategic political purposes, for instance by freezing the reserves of several countries, including Iran, Venezuela, and Afghanistan. Most conspicuously, the USA froze a large part of the enormous reserves of Russia during the Russo-Ukrainian War in 2022. The actions of the US government left no doubt that the dollar as world money is a cardinal instrument of imperial power for the USA.

Equally striking was US deployment of the dollar as an economic weapon by taking advantage of its accounting and paying functions among internationally active banks. Clearing and settlement of obligations among banks is fundamental to pursuing cross-border transactions. The Society for Worldwide Interbank Financial Telecommunication (SWIFT) is supposed to be a neutral communication channel among banks, headquartered in Belgium and based on the dollar. Ostensibly, SWIFT is a non-political, purely economic, electronic software that standardises the information available to banks about transactions, which then allows for clearing and settlement.

In reality, the institutional mechanisms of SWIFT are controlled by the USA. The communication protocol required for international banking clearing and settlement by international banks is used by the USA in the same way as dollar reserves – that is, as an instrument of imperial power. Through SWIFT, the USA controls the banking 'language' required for international clearing and settlement and is able to monitor all the relevant international transactions. The imperial use of SWIFT was demonstrated in 2022, when Russian banks were excluded from its facilities, as Iranian banks had been in 2018.

The aggressive use of the dollar by the USA is, nonetheless, a double-edged sword. Reserves of world money are supposed to be a secure abode of value, and use of the dollar as means of payment and unit of account is supposed to serve the interests of international capital in

---

75 For an extensive discussion on the private–public linkage of financial markets, see, for instance, K. Pistor (2013) 'A Legal Theory of Finance', *Journal of Comparative Economics* 41 (2): 315–30; R. C. Hockett and S. T. Omarova (2016) 'The Finance Franchise', *Cornell Law Review* 1143; S. Ugolini (2017) *The Evolution of Central Banking: Theory and History*, Palgrave Macmillan: London; and M. Ricks (2018) 'Money as Infrastructure', *Columbia Business Law Review* 757.

general. When the ability of the dollar to deliver the tasks of world money depends explicitly on the strategic choices of the US ruling bloc, its role is directly undermined. As was noted above, there are still no major competitors to the dollar in this regard among the leading currencies. But the rapid technological developments of recent years have impacted on the domestic form of money in ways that could prove important at the world level.

Digital world money?

Digital technologies have given rise to new forms of money that have already become prevalent in the sphere of domestic circulation of core countries and increasingly of peripheral countries. Two of these forms of digital money (or e-money), namely 'access e-money' and 'e-money proper', have already been analysed in political economy and pose few theoretical difficulties.[76]

Access e-money is simply the electronic (digital) form of credit money (credit and debit cards, credit transfers, direct debits, etc.). It presents no problems for economic analysis, since it is simply the liability of the issuer that returns when assets mature. Access e-money reflects merely the continuing shift of credit money away from paper and toward an incorporeal form.

In contrast, e-money proper, although still the liability of the issuer, is not created through the advance of credit. Rather, it is privately issued money stored on electronic devices and purchased with ordinary money at par value. Some examples are 'prepaid cards, or prepaid software programmes used on the internet, often called server-based e-money'.[77] These forms of money are frequently issued by industrial and commercial enterprises; of note among these are mobile telephony providers, which have risen to the fore in peripheral countries in recent years, facilitating monetary transactions locally or even nationally.

For the purposes of world money, however, neither of these digital forms of money is of great consequence. The development that matters is the emergence of cryptocurrencies, yet another digital form of money.

---

76 See Lapavitsas (2013) *Profiting without Producing*, pp. 87–100.
77 Ibid., p. 97.

Cryptocurrencies are not liabilities of an issuer created through the advance of credit and returning to the issuer when loans mature and are repaid – they are not credit money. They are also not liabilities of an issuer bought at par by using regular money – they are not e-money proper. Instead, they are potential digital commodity monies.

Cryptocurrencies are properly considered as digital assets (peculiar commodities). To be sure, they lack corporeality but there is a huge range of non-digital commodities which also lack corporeality, such as services. A haircut is as incorporeal as a website – both lack a physical body. However, cryptocurrencies are certainly material, if one properly understands the digital world to be a physical entity, rather than a meta-physical, mental, or even spiritual universe.[78] Put differently, the 'cyber-space' is a material reality of computers, cables, energy, specialist techni-cians, and users that are subject to the restrictions of matter. Its material reality includes thousands of kilometres of submarine cables, and cryp-tocurrencies are a product of it.[79]

In this light, the digital process that underpins cryptocurrencies, i.e. distributed ledger technology (DLT), is a software that functions as a database creating a digital double-entry bookkeeping system. For our purposes, the most appropriate form briefly to consider is a distributed ledger system that is based on a blockchain and is freely open to partici-pants ('permissionless'). Such a system would be programmed as a chain of blocks among nodes (each node being, for instance, a transactor). If a node initiated new data, a predefined algorithmic method would vali-date the data additions, creating a new block and adding it to the digital ledger.[80] A full history of all transactions among nodes would be publicly available at all times.

There is an obvious resemblance between such 'permissionless' cryp-tocurrencies and the chains of credit money. When credit money is deployed, a new transaction among two agents adds fresh obligations to the totality of promises and counter-promises comprising the chain. However, in a chain of credit money the fresh obligations could only be

---

78 Jean-François Blanchette (2011) 'A Material History of Bits', *Journal of the American Society for Information Science and Technology* 62 (6): 1042–57.

79 See Andrew Blum (2013) *Tubes: A Journey to the Center of the Internet*, Ecco: New York.

80 World Bank (2017) 'Distribute Ledger Technology (DLT) and Blockchain', *FinTech Note* No. 1, pt. 2. There are also DLTs that do not work with this type of block dynamics.

generally trusted if a third party guaranteed their validity. This typically means that the credit instrument used in one transaction could not be simultaneously or subsequently used by the same transactor in another. The task of ensuring the validity of the credit instruments is assumed by financial intermediaries, and ultimately by the central bank, providing the asset into which all others are finally convertible.

In contrast, within a blockchain there is no need for a third party. The validity of the new block is established through cryptography, which ensures that the information stored in the software cannot be hacked, and thus cannot also be used by others.

After being designed, some cryptocurrencies could be 'mined' – that is, fresh units could come to light through algorithmic processes that require enormous computer power and consume vast amounts of electricity – but this does not hold for centralised cryptocurrencies, for instance. A transactor could buy a cryptocurrency from a broker, or in a market (an exchange), by using regular money. The cryptocurrency would then be placed in a digital wallet, and each wallet could send and receive units as the holder required.

There is, in this respect, an evident similarity with the use of commodity money among transactors. A gold coin generates its own trust, since it possesses value, while the same coin cannot be used simultaneously in more than one transaction, since it becomes the property of the seller. There is no need for a third party to validate transactions. It is, thus, natural for cryptocurrencies to be referred to as 'digital gold'.

But cryptocurrencies are also profoundly different from gold, and that has nothing to do with their lack of a natural body. Indeed, the lack of corporeality is altogether a trivial issue with regard to the ability of cryptocurrencies to act as money. The real point of difference is that cryptocurrencies, unlike gold, do not have an intrinsic use value. They are digital entities that could potentially become money or be used for financial speculation, without any other usefulness imparted to them through production. In terms of the discussion of money in part II of this book, cryptocurrencies are digital entities that are merely able to acquire the formal use value of being money.

For that to become a reality, however, two conditions are paramount, which also hold for gold: first, cryptocurrencies must possess certain physical characteristics, such as homogeneity, durability, divisibility, and so on; second, cryptocurrencies must command sufficient social custom, allowing them to act as the universal equivalent.[81] Such social custom typically relies on the explicit backing of the state through a range of legal and other means, as was discussed for the domestic functioning of money in part II.

The special physical characteristics required for 'moneyness' are socially programmed into cryptocurrencies – that is, they are already encoded in the blockchain by design. The second condition, however, is of an entirely different order of difficulty. Fundamental to the inability of cryptocurrencies to make the full transition to money is the lack of a social custom of use that is vitally reinforced by systematic state intervention.

This deficiency is particularly pronounced, as cryptocurrencies have no intrinsic use value that could separately familiarise people with their deployment. Unlike precious metals, cryptocurrencies cannot rely on their social use or on plain tradition arising from use, as happened for instance with gold and silver, used for jewellery, ornaments, and so on. Lack of social custom of use also contributes to high transaction fees. In practice, therefore, most cryptocurrencies are used as financial assets for speculation rather than as money. They will remain merely potential money until mechanisms emerge that could also satisfy the second prerequisite of 'moneyness'. It is hard to see how this could happen without the direct involvement of the state.

In this connection it is important to note that there are also 'permissioned' cryptocurrencies, in which the participants are controlled. For such cryptocurrencies, the centralising authority of the state and its central bank is perfectly compatible with DLT and blockchains. Consequently, as cryptocurrencies began spontaneously to proliferate during the last decade, central banks and transnational financial institutions became increasingly involved in developing and using them.[82]

---

81 On these paramount requirements of money, see C. Lapavitsas (2005) 'The Emergence of Money in Commodity Exchange, or Money as Monopolist of the Ability to Buy', *Review of Political Economy* 17 (4): 549–69.

82 For a more detailed discussion, see, for instance, M. Bech and R. Garratt (2017) 'Central Bank Cryptocurrencies', *BIS*, Quarterly Review, September, pp. 55–70; S. Riksbank (2017) 'The Riksbank's e-krona Project. Report 1', at riksbank.se; S. Riksbank (2018) 'The Riksbank's e-krona Project. Report 2', at riksbank.se; Norges Bank (2018) 'Central Bank Digital Currencies', Norges Bank Papers No. 1; Bank of Israel (2018) 'Report of the Team to Examine the Issue of Central Bank Digital Currencies', at boi.org.il/en; T. Mancini Griffoli et al. (2018) 'Casting Light on Central Bank Digital Currency', *Staff Discussion Notes* 18 (8): 1; ECB (2019) 'Exploring Anonymity in Central Bank Digital Currencies', *InFocus* 4; C. Boar, H. Holden, and A. Wadsworth (2020) 'Impending

Several state-backed cryptocurrencies have already emerged.

The most important among these state-backed forms is the Chinese Digital Currency Electronic Payment (e-CNY), or digital renminbi, a cryptocurrency that can be legally used for the settlement of obligations, which is already in the testing phase. This is a form of Central Bank Digital Currency: a liability of the central bank that is created directly on the balance sheet without engaging in credit transactions. In short, state-backed cryptocurrencies can be thought of as a kind of 'crypto fiat money'. They are created by the state and are constantly in circulation without following the circular path of credit money. The Law of Reflux does not apply to such money.

In contrast to 'permissionless' cryptocurrencies, the 'moneyness' of which remains deeply compromised by lack of use value and broader customs of use backed by state support, the Chinese e-CNY is money. Like other cryptocurrencies, it is designed and produced with the physical characteristics required to become money already encoded in its software. But it is also able to rely on the requisite social custom since e-CNY is formally backed by the state in settling obligations. Moreover, the Chinese people are already widely accustomed to using access e-money and e-money proper through a range of internet innovations, and this would facilitate the social acceptability and customary practice that are required for a state-backed cryptocurrency to become fully established as money.

This new type of money could potentially act as an international reserve currency, even if it was originally designed for domestic purposes.[83] In principle, it is conceivable that internationally active agents, including states, could keep value in such fiat money, the use of which would be validated through cryptography. It could potentially be independent of the existing international banking mechanisms, including international clearing, which remains under the dominant control of the USA with reference to the dollar.

For these reasons, digital money is likely to be a field of intense

---

Arrival – A Sequel to the Survey on Central Bank Digital Currency', BIS Working Paper No. 107; R. Auer and R. Böhme (2020) 'The Technology of Retail Central Bank Digital Currency', *BIS Quarterly Review*, 85–100; R. Auer, P. Haene, and H. Holden (2021) 'Multi-CBDC Arrangements and the Future of Cross-border Payments', BIS Working Paper No. 115.

83 See J. J. Duque (2020) 'State Involvement in Cryptocurrencies. A Potential World Money?', *The Japanese Political Economy* 46 (1): 65–82.

hegemonic competition in the years ahead. Chinese 'crypto fiat' created independently of credit processes might allow for limited control by the Chinese state after entering global circulation. It could thus prove an important instrument in the hegemonic contest with the USA. However, that would depend on the Chinese state creating a framework of trust for such money through its political and military relations with other states in the world economy. Though such a development is possible, its feasibility remains dubious for reasons that will become clearer after considering the rise of China in chapter 14.

14

The Chinese Hegemonic Challenge

Domestic class dominance and world hegemony

The early 2020s witnessed intensified economic, political, and military tension, as US pre-eminence came under a sustained challenge. Historical analogies never work perfectly, but the emerging hegemonic contests resemble those prior to 1914, for the current contests have a multiplicity of political and national causes, but they are also profoundly economic. As was established in the preceding chapters, hegemonic competition turns on who has the power to shape the international realm of capitalist activity, dictating the framework of the flows of productive, commercial, and financial capital across the world economy. Pivotal to it is control over world money.

In all these regards, the contemporary struggle for hegemony is qualitatively different from the political, ideological, and military contest between the USA and the Soviet Union that lasted until 1991. Several powers are already positioning themselves, including Russia, India, and others. The contestants come from the periphery, and all seek a greater independent say in shaping the international realm. There is no doubt, however, that the main challenger is China. The relationship between the USA and China took a turn for the worse in the 2010s, and the health emergency deepened the divide.

Strikingly, the economic dimension of the contest between the USA and China hinges on the role of the state in both countries. However, both the mode and the extent of state intervention in China are profoundly different from those adopted by the USA. The US state provides support to financialised capitalism by drawing chiefly on command over fiat money, while also mobilising its intimate links with private corporations. The Chinese state has certainly catalysed the meteoric rise of China during the last four decades but its interventions are based on direct ownership and command over both productive resources and finance. The difference is of great importance for the emerging hegemonic contest.

The following sections show that China has already achieved a leading position in manufacturing and trade in the world economy, while developing new institutions with a significant impact on the global flows of capital. However, the road to hegemony is long, twisted, and risky. China has become pre-eminent in manufacturing and trade in the world economy, but its position in the global financial networks and its ability to exercise command over world money are not on the same level.

If China is to become truly hegemonic, it will have to tackle its weaknesses in world finance and money, and the task is Herculean, given the international trends discussed in previous chapters. But that is not all, for China's difficulties with finance and money in essence reflect the deeper problem it faces within the world economy. Namely, should China attempt to integrate further into the existing international economic order by implicitly accepting US hegemony, or should it continue to create diverging institutions that implicitly contest US hegemony but perhaps limit Chinese access to the world market as a whole? The challenge posed to China by the dollar as world money is ultimately a condensed form of this dilemma.

The international predicament of China corresponds directly with tough domestic choices, as is always the case with capitalist development. The Chinese economy faces onerous domestic problems in the 2020s, including uneven development across the country's regions, a profound divergence between rural and urban economy, a heavy preponderance of investment over consumption, a rapidly ageing population, and long working hours for those who are employed. The years of exceptionally rapid capitalist accumulation are in the past, and the rate of return on Chinese capital is on a downward path, as is shown in the following sections. These structural problems are compounded by a vast load of debt generated by the financial system during the last two decades, including China's peculiar 'shadow banks'.

The Chinese ruling bloc has not escaped the acute social and economic tensions that typically emerge as capitalist relations dominate economic activity. The domestic problems of the Chinese economy relate to the balance between public and private control over resources, the nature of property rights over key enterprises, and the resultant opposition between capital and labour. China has not taken the same neoliberal path as other core and peripheral countries during the last four decades, its policy choices rebounding in favour of domestic growth and raising the country's international weight. Nevertheless, the tension between public and private (as well as potentially private) control over resources has not been eliminated and will dictate the country's direction in the future.

Transforming the functioning of the domestic economy and thus altering the position of a country in the world economy is never merely a technical issue. For China to become a hegemonic power, it will have to raise the productivity of its labour force still further, rebalance domestic investment and consumption, accelerate technological innovation, reorganise the allocation of loanable money capital, retain its position as a leading trading nation, sustain the flows of FDI in both directions, and so on. These are momentous tasks that will have to be completed in the face of sustained US opposition and hostility. They necessarily involve shaking up the forms of organisation of Chinese production, while altering the relationship between capital and labour. Ultimately, they pivot on who owns and commands the core productive forces of an economy that is already largely organised on capitalist principles.

Lest it be misunderstood, it is highly unlikely that there will be an explicit conflict between publicly and privately owned capitals in China in the coming future. There is no independent private capitalist class in China capable of directly challenging the command of the state over the core of the Chinese economy. Indeed, it is shown in this chapter that the interpenetration of private and public control over capital in China has grown in recent years. Rather, tensions are likely to appear within the public mechanisms commanding the enormous enterprises that are the backbone of the Chinese economy, which are integrally linked to the Communist Party of China. Power fiefs have already emerged that exercise vast power and which are not necessarily in line with overall state economic policy.

For the time being the Chinese ruling bloc appears to have decided to continue with public control over strategic productive forces, marshalled by the Communist Party. However, the pressure to move toward private ownership and control has far from disappeared. The conduct of China in the emerging hegemonic contest with the USA will depend on the outcomes of the domestic struggle, which will also involve labour. If privatisation somehow prevailed within the ranks of the ruling bloc and a profit-driven bourgeois class emerged at the helm, it is hard to see how the Chinese challenge to US hegemony would be sustained. To substantiate these points, several key aspects of the Chinese economy are considered in the rest of this chapter.

China in the ascendant economically and militarily

The USA and most of its Western allies refused to recognise the People's Republic of China after its establishment in 1949, and the new Chinese state soon adopted the Soviet type of command economy. In the late 1970s, however, China took the historic decision to engage in a transition toward what its elite currently calls a 'socialist market economy'. The debate on the nature of the reshaped Chinese economy – that is, whether it is state capitalism, market socialism, or other – has never stopped.[1]

For our purposes, it is not necessary to enter this debate since it is indisputable that a powerful and dynamic capitalist sector lies at the core of the Chinese economy. Equally important is that capitalist principles of organising economic activity also permeate sectors of the economy in which capitalist property rights are not established. What matters more, however, is to consider the mechanisms through which the Chinese state and the Communist Party of China support, promote, and manipulate capitalist economic relations, thereby intensifying the emerging hegemonic contest with the USA.

Once capitalism was unleashed, China advanced with extraordinary speed across a broad front, including industrial production, financial flows, and technology. The Chinese economy is currently the second largest in the world, and Chinese GDP in 2020 was almost one hundred times bigger than in 1978. China also has the largest manufacturing sector in the world and is the only country whose economy registers all the industrial categories contained in the United Nations (UN) International Standard Industrial Classification.

Figure 14.1 brings out the stark contrast in manufacturing value added between China and the five core countries considered in part II; Russia was

---

1 For several measured observations from different radical perspectives, see, for instance, N. Yokokawa, J. Ghosh, and R. Rowthorn (eds) (2013) *Industrialization of China and India*, Routledge: London.

also included to place the hegemonic struggle in fuller context. Starting from third place in 2004, when the pandemic struck in 2019 Chinese manufacturing output was roughly equal to that of the USA, Japan, and Germany taken together. During that period, relative stagnation at a significantly lower level was manifested for France, the UK, and Russia.

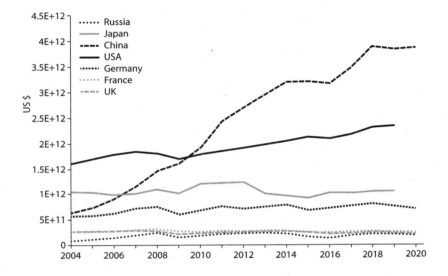

Figure 14.1. Manufacturing value added, 2004–20, current US $.
Source: Constructed from World Bank data.

The manufacturing data is consistent with China becoming the largest trading economy in the world, as is shown in figure 14.2, and the chief trading partner of many more countries than the USA can boast. It is apparent from the figure that exports became an even more important part of the Chinese economy during the pandemic, precisely at a time when the exports of its competitors declined precipitously.

Crucially for the hegemonic contest, the Chinese domestic defence sector has also advanced in leaps and bounds during the last two decades as the country's manufacturing and technological capabilities have escalated. As is shown in figure 14.3, China is currently the second-largest military spender in the world, though still some way behind the USA, which has also greatly increased its military spending since the early 2000s.

A substantial part of US military expenditure is to pay for personnel, since the hegemon is obliged to maintain a vast military presence across

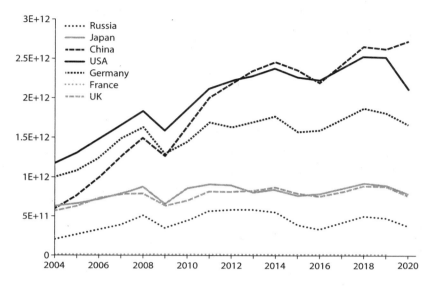

Figure 14.2. Exports of goods and services, 2004–20, current US $.
Source: Constructed from World Bank data.

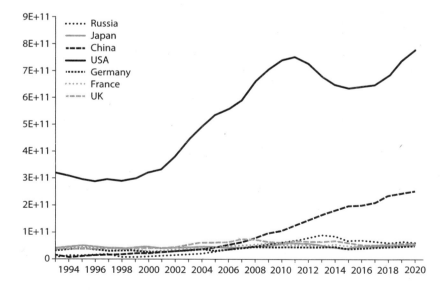

Figure 14.3. Military expenditure, current US $.
Source: Constructed from World Bank data.

the world, and it is likely that there are also significant hidden expenditures that are not shown in figure 14.3 for all countries. Nonetheless, China is the USA's only major challenger in terms of military expenditure, spending as much as Russia, the UK, France, Germany, and Japan combined. If examined relative to GDP, the rankings would look quite different, since rapid growth has kept Chinese military spending below 2 per cent during this period, in contrast to the USA and Russia, where spending has fluctuated between 3 and 5 per cent, but the overall outlook is not in doubt.

The US Department of Defense is tasked with submitting an annual report to the US Congress regarding China's military development and tracking Chinese military power. According to the report for 2021, the Chinese armed forces had the largest navy and the third-largest air force in the world, while China continued rapidly to upgrade its nuclear capability and gradually to acquire an international military presence.[2] China can already compete with the USA across a range of military fields, including naval shipbuilding, land-based conventional ballistic and cruise missiles, integrated air defence systems, and so on. The US Department of Defense expects China's armed forces to expand their capabilities significantly in the coming two decades, including through the adoption of new technologies, thus becoming 'informatised'.

It is vital to note, however, that military power is more than a simple reflection of military spending, since it also depends on cutting-edge war technologies and nuclear capabilities. In these regards, the Russian state retains considerably more hegemonic clout than its plain military spending, or even its manufacturing and trading statistics, would convey. A hegemonic military presence, furthermore, also depends on the ability to project power across the world through military bases and military equipment. The USA is in a league of its own in this respect, with hundreds of bases and military capability encircling the globe. China has a lot of distance to cover.

Military power aside, China has been gradually mounting a challenge to US hegemony in the world economy by steadily forming separate institutional mechanisms that diverge from those created by the USA. The economies of both core and peripheral countries are thereby becoming increasingly integrated with China, but still within the framework of

2 See US Department of Defense (2021) *Military and Security Developments Involving the People's Republic of China: A Report to Congress*, November, chs 2 and 5, at media.defense.gov.

the world market. The list of steps taken by China in this regard is long and continues to expand, often involving established US political allies.

In 2020, for instance, China concluded the EU–China Comprehensive Agreement on Investment, which opened Chinese markets and financial services to EU countries, along with health services (private hospitals), telecommunications, and research and development.[3] In the same year, China and several countries of the Pacific Rim, including Japan, South Korea, Australia, and New Zealand, signed a Regional Comprehensive Economic Partnership, an agreement that could potentially result in the largest free trading area in the world.

Along similar lines, since 2013, China has systematically promoted the Belt and Road Initiative. This aims to link the entire Eurasian continent via motorways, railways, ports, energy infrastructure, and trade networks, providing 'public goods' to the world.[4] Member countries of the initiative would presumably cooperate in five areas: policy coordination, facility connectivity, unimpeded trade, financial integration, and people-to-people bonds.

In 2013, China also promoted the establishment of the Asian Infrastructure Investment Bank (AIIB), a multilateral development bank focusing on infrastructure in Asia. In theory, this would serve the financial needs of countries in Asia without the stringent conditionality of the IMF or the World Bank – that is, it would advance loans without insisting on liberalisation or imposing detailed structural reforms. In practice, however, the role played by the AIIB in the years since its establishment has been modest.

More important has been the direct provision of aid to developing countries by creating special institutions associated with nearly all major multilateral development banks. Thus, the Growing Together Fund was set up at the African Development Bank, while a co-financing fund was established for Latin America and Caribbean countries with the Inter-American Development Bank.[5] The bulk of Chinese aid in the 2010s

---

3 This is the result of a long process that began in 2012; see European Commission 'EU-China Agreement: Milestones and Documents', at policy.trade.ec.europa.eu.

4 Stated with charming simplicity by the State Council Information Office of the People's Republic of China (2019) *China and the World in the New Era*, section 2.3, while section 3.5 asserts, equally charmingly, that 'China will never seek hegemony', at english.www.gov.cn.

5 L. Calabrese, B. Willitts-King, and Y. Chen (2021) 'How China's New White Paper Defines a Decade of Development Cooperation', Overseas Development Institute, at odi.org.

went to low- and middle-income countries, mostly in Asia and Africa, through bilateral agreements.

These policies are a challenge to the international institutional framework and the neoliberalism promoted by the hegemonic USA in recent decades. Peripheral countries have long resented the one-size-fits-all policies implemented by the multilateral institutions created by the USA, which have frequently entailed catastrophic results.

At the same time, the economic interpenetration between China and core countries has also proceeded in leaps and bounds. Suffice it to note that France and Italy are members of the Belt and Road Initiative. Even the UK, the closest political and military ally of the USA, is a founding member of the AIIB. With admirable ambition, the UK intends to 'deepen the economic ties with Asia and to create opportunities for British businesses', according to an official statement made in 2018 by the Chancellor of the Exchequer, Philip Hammond, who fully ignored US complaints that the initiative would undermine the role of the World Bank.[6]

The broad parameters of China's hegemonic challenge to the USA are already in place. The question remains, however, how the country will position itself when the contest begins to unfold in earnest. Hegemonic and imperialist drives, as was discussed earlier, are ultimately grounded in the domestic economy and the associated relations of production. For China, the path will depend on the balance between public and private command over the domestic forces of production and will be shaped by the policy decisions of the Chinese state and the Communist Party.

The state foundations of the rise of China

It is certainly possible to approach the functioning of the Chinese economy through the prism of a putative opposition between the market and the state. That, however, would lead to deeply misleading results. The relationship between the public and the private sectors of the Chinese economy is far more complex than this shallow ideological construct implies.

The establishment of the People's Republic in 1949 allowed China to recover from continuous wars sparked off by European imperialists entering its territories in the 1840s. The country rebuilt its transport system,

6 See UK Parliament (2018) *UK Contribution to the Asian Infrastructure Investment Bank Special Fund*, statement made on 21 March, Statement UIN HCWS573.

constructed a tax base, slowly rehabilitated elementary market transactions, and from the outset placed the public sector at the centre of economic activity.[7] In 1955, the first Five-Year Plan was introduced, laying foundations for economic development based on the expansion of heavy industry.[8]

The results of the first Five-Year Plan were modest, while significant sectoral imbalances emerged between agriculture, light industry, and heavy industry. China remained overwhelmingly agrarian, with low levels of technology, poor productivity, and shortages of key commodities. Further state-led efforts at industrial development, including the Great Leap Forward in the late 1950s and the Cultural Revolution in the late 1960, also had limited economic success. Three decades after the victory of the revolution, the country had a low income per capita and low levels of industrialisation.[9] Nevertheless, it must be stressed that significant welfare gains had been made by the Chinese people, for instance in health and education provision. And, as is shown below, the foundations of future industrial growth were also laid during those years.

Things began to change dramatically in the late 1970s, when Deng Xiaoping assumed power and altered economic policy to promote capitalist development. By that time, the USA and Japan had already normalised relations with China, and the People's Republic had replaced the Republic of China (Taiwan) as a member of the UN in 1971. The People's Republic also became a permanent member of the UN Security Council, gaining recognition within the international system of states. Meanwhile, Sino-Soviet relations had already begun to deteriorate in the 1960s. The consolidation of power by Deng Xiaoping along with improved relations with the USA allowed China to launch Opening and Reform in 1978, signalling the beginning of its structural transformation.

The first measures of economic reform focused on altering the balance between agriculture and light and heavy industry. The government reduced direct intervention and control of economic activity, aiming to introduce a domestic market mechanism that would regulate the output of light industry through price signals. Policy paid close attention to the poor availability of consumer goods in the domestic

---

7 A. Maddison (1998) 'Chinese Economic Performance in the Long Run', OECD Development Centre, at oecd-ilibrary.org.

8 Y. Zheng and Y. Huang (2018) *Market in State: The Political of Domination in China*, Cambridge University Press: Cambridge, UK.

9 Maddison (1998) 'Chinese Economic Performance in the Long Run', ref. 8.

market, especially in food and clothing.[10] Private enterprises were widely established, and light industrial output increased substantially from 1978 to the mid-1990s.

The liberalisation of the domestic market accelerated in the mid-1990s, at a time when the hegemonic USA was systematically imposing neoliberal policies across the developing world. The Chinese government also encouraged resources to be allocated and output to be determined increasingly through price signals emanating from the domestic market. State-owned banks began to adopt commercial practices, and state-owned enterprises (SOEs) – which were the backbone of the planned economy – started to acquire a corporate outlook.[11] At the time, it looked as if China was entering the path of globalisation and financialisation that was promoted by the USA across the world. Things turned out very differently in practice.

The Chinese ruling bloc has consistently rejected the economic doctrines advocated and implemented by the multilateral institutions of the Washington Consensus that were instrumental to US hegemony.[12] Instead, the Chinese state has systematically created public enterprises, often of a gigantic size, in the sphere of productive accumulation and in finance. At the same time, it has steadily reshaped its economy in a capitalist direction, aiming for further integration in the world market. Capitalist liberalisation is certainly prevalent in China compared with the decades after the revolution, but the commanding role of the state is also undeniable. On this basis, in the last four decades the Chinese economy became indispensable to the internationalisation of productive capital and to the global expansion of trade.

Capitalist reforms inevitably brought a profound transformation to domestic labour. A critical decision was the gradual abolition of lifetime employment and the phased introduction of employment contracts.[13] A labour market began to be created in the 1980s, the true foundation stone of capitalism. This spurred mass migration from the countryside

---

10 Y. Wang (2014) *Development of China's Industries and Industrial Restructuring*, Routledge: London, pp. 35–48.

11 See Zheng and Huang (2018) *Market in State*.

12 An excellent analysis of the political and economic debates that helped China avoid the disastrous path of neoliberalism can be found in I. Weber (2019) *How China Escaped Shock Therapy: The Market Reform Debate*, Routledge: London. China advanced slowly by trying out reforms that could bring results within its own historically specific conditions.

13 T. G. Rawski (1999) 'China: Prospects for Full Employment', ILO Employment and Training Papers No. 13.

to urban centres which continued throughout the 2010s. Chinese growth involved reallocating labour from agriculture to industry on the grandest of scales. Foreign-owned enterprises and domestic private capitalists were particularly active in hiring migrant labour. In 2020, the World Bank estimated the Chinese labour force to be roughly 770 million people out of a population of 1.4 billion.[14] A little less than a quarter are employed in agriculture and slightly more than this in industry, while the rest work in services. Perhaps between 250 and 300 million are either migrants from rural areas, or the offspring of migrants.[15]

As a result of this major shift, urbanisation proceeded at extraordinary rates and enormous population centres have emerged across the country, although urbanisation is still considerably below that of the USA. The massive influx of rural migrant workers drove down labour costs in the newly emerging labour market. Low wages and rampant exploitation prevailed in the early years of Chinese transformation, with migrant workers bearing the brunt of exploitative abuses, including by foreign-owned enterprises.

Still, as Chinese capitalism took firmer shape, labour skills began to improve, professional specialisation expanded tremendously, and real wages began to rise. Between 2000 and 2017, the real urban wage rate and the real wage rate for migrant workers increased substantially more than the equivalent rates across the world.[16] Nonetheless, the vast working class that has emerged during the last four decades, including layers of professional workers, remains subject to heavy exploitation. It is currently common in China to refer to the '996' working pattern – work from 9am to 9pm, six days a week. This was originally prevalent among enterprises associated with the internet but has gradually become almost a social norm among professional young workers.

The Chinese state has continually promulgated legislation on labour protection, but enforcement has remained shoddy and inconsequential. Migrant workers have long been discriminated in public provision, including health care and children's education.[17] The new layers of urban workers appear to be in a better position, although they face heavy costs

14 World Bank, 'Data: Labor force, total – China', at data.worldbank.org.

15 This is a rough estimate based the data of the 2010s. By 2010, there were 260 million migrant workers in China; see Zheng and Huang (2018) *Market in State*.

16 D. Lo (2020) 'Towards a Conception of the Systemic Impact of China on Late Development', *Third World Quarterly* 41 (5): 860–80.

17 See Zheng and Huang (2018) *Market in State*.

of housing in big cities. The future of the Chinese economy will depend on relations between the newly formed working class and the mechanisms of state that have overseen capitalist development during the last four decades.

In sum, Chinese reforms promoted coordination of the economy through the market, encouraged private property in several sectors, liberalised trade flows, and created an enormous class of wage labourers. At the same time, public ownership and control over strategic forces of production remained fundamental to the economy. China followed its own path of development, creating a state-led form of capitalism where SOEs dominate the economy, including the financial system. There is no comparison with the neoliberal experiments in the peripheral countries of Latin America, South-East Asia, and elsewhere, which have produced outcomes varying from the mediocre to the downright disastrous during the last four decades.

The decisive role of SOEs and the public sector

The SOEs that play a determining role in the Chinese economy are a legacy of the Soviet type of command economy. Public enterprises – indeed entire ministries – began to be transformed in the early 1980s with the intention of turning 'into shareholding companies with limited liability with the objective of protecting SOE management from government interference'.[18] In the early 1990s, even deeper institutional reform of SOEs was promoted, aiming to build a publicly owned system of enterprises that could compete globally, often referred to as 'national champions'. [19]

Currently there are more than 150,000 SOEs in operation, varying greatly in specialisation and having national or regional coverage. The leading enterprises of the Chinese economy – the so-called 'centrally managed SOEs' or 'central SOEs' – are under the direct control of the central government. Most of the national champions are centrally

18 I. Hasan, P. Wachtel, and M. Zhou (2009) 'Institutional Development, Financial Deepening and Economic Growth: Evidence from China', *Journal of Banking & Finance* 33 (1): 157–70.

19 See for example, D. Sutherland (2003) *China's Large Enterprises and the Challenge of Late Industrialization*, 1st edition, Routledge: London; Y. Huang (2008) *Capitalism with Chinese Characteristics: Entrepreneurship and the State*, Cambridge University Press: New York.

managed SOEs dominating the sectors of energy, telecommunications, transportation, aviation, and construction, among others.[20] In addition, there are thousands of SOEs controlled by regional governments and other parts of the state – the so-called 'local SOEs'.

The national champions are conglomerate groups that contain at least one parent enterprise and one functioning subsidiary, but normally have several separately listed subsidiaries in various industries. The parent enterprise would be state-owned and act as the shareholding company; the subsidiaries would issue shares mostly held by the parent enterprise but which would also be available for purchase by private capitalists through the stock market.[21] A conglomerate would also contain its own institute to coordinate research and development as well as a financial intermediary to cover its needs.[22]

The institution that has overall control of SOEs is the State-owned Asset Supervision and Administration Commission of the State Council of China (SASAC), established in March 2003. SASAC is a hybrid agent acting as investor, owner, and regulator of SOEs. It is the designated authority exercising ownership on behalf of the State Council – that is, of the central government of China.

The original mode of operation of SASAC was declared to be 'managing personnel, managing affairs, and managing assets'.[23] SASAC would manage the assets of centrally administered SOEs as well as overseeing the assets of other SOEs under its supervision. Its primary concern was, presumably, to ensure conformity of SOE investment and financing plans with China's national development plans and industrial policies. Moreover, SASAC was given power to appoint and remove the executive officers of the main SOEs. It would not be involved in the day-to-day operations of enterprises but would have a very strong say in significant events, such as company mergers, demergers, and bankruptcy.

In time, the declared mode of operation of SASAC became

20 M. M. Pearson (2015) 'State-Owned Business and Party-State Regulations in China's Modern Political Economy', in B. Naughton and K. S. Tsai (eds) *State Capitalism, Institutional Adaptation, and the Chinese Economic Miracle*, Cambridge University Press: Cambridge, pp. 27–45.

21 L. W. Lin and C. J. Milhaupt (2013) 'We Are the (National) Champions: Understanding the Mechanisms of State Capitalism in China', *Stanford Law Review* 65: 697–759.

22 Ibid., ref. 18.

23 SASAC (2019) 'Change Towards "Managing Capital": Why and How? [向以'管资本'为主转变：为何转与如何转？]' at sasac.gov.cn.

'managing capital', which primarily means ensuring high returns for shareholders.[24] This was supposed to reduce bureaucracy and allow enterprises to follow market signals more closely. In practice, it signalled the growing prevalence of capitalist principles in the operation of SASAC: SOEs remained under the control of state authorities, but control began to be exercised less directly. The emphasis on 'managing capital' is a sign of the underlying tension between public and private property and control over strategic resources, which presents the Chinese ruling bloc with one of its hardest dilemmas.

It is crucial to note, in this connection, that the boundary between SOEs and purely private enterprises has also become blurred over time. In practice, and in law, there is mixed ownership, which allows the 'bi-directional flow of stake-acquiring investment' between the SOEs and private enterprises – that is, SOEs are allowed to acquire equity stakes in non-SOEs, and vice versa.[25] In 2019, the Chinese state held equity stakes in roughly two thirds of the thousand largest private enterprises – in effect, these enterprises were partly public.[26] In the two decades since 2000, the number of private enterprises with some public equity has tripled. Far from the rise of private capitalism undermining and limiting the role of the state in the economy, private and public interests have become increasingly intertwined as China has ascended to a leading position in the world economy. The balance between the two, however, is far from stable and is a constant source of tensions within the ruling bloc.

The transformation has been similarly profound in the financial sector. Until the late 1970s, China had a single bank, the People's Bank of China, fulfilling conventional banking functions and allocating resources in line with government directives, serving as a 'cash agent for the government'.[27] By 1984 a two-tier banking structure had emerged, separating commercial banking activities from the People's Bank of China and establishing four publicly owned commercial banks with sectoral specialisations.

---

24 See SASAC (2019) 'Change Towards "Managing Capital"'.

25 D. Lo, L. Gao, and Y. Lin (2022) 'State Ownership and Innovations: Lessons from the Mixed-Ownership Reforms of China's Listed Companies', *Structural Change and Economic Dynamics* 60: 302–14.

26 C.-E. Bai et al. (2021) 'The Rise of State-Connected Private Owners in China', NBER Working Paper No. 28170.

27 P. Bottelier (2009) 'The Evolution of Banking and Finance in China: Domestic and International Aspects', in M. Zhu, J. Cai, and M. Avery (eds) *China's Emerging Financial Markets: Challenges and Global Impact*, Wiley: New York, pp. 53–70.

The Agricultural Bank of China specialises in financial support for rural development; the Bank of China provides financial support to foreign trade and the foreign exchange market; the China Construction Bank finances long-term, capital-intensive projects; the Industrial and Commercial Bank of China serves the financial needs of the rest of the economy. Finally, the People's Bank of China was designated as the central bank of China. During the reform period, the Chinese government also promoted the establishment of several joint-stock banks and regional banks, creating a multi-tier banking system.

After 1993, the four state-owned banks moved toward a system of self-management, bearing responsibility for risk-taking, losses, and profits. However, in 2003, the Chinese state created Central Huijin Investment Limited, a corporate structure that is the main shareholder of the big four banks, acting as owner on behalf of the state. The leading personnel of Central Huijin, including the board of directors and the board of supervisors, are appointed by the State Council of China.[28]

China has a bank-based financial system dominated by the state. Moreover, the frequently mentioned shadow banks of China bear no relation to the shadow banks of core countries – that is, portfolio managers engaging in securitisation based on obtaining wholesale market liquidity. Chinese shadow banks are traditional financial intermediaries that collect funds and advance loans to enterprises and households.[29] To refer to them as 'off-balance-sheet businesses' is merely to indicate that their loans and deposits are often not recorded on balance sheets to evade regulation.[30]

Chinese shadow banks are important in two respects. First, they engage in 'shadow lending', transferring spare funds to borrowers independently of established commercial banks but still broadly within the law. In this connection, they could act as vehicles for speculative investment across sectors, while offering access to loans for small and medium enterprises. Second, they facilitate 'shadow saving', collecting funds from households and individuals by issuing financial assets that offer

---

28 As is plainly stated on Huijin's official website; see Central Huijin Investment Limited (2008) 'About us', at huijin-inv.cn.

29 Thus, they could be appropriately referred to as 'shadow of banks' or 'banks in the shadow'. See T. Ehlers, K. Steven, and F. Zhu (2018) 'Mapping Shadow Banking in China: Structure and Dynamics', BIS Working Papers No. 701, BIS at bis.org. D. Bulloch (2018) 'BIS Report on China's Shadow Banking Sector Suggests a Problem That's Not Going Away', *Forbes*, 21 February, at forbes.com.

30 K. Chen, J. Ren, and T. Zha (2018) 'The Nexus of Monetary Policy and Shadow Banking in China', *American Economic Review* 108 (12): 3891–936.

higher returns than bank deposits. Savers are attracted into a risky and unregulated world, with all that this implies for possible losses.

Banking aside, the clearest evidence of state control in finance is given by regulations on cross-border flows of capital. In 1979, the State Administration of Foreign Exchange (SAFE) was set up to manage foreign exchange, thus starting a process of market reform. Currency convertibility for current account purposes had been fully implemented by the end of 1996.[31] However, the bulk of the capital account has remained under severe restrictions, and several key items are tightly controlled, including cross-border portfolio investment.[32]

To be more precise, Chinese authorities allow limited access to domestic financial markets for qualified foreign institutional investors, who may use any currency, as well as for renminbi qualified financial institutional investors, who must use the renminbi. However, the sums are capped at low levels, except for sovereign funds, central banks, and governments. Similarly, the authorities allow only qualified domestic institutional investors, including banks, securities firms, and insurance companies, to invest in overseas financial markets. FDI, on the other hand, is one of the categories of capital flows least controlled by the Chinese government.[33] China has become one of the largest FDI providers across the world, as was shown in chapter 13. Inward FDI, in contrast, is directed toward preferred areas by the authorities, or is altogether prevented on grounds of national security.

For the Chinese hegemonic challenge to carry true weight in contemporary capitalism, it must include a bid to gain the status of world money for the renminbi, or at least to join the top tier of the currency hierarchy. Attempts in that direction began in 2009, mainly by using the renminbi in settlement of cross-border trades and as part of China's response to the huge losses in its dollar reserves.[34] In addition, the central bank of

31 Y. Huang (2020) 'Introduction: Proactively and Steadily Advancing China's Financial Opening', in H. Bing et al. (eds) *The Jinshan Report: Opening China's Financial Sector*, Australian National University Press: Canberra, pp. 1–24.

32 K. F. Habermeier et al. (2017) 'Capital Account Opening and Capital Flow Management', in R. W. Lam, M. Rodlauer, and A. Schipke (eds) *Modernizing China: Investing in Soft Infrastructure*, IMF: New York.

33 M. McCowage (2018) 'Trends in China's Capital Account', Bulletin of Reserve Bank of Australia, at rba.gov.au.

34 Z. Wang (2017) 'The Resumption of China's Exchange Rate Reform and the Internationalization of RMB between 2010 and 2013', *Journal of Contemporary China* 26 (108): 852–69.

China signed bilateral currency swaps with several countries to promote use of the renminbi in trade and investment. The war in Ukraine, with the aggressive use of the dollar as a level of imperial power by the USA, particularly in freezing the dollar reserves of the central bank of Russia, will probably boost these efforts, as will the gradual emergence of Central Bank Digital Currencies that was discussed in chapter 13.

However, as was also shown in chapter 13, the renminbi accounts for an insignificant proportion of international reserves – and of global settlements – by value.[35] In contrast, the US dollar currently supplies roughly 60 per cent of world reserves and dominates the setting of prices for key commodities as well as the denomination of assets and liabilities of internationally active banks.[36] The dollar remains the reference point of the monetary operations of internationalised productive capital and the lifeblood of globalised finance. There is still no comparison between the USA and China in this respect, nor is the balance going to change in a short space of time.

To recap, the rise of capitalism in China is inextricably linked to the Chinese state's power to decide which markets would open domestically as well as to determine the precise meaning of market openness in each case. The partial rejection of neoliberalism by China was not merely, or even primarily, a result of socialist or other ideology. It was, rather, a matter of *realpolitik* by the upper echelons of the Communist Party of China aiming to ensure the success of economic reforms and to protect the national interest. The role of the Communist Party as a countrywide mechanism of power over both the economy and society was decisive.

Communist Party control

The power of Chinese state authorities over both economy and society ultimately rests on the country's one-party political system. Upon the establishment of the People's Republic, a centralised system of political control allowed the Communist Party to act as overseer of both state bureaucracy and government, while integrating military structures and economic institutions into a single system. The mechanisms of the Party and the mechanisms of the state and the government became

35 See also People's Bank of China (2020) *RMB Internationalization Report*, at gov.cn.
36 See C. Bertaut, B. von Beschwitz, and S. Curcuru (2021) *The International Role of the US Dollar*, Federal Reserve Notes, 6 October, at federalreserve.gov.

inextricably intertwined in ways that could be understood through the old Soviet methods of the *nomenklatura*.[37]

This term, which was at one time widely deployed to analyse the political workings of the Eastern Bloc, translates into a hierarchical list of posts with a description of the duties of each office.[38] It remains essential to the functioning of contemporary China, including the economy. The methods of the *nomenklatura* are instrumental to selecting, appointing, and evaluating the organisational structures of the Communist Party, the government administration, and other state institutions.[39]

Senior Chinese officials normally hold positions in both Party and government. Thus, the General Secretary of the Communist Party of China also serves as the head of state and the head of the armed forces, and together with another four to eight officials participates in the Standing Committee of the Politburo, the highest echelon of collective leadership. The central government of China is led by a premier who heads the equivalent of the cabinet and is appointed by the National Congress of the Communist Party every five years. Regional governments are similarly controlled by the Communist Party.

Being a member of the Communist Party is an unwritten requirement for advancing within the mechanisms of state and government, and certainly for attaining the higher posts. This requirement also holds for the management structures of SASAC, the SOEs, the large banks, and other institutions with a direct economic role. Chinese economists have claimed that a 'revolving door' exists between the top management of SOEs and the leading government posts.[40] Perhaps a third of government officials above the vice-ministerial level have held positions in SOEs in the past, while scores of senior executives of SOEs have previously worked in government.[41]

37 M. Manion (1985) 'The Cadre Management System, Post-Mao: The Appointment, Promotion, Transfer and Removal of Party and State Leaders', *The China Quarterly* 102: 203–33.

38 The literature is large; see, for instance, B. Harasymiw (1969) 'Nomenklatura: The Soviet Communist Party's Leadership Recruitment System', *Canadian Journal of Political Science* 2: 493–512.

39 H. S. Chan (2004) 'Cadre Personnel Management in China: The Nomenklatura System, 1990–1998', *The China Quarterly* 179: 703–34.

40 See Zheng and Huang (2018) *Market in State*. See also A. H. Zhang (2015) 'Antitrust Regulation of Chinese State-Owned Enterprises', in B. L. Liebman and C. J. Milhaupt (eds) *Regulating the Visible Hand? The Institutional Implications of Chinese State Capitalism*, Oxford University Press: New York, pp. 85–108.

41 See Zhang (2015) 'Antitrust Regulation of Chinese State-Owned Enterprises'.

Recent government releases state that SOE executives and SOE Communist Party branch leaders would be allowed to 'cross-serve' between posts.[42] This would be possible only if the executives were also Party members, which is typically the case. The centralised one-party system systematically blurs the boundaries of 'state', 'government', and 'party' across Chinese society and economy.

Communist Party branches exist across domestic enterprises and are established even in foreign-owned enterprises. Staff who hold leading Party positions always have decisive power within the hierarchical level at which they operate in an enterprise or other economic institution. They are vital cogs in the Party's efforts to impose the broad parameters of its chosen economic policy as well as to mobilise people and resources when required. Fundamental to this mechanism is 'bottom-up' accountability – that is, formally accounting for public actions from the lowest level upward. This type of accountability permeates the Chinese political system and facilitates 'top-down' commands and the assignment of tasks.[43]

Similar chains of command characterise regional governments, allowing for the coordination of central and regional state power. At local and regional levels, it is still the Party branch that is the ultimate repository of political power. There are thirty-one provincial-level administrative divisions in mainland China and each has a full set of Party as well as government structures mirroring those at the centre, with a lower political rank.

Government bodies below the central level can be broadly categorised as 'local government', and the governor of a province ranks equal to a central government minister. However, local governments are far from mere executors of the will of the central government. Considerable autonomy exists, particularly after the fiscal reform of 1994 that gave local governments command over local resources.[44] Local governments have become powerful economic agents with close relations to local enterprises, particularly large corporations.[45]

---

42 The Central Committee of the Communist Party of China issued the 'Regulations on the Work of the Grassroots Organizations of State-Owned Enterprises of the Communist Party of China (for Trial Implementation)' [中共中央印发《中国共产党国有企业基层组织工作条例（试行）》], at gov.cn.

43 X. Zhou (2020) 'Organizational Response to COVID-19 Crisis: Reflections on the Chinese Bureaucracy and Its Resilience', *Management and Organization Review* 16: 473–84.

44 See Zheng and Huang (2018) *Market in State*.

45 J. C. Oi (1992) 'Fiscal Reform and the Economic Foundations of Local State Corporatism in China', *World Politics* 45: 99–126.

China has retained various elements of central planning, including five-year plans and a variety of economic targets and goals set by different authorities. The national plans, approved by the Communist Party, determine the broad framework of transformation and development of the Chinese economy. The implementation of national plans, on the other hand, relies on state ownership of productive resources, dominated by SOEs. Even though the SOEs operate through market signals, they are crucial instruments of the state to achieve development goals.

SOEs often function with soft budget constraints, receiving privileged access to cheap bank credit, and some even have implicit government guarantees.[46] They are tasked with huge public infrastructure projects, such as constructing the network of high-speed trains that has rapidly spread across the country, often without direct concern for profits. Moreover, until the 2000s, in practice, SOEs functioned as public welfare units, with their own hospitals, schools, and housing. Social responsibilities remain, even though the provision of housing and other basic goods has been heavily subjected to market processes during the last two decades.

State-owned financial institutions, especially state-owned commercial banks, also serve as instruments to achieve centrally determined development goals. State-owned banks provide cheap credit to SOEs to finance projects deemed important for national policy goals. As the mode of intervention in the economy shifted toward 'managing capital', financial support for enterprises also started to come from public 'Industrial Guidance Funds'. These are 'funds set up solely by governments at all levels through budgetary investment or jointly by governments together with private capital'; the distribution of credits among investment projects is determined by the Ministry of Finance.[47]

If there are going to be frictions and political tensions within the ruling elite in China in the coming years, these will not originate in an imaginary opposition between private capitalists and the state. Elite conflicts are more likely to emerge among state functionaries within the hierarchical relations of managing the economy. 'Small kingdoms' are regularly formed within the public sector, which aim to bypass centrally

46 L. Tian and S. Estrin (2007) 'Debt Financing, Soft Budget Constraints, and Government Ownership: Evidence from China', *Economics of Transition and Institutional Change* 15 (3): 461–81.

47 F. Pan, F. Zhang, and F. Wu (2021) 'State-Led Financialization in China: The Case of the Government-Guided Investment Fund', *The China Quarterly* 247: 749–72.

determined policy goals or even to undermine the authority of the central authorities.

SASAC and Central Huijin are the owners of the largest conglomerate groups, holding property rights on behalf of the State Council of China. But as a hybrid agent, blending ownership and control, SASAC does not have full controlling power over conglomerate management. Characteristically, central SOEs are only obliged to transmit 5 to 10 per cent of their profits to the central government, while some of the largest SOEs are entirely exempt from this obligation for significant periods of time.[48] Thus, SOEs are in command of vast profits that fuel their economic power and strengthen their political bargaining power. Similar points hold for the financial sector. Moreover, the tendency to create power centres within the financial sector is exacerbated by the multiplicity of regulating authorities, including the Ministry of Finance, which occasionally issue conflicting directives.

In sum, Chinese capitalism has emerged under the Communist Party guidance of both economy and society, while the state has maintained ownership and command over productive resources. In fundamental ways, the Chinese economy operates differently from the financialised capitalism of the core countries of the world economy. But as capitalism matures in China and acquires society-wide dimensions, the mechanisms of public ownership and control face growing internal strains.

Even so, there is no doubt that the Chinese way has been enormously successful in promoting capital accumulation, propelling the country toward a hegemonic position. The USA has already picked up the gauntlet, and its actions will have a profound effect on China and the rest of the world economy.

The US–China trade war

Chinese officials naturally claim that China's rise and its weighty global presence are beneficial to international welfare and do not signal hegemonic intent. Just as naturally, the US ruling elite perceives the rise of China and its increasingly assertive economic role as a hegemonic challenge. In the second half of the 2010s, under the Trump administration,

48 Huang (2008) *Capitalism with Chinese Characteristics*; K. E. Brødsgaard (2012) 'Politics and Business Group Formation in China', *The China Quarterly* 211: 624–48.

the USA shifted from regarding China as a 'strategic partner' to a 'major strategic competitor of the United States', marking a clear shift in Sino–US relations.[49] In the 2020s, during the first years of the Biden administration, the USA did not change course on China despite Biden's broad dismissal of Trump's policies.

Given the position of China in the world market, the US ruling elite faces a truly complex problem in confronting the hegemonic challenge. A plausible initial response would be to reduce economic links with China, while protecting US military superiority and hoping to prevent a comprehensive rupture in the world market. The difficulty of this task can be appreciated by casting a glance at the trade war launched by the Trump administration against China.

The trade war began in January 2018, when President Trump announced tariffs on imported solar panels and washing machines on the grounds of China's 'unfair trade practices' and intellectual property theft. Both countries subsequently escalated trade friction by increasing the volume of goods subject to tariffs as well as the level of tariffs. By 2021, roughly two thirds of Chinese exports to the USA were subjected to new tariffs, and the same held for almost 60 per cent of US exports to China; the average level of tariffs was about 20 per cent for both countries, several times higher than the tariffs on commodities from the rest of the world.[50]

For the USA, the objectives of the trade war were transparent. The hegemon aimed to reduce its trade deficit with China, boost and repatriate manufacturing and other capacity (reshoring), force China to open its economy further, and weaken the interventionist approach of the Chinese state. In January 2020, following two years of trade tensions, the two countries concluded the 'US-China Phase One' trade deal, which reduced tariffs somewhat in both directions. China was also committed to purchasing an additional 200 billion dollars' worth of US products in 2020 and 2021 compared with 2017.

More than a year after the 'US-China Phase One' deal, the USA had achieved practically none of its objectives. The trade deficit of the USA with China had declined after 2018, but soon began to rise again, and in 2020 reached new heights. Moreover, the overall trade balance of the

---

49 A. Tellis (2020) 'The Return of U.S.–China Strategic Competition', *Strategic Asia 2020*, at nbr.org.

50 C.Bown (2021) 'The US–China Trade War and Phase One Agreement', Peterson Institute for International Economics (PIEE), Working Papers No. 02, at piie.com.

USA did not improve, partly due to the significant weakening of US exports. It appears that the input costs of US exporters drastically increased, damaging their competitiveness.[51] China was also unable to make good on its commitment of extra purchases of US goods, in part because of the pandemic, and did not even reach two thirds of the target for 2020.[52]

Reshoring also did not materialise on a significant scale. Indeed, it appears that US importers shifted partly to other East Asian as well as Central and Latin American countries, indicating a reorganisation of production networks in response to the trade conflict with China.[53] It also seems that US domestic manufacturing was altogether hurt by the imposition of tariffs, and manufacturing employment declined marginally.[54] US manufacturing exports to China, which had risen strongly between 2009 and 2017, flattened in 2018 and declined significantly in 2019.[55]

As for transforming Chinese domestic economic practices and policies, once the trade deal was signed, China took steps to open its financial markets to US enterprises. It also announced other measures, including an intellectual property action plan to strengthen the protection of property rights.[56] However, the country did not relent on the main demand by the USA – that is, to limit the role of SOEs in the economy and to attenuate their links with government. In practice, the Chinese government boosted imports from the USA, as it was obliged to do, by taking administrative measures that granted special exemptions for domestic enterprises from the counter-tariffs it had imposed on US imports.[57]

---

51 K. Handley, F. Kamal, and R. Monarch (2020) 'Rising Import Tariffs, Falling Export Growth: When Modern Supply Chains Meet Old-Style Protectionism', NBER, Working Paper No. 26611, at nber.org.

52 C. Bown (2020) 'US-China Phase One Tracker: China's Purchases of US Goods', PIIE, at piie.com.

53 E. Bekkers and S. Schroeter (2020) 'An Economic Analysis of the US-China Trade Conflict', WTO, Working Paper No. ERSD-2020-04, at wto.org.

54 A. Flaaen and J. R. Pierce (2019) 'Disentangling the Effects of the 2018–2019 Tariffs on a Globally Connected U.S. Manufacturing Sector', Federal Reserve Board Finance and Economics Discussion Series No. 086.

55 C. Bown (2021) 'Anatomy of a Flop: Why Trump's US-China Phase One Trade Deal Fell Short', PIIE, at piie.com.

56 M. Cohen (2020) 'Is It in There – CNIPA's "Phase 1" IP Action Plan?', China IPR – Intellectual Property Developments in China, at chinaipr.com.

57 C. Bown and M. Lovely (2020) 'Trump's Phase One Deal Relies on China's State-Owned Enterprises', PIIE, at piie.com.

The trade war appears to have had a negative impact on economic activity in both countries. US agricultural exports to China declined significantly, although farm income rose compared with the pre-trade-war period due to subsidies by the US government. In China, the conflict contributed to a slow-down of growth as well as impacting negatively on general welfare.[58]

The hegemonic contest between the USA and China will not be settled through a hastily put together trade war by the US government. It is apparent that the Chinese challenge will be far from easy for the USA to confront, as was further shown by the two contestants' sharply different responses to the Pandemic Crisis.

Tackling the health emergency: Efficiency and authoritarianism

There is no doubt that Chinese state mechanisms proved far more effi-cient than those of the USA – and most of its European allies – in deal-ing with the public health aspects of the Pandemic Crisis. By February 2023, China had registered a little more than 2 million confirmed cases of the disease and a little under 90 thousand confirmed deaths, in cumu-lative terms. The USA, in contrast, had registered more than 100 million confirmed cases and over 1 million confirmed deaths, again in cumula-tive terms.[59]

The bulk of the confirmed cases and most of the confirmed deaths in China occurred in early 2023 as the Zero Covid policy was abandoned. In early 2022 there was a fresh outbreak of the disease across the world due to the Omicron variant of the virus. The Chinese authorities confronted the new wave by reimposing harsh localised lockdown measures, especially in Shanghai. The economic and social impacts of the measures were very heavy on a population that had already been subjected to severe restrictions during the preceding two years as part of the country's Zero Covid policy, discussed in chapter 2. Since much of the rest of the world had practically abandoned restrictions by early 2023, a burgeoning popular reaction to the new measures forced the Chinese government to abandon Zero Covid. The result was a rapid

58 M. Li, E. J. Balistreri, and W. Zhang (2020) 'The U.S.–China Trade War: Tariff Data and General Equilibrium Analysis', *Journal of Asian Economics* 69: 101216. See also Bown (2021) 'The US–China Trade War and Phase One Agreement', ref. 32.

59 All figures taken from 'Our World in Data', a project of the Global Change Data Lab, a non-profit organisation based in the UK; see ourworldindata.org.

escalation of cases and deaths, which appeared to subside equally rapidly in February 2023. Nevertheless, the overall harm caused by the disease still bore no comparison to the disaster that befell the USA, even if there are doubts about the reliability of the Chinese data.

The extraordinary difference in performance compared with the USA was partly due to the power of the Chinese central government based on the one-party system, which reduced frictions between central and local authorities. The characteristic Chinese combination of top-down deployment of tasks (setting rigid goals within fixed deadlines) and bottom-up accountability allowed for an integrated state response that rapidly suppressed the pandemic.[60] Since the Communist Party is the overarching political authority, containment of the virus became a political task across society.

As soon as the pandemic broke out in Wuhan in late 2019, China formed the Working Group on Epidemic Control, led by the Standing Committee of the Politburo of the Communist Party. Its first meeting was held on 25 January 2020 to discuss the tasks of preparing the nationwide campaign of epidemic prevention and control and ordering local governments to set up working groups ensuring policy implementation. In the months that followed, specific tasks and instructions were continually sent to local governments, SOEs, and all other public institutions.

Regular leadership visits to infected areas, meetings, and speeches soon elevated the disease into a political priority and not merely a public health emergency.[61] National mobilisation proved crucial to complying with fundamental precautions and applying basic pandemic suppression measures. Strict lockdowns were imposed on affected provinces and other areas, but China avoided a nationwide lockdown.

Moreover, there was a rapid and coordinated national mobilisation of health care resources, together with the required logistics, to support stricken provinces. Mass testing was also quickly introduced and implemented.[62] The policy of managed quarantine was probably the clearest

---

60 See T. Moraitis and Y. Shi (2020) 'When State Intervention Saves "the Economy", but Not You', *Jacobin*, 6 July, at jacobin.com.

61 D. Lo and Y. Shi (2020) 'China Versus the US in the Pandemic Crisis: Governance and Politics Confronting Systemic Challenges', *Canadian Journal of Development Studies/Revue Canadienne d'études du Développement* 42 (1–2): 90–100.

62 State Council (2020) 'The State Council Responds to the Coronavirus in a Joint Prevention and Control: Further Advance the Nucleic Acid Testing Capacity' [国务院应对新型冠状病毒感染肺炎疫情　联防联控机制关于印发进一步推进新冠病毒核酸检测能力建设工作方案的通知], at gov.cn.

example of the efficacy of state mobilisation, including complex coordination among different state mechanisms. Severe quarantine conditions were imposed in March 2020, including for travellers from abroad, and continued into the beginning of 2023, when the quarantine policies were finally abolished.

SOEs played a major role in addressing the health emergency. Following SASAC instructions, SOEs rapidly expanded – or created afresh – production lines for critical medical supplies, including surgery masks, disinfectants, and latex gloves. China was also the first country to develop vaccines:[63] Sinopharm, a leading central SOE in the provision of medical and health services, was the first to produce two vaccines based on an inactive form of SARS-CoV-2.[64] Three more vaccines followed, produced by private biomedical enterprises. The government paid vaccine developers at market prices and distributed the jabs for free, using the fiscal budget and public health insurance funds to cover the costs.[65] The Chinese state made its vaccines widely available to peripheral countries as the pandemic intensified the hegemonic contest.

The effective intervention of state mechanisms relied heavily on social mobilisation at grass-roots level. Communal networks, including the community/neighbourhood council, a socialist legacy, played a significant role in delivering care services to households during the early period of Covid-19.[66] To be effective, social care services need an infrastructure, extending beyond the family and the private provision of care. China was able to draw on a social infrastructure that is centred on local communities and which mobilises state, family, and local resources. Some of the older traditions of socialist solidarity were partially reactivated as China confronted the virus as a social threat.

However, not everything in the Chinese state's response to the pandemic was efficient or laudable. At the very start of the health emergency, for instance, local authorities had an incentive to ignore, suppress, or even distort information to protect themselves and cover errors or

---

63 Y. Hu and S. Chen (2021) 'What Can We Learn from COVID-19 Vaccine R&D in China? A Discussion from a Public Policy Perspective', *International Society of Travel Medicine* 28 (4): 1–3.

64 C. Baraniuk (2021) 'What Do We Know about China's Covid-19 Vaccines?', *The British Medical Journal* 373: n912.

65 See State Council (2021) 'Covid-vaccine Is Free for Everyone [新冠疫苗免费接种，医保基金和财政共同负担]', at gov.cn.

66 Z. Li, Y. Chen, and Y. Zhan (2022) 'Building Community-Centered Social Infrastructure: A Feminist Inquiry into China's COVID-19 Experiences', *Economia Politica* 39: 303–21.

inaction.[67] There were also significant tensions between commands given from the top and accountability exercised from the bottom upward. Despite the experience that China already had in applying epidemic protocols due to the SARS outbreak a decade earlier, medical doctors' reports were initially ignored or suppressed by local authorities.[68]

Moreover, as restrictions and lockdowns were imposed, the denial of individual rights assumed great dimensions and took on authoritarian forms. This was exemplified by cases related to contact tracing, especially for 'super-infectious' individuals (those who had passed the virus to many others) and to cases arriving from abroad. For the 'super-infectious', the authorities even publicised family names, home addresses, workplaces, and recent travel history, although full names were not revealed. The information was meant to help locate the close contacts, but in practice it caused brutal public shaming.

The social problems and the disruption caused by the Zero Covid strategy started to become apparent in 2022 as the Omicron variant proved less susceptible to vaccines across the world. There was a sustained accumulation of confirmed cases in China, and the authorities were led to impose severe localised lockdowns at a time when the rest of the world had effectively abandoned restrictions. The costs for China were great in terms of economic output and there was a further heavy impact on social and family life. It soon became clear that the policy had become untenable. Workers and students in big cities began to demonstrate, forcing the government initially to ease the restrictions and soon to abandon Zero Covid in early 2023.

In all these respects the contrast between China and the core states of the world economy was very sharp. The US response to the pandemic, as was shown in part I, relied on Big Pharma. It was also marked by a lack of cooperation between the federal state and individual states, as the federal government was unable to give strong direction to individual states, and friction soon emerged. Lack of central coordination was coupled with the neoliberal ideology that has permeated US state institutions in recent decades, leading several states to rely on market mechanisms to obtain key equipment and other resources with which to

---

67 See D. Lo and Y. Shi (2020), 'China Versus the US in the Pandemic Crisis', *Canadian Journal of Development Studies* 42 (1–2): 90–100.

68 See Zhou (2020) 'Organizational Response to COVID-19 Crisis: Reflections on the Chinese Bureaucracy and Its Resilience'.

confront the emergency. The contrast with the centrally coordinated distribution of medical resources in China was striking, and the health outcomes for the US people dramatically worse.

In sum, there is no contest regarding the overall efficacy of the responses of both countries to the health emergency, and no comparison in the social costs borne by each. China was far more successful than the USA in confronting the disease. But the relative success and efficiency of Chinese state mechanisms in the face of the health emergency should not obscure the profound problems China will face as the hegemonic contest unfolds.

Hegemony is far from a settled issue

In key respects, and despite its astonishing rise, China still barely qualifies as a developed country. Agriculture employs almost a quarter of the labour force, far above the few decimal points characteristic of core countries. Moreover, according to World Bank data, in 2020, Chinese GDP per capita stood at 10,500 current US dollars, a mere fraction of the US figure of 63,500.[69] There is, similarly, no comparison with the other core countries, which all have a per capita income of more than 40,000 dollars.

For huge numbers of Chinese people, especially in rural areas but also among the urban working class, deep poverty is the reality of life.[70] Rapid capitalist development has generated enormous income inequalities which are exacerbated by inadequate welfare provision. In the days of the planned economy, both the rural and the urban population had guaranteed access to basic medical services, practically free education, and subsidised housing provision.[71] As capitalism galloped ahead, housing became inaccessible to broad layers of urban workers, despite rising wages. Access to other basic services is also marked by pronounced inequalities.

Moreover, long before the pandemic, the Chinese economy began to confront a slowdown in growth as well as rising labour costs. The term

---

69 See World Bank Data: 'GDP per capita (current US$) – China, United States, Greece, Turkiye', at data.worldbank.org.

70 As the pandemic spread in 2020, the Chinese premier, Li Keqiang, stated that for about 600 million Chinese people, more than 40 per cent of the population, monthly income was less than 140 US dollars. See S. Yu (2020) 'China Faces Outcry after Premier Admits 40% of Population Struggles', *Financial Times*, 11 June, at ft.com.

71 C. K. Wong (2013) 'The Evolving East Asian Welfare Regimes: The Case of China', in L. Zhao (ed.) *China's Social Development and Policy*, Routledge: New York, pp. 224–5.

'new normal' was coined to describe its condition, especially in the second half of the 2010s. An important factor is the changed outlook of non-financial enterprises, including the leading SOEs, in the period since the Great Crisis of 2007–09. The supply side of the Chinese economy has begun to exhibit symptoms of weakness, which are reflected in low profitability.

Figure 14.4 shows the general rate of profit in China in the two decades since the mid-1990s. The important point here is not the level but the trend, which indicates that Chinese profitability has been weak since the early 2010s.[72]

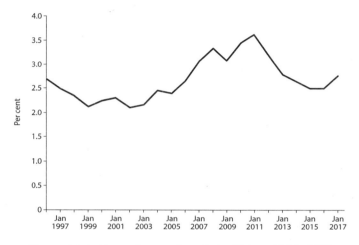

Figure 14.4. General rate of profit in China, 1996–2017.
Source: Authors' calculation based on data from Wind, China National
Statistics Yearbook, and the Federal Reserve Bank of St Louis.

72 The calculation of rate of profit followed the method proposed by M. Li (2017) 'Profit, Accumulation, and Crisis: Long-Term Movement of the Profit Rate in China, Japan, and the United States', *The Chinese Economy*, 50 (6): 381–404 – that is, r = (GDP – labour cost – taxation cost – depreciation of fixed capital) / capital stock. The level calculated is considerably lower than for other estimates, such as Z. Li and M. Li (2015), 'China's Falling Rate of Profit and the Coming Economic Crisis', *Economic and Political Weekly* 50 (41): 27, 29–31; Li (2017), and even A. A. Marquetti et al. (2021) 'Rate of Profit in the United States and in China (2007–2014): A Look at Two Trajectories and Strategic Sectors', *Review of Radical Political Economy* 53 (1): 116–42. However, the general trends are consistent throughout: the rate of profit of the Chinese economy reached a mini peak around the Great Crisis of 2007–09, and then went down after 2011. The difference in levels is due to different data sources, especially for the capital stock. In this chapter, the data for the capital stock from 1960 to 2017 was retrieved from the Federal Reserve in St Louis, originally published in R. C. Feenstra, R. Inklar, and M. P. Timmer (2015) 'The Next Generation of the Penn World Table', *American Economic Review* 105 (10): 3150–82.

Fundamental to the weakness of profitability is the trajectory of labour productivity, as is shown in figure 14.5. Two points stand out in this respect. First, there was an extraordinary increase in the level of productivity after the early 1990s, and this was ultimately the foundation of Chinese global ascendancy. The growth in Chinese productivity is also an important reason why workers in core countries have been able to support their consumption despite generally weak wage growth. Cheap Chinese (and other Asian) consumer goods imported into core countries supported worker access to use values, while keeping real wages low and thus propping up the rate of profit. Second, the rate of growth of productivity has been on a sustained downward path since the middle of the 2000s. Productivity growth in China has varied significantly since the early 1990s, but its recent weakness seems more severe. The internal mechanism of capitalist accumulation, discussed in chapter 4 for core countries, appears to have also malfunctioned in China during the last decade.

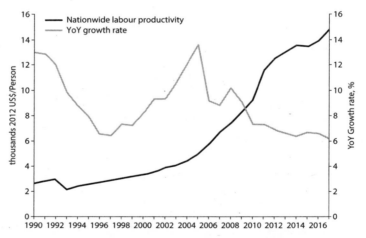

Figure 14.5. Average labour productivity in China,
level and rate of growth, 1990–2018.[73]
Source: Authors' calculation based on data from
China National Statistical Yearbook.

---

73 Labour productivity is measured as the ratio of GDP to employed population in the China National Statistical Yearbook. Here it is recalculated as the ratio of real GDP (in 2012 US $) to employed population. The YoY growth rate is reported by the China National Statistical Yearbook.

Unlike core countries, however, weak productivity growth is not connected to weak investment. Figure 14.6 shows a relative weakening of aggregate investment in China after the Great Crisis of 2007–09, but the level is still exceptionally high compared with the core countries. The problem for China appears to be not the level of investment but the efficiency with which investment is used for productive purposes. The volumes of investment are also related to China's vast construction sector, which is spearheading the urbanisation of the country. It is evident that China needs to rebalance the sources of aggregate demand toward consumption, and to deploy investment more efficiently than hitherto.

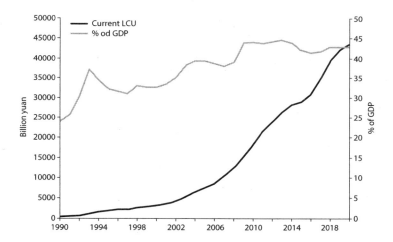

Figure 14.6. Gross fixed capital formation in China, 1990–2020.
Source: The World Bank.

Finally, profitability has also been under pressure from rising real wages, the escalation of which has prevented any further increases in the rate of exploitation. Figure 14.7 shows the trajectory of real wages in the private and non-private sectors of the economy, respectively, and the gap between the two appears to be increasing.[74] The popular thesis that

74 There is a debate over whether the rise in wages acted as a squeeze on profitability or contributed to economic growth by boosting consumption; see, for example, C. Piovani (2014) 'Class Power and China's Productivity Miracle: Applying the Labor Extraction Model to China's Industrial Sector, 1980–2007', *Review of Radical Political Economics* 46 (3): 331–54; H. Qi (2017) 'Dynamics of the Rate of Surplus Value and the

China's development is based upon cheap labour has been untenable since the late 2000s.[75] Rising real wages and a declining productivity growth rate have undoubtedly put pressure on the competitiveness of Chinese output and probably encouraged the substantial outward flow of FDI in the 2010s, as was noted in chapter 13.

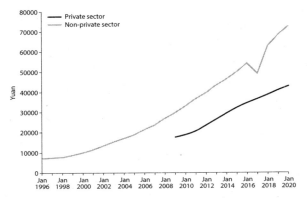

Figure 14.7. Real wages of private and non-private
sectors of China, 2008–2020.
Source: China Statistical Yearbook, various
issues, and the World Bank.[76]

The declining rate of profit greatly complicates the issue of economic restructuring in China. Chinese growth has been fuelled by high investment for several decades, resulting in profound imbalances in the domestic economy. The components of aggregate demand ought to be rebalanced in favour of consumption, reducing the weight of the

"New Normal" of the Chinese Economy', *Research in Political Economy* 32: 105–29; Martin Hart-Landsberg and Paul Burkett (2011) 'The Chinese Reform Experience: A Critical Assessment', *Review of Radical Political Economics* 43 (1): 56–76.

75 For further discussion, see Dic Lo (2013) 'China and World Development – Beyond the Crisis', in Yokogawa, Ghosh, and Rowthorn (eds) *Industrialization in China and India*. Lo has also argued that since the turn of the century, the character of China's development has changed as wage growth has become higher than productivity growth; see D. Lo (2016) 'China Confronts the Great Recession: "Rebalancing" Neoliberalism, or Else?' in P. Arestis and M. Sawyer (eds), *Emerging Economies During and After the Great Recession*, Palgrave Macmillan: London, pp. 232–69.

76 The wages of the private sector were reported only after 2008. The real wage was not reported directly and was calculated as real wage = nominal wage/consumer price index * 100.

construction sector and allowing Chinese workers to obtain more of the fruits of their own labour. But rising wage costs and lower returns to capital present a major problem for Chinese public and private enterprises, making it difficult to rebalance aggregate demand. One obvious path for private capital would be to relocate production domestically to areas in which labour is less capable of ensuring rising wages. Another would be to accelerate the internationalisation of Chinese productive capital, including further growth of outward FDI. Neither would be easy to accomplish within the current framework of ownership and control of capital.

The task is acutely difficult for the Communist Party, since confronting the weakening of accumulation while shifting the composition of aggregate demand could prove socially explosive and politically dangerous. This is particularly so as the Chinese population is rapidly ageing, thus increasing the need for welfare provision. Ageing also lessens the comparative advantage that China has enjoyed for years in labour-intensive industries, even if there still are huge numbers of people engaged in agriculture. To tackle the ageing population and low birth rate, the Chinese government has reversed its one-child policy in recent years. However, the ageing of the population cannot be solved solely through population policy and requires systemic change, including housing and the unequal distribution of income, which is a political minefield.

Confronting the fall in the rate of return on capital, while maintaining a globally pre-eminent position in trade and investment, will also require a further leap in the productivity of labour. To that purpose, China will need to accelerate its technological progress. The country appears to be catching up in high technology, including quantum computers and supercomputers, 5G telecommunications, high-speed railways, and artificial intelligence.[77] However, basic research, which is fundamental to technological development, is structurally weak and remains a key obstacle to China attaining technological self-reliance, particularly in relation to the USA.

The USA has long been the leading global force in basic scientific research, followed at some distance by Japan and European powers. Its hegemonic position relies on its universities and research institutes

---

77 Noted with justified trepidation by several leading US institutions; see, for instance, T. Chhabra et al. (2020) 'Global China: Technology', Brookings Institution, Brookings Foreign Policy's 'Global China' project, at brookings.edu.

working closely with big business and supported by the state, particularly in connection with military applications. China has a much lower rate of technology transfer among its corporations, universities, research centres, and government institutions than the USA.[78] The country essentially lacks the vast network of public research institutions and private enterprises that is fundamental to US technological prowess. It will be far from easy for China to overcome this deficiency in the face of sustained US hostility in the years ahead.

Confronting the 'new normal' will also be greatly complicated by the hugely inflated debts of the corporate sector. In 2018, China's total domestic non-financial debt exceeded 250 per cent of GDP, a drastic increase from just over 140 per cent in 2008. Of this debt, 60 per cent is owed by corporations, while government and households account for 20 per cent each.[79] This is a very different composition of aggregate debt from that of the USA, as was discussed in earlier chapters. It reflects the different structure of Chinese capitalism and the relative absence of financialisation along the lines of core countries. But capitalism is intrinsically prone to credit booms that ultimately weaken accumulation, irrespective of financialisation. Dealing with the domestic debt mountain in China will act as a drag on accumulation, even if the banking system remains publicly controlled and supported by a directed central bank.

Last, but not least, a hegemonic struggle will at some point also require an ideological dimension, even if the struggle is largely economic. For the USA and its close allies, that ideology has long been based on the keywords of human rights and democracy. There is no doubt that their stance is cynical both domestically and internationally, but the West can be expected to mobilise the same tired set of cliches against China in the future, also raising the spectres of authoritarianism and national oppression. Chinese society certainly faces profound problems of democratic expression, equality, and the free development of its people. The lack of an alternative ideological narrative to offer on a global scale remains a deep problem for the hegemonic aspirations of China.

In sum, the hegemonic contest is far from settled, and China must deal with profound domestic problems of capitalist accumulation as it

78 See State Council (2019) 'Establishing a Demand-Oriented Mechanism for Transforming Scientific and Technological Achievements', at gov.cn.

79 All figures taken from BIS (2022) 'Statistics of Credit to the Non-Financial Sector', at bis.org.

vies with the USA internationally. The answer will depend on the domestic balance of class forces. In part, it will be determined by the tug of war within the ruling bloc, as the dilemma between public and private command over the forces of production will continue to create tensions. It will also be determined by the accumulating tension between the ruling bloc and the vast new working class that demands better wages and improved living conditions. China's hegemonic challenge to the USA will ultimately have domestic determinants.

15
The Sickness of Europe

Conditional German hegemony meets the Pandemic Crisis

When Covid-19 struck, the European Union (EU) had already registered several years of poor economic performance. Moreover, it lacked adequate mechanisms to enable a coordinated fiscal response to the pandemic shock, mostly because the German government had resisted proposals for a common fiscal policy and an effective banking union throughout the 2010s.[1]

EU member states initially attempted to confront the turmoil by relying on their own strength and resources. Fiscal deficits expanded, augmenting public debt and making it difficult for already heavily indebted EU states to access international financial markets. The fissiparous tendencies that wracked the EU during the Eurozone Crisis in the 2010s, and were effectively pacified by European Central Bank (ECB) intervention in 2012, rapidly re-emerged. The tremors were felt particularly acutely in Italy, as its borrowing rates escalated in March 2020.

The immediate cause was the stance of Christine Lagarde, the president of the ECB. On 12 March, Lagarde announced a modest programme of long-term asset purchases until the end of 2020, declaring that '[w]e are not here to close spreads. This is not the function or the mission of

---

1 This chapter draws on C. Lapavitsas and S. Cutillas (2021) 'National States, Transnational Institutions, and Hegemony in the EU', *Evolutionary and Institutional Economics Review* 19: 429–48.

the ECB. There are other tools for that, and there are other actors to actually deal with those issues.'[2] This statement was remarkable for its short-sightedness; it exacerbated market concerns about Italy's ability to finance its public debt, and thus posed a direct threat to the common currency. As soon as that threat was felt, the policy was rapidly altered, and by 24 March the ECB had launched the Pandemic Emergency Purchase Programme (PEPP), which soon acquired great dimensions similar to the US Federal Reserve policy.

The adoption of loose monetary policy by the ECB, driving interest rates close to zero, went together with expansionary fiscal policy by several member states of the EU, abandoning the policy of austerity that had plagued the Union throughout the preceding decade. As deficits mounted, the EU Stability and Growth Pact was suspended together with regulations of state aid to industry. However, several peripheral countries burdened with high public debt were still constrained in expanding fiscal expenditure. Their reaction, supported by France, was to push for a joint EU fiscal response.

The health emergency forced the EU to abandon its rigid rules of monetary and fiscal policy in favour of greater discretion by member states and by the Union as a whole. This significant change had been in train for several years, but Germany, the conditional hegemon of the EU, had shown reluctance to complete it in the 2010s. It relented in 2020, because the pandemic blow posed a crippling threat to the European Economic and Monetary Union (EMU) and the EU, both of which are vital to German industry. A joint fiscal response to the pandemic – the 'Next Generation EU' programme – was proposed, and although the magnitude of the fiscal expansion in the EU never reached the dimensions of the US boost, the political symbolism was not in doubt.

The hegemonic position of Germany in Europe is highly unusual because it depends on the existence of EU institutions, particularly the EMU. In contrast to the USA and the mechanisms of the world economy, Germany has not created the EU institutions. Rather, it constructed its hegemony by taking advantage of these institutions – at times without prior planning – to suit the interests of its productive and financial capital. German hegemony is conditional on the mechanisms of the EU,

---

2 See ECB, Press Conference, Christine Lagarde, President of the ECB, Luis de Guindos, Vice-President of the ECB, Frankfurt am Main, 12 March 2020, at ecb.europa.eu.

and its power is primarily economic and to a far lesser extent political. When the pandemic struck, it became imperative for Germany to accede to institutional changes in the Union to protect its hegemonic position.

At the global level, however, Germany is subservient to the USA and appears incapable of defending its interests relative to the global hegemon. The weakness of Germany was strikingly demonstrated in the Russo-Ukrainian War in 2022, when the German ruling bloc acceded to US-inspired natural gas and oil sanctions on Russia that would have a severely negative impact on German industry and society at large. Germany's docile stance toward the global hegemon threatened the very basis of its local hegemony.

The peculiar hegemonic structures of the EU cast additional light on the nature of contemporary hegemony in the world economy. German hegemony in the EU is not aimed at creating a separate trading bloc in opposition to the USA. The EU is thoroughly neoliberal, and German industrial and financial capital remain global in outlook. Germany's local hegemony in Europe allows it to maintain a stronger presence in the world market without mounting a true challenge to the USA.

The global hegemon tolerates locally hegemonic powers if they contest neither the institutional framework of the world economy nor the pivotal role of the dollar as world money. In these regards, the EU poses no threat to US hegemony. Indeed, the Union was effectively forced by the hegemon to accept enormous costs by switching its energy supplies away from cheap Russian fossil fuels in 2022. The impact will be felt by broad layers of workers and others across Europe, exacerbating the sickness of European capitalism. A further sharpening of social tensions in the years ahead is likely within and among the member states of the Union. Analysing these likely tensions requires focusing on the peculiar structures of core and periphery in the EU.

Integration and divergence in the EU

Political and social theorists have engaged in debates about the character and direction of the EU since the 1950s, especially regarding the relationship between sovereign nation states and the transnational institutions of the Union. The vast majority have advocated different ways in which the EU could, presumably, promote integration. But, as the transnational institutions of the EU, particularly its legal framework and monetary mechanisms, became more entrenched, greater divergence has prevailed among the members of the Union. Far from heading toward greater integration, the EU is marked by novel forms of hegemony and fresh divisions between core and periphery.

Little in the lengthy debates on the EU would have led to this conclusion. Take, for instance, the well-known 'neo-functionalist' current launched by Ernst Haas, who argued in the 1950s that transnational bodies operating in one field within the EU would generate 'spillovers' into other fields, thus gradually expanding the transnational domain.[3] This neo-functionalist view implied that the nation state would be steadily overcome as integration proceeded, and it fitted well with the mindset of an army of EU bureaucrats in Brussels. However, it gradually became apparent that spillovers were in practice quite limited. The technocratic transnational space of Brussels did not inexorably encroach upon the domain of national sovereignty.[4]

'Intergovernmentalism', the main theoretical challenge to neo-functionalism, particularly in its 'liberal' version associated with Andrew Moravcsik, has not fared much better.[5] This approach departed from the indisputable observation that the EU is a treaty-based alliance of nation states. For Moravcsik, nation states are agents interacting within a game theoretic framework – largely borrowed from neoclassical economics – that also allows for asymmetrical information. The upshot is clear: at the heart of the EU lie nation states driven by domestic and international interests and not transnational mechanisms with their own independent functioning.

This political theory is in effect a disciplinary spillover from the original treatment of the EU by the British historian Alan Milward.[6] For Milward, the EU was a creation of the nation states of Europe after the

3 See E. Haas (2004) [1968] [1958] *The Uniting of Europe: Political, Social, and Economic Forces, 1950–1957*, University of Notre Dame Press: Notre Dame, Indiana.

4 Haas came to appreciate this point, as is clear from the new introduction of his book in 2004. His theory still retained the power to account for particular instances of institutional and political development in the EU. See, for instance, the arguments of one of the most prominent supporters of this approach, P. Schmitter (2005) 'Ernst B. Haas and the Legacy of Neofunctionalism', *Journal of European Public Policy* 12 (2): 255–72.

5 See A. Moravcsik (1998) *The Choice for Europe: Social Purpose and State Power from Messina to Maastricht*, Cornell University Press: Ithaca, NY.

6 See A. Milward (1992) *The European Rescue of the Nation-State*, Routledge: London.

Second World War, allowing these states to regain legitimacy in the eyes of their people following the disasters of war. At all critical junctures of the creation and deepening of the EU, the main concerns of member states were economic, including mostly trade relations and industrial policy. The European nation state, far from surrendering its sovereignty, in practice enhanced it via the institutions and policies of the EU.[7]

It is vital to stress in this connection – and irrespective of the treatment of EU states by political theorists and historians – that the emergence and subsequent history of the EU have been marked by political expediency from the beginning, often determined by military considerations. The USA was instrumental to the emergence of 'Europe' as a counterweight to the Soviet Union during the Cold War, and an anti-communist strain is deeply ingrained in the EU.[8] Moreover, the entire European 'project' had a strongly haphazard element from the start and included a multitude of Cold War organisations that failed to grow during the subsequent decades.[9] Above all, the decisive political acts in the construction of the EU were without exception imposed from the top on an unsuspecting public, and even in the face of popular opposition.[10]

Milward's analysis had the great merit of being historical instead of proposing abstract theories of international relations among nation states. To be sure, there were plenty of European states that did not need 'rescuing' by the EU after the Second World War, thus not easily fitting into Milward's schema. However, once he had hacked his way through the dense undergrowth of EU integration theory, it became hard for others to maintain an analysis of the EU without seeking foundations in political economy.

This point holds even for the most recent and innovative analyses of the EU in political theory, as these are found in the work of both Chris Bickerton and Peter Mair.[11] Summarily put, the EU has transformed the way in which

---

7 See, for instance, A. Milward and V. Sørensen (1993) 'Interdependence or Integration? A National Choice', in A. Milward et al. (eds) *The Frontier of National Sovereignty*, Routledge: London, pp. 1–32.

8 See J. Gillingham (2016) *The EU: An Obituary*, Verso: London and New York.

9 As is shown by K. K. Patel (2020) *Project Europe*, Cambridge University Press: Cambridge, UK.

10 Without even a trace of self-awareness, the ardent Europeanist Middelaar refers to several of these acts as 'coups'; see L. van Middelaar (2013) *The Passage to Europe*, Yale University Press: New Haven and London.

11 See C. Bickerton (2012) *European Integration: From Nation-States to Member States*, Oxford University Press: Oxford. See also, P. Mair (2013) *Ruling the Void: The*

European elites derive their political legitimacy, as democracy has become steadily attenuated within the Union. The national mechanisms of legitimation – operating through the machinery of parliament, the law, and the executive branch of the state – have lost weight relative to the transnational mechanisms of legitimation – operating through the machinery of the EU. Nation states in the EU have become member states, and a political void has emerged between national governments and the citizenry. The national elites of the EU draw legitimation and political direction from each other.

There is more than a grain of truth to this political analysis, but accounting for the withering of democracy and national sovereignty in Europe calls for fuller reference to the underlying conduct of capitalist accumulation. At the very least, the political economy of capitalist development in the EU should be able to shed light on the growing divergence among member states and the emergence of novel divisions between core and periphery in Europe.

From this perspective, a critical moment for both national sovereignty and transnational relations in the EU was the establishment of the common currency in the 1990s. A distinct – if often unspoken – aim of monetary integration was to create mechanisms that could limit US monetary hegemony over European countries, thus contesting the role of the dollar in the world market.[12] To achieve this aim, the EU opted for a monetary union that was theoretically based on the pooling of sovereignty by member states. Presumably, greater integration would also follow, pivoting on the common currency. What occurred in practice was Germany's accretion of hegemonic power and the accelerating divergence of member states.

German local hegemony is rooted in the domestic class relations of Germany but is articulated through the mechanisms and institutions of the EU, particularly those of the monetary union. The creation of the euro propelled Germany to local and conditional hegemony while also encouraging the division of the EU into core and several peripheries. The division remains shifting and loose but is nonetheless real. The core contains Germany and France – locked in contest with each other but

Hollowing of Western Democracy, Verso: London. For a discussion of the withering of democracy in the EU, see C. Bickerton and L. Jones (2018) 'The EU's Democratic Deficit: Why Brexit Is Essential for Restoring Popular Sovereignty', 11 June, at thefullbrexit.com.

12 See C. Lapavitsas (2013) 'The Eurozone Crisis through the Prism of World Money', in M. Wolfson and J. Epstein (eds) *The Handbook of the Political Economy of Financial Crises*, Oxford University Press: Oxford and New York, pp. 378–94.

with the former in the leading position – as well as smaller countries such as the Netherlands, Finland, and Austria. The patterns of dominance over the periphery derive, first, from the common currency with its extensive battery of institutions and, second, from the spread of German industrial capital across much of the EU.

Suffice it in this respect to mention two EU peripheries: the first is in Southern Europe, formed by Spain, Portugal, and Greece, which operates within the EMU but has a weakened industrial sector and is heavily indebted to the core; the second is in Central and Eastern Europe, formed by Poland, Hungary, Czechia, Slovakia, and Slovenia, which operates partially outside the EMU and comprises countries that are integrated in Germany's industrial production chains.

Much of the discussion in the rest of this chapter focuses on the southern periphery, since the role of the transnational mechanisms of the EMU in entrenching the dominant position of the core was clearly demonstrated during the Eurozone Crisis.[13] Two of these mechanisms proved crucial. The first was institutional, deriving from the monopoly of the ECB over the creation of liquidity in the EMU, which allowed the central bank to put entire national economies in a stranglehold. The second was partly ideological, namely the threat felt by millions of people that they would lose their savings as well as their identity if their country were to exit the EMU.

Monetary union, neoliberalism, and hegemony in the EU

The euro is the domestic money of all member states of the EMU and is thus supposed to perform a coordinating and homogenising role in each domestic economy. However, the point is that the euro is not truly

---

13 Quite naturally, then, the Eurozone crisis was a testing ground for 'liberal intergovernmentalism', as the original author of this approach and his collaborators fully realised; see A. Moravcsik and F. Schimmelfennig (2019) 'Liberal Intergovernmentalism', in A. Wiener, T. Börzel, and T. Risse (eds) *European Integration Theory*, 3rd edition, Oxford University Press: Oxford, pp. 64–84. Moravcsik and Schimmelfennig claimed that the crisis largely confirmed the theory, since the adjustment costs were shifted onto the southern periphery and the reforms that occurred suited the interests of Germany. There is no doubt about the unbalanced response of the EU, but the point is that the asymmetry between 'north' and 'south' in the EU arose in large measure because of the very structures of the EMU. Deeper processes than 'intergovernmentalism' were involved in creating the EMU, which subsequently led to a paroxysm of imbalances among member states.

domestic, since it is governed transnationally, and its role can be devastating for peripheral countries. This is because the euro still acts as a tacit form of world money among the member states, settling transactions and facilitating capital flows across the internal borders of the EMU, even if it is formally the domestic currency of all.

A crucial result of this contradictory arrangement is the accumulation of TARGET2 imbalances deep at the heart of the EMU. TARGET2 imbalances became gigantic in the early 2020s, reflecting the entrenchment of core and periphery in the EU and creating a problem with no immediate solution, as is shown in the subsequent sections of this chapter. At the same time, the euro has effectively failed to become a form of world money capable of challenging the US dollar as the global reserve currency and international means of payment. The common currency of the EU does not pose a significant threat to the dollar, and its second-rank position fits with the political dominance of Atlanticism over the EU.

The German ruling bloc did not plan these developments when the EMU took shape in the 1990s. For decades, the chief concern of German policy makers had been to prevent sharp appreciations of the Deutsche Mark that could cripple industrial exports. This meant, above all, maintaining independence in conducting monetary policy for the Bundesbank.[14] In contrast, France and smaller countries aimed to avoid severe depreciations by creating a framework for stabilising exchange rates that would also allow for a powerful say in decision-making.[15]

The main push toward monetary union came from the French ruling bloc, whose interest in transnational monetary controls long predated the Treaty of Maastricht in 1992 that formally opened the way toward monetary union. The EU shifted its exchange rate policy from stabilising rates within a band via systematic intervention in the foreign exchange markets toward eliminating exchange rates altogether by deploying a common currency both domestically and internationally. Establishing the EMU in the 1990s was a qualitative leap compared with plain exchange rate controls, not least since member states became formal partners in the monetary union, with pooled sovereignty.

---

14 See F. Scharpf (2011) 'Monetary Union, Fiscal Crisis and the Pre-emption of Democracy', *Journal for Comparative Government and European Policy* 9 (2): 163–98.

15 See Flassbeck and Lapavitsas (2015) *Against the Troika*.

But competition among member states has not been eliminated and in practice permeates the structures of the monetary union, resulting in deep asymmetries. National competition results from the flows of commercial capital across borders as well as from the flows of loanable capital. It reflects the solidity and depth of national financial structures and the commitment of each member state to the EMU in its entirety. The financial markets of Europe continually account for this commitment in terms of what is called the redenomination risk (that is, the risk of shifting back to a national currency) and the spread in interest rates between the public bonds of Germany and each member state.

Within the framework of the EMU, the ECB determines a common monetary policy, implemented in a decentralised manner by national central banks, while responsibility for fiscal policy was originally left to national governments. Member states are thus exposed to opposing dynamics. On the one hand, the integration of monetary systems hinges on the liberalisation of capital flows and the homogenisation of financial markets to sustain the value of the euro internationally. On the other, persistent national differences in the functioning of financial markets as well as the historical characteristics of domestic economies continually enter the calculus of internationally active financial enterprises, often resulting in reverse flows of loanable capital from periphery to core.

The role of the EMU in inducing divergence within the EU is a component part of the broad neoliberal turn of the EU during the last four decades. In its early period, from the 1950s to the 1970s, the EU was marked by state management of aggregate demand, public ownership of economic resources, and a degree of social democratic considerations. The Union shifted decisively toward neoliberalism in the 1980s, culminating in the Maastricht Treaty of 1992, which drew on the Single European Act of 1986. Constructing the EMU was a prime institutional step in this shift.

More broadly, the neoliberal turn of the EU relied on the steady mutation of the so-called 'four freedoms' enshrined in the original Treaty of Rome of 1957, namely the freedom to move goods, services, capital, and labour across the internal borders of the Union. In the decades since Maastricht, the 'four freedoms' have been firmly transformed into freedoms of the individual. In this guise, they underpin the legal framework of the EU, which transcends national sovereignty and supports the functioning of EU transnational mechanisms.

European law, in practice, dominates national law and is impervious to national executive and legislative power.[16] Its neoliberal tenor is not in doubt, and nor are the barriers it would place in the path of a national government that opted for economic policies directly opposing neoliberalism. In effect, EU law has a constitutional dimension that acts as a binding external constraint on member states.[17]

Constitutional or not, EU law has gradually acquired vast dimensions, including the 'primary' law of EU treaties and the 'secondary' law of EU directives, regulations, decisions, and international agreements. The principal institution, in this respect, is the European Court of Justice (ECJ), which has gradually arrogated to itself the power of interpreting the law (thus also making it) without encroachment by a separate legislative power. The ECJ resembles the ECB insofar as it is a transnational body that holds itself up by its own bootstraps, as it were. It possesses enormous power to shape the legal cogwheels of the EU, which are crucial to the operations of the single market and the EMU.

The overall result of the neoliberal turn of the EU, marked by the construction of the common currency, was steady divergence among member states, leading to the emergence of core and periphery, a division that has become an entrenched source of tension and crisis. At the same time, Germany was propelled into a position of peculiar hegemonic power over the EU.

Germany rises to conditional and local hegemony

Germany has long been the leading economy of the EU, but that did not translate into assuming a hegemonic position until the 1990s, when the country emerged as a tremendous net exporter, generating unprecedented imbalances on current account within the EMU. Stringent wage restraints since the late 1990s gave German industrial exporters a competitive advantage relative to several other countries in the EU. Together with the fiscal austerity imposed by Maastricht and ECB

---

16 The classic legal analysis of this extraordinary development was given by J. H. H. Weiler (1999) *The Constitution of Europe*, Cambridge University Press: Cambridge, UK.

17 These constraints were hotly contested at the peak of the Brexit controversy in the UK, and were set forth with great clarity by R. Tuck (2020) *The Left Case for Brexit: Reflections on the Current Crisis*, Polity Press: London. See also, C. Lapavitsas (2018) *The Left Case against the EU*, Polity Press: Cambridge, UK, and Medford, MA.

monetary policy, which lowered interest rates for member states, the divergence in competitiveness created highly unstable conditions in the Eurozone and solidified its division into core and southern periphery.

At the same time, the reunification of Germany in 1990 and the collapse of the Eastern Bloc allowed German industrial capital to establish productive capacity in surrounding countries, creating a further periphery in Central and Eastern Europe through supply chains and financial flows. Countries in the Central European periphery entered a process of renewed industrialisation pivoting on the German industrial complex. In contrast, the productive sector of the Southern European periphery came under strain, veering toward areas of low productivity and low exporting capacity.

In the 2000s, the deregulation of capital flows within the EU, together with low interest rates also encouraged growth of the financial sector and favoured financialisation.[18] The banks of core countries, particularly in Germany and France, were heavily involved in lending to southern peripheral countries, and the resulting capital flows balanced the current account deficits of peripheral countries while increasing their indebtedness. Moreover, access to the money market of the EMU facilitated credit creation by peripheral banks in the south, promoting subordinate financialisation and creating domestic bubbles, most notably in Spanish real estate.

The burst of the US bubble in 2007–09 gradually morphed into the Eurozone Crisis. Large fiscal deficits emerged in the southern periphery of the EU as the automatic stabilisers were activated and domestic banks received public funds to avoid collapse. Public debt escalated rapidly, core banks became greatly concerned about the solvency of peripheral states, and the financial flows that had supported the current account deficits of peripheral countries dried up completely in 2010.

A sudden stop occurred in 2010, indeed a reversal of capital flows, as core country banks sought to pull out of the southern periphery. The euro came under severe pressure and the ECB was forced to intervene by providing liquidity to banks, thus entering a path of transformation that became evident in the Pandemic Crisis. During this period, the deeper structures of the EMU also came under sharp scrutiny, especially the imbalances among the accounts of member-country central banks

---

18 The analysis of EMU imbalances in this section draws heavily on C. Lapavitsas et al. (2012) *Crisis in the Eurozone*, Verso: London and New York.

– that is, the TARGET2 accounts discussed in the following sections.

The fundamental asymmetry in the Eurozone, however, lay not only in the volume and direction of financial flows but also in the profound imbalances on current account, especially in German surpluses that reflected divergences in national competitiveness. At the root of the divergences lies a ferocious wage restraint in Germany, which started in the second half of the 1990s and resulted in huge gains in competitiveness for German industrial exporters. Severe domestic austerity propelled the German industrial oligarchy into a hegemonic position in the EU on the back of EMU mechanisms.

Germany's rise to unprecedented export dominance can also be seen in terms of the variations in inflation within the EMU. Prior to the establishment of the Eurozone, higher inflation in EU countries relative to that of Germany, other things equal, would have led to a fall in exchange rates. The Eurozone eliminated that channel of adjustment, and thus higher inflation rates meant that the real effective exchange rates of peripheral countries remained high. Consequently, several countries in the Eurozone, particularly in the southern periphery, faced a dramatic loss of competitiveness.

When the Eurozone Crisis burst out in 2010, the German ruling bloc came gradually but resolutely to the conclusion that it had to defend the EMU, on which its hegemony relies. It chose to operate through the institutions of the EU, while also inviting the IMF to play a technical role in dealing with the crisis. Nevertheless, the key decisions were made in Berlin and the testing ground was Greece, the weakest of the countries in the southern periphery.

During the first stages of the Eurozone Crisis, the ECB refused to intervene in the secondary markets for public debt, even though it already had an active bond purchase programme.[19] Still, it provided substantial liquidity to banks to confront the shock of the crisis. Furthermore, bailout programmes followed in 2010–12 for peripheral countries that were temporarily shut out of financial markets. Public funds were advanced to Greece, Portugal, and Ireland on the condition that they implement policies of austerity and deregulation, supervised by the 'Troika' of the Commission, the ECB, and the IMF.

The chief aim of the bailouts was to prevent sovereign defaults that would have created major losses for French and German banks already under pressure from the burst of the US bubble, thus threatening the

---

19 As was noted by A. Tooze (2017) 'Notes on the Global Condition: Of Bond Vigilantes, Central Bankers and the Crisis, 2008–2017', at adamtooze.com.

viability of the euro. In effect, the bailouts rescued the banks of core countries, which were in danger of bearing the brunt of state defaults.

The Greek bailouts led to a disastrous contraction of GDP in the country by imposing fiscal cuts, reducing wages, and destroying the conditions for private investment. Eventually, a haircut was imposed on lenders to the Greek state in 2011–12, but even that fell heavily on domestic Greek institutions, particularly as French and German banks had already reduced their exposure to Greece. The bailouts were imposed ostensibly by the Troika but were in practice determined by Berlin acting as the *de facto* government of the Eurozone. In 2011–12, Athens even had to submit to the replacement of its prime minister by an unelected central banker who had the confidence of Berlin. German hegemony was unbending but still preferred to hide behind the institutions of the EU.

Berlin opted to channel its decisions via the transnational mechanisms of the EU, and the main conduit in this respect was the ECB. The point is, however, that the operations of the ECB – and of the EMU more generally – are not directly controlled by Germany, or by any other individual member state. The ECB is not the Bundesbank, and it does not rely on any individual member state to give it legitimacy to create money on its balance sheet. Germany is forced to mediate its hegemony via the transnational mechanisms of the euro, and that is an inherently uncertain process. The power of the ECB in this context is considerable and has increased substantially in the 2010s, as is shown in the following sections.

The institutional transformation of the EU in the 2010s

The Eurozone Crisis set in train a series of institutional transformations that proved crucial to the EU when the pandemic struck. In 2010, the EU adopted a strategy that avoided the imposition of costs on Germany and forced internal deflation – essentially, a fall in wages and prices – onto southern peripheral countries. Severe austerity was expected to eliminate the fiscal and current account deficits, while deregulation of labour and product markets would presumably restore international competitiveness.

Several institutional transformations of the EU ensued upon adoption of this strategy. Germany entrenched its local hegemony and simultaneously led the EU into an economic and political quagmire. Between mid-2011 and early 2012, the Fiscal Pact and the 'Six-Pack' and 'Two-Pack' reforms were signed, further hardening the terms of fiscal policy and public debt in the EU. These reforms inscribed austerity into the constitutional framework of the EU, but were also complex, detailed, and inherently dysfunctional, thus in practice leaving member states with room for manoeuvre.

New institutions were also created to manage the bailouts and their financial repercussions. In May 2010 the European Financial Stability Fund and the European Financial Stability Mechanism came into existence. The former was the more important of the two; it was created as a private institution, located in Luxembourg, and operated under British law. The intention was to avoid explicitly contravening the so-called no-bailout clause – that is, article 125 of the Treaty on the Functioning of the EU. This action was typical of how the institutional transformation of the EU proceeded in the wake of the Eurozone Crisis: the letter of the Treaties was formally observed but their spirit was ignored when urgent action had to be taken. No institution demonstrated this more clearly than the ECB, as is shown below.

Two further institutional changes were, however, resisted by Germany. First, there would be no formal lender of last resort in the Eurozone: the mandate of the ECB remained formally the same and continued to forbid the financing of state deficits. Second, there would be no issuing of Eurobonds that would formally create mutual responsibility for public borrowing within the EU. Germany strongly resisted taking responsibility for the costs of public finance in other member states.

Still, in July 2012 the president of the ECB, Mario Draghi, proclaimed that he would do 'whatever it takes' to save the euro. This step pacified the Eurozone Crisis and was a defining moment, not least because it ushered in the gradual transformation of the ECB, laying the ground for its intervention when the pandemic struck. The changed role of the ECB must be seen in conjunction with steps taken to reform the banking and financial sectors across the EU with a view to preventing a repetition of the phenomena of the Eurozone Crisis.

The financial reforms focused, first, on strengthening the capital and liquidity requirements of banks; second, on implementing recovery and resolution regulations on failing banks to limit the liability of taxpayers for losses; and third, on legally separating risky financial activities from the practices of deposit-taking banks.[20] They were part of a putative drive toward a banking union, the objective of which was to integrate

20 See E. Liikanen et al. (2012) 'High-Level Expert Group on Reforming the Structure of the EU Banking Sector', press release, Brussels, October, at ec.europa.eu.

the banking sector across the EU and to eliminate public bailouts of private banks as well as countering the fragmentation of banking sectors along national borders, thus supposedly 'completing' the monetary union.[21]

Despite these ambitions, progress toward a banking union was very limited. In practice, the functioning of the money market in Europe remains deeply deficient. The ECB currently dominates it, and the profound imbalances within the monetary union are reflected in the balance sheets of the central banks of member states via the TARGET2 balances.

Since the Eurozone crisis, the ECB has emerged as the pre-eminent economic institution of the EU, acting in ways that digress from its original statutes. It gradually accrued powers of intervention reminiscent of the Federal Reserve, engaging in quantitative easing in the 2010s and enormously expanding its balance sheet. Germany acceded to the transformation of the ECB essentially for the same reason that it acceded to the bailouts during the Eurozone crisis – that is, to protect the euro. The hegemonic position of the German ruling bloc within the EU depends on the survival of the EMU, which, in turn, relies on the ECB as a transnational entity with powers of discretion.

The nature of the change in the ECB started to become clear in the middle of the 2010s. The Lisbon Treaty of 2007 forbids the ECB from buying state debt, but its provisions were sidestepped in 2014–15, under the presidency of Mario Draghi, when the ECB systematically engaged in quantitative easing via the so-called Asset Purchase Programmes (APP).[22] The impact of quantitative easing can be seen in the consolidated balance sheet of the Eurosystem, which is the broader central banking institution of the EMU containing the ECB as well as the national central banks (NCBs) of member states. The NCBs operate as branches of the ECB and implement the common monetary policy designed by the ECB.

Figures 15.1 and 15.2 show, respectively, the asset and the liability side of the balance sheet of the Eurosystem:

---

21 See M. Bellia and S. Maccaferri (2020) 'Banks' Bail-In and the New Banking Regulation: An EU Event Study', European Commission JRC Technical Report, JRC Working Papers in Economics and Finance No. 07.

22 The APP consists of four smaller programmes, namely the corporate sector purchase programme, the public sector purchase programme, the asset-backed securities purchase programme, and the third covered bonds purchase programme. See ECB (2021) 'Asset Purchase Programmes', at ecb.europa.eu.

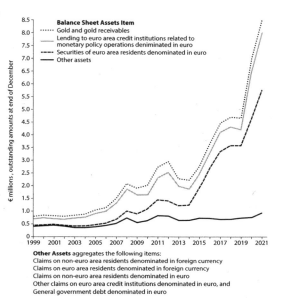

Figure 15.1. Eurosystem consolidated balance sheet:
assets, December 1999–December 2022.
Source: ECB.

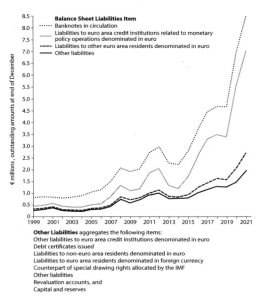

Figure 15.2. Eurosystem consolidated balance sheet:
Liabilities, December 1999–December 2022.
Source: ECB.

The assets and liabilities of the Eurosystem grew steadily after the outbreak of the Great Crisis of 2007–09 but escalated rapidly after 2014, when quantitative easing was implemented. The main components of change were, on the asset side, the acquisition of vast volumes of securities issued by residents of the euro area and, on the liability side, the increase in deposits of Eurozone banks held by the Eurosystem. In brief, the Eurosystem provided huge volumes of liquidity to banks by acquiring equally huge volumes of securities.

The escalation of assets and liabilities assumed enormous proportions after the outbreak of the Pandemic Crisis. The increase was partly due to provision of liquidity to banks via the ECB's Long-Term Refinancing Operations, but mostly through the PEPP, which was effectively the continuation and considerable enlargement of APP.[23] Moreover, the regulations constraining ECB acquisitions were greatly relaxed in 2020. In effect, the PEPP acted as an emergency APP, and by the spring of 2022 it had resulted in the Eurosystem holding nine times as many public bonds by value as in the spring of 2021.

The extraordinary intervention by the ECB after 2020 compressed interest rate spreads between core and periphery within the EMU, and the central bank acted once again as guarantor of the euro. Nonetheless, the expansion of the balance sheet of the Eurosystem still had a strong national character, with NCBs carrying most of the burden of buying securities and lending to banks in their national territory. In early 2021, the ECB held less than 20 per cent of the balance sheet of the Eurosystem, the rest being held by the NCBs.[24]

Quantitative easing in the EMU was a particularly important development. The acquisition of public bonds via the creation of central bank liabilities has given rise to enormous imbalances among member states. These imbalances cast light on the nature of hegemony in the EU but are not immediately apparent in the consolidated balance sheet of the Eurosystem; for this, we must take a careful look at TARGET2.

---

23 The major differences between the two were the waiver of eligibility requirements for Greek government debt, which was excluded from the APP due to its low quality, and the removal of any self-imposed purchase limits by the ECB.

24 See ECB (2022) 'Statistical Data Warehouse: Breakdown of the Eurosystem Aggregated Balance Sheet', at sdw.ecb.europa.eu.

The significance of TARGET2

Central banking in the EU is highly peculiar by construction. For our purposes, the EMU has no such thing as one central bank with one balance sheet. Instead, the Eurosystem and the ECB have their own balance sheets, as does each of the NCBs. The separation of balance sheets reflects the imbalances generated when money moves among EMU member states, whether the money flows are caused by commodity flows, loanable capital flows, or simple transfers between countries.

If a sum of money moves across the internal borders of the EMU, the accounting practice of the Eurosystem requires the central bank of the receiving country to register the sum on its balance sheet as an additional liability, while the asset stays on the balance sheet of the central bank of the remitting country. The receiving central bank must add a balancing item to reflect holding more euros on its balance sheet, while the remitting central bank must add a balancing item to reflect holding fewer euros on its balance sheet.

The balancing item is called a TARGET2 balance. It encompasses potentially all cross-border intra-EMU transactions that are cleared through the main payments system of the EMU, the TARGET2 system. This is a pivotal mechanism at the heart of the monetary union, allowing for the settlement of obligations among central banks but also among private banks and private non-bank enterprises. It makes it possible to settle transactions between capitalist enterprises straddling the internal borders of the EMU via the exchange of reserves at their respective NCBs. Each TARGET2 balance is an asset for the receiver and simultaneously a liability for the sender within the Eurosystem, both in relation to the ECB.

Take, for instance, a private transaction arising from an Italian resident purchasing a commodity (or a financial security) from a German resident. The Italian would normally send money via an Italian bank to a German bank and the payment, as in any monetary system, would generate a flow of central bank money (that is, of central bank reserves) from the Italian bank's account at the Banca d'Italia to the German bank's account at the Bundesbank. The flow of reserves from Banca d'Italia to the Bundesbank would decrease the liabilities of the former on its balance sheet, while increasing the liabilities of the latter on its balance sheet. To 'balance' their balance sheets, other things being equal, the two NCBs will generate TARGET2 balances: Banca d'Italia will have an increase in TARGET2 liabilities, while the Bundesbank will have an increase in TARGET2 assets, thus equalising assets and liabilities on both balance sheets.

In technical terms, consequently, TARGET2 balances are net positions of single NCBs against the ECB and thus against the rest of the Eurosystem. They resemble overdraft facilities made available by the Eurosystem to ensure that payments by enterprises and NCBs go through the clearing process without hindrance and regardless of the jurisdiction of the original payer. This is absolutely necessary to ensure that the euro has the same exchange value across EMU member states. It appears, then, that TARGET2 balances are nothing more than accounting devices to ensure the practical functioning of the euro. But the reality is far more complex than that.[25]

TARGET2 reflects the inner workings of the euro as means of payment and hoarding among EMU members, mirroring the Union's division between core and periphery. If the EMU did not exist, member states would relate to each other through their own currencies. A current account deficit or a net outflow of loanable capital for a country would entail a loss of reserves of world money, typically at the central bank. If the loss persevered, the country would be confronted with exchange rate depreciation, possibly leading to a foreign exchange crisis; the opposite would obviously hold for a current account surplus or a money capital inflow.

Within the EMU, this mechanism has been eliminated. A country with a current account deficit or a capital outflow will not lose reserves of world money but instead its central bank will acquire TARGET2 liabilities. On the other hand, the central bank of a country with a

25 The argument put forward in this section draws on the ECB's institutional view that TARGET2 balances are integral to the operations of the APP (see J. Eisenschmidt et al. (2017) 'The Eurosystem's Asset Purchase Programme and TARGET Balances', ECB Occasional Paper Series No. 196; and V. della Corte, S. Federico, and E. Tosti (2018) 'Unwinding External Stock Imbalances? The Case of Italy's Net International Investment Position', Bank of Italy Occasional Papers No. 446. It also draws on the argument that TARGET2 balances result from intra-EMU capital flows, developed in different forms by K. Whelan (2014) 'TARGET2 and Central Bank Balance Sheets', *Economic Policy* 29 (77): 79–137, and by M. Minenna, G. Dosi, and A. Roventini (2018) 'ECB Monetary Expansions and Euro Area TARGET2 Imbalances: A Balance-of-Payment-Based Decomposition', *European Journal of Economics and Economic Policies: Intervention* 15 (2): 147–59.

current account surplus or a capital inflow will accumulate TARGET2 credits. In short, private intra-Eurozone flows of money across borders are continually cleared via adjustment of the TARGET2 position of member states' NCB. The private flows of money arising for whatever reason result in changes in the intra-Eurozone liabilities and assets of the national central banks.

The process resembles the movement that would have taken place in the reserves of world money if the EMU did not exist, but there are also substantial differences. For one thing, in contrast to reserves, a member state of the EMU cannot make the accumulation of TARGET2 assets its conscious public policy. Indeed, a member state would be altogether unlikely to change its TARGET2 position (both claims and liabilities) as a matter of choice. The TARGET2 balances of NCBs have an automatic dimension reflecting deeper underlying processes, including most importantly the contradictory role of the euro as simultaneously the domestic and the international money of EMU members.

A comparison with the dollar is instructive at this point. Dollar reserves play a largely passive role for long periods of time among countries, particularly when commodity and money capital flows are behaving 'normally'. In times of crisis, however, control over reserves, and especially access to emergency reserves, becomes a matter of sovereign and ultimately hegemonic power. Shortage of reserves could lead to the collapse of both commercial and capital flows, with potentially catastrophic results for financial institutions operating internationally. Managing the reserve role of the dollar internationally is an integral element of US hegemony, in good part via allowing other countries to access the Federal Reserve balance sheet through swaps, as was discussed in previous chapters.

TARGET2 balances also normally play a passive role among member states, but their difference with regular reserves of world money becomes apparent in times of turmoil, for TARGET2 would preclude the emergence of a sharp domestic crisis due to cross-border flows. A member state of the EMU with a persistent current account deficit or net capital outflows would not run out of reserves, but instead its central bank would accumulate liabilities ('red ink') within the TARGET2 system. Analogously, a country with a current account surplus or net capital inflows would accumulate credits ('black ink').

These could be tolerated within the Eurosystem, since there is no legal obligation to settle open positions among central banks. Thus, instead of reserve flows leading a country to the brink of a crisis and forcing financial enterprises to make catastrophic adjustments, member states of the EMU would be accumulating TARGET2 assets and liabilities. In effect, the ECB would be accommodating the pressures of the underlying imbalance in commodity and capital flows on its balance sheet.

At the same time, however, the euro is supposed to be the domestic money of EMU members, and TARGET2 casts a sharp light on the Union's putative homogeneity. For, if the euro was indeed truly the domestic money of, say, both Italy and Germany, the transaction between the Italian and the German residents in our earlier example would have had further dimensions.

The Italian bank, after transferring the money to the German bank, would have found itself short of reserves, for reasons discussed in the brief analysis of banking in part II. Naturally, it would have sought reserves in the money market, possibly through repo transactions. Other things being equal, if the euro was genuinely the domestic money of the EMU, the Italian bank would have borrowed the required reserves from the German bank, since the latter would have found itself with extra reserves after receiving the payment in the first place. In that case, the money flows between Italy and Germany would have been reversed and there would have been no TARGET2 imbalances.

But such an automatic rebalancing of banking positions via the money market has simply not been taking place since the outbreak of the Eurozone Crisis. Its absence is reflected in the enormous accumulation of TARGET2 assets and liabilities. Instead of transacting with each other in the money market, the Italian bank would seek to obtain the necessary reserves from the Banca d'Italia, while the German bank would keep its additional reserves with the Bundesbank. The NCBs of member states would thus dominate their respective money markets, and the ECB the overall market, all acting as indispensable counterparties for private banks. The result would be the accumulation of TARGET2 imbalances within the Eurosystem.

The trajectory of TARGET2 balances since the Great Crisis of 2007–09, shown in figure 15.3 for five key participants, casts light on these deeper workings of the EMU and foregrounds the hierarchical structure of the EMU.

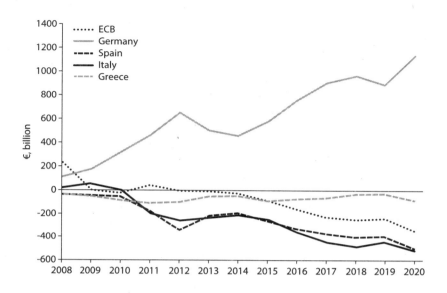

Figure 15.3. TARGET2 balances, euro, bn.
Source: ECB

The TARGET2 assets of the German Bundesbank have reached gigantic proportions in the decade and a half since the outbreak of the Great Crisis of 2007–09. During the same period, the liabilities of the central banks of Italy, Spain, and Greece have been almost the mirror image of the German assets. Following the outbreak of the pandemic and the surge in quantitative easing by the ECB, the credits of the Bundesbank exceeded 1.1 trillion euro in early 2021, while the liabilities of the Bank of Italy and the Bank of Spain were roughly 500 billion each, and those of the Bank of Greece escalated toward 90 billion.

These vast imbalances – partly accounted for in terms of current account deficits in the periphery compared with current account surpluses for Germany, but also reflecting the flows of loanable capital out of peripheral countries while capital was flowing into Germany – were integral to the Eurozone Crisis. Since 2014, however, TARGET2 imbalances have resulted from the ECB implementing quantitative easing.

The vast creation of liquidity by the ECB encouraged the export of loanable capital from the periphery and facilitated intra-EMU flows of loanable capital into Germany, including flows that occurred indirectly from the periphery to Germany. At the same time, the ECB became ever more dominant in the money market of the EU, while accumulating huge TARGET2 liabilities through buying securities to implement quantitative easing. The vast divergences of TARGET2 show that the Bundesbank is considered a safer abode of reserves than the rest of the Eurosystem by the commercial banks and financial institutions that have access to it. German TARGET2 credits signal the hierarchical pre-eminence of the Bundesbank, even if the German NCB implements monetary policy operations only within the German jurisdiction.

The peculiar hegemonic position of Germany in this regard is expressed as tacit support for the quantitative policies of the ECB through the huge accumulation of 'black ink' by the Bundesbank within the Eurosystem. The Bundesbank does not operate like the Federal Reserve in providing reserves of international money to countries that are short of it, but instead tolerates the enormous deficits of others within the clearing system. TARGET2 surpluses are thus a token of German hegemony. The claims of the Bundesbank within TARGET2 are not at all a case of German taxpayers subsidising the feckless periphery of the EMU, as was once claimed within the German establishment.[26] Without the 'black ink' of the Bundesbank in the Eurosystem, there would have been no euro and no German hegemony in the EMU.

This still leaves open the question of what would happen to these balances in the case of a country exiting the EMU. The answer is still far from clear, but it is no coincidence in this respect that TARGET2 is under the jurisdiction of the Frankfurt am Main tribunals.[27] It would be extremely difficult for 'red ink' countries to exit the framework of the EMU without incurring major costs. And that is without even mentioning the considerable costs that would emerge from attempting to establish an alternative national payment system to replace TARGET2 for the exiting country. The EMU is a trap with no easy exit, a mechanism creating divergence and core–periphery divisions while also binding the hegemonic power into it.

26 The most prominent exponent of this view was Hans-Werner Sinn. See H.-W. Sinn and T. Wollmerhäuser (2012) 'TARGET Loans, Current Account Balances and Capital Flows: The ECB's Rescue Facility', *International Tax and Public Finance* 19 (4): 468–508. See also H. W. Sinn (2022) 'Target Debate', at hanswernersinn.de.

27 See C. Lapavitsas (2018) 'The Redenomination Risk of Eurozone Exit for Greece', *ifo* [ifo Institute – Leibniz Institute for Economic Research at the University of Munich] *DICE Report* 16 (3): 31–4.

The lifting of austerity

As the destructive force of the pandemic became readily apparent, the EU was forced not only to loosen monetary policy but also to lift the fiscal straitjacket of austerity. The Stability and Growth Pact setting the stringent terms of fiscal policy for member states, which had come to include a range of new restrictions after the Eurozone crisis, was suspended. Individual member states gained considerable fiscal discretion and deficits escalated rapidly, although remaining generally lower than in the USA, or the UK, as was shown in chapter 4.

Moreover, the EU suspended regulations governing state aid to industry as well as other rules that presumably provided a 'level playing field' of competition. Member states were able to support their industries according to their resources and discretion. Germany immediately engaged in large state support, as did Italy, with France following at some distance behind.

For countries in the southern periphery of the EU, including Italy, these policies afforded scope to support domestic demand, partly through automatic stabilisers and partly through active fiscal intervention. Peripheral states also obtained greater freedom to intervene on the side of supply and to offer support to selected industries. However, member states in the southern periphery remained burdened with high public indebtedness, which remained a major constraint despite the fall in interest rates. The reaction of peripheral countries, supported by France, was to push for a joint EU fiscal response.

The key move in this respect was made by Germany, which took an important and symbolic decision: Germany backed France to devise a joint fiscal response to the pandemic that took the form of the 'Next Generation EU' programme. Summarily put, the programme is supposed to provide 750 billion euro, obtained by the EU Commission through borrowing in the open financial markets. This would be a significant step toward debt mutualisation, since a version of joint bonds would be finally issued for the first time, even if in limited amounts.

A significant breach was made in the spirit of the EU Treaties, according to which the Union is not allowed to operate with jointly borrowed funds.[28] The funds will be split into 360 billion euro of loans and 390

---

28 EU 'primary law' was circumvented by relying on the loose phrasing of article 311 of the Treaty on the Functioning of the European Union; see EU,

billion euro of grants that will be heavily directed toward member states in the peripheries of the EU. The monies will become available for entrepreneurial projects, preferably public–private partnerships, submitted by individual countries and aiming at a 'green', 'digitalised', and 'inclusive' transformation of their economies.[29]

The crucial component of the programme is the grants, representing fiscal transfers to peripheral countries. The planned size of the transfers is not large compared with the GDP of the EU, which stood at around 14 trillion euro after the formal departure of Britain in 2020. Indeed, the programme is decidedly modest, and its importance is primarily political. The fiscal grants that the southern periphery of the EU will receive for three years are unlikely to exceed 2 per cent of GDP annually. As for the loans made available to peripheral states, they will probably have a lower rate of interest than for sovereign debt in the open markets, given the top credit rating of the European Commission.

Three further issues stand out with regard to the fiscal programme of the EU. First, the objectives of the programme are not based on the development needs of peripheral countries. As is made clear in the technical analysis accompanying the programme, the sectors that will absorb the bulk of the funds have largely been determined by their export potential for core countries as well as with the intention of supporting the position of the EU in the world market.[30] There is no evidence that the optimal industrial strategy for, say, Spain and Greece, following the pandemic and the preceding decade of weak growth, ought to comprise 'greening' the economy and promoting 'digitalisation'. Second, given the opacity of the programme and the lack of democratic control over it, there is reason to expect that the funds will be distributed by member state governments in favour of powerful domestic capitalist groups. Third, peripheral countries that decide to obtain the loans of the programme would do well to remember the harsh conduct of the EU as a lender, as was shown to Greece in the 2010s.

Lifting austerity during the pandemic demonstrated a degree of tactical flexibility on the part of Germany in defending its local hegemony. Yet neither monetary nor fiscal policy in the pandemic truly tackled the

---

'Consolidated Version of the Treaty on the Functioning of the European Union, at data.europa.eu.

29 Repeated frequently at the website for 'Recovery Plan for Europe', at ec.europa.eu.

30 See, European Commission (2020) 'Identifying Europe's Recovery Needs', Commission Staff Working Document, No. 98, at eur-lex.europa.eu.

weakness of productive accumulation in Europe, which is even more pronounced than in the USA, as was discussed in part II. Inflation also rose substantially in the EU in 2021–22, and the prospect of raising interest rates and moving toward reintroducing austerity raised its head already in 2022.

Above all, the war in Ukraine witnessed the extraordinary spectacle of Europe opting to bear the heaviest burden of the contest between the USA and Russia. Germany is due to receive a body blow to its industrial strength, while the loss of income for broad swathes of workers and others across the Union will take on major dimensions. German conditional and local hegemony proved utterly inadequate at the global level, the country submitting to US demands and even undermining itself. The sickness of Europe shows no signs of abating and calls for radical alternative policies.

16

Coda: The 'Greening' of Capitalism?

The pandemic offered fresh evidence regarding the deleterious impact of private capital on the natural world, as was discussed extensively in chapter 2. The domination of society by capital poses severe dangers for human health, due especially to the pernicious role of Big Pharma and its entanglement with medicine. The policies to confront Covid-19 were determined by economic, political, and ideological relations across the world, but had to be set against the material canvas of the viral threat to human health.

By analogy, the strategies to confront the havoc of the current interregnum will ultimately be determined by the economic, political, and ideological relations that were the focus of analysis in the preceding chapters. However, all strategies must be set against the material canvas of the environmental and climate disasters, the ecological crisis that has steadily developed as capitalism has encircled the globe.

Analysing the interaction of capital with nature and discussing the deeper causes of the unfolding ecological crisis are obviously beyond the ambit of this book. Nonetheless, the interregnum has been marked by the 'green turn' of multilateral organisations, governments, and, significantly, multinational corporations. A brief analytical discussion of this development, affording further insight into the pernicious relationship of capital to nature, could more sharply identify the factors that are likely to shape the path ahead.

The rise and rise of sustainability

Accelerated capitalist integration has had dramatic consequences for the natural environment. Global production chains rely on the huge expansion of shipping, road transport, and air travel, which have a severe impact on the environment. Agribusiness, integral to production chains, dominates vast tracts of land in core and peripheral countries and commits these to monoculture or cattle raising. The digital universe that ties together states, giant corporations, and households has gargantuan energy demands. Fossil fuel consumption continues to escalate, contributing to global warming, and pollution is visible to the naked eye across land and water. The list could easily be extended.

The environmental and climate impact has engendered a powerful reaction by multilateral organisations and governments during the last three decades, a 'green turn' crucially shared by corporations and resulting in a veritable 'greening' of private capital. It cannot be overstressed that the reaction of corporations has not emanated from an inner drive, or some belated incorporation of the costs of destroying nature into the circuit of capital. As was mentioned in the opening chapters of this book, the pursuit of profit subordinates all other motivations and leads capital to treat nature as a territory to be plundered for free wealth. This remains the fundamental outlook of the giant multinationals, banks, and shadow banks dominating the world economy.

The 'greening' of private capital has arisen in response to pressures external to the circuit of capital and is more appropriately characterised as 'greenwashing'. To be sure, it is the product of forces broadly internal to the development of contemporary capitalism, the result of social and ideological tensions built up over a long time as private capital continued to exploit nature. But no essential component of the fundamental circuit of capital would ever lead to its 'greening'. Left to its own internal mechanisms of exploitation and accumulation, private capital would relentlessly destroy the natural world.

What has changed during the last three decades is the burgeoning of popular concern about the impact of economic activity on the environment, and particularly on the climate. In core countries, concern has taken the character of a mass movement, especially among young people, while growing disquiet is apparent in several peripheral countries. This external force has led private capital to engage in a 'green turn'.

Vital to the 'green turn' of private capital have been the concerted efforts of multilateral organisations aiming ostensibly to create conditions of sustainability for the environment and the climate. From the standpoint of multilateral organisations, these conditions would be presumably achieved by mobilising the power of giant corporations. Consistent with neoliberal thinking, several initiatives were undertaken to create a propitious institutional framework for enterprises across the world, and market mechanisms were promoted as the preferred method of confronting the ecological crisis. The power of core countries, particularly the hegemonic USA, could be detected behind these efforts.

The UN has played a particularly important role in this regard. Since the 1990s, the UN has systematically promoted the notion of sustainable development, linking the ecological crisis to the persistence of poverty across a broad swathe of peripheral countries. A defining moment was the Earth Summit of 1992 in Rio de Janeiro, which crystallised global concerns about the ecological crisis. During the ensuing decades, the UN created a multitude of agencies and initiatives to facilitate coordination between corporations and governments, mediated by markets, to support its sustainability agenda.

UN initiatives included the Millennium Development Goals, a set of categories that could generate measurable indicators of economic, social, welfare, and environmental conditions, which were supposed to act as shared standards across the world economy.[1] These goals resulted from a long institutional process, including a Millennium Summit held in 2000, and were meant to be achieved by 2015. In preparation for the summit, Kofi Annan, the General Secretary of the UN, produced a report that framed the debate of sustainability by seeking to turn globalisation into a 'positive force' that would help pull people out of poverty across the world.[2]

The natural successor of the Millennium Development Goals were the Sustainable Development Goals, which were even more ambitious and expected to be achieved by 2030. Specific measurable targets were set for each goal, together with indicators to measure progress toward

1 See D. Hulme and J. Scott (2010) 'The Political Economy of the MDGs: Retrospect and Prospect for the World's Biggest Promise', The University of Manchester Brooks World Poverty Institute Working Paper No. 110, pp. 3–5.

2 Kofi A. Annan (2000) 'We the Peoples: The Role of the United Nations in the 21st Century', United Nations, at un.org.

achieving the targets.[3] Both sets of goals have come under sustained criticism by political economists and committed critics of the ecological disasters of capitalist accumulation. It was pointed out, for instance, that their heavy focus on private enterprises and the concomitant ignoring of the collective interest – the commons – has legitimised and even facilitated the grabbing of natural resources by corporations and states.[4]

Cooperation with the World Bank was important in creating both the Millennium Development Goals and the Sustainable Development Goals. For our purposes, however, the crucial aspect of these plans is that they helped establish the broader framework of environmental, social, and governance (ESG) criteria. These are currently integral to the global operations of industrial and financial enterprises, and hence to the greenwashing of private capital, as is shown in the next section. The funding required to achieve the Sustainable Development Goals would probably run into trillions of US dollars annually, and thus the scope for financial and other transactions based on ESG is potentially enormous.[5]

Equally important in this respect was another UN initiative, the UN Global Compact, a platform with a very high private sector involvement across the world. At the Davos World Economic Forum in January 1999, UN General Secretary Kofi Annan called upon the massed ranks of chief executives of globally active enterprises to give a human face to the world market by adopting appropriate moral values, including protecting the environment.[6] The UN stood ready to develop these ideas and facilitate dialogue between corporations and broader social groups as well as political actors.

The result was the UN Global Compact, officially launched in 2000. The Global Compact is both a policy platform and a practical framework for globally active corporations to develop strategies related to sustainability and social responsibility. In 2004, the Compact launched

---

3 See United Nations (2017) Resolution Adopted by the General Assembly on 6 July 2017, Work of the Statistical Commission Pertaining to the 2030 Agenda for Sustainable Development (A/RES/71/313 Archived 28 November 2020 at the Wayback Machine Internet Archive).

4 Peter Bille Larsen, Tobias Haller, and Ashish Kothari (2022) 'Sanctioning Disciplined Grabs (SDGs): From SDGs as Green Anti-Politics Machine to Radical Alternatives?', *Geoforum* 131: 20–6.

5 See OECD (2020) 'Global Outlook on Financing for Sustainable Development 2021: A New Way to Invest for People and Planet', OECD Publishing: Paris.

6 See United Nations (1999) 'Kofi Annan's Address to World Economic Forum in Davos', at un.org.

its framework of financial transactions based on ESG, focusing on how international managers of money capital – especially shadow banking institutions – could influence the behaviour of corporations regarding sustainability and other related issues.

The institutional framework of ESG practices also crucially relied on a further initiative by the UN Environment Programme (UNEP), the main authority within the UN system that focuses on strengthening environmental standards and practices across the world. In 1991, shortly before the Rio Summit, UNEP met with a group of large banks to prepare for the summit, and the result was the Statement by Banks on the Environment and Sustainable Development launched in May 1992. In 1997, it was redrafted to broaden its appeal to the wider financial sector and became the UNEP Statement by Financial Institutions on the Environment and Sustainable Development. Banks, insurance, and reinsurance companies became steadily involved and in 2003 formed the UNEP Finance Initiative.[7]

The mission of the UNEP Finance Initiative is, apparently, to promote the adoption of best environmental and sustainable practices at all levels of operations by financial institutions. The Initiative aims to cooperate with globally active financial institutions to create a basis for integrating sustainability into financial market practices. Together with the UN Global Compact, it promotes the Principles for Responsible Investment (PRI), an organisation which seeks to establish norms for sustainable finance and set standards for private financial enterprises to contribute to sustainable development. The PRI was launched in April 2006 at the New York Stock Exchange and the number of private signatories has grown greatly since then;[8] it has been instrumental to the greenwashing of big business across the world.[9]

Multilateral organisations were early to set the scene of sustainable

---

7 S. Park (2006) 'UNEP's Finance Initiative: Beyond Bluewash?', International Studies Association 47th Annual Convention, ISA: Tucson, AZ. See also S. Park (2012) 'Bankers Governing the Environment? Private Authority, Power Diffusion and the United Nations Environment Programme Finance Initiative', in S. Guzzini and I. Neumann (eds) *The Diffusion of Power in Global Governance*, Palgrave Macmillan: London, pp. 141–71.

8 For a short historical account of ESG, see R. G. Eccles and J. C. Stroehle (2018) 'Exploring Social Origins in the Construction of ESG Measures', at ssrn.org.

9 See, for instance, S. Kim and A. Yoon (2022) 'Analyzing Active Fund Managers' Commitment to ESG: Evidence from the United Nations Principles for Responsible Investment', *Management Science* 69 (2): 741–58.

development for private corporations, but national governments also came under pressure to respond to popular concerns, particularly when faced with mass movements carrying substantial electoral weight. The result was the gradual introduction of so-called 'green deals' with fiscal, monetary, and industrial aspects.[10] The policies of key states differ among themselves, but all apparently seek to construct a 'green economy'.[11] It cannot be overstressed that mobilising the mechanisms of large corporations is usually an integral part of government plans.

The term 'Green New Deal' was coined in the 2000s in the USA as a set of programmes to address the complex climate, economic, and social problems faced by the hegemon. A Green New Deal was presented in a Resolution to the US Congress in 2018 focused on achieving growth while maintaining sustainable environmental and climate conditions.[12] The long list of goals included net-zero emissions of gases causing global warming, securing clean air and water, improving climate and community resilience, achieving the production of healthy food, creating jobs, investing in infrastructure and industry, and even promoting social justice. In 2019, members of the US Senate voted against proceeding with the resolution, and in 2020, President Joe Biden also declined to support it. Nonetheless, a further plan related to environment and climate, titled 'A Clean Energy Revolution', was proclaimed by Biden with similar but less ambitious goals.[13]

Similar policy proposals were made by other core governments during this period. Thus, in the UK, a Green Deal was launched as a policy initiative focusing mostly on energy-saving improvements for homeowners and aiming to produce energy that did not worsen the climate. The policy was implemented through the Energy Act of 2011, with a second and third version implemented in 2014 and 2017, respectively. Peripheral countries also proved willing to move in the same direction. In 2020, the South Korean government announced a Digital

---

10 See M. Smol (2022) 'Is the Green Deal a Global Strategy? Revision of the Green Deal Definitions, Strategies and Importance in Post-COVID Recovery Plans in Various Regions of the World', *Energy Policy* 169: 113152.

11 See A. D. Boyle et al. (2021) 'Green New Deal Proposals: Comparing Emerging Transformational Climate Policies at Multiple Scales', *Energy Research & Social Science* 81: 102259.

12 See US Government (2018) 'Resolution: Recognizing the Duty of the Federal Government to Create a Green New Deal', *H Res.* 109 (2018), at congress.gov.

13 See J. Biden and K. Harris (2020) '9 Key Elements of Joe Biden's Plan for a Clean Energy Revolution', Joe Biden Press Office, at biologicaldiversity.org.

New Deal together with a Green New Deal, an initiative that was the first of its kind in East Asia. The 'green' part included the production of renewable energy, moving away from fossil fuels and reducing the pressure on the climate, 'greening' the country's infrastructure and its industry, and encouraging citizens to buy cars that do not rely on fossil fuels. All that would be achieved while creating almost 2 million new jobs.[14]

Finally, the EU also began to discuss the idea of a Green New Deal within its political mechanisms in the 2000s.[15] A European Green Deal was officially designated by the European Commission as part of its economic strategy in 2019.[16] The plan, strongly related to the Sustainable Development Goals, aims at net-zero emissions of gases that induce global warming by 2050. It includes changes in industrial policies, a proposed transformation of production and consumption, and ambitious aims for food and agriculture, transport, construction, taxation, and social benefits.

Taken at face value, the successive initiatives, proclamations, and plans by multilateral organisations and governments appear to be a historic development, the acquisition of a 'green' conscience by contemporary capitalism. But their true measure can be quickly ascertained. Since the vaunted UN Rio de Janeiro Earth Summit in 1992, none of the environmental and climate targets have been met. The outcome of these efforts over three decades has been consistently to miss the targets, especially regarding climate.

During the same period, the dominant multinationals in production chains, the large banks and financial institutions, and even the giants of fossil fuel production have engaged in an extraordinary transformation within the institutional framework steadily created by multinational organisations and governments. The more environmental and climate targets were missed at the global level, the 'greener' capital, and particularly big business, apparently became at the micro level. Corporations learned to find profit-making avenues in the new framework by dressing investment in 'green' clothes and seeking 'green' credentials.

14 S. Chowdhury (2021) 'South Korea's Green New Deal in the Year of Transition', UNDP Seoul Policy Centre, at undp.org.

15 P. Schepelmann et al. (2009) 'A Green New Deal for Europe', Green European Foundation, Green New Deal Series, vol. 1.

16 European Commission (2019) 'Communication from the Commission: The European Green Deal', COM No. 640.

The greenwashing of private capital

Private capital is acutely aware of the need to present itself as a champion of the environment and protector of the climate, while also seeking new sources of profit, as is its wont. The institutions and policies introduced at global and national levels have facilitated the greenwashing of private capital, in line with the internationalisation of production, the global spreading of finance, and the growth of digital technology.

Nothing demonstrates this cynical stance more clearly than the meteoric rise of the ESG criteria in the private sector and increasingly among central and local state authorities. ESG is prevalent in the design of policy by multilateral organisations, and ubiquitous in the lexicon of the multinationals and financial institutions that dominate the world economy.

ESG criteria exemplify the symbiotic relationship of internationally active productive capitals (as issuers of securities) with global financial capitals (as portfolio managers and mediators of securities transactions) behind an ideological façade that offers fresh opportunities for profit making. The apparent 'greening' of global financial capitals proceeded together with the apparent 'greening' of internationalised productive capitals, creating enormous scope for profitable 'green finance'.[17]

The approach of ESG emerged from innovations introduced within private finance in cahoots with the academic world. Commercial ESG ratings appeared in the 1980s, initially targeting highly specialised buyers of securities but gradually becoming mainstream. Shadow banking was instrumental to the proliferation of ESG practices in the 2010s.[18] Institutional investors, such as pension funds and insurance companies, collecting the idle money of large numbers of workers and other social strata, sought the high moral ground by purchasing financial assets that ostensibly complied with a range of 'values', none more exalted than 'protecting the environment'. Multinational and domestic enterprises also wanted to appear responsive to social concerns regarding environmental degradation and climate change.

---

17 See, for instance, N. Badenhoop, (2022) 'Greening Supply Chains and Their Financing under EU Law', forthcoming in D. Snyder and S. Maslow (eds), *Contracts for Responsible and Sustainable Supply Chains: Model Clauses, Legal Analysis, and Practical Discussion*, American Bar Association: 2023.

18 See Eccles and Stroehle (2018) 'Exploring Social Origins in the Construction of ESG Measures'.

The growth of ESG-based securities during the 2010s was tremendous. Take, for instance, ESG 'labelled' bonds, which are ear-marked to finance projects with environmental or, presumably, other social benefits. In 2021, their volume exceeded 2 trillion US dollars, having grown more than tenfold during the preceding five years, and the great bulk were so-called 'green' bonds – that is, securities that presumably confer explicit benefits to the environment. During this period, shadow banks that flaunt their ESG credentials also witnessed enormous growth of their assets under management (AUM). Mutual funds with ESG mandates held mostly equities (more than 60 per cent of AUM) but also bonds (around 20 per cent of AUM); ETFs with ESG policies also grew rapidly, again focusing on equities.[19]

As ESG practices became entrenched in securities trading, a complex institutional universe emerged within international portfolio finance. For one thing, the great volume of securities drawing explicitly on ESG principles requires the systematic provision of ESG ratings, indexes, and associated services. Thus, in addition to asset managers, institutional investors, multinational enterprises, and public authorities deploying ESG principles in issuing and purchasing securities, there emerged countless providers of ESG ratings and indexes who are globally active.[20] Moreover, framing and guidance mechanisms for the use of ESG took firmer shape, including by the authorities of securities markets. Finally, leading state institutions – central banks in particular – began to set regulations and standards.[21]

ESG ratings are attached to securities in a manner similar to the creditworthiness scores given by credit rating agencies. The ratings are registered on different ordinal scales, for instance from CCC to AAA, sometimes from brown to green, or bearing positive, neutral, and negative assessments. Ratings providers rank different aspects of the performance and structure of the issuer, subsequently aggregating these to create metrics that define the elements of the three pillars of the

19 See M. Scatigna et al. (2021) 'Achievements and Challenges in ESG Markets', *BIS Quarterly Review*, December: 83–97.

20 Original ESG providers were aggressively acquired in the 2010s by the main providers of general financial ratings; see F. Berg, J. F. Koelbel, and R. Rigobon (2022) 'Aggregate Confusion: The Divergence of ESG Ratings', *Review of Finance* 26 (6): 1315–44.

21 For an exhaustive overview of the landscape of ESG methodologies and providers, see R. Boffo and R. Patalano (2020) 'ESG Investing: Practices, Progress and Challenges', OECD: Paris, pp. 19–20, at oecd.org.

approach, namely E (Environmental), S (Social), and G (Governance). The scores supposedly measure the degree of sensitivity of private corporations and public administrations to the three pillars.

Securities buyers were thus able to incorporate ESG data in their investment strategies alongside standard financial analysis of risk and return. Enterprises issuing securities could potentially be excluded from the strategies, if they engaged in activities that did not align with the moral values of the securities buyers, or with legal and other standards relating to human rights, employment practices, protecting the environment, and fighting corruption. On this basis, securities buyers could actively seek to change the conduct of enterprises in relation to climate change, gender diversity, criminal behaviour, and so on.[22]

The definition of ESG performance is, however, far murkier than the assessment of enterprise creditworthiness. Moreover, ESG performance is open to widely varying interpretations that reflect different factor categories, subcategory metrics, indicator weightings, and a host of other factors that are specific to each provider of ratings.[23] Despite the enormous growth of ESG practices, there is no clarity regarding what would generally be expected, or priced, by the securities markets. Above all, there is no firm set of ESG standards that could be considered official or established by law across the world.

In practice, therefore, an open international market has emerged, with a vast array of private providers of ratings and indexes who supply their own ESG measurements.[24] Private enterprises and other issuers of securities engage in 'ESG shopping', looking for providers that could maximise their ratings. Private providers, in turn, attempt to control the terms of assessment, seeking to protect customers from regulations and other risks.[25] Opacity and 'ESG washing' have become bywords of deploying ESG criteria in financial and other investment. Providers of ESG ratings and indexes are able to tilt the vast portfolios of international finance

---

22 See G. Inderst and F. Stewart (2018) 'Incorporating Environmental, Social and Governance (ESG) Factors into Fixed Income Investment', World Bank: Washington, DC.

23 See, for instance, F. Berg, K. Fabisik, and Z. Sautner (2020) 'Rewriting History II: The (Un)predictable Past of ESG Ratings', European Corporate Governance Institute–Finance Working Paper No. 708.

24 See Boffo and Patalano (2020) 'ESG Investing'.

25 Gabor (2021) 'The Wall Street Consensus'.

toward specific issuers or thematic areas by offering a range of stylised benchmarks that allow financial enterprises (typically shadow banks) to appear to focus on climate and environmental sustainability.

The disingenuous aspect of ESG is hardly surprising, considering that its practices have arisen for reasons of social pressure external to the inner drive of the circuit of capital. The profits of domestic and international producers would be substantially squeezed if the costs of the ecological crisis were brought back onto company accounts and enterprises had to confront them directly.

For the managers of multinational corporations, ESG ratings are a convenient means of appearing to meet environmental and other social concerns, while attracting capital and minimising the costs of borrowing or issuing equity.[26] ESG ratings are also an excellent ticket into the extensive 'green' programmes that leading governments have gradually introduced under social and political pressure. Fresh avenues of profitability have emerged purely by manipulating popular concerns about the ecological crisis.

Inevitably, ESG practices have become integral to the institutional structures of the world economy. Multilateral organisations increasingly accept privately constructed ESG criteria while assessing the environmental sustainability of development projects.[27] The World Bank has created its own Environmental and Social Framework, which became effective in 2018, to support its Investment Project Financing.[28] The European Commission and the People's Bank of China recently jointly released a Common Ground Taxonomy, which identifies a set of economic activities recognised as environmentally sustainable by both the EU's and China's own classification systems.[29] Particularly important in this respect is that central banks are also discussing ways to include

26 See Kim and Yoon (2022) 'Analyzing Active Fund Managers' Commitment to ESG'. See also N. Apergis, T. Poufinas, and A. Antonopoulos (2022) 'ESG Scores and Cost of Debt', *Energy Economics* 112: 106186. Some of the largest ESG-conscious funds invest in the world's largest carbon emitters; see Gabor (2021) 'The Wall Street Consensus'.

27 See D. Gabor (2019) 'Securitization for Sustainability: Does It Help Achieve the Sustainable Development Goals?', Heinrich Böll Stiftung North America: Washington, DC, October.

28 But it has been accused of 'greenwashing'; see A. Hattle (2021) 'Climate Adaptation Finance: Fact or Fiction?', The CARE Climate Justice Center Report, January, at careclimatechange.org.

29 See Scatigna et al. (2021) 'Achievements and Challenges in ESG Markets'.

climate concerns within their policy scope, thus making ESG criteria a component of monetary policies.[30]

In sum, a global framework has gradually emerged based on ESG criteria, consonant with the interests of internationally active capital and seeking to force compliance across the world. Several private agencies currently provide ESG ratings for entire countries to deploy in trading government securities and other assets. ESG criteria are increasingly applied to public administration, including rules, laws, and policies that relate to environmental sustainability.[31] Having an ESG rating might even become a *de facto* obligation for countries to enter financial markets in the years ahead.

ESG criteria reflect the inability of contemporary capitalism to engage in meaningful reform with regard to the environment. Instead, a façade is created to hide the essential incompatibility of neoliberal financialised capitalism with ecological stability and, more broadly, with social needs. The greenwashing of capital has reached enormous dimensions, resting on global structures that provide ideological cover while sustaining the profit-making activities of private enterprises. Any consideration given to alternative strategies for the future must take into account this malignant development.

---

30 The aim appears to be to reorient credit toward green activities, in the process reducing both the impact of extreme climate events on financial agents and the financing of high-carbon activities. See Y. Dafermos, D. Gabor, and J. Michell (2020) 'Institutional Supercycles: An Evolutionary Macro-Finance Approach', unpublished manuscript, University of West of England, Bristol.

31 See A. Georgieva and J. Sloggett (2019) 'A Practical Guide to ESG Integration in Sovereign Debt', at unpri.org.

17

Turbulence Ahead

The predicament of the interregnum

In the early 2020s Covid-19 sparked a profound social, economic, and political crisis, exacerbating tensions and weaknesses that had built up over a long time. Further worsening matters, sharp hegemonic contests broke out as the USA faced challenges from beyond the historic centres of capitalist accumulation, while the war in Ukraine threatened a broader conflagration.

The contradictions of contemporary capitalism, led by international-ised production and global finance, have become spectacularly apparent during the interregnum that began with the Great Crisis of 2007–09.[1] Political actors in core and peripheral countries responded to the prolif-erating emergencies of the period by extending the powers of the state, while exhibiting ever stronger anti-democratic tendencies. Authoritarianism, however, offers no cure for the malaise induced by pervasive capitalist social relations – it merely postpones the day of reckoning.[2] It is even less a means of confronting the great upsurge of international tensions and hegemonic contests as capitalism encircles the globe.

---

1 For a clear analysis of these inherent contradictions, see Harvey (2014) *Seventeen Contradictions and the End of Capitalism.*

2 It buys time, in the apt phrase of Wolfgang Streeck analysing the relentless hollowing out of democracy in contemporary capitalism; see W. Streeck (2014) *Buying Time: The Delayed Crisis of Democratic Capitalism*, Verso: London.

The bipolar world, born in the aftermath of the Second World War and installed through a Cold War filled with tension, came to an end with the collapse of the Eastern Bloc and the Soviet Union itself in 1991. The ensuing years of US hegemony were accompanied by a cascade of economic and geopolitical crises as the USA aggressively promoted capitalist expansion across the world, while engaging in endless military interventions and wars.[3] To serve the hegemon's aims and commands, NATO, the main instrument of US military power, was reshaped and expanded.[4]

For much of the world, these developments constituted a resurgent aggressive imperialism. It is an open question how far into the future the USA can maintain its hegemonic position. Alternative centres of capitalist accumulation have emerged across the historic periphery of the world economy, and the challenge of China has only just begun.[5] International relations theorists from the emerging powers already talk of complex multipolarity, in which hierarchically ordered states, ranging from the American and Chinese superpowers, to great powers such as India and Russia, and to medium and small states with little influence, engage in different degrees of cooperation, ultimately defining 'a multipolar structure with bipolar forces rising and unipolar forces declining'.[6]

The relative retreat of US hegemony is ultimately due to the underlying weakness of capitalist accumulation in the core countries of the world economy. Suffice it to mention that life expectancy, a plain indicator of social wellbeing, plunged in the USA in 2019–21 and now stands below that of China.[7] The rich benefited further from government

3 See S. Kushi and M. D. Toft (2022) 'Introducing the Military Intervention Project: A New Dataset on US Military Interventions, 1776–2019', *Journal of Conflict Resolution* 67 (4): 752–79. The authors estimate that there have been roughly four hundred US military interventions since 1776. Half of these were undertaken between 1950 and 2019, and about one hundred after the end of the Cold War.

4 See H. B. L. Larsen (2020) *NATO's Democratic Retrenchment: Hegemony After the Return of History*, Routledge: Abingdon, New York, pp. 17–18.

5 For a wide-ranging discussion, see M. Hudson (2022) *The Destiny of Civilization: Finance Capitalism, Industrial Capitalism or Socialism*, ISLET—Verlag: Dresden.

6 Z. Huasheng (2020) 'Bipolarity and Its Relations with Multipolarity and Unipolarity', Russian International Affairs Council, 15 October, at russiancouncil.ru.

7 The decline was most prominent among marginalised social and ethnic groups; see E. Arias et al. (2022) *Provisional Life Expectancy Estimates for 2021*, Vital Statistics Rapid Release Report No. 23, August, at cdc.gov.

support given to finance, while rapid inflation in the early 2020s facilitated enormous transfers of income from labour to capital.

The privileged elite at the core shows scant awareness of the economic, political, and social turmoil that is gradually enveloping the world. On the opposite side, workers, and the poor, although riven with discontent, lack the consciousness and organisation to force change from below. While ruling blocs in peripheral countries are able to pose challenges to US hegemony, they are not strong enough to set new terms of operation for the world economy, including by changing the form of world money.

Times are highly charged as the old order is discombobulated but the new struggles have yet to be born. Neoliberal financialisation is in deep trouble without visibly mutating into a new form of capitalism, as core states intervene heavily to support accumulation without altering its fundamental underpinnings. Nascent industrial capitalism in peripheral countries has shifted the centre of gravity of productive accumulation in the world economy but does not yet possess the vigour to impose alternative configurations in economy, society, and politics.

The period ahead is likely to be marked by persistent domestic unrest and global hegemonic contests, with a high risk of military conflagration. The onus is on workers' organisations, social movements, and left-wing political organisations to offer ways out. Fundamental to any coherent alternatives will be a clear understanding of the role of the state domestically and internationally as the interregnum continues to unfold.

Gigantic domestic state intervention

National states are prime actors in contemporary capitalism. As Marx famously noted, states owe their autonomy to the internal dissensions among the various groupings of the ruling class – landlords, industrialists, financiers, and others.[8] Notwithstanding easy talk about all-powerful markets during the years of neoliberal ascendancy, states continue to shape the world together with private capital.

Repositories of huge social and ideological power, states are the

8 See K. Marx (1996) 'Eighteenth Brumaire of Louis Bonaparte', in *Later Political Writings*, edited by Terrel Carver, Cambridge University Press: Cambridge, ch. 7.

enforcers of last resort not only through the mechanisms of the military, the police, and the courts, but also through their economic power that rests on command over money, the ability to tax, and even direct owner-ship over productive resources.[9] But states also differ greatly among themselves depending on the internal constellation of social classes as well as on the global divisions of core and periphery, as was shown in parts II and III of this book.

These differences matter greatly because the driving motives of states are intertwined, but do not coincide, with those of private capitals. Powerful state mechanisms, especially those of the hegemonic state, are able strongly to influence the motion of capitalist accumulation. And yet, since the Great Crisis of 2007–9, core states as well as emerging challengers have been unable to shape a new path ahead.

The debility of the neoliberal financialised order was sharply revealed in 2020, since it proved impossible to confront the common threat to humanity posed by Covid-19 in a coordinated and coherent way. Core states, including the USA, were incapable of offering global leadership or even adequately protecting their own populations. Peripheral states were forced to cope with the viral onslaught by relying mostly on their own strengths. For some, the path was disastrous, but, remarkably, several others performed better than the wealthier core. The pandemic confirmed that contemporary capitalism is marked by global divergence rather than convergence.

Class interest was the main reason for the failures of the core and for the catastrophes that befell several countries in the periphery. The defi-ciencies of health systems in even the richest countries became apparent as infection cases swelled. Workers and the poor took the brunt of the pandemic through loss of life and long-term damage to health as well as through the sustained psychological and mental damage from lock-downs and restrictions.

The clear winner of state intervention was Big Pharma, which prof-ited from the strategy of mitigation and vaccination that eventually prevailed across broad swathes of the world. Huge multinationals now parade as saviours of humanity despite their appalling record in dealing

---

9 In the words of Charles Tilly, they are 'relatively centralized, differentiated organizations whose officials more or less successfully claim control over the chief concentrated means of violence within a population inhabiting a large, contiguous territory'; see Tilly (1982) 'War Making and State Making as Organized Crime', p. 3.

with public health, and despite the death toll of the pandemic in the hegemonic USA exceeding one million.

Debility was equally apparent in the economic response to the pandemic. Core states engaged in unprecedented policies of monetary and fiscal expansion. They were thus able to forestall the generalised collapse of capitalist accumulation that loomed ominously as restrictions and lockdowns spread rapidly in the first half of 2020. But there is no evidence that they have put capitalist accumulation on a new path of sustained growth.

Fiscal expansion in 2020–21 was tremendous, and even included partial nationalisation of the wage bills of a vast array of enterprises in several core countries. It became clear that the severe austerity of the 2010s across the core of the world economy was a matter of political choice and not an economic necessity, much less a matter of economic 'orthodoxy'. The existential threat of Covid-19 forced even the EU, the fiscal citadel of the core, to relax austerity. The abandonment of austerity, however, showed that the trouble with capitalist accumulation went far deeper than mere deficiency of aggregate demand, for as demand was boosted the weakness of aggregate supply became apparent, and the outcome was accelerating inflation.

The monetary response of core states, on the other hand, was to continue practices that had already been tried during and after the Great Crisis of 2007–09. The provision of liquidity and the widespread adoption of quantitative easing in the early 2020s left no doubt that the economic power of core states derives largely from control over domestic money. The main economic institution of mature financialised capitalism is the central bank, which dominates the money market, regulating interest rates, supervising the financial system, and acquiring enormous volumes of public debt.

Behind the ideology of liberalisation, prevalent during the last four decades, lies monopoly state control over money as the final means of payment, managed by an unelected army of technocrats in close cooperation with oligarchic financial interests. Control over domestic money affords to core states immense powers of intervention in the economy, notably on the side of aggregate demand. It creates great scope for monetary policy and facilitates fiscal expansion by monetising the growth of public debt as central banks stretch their balance sheets.

Monetary and fiscal interventions by core states throughout the interregnum have aimed primarily at sustaining financialised capitalism, first and foremost by supporting financial profits. Central bank control over domestic money proved crucial to buttressing financialisation, particularly as shadow banking continued to grow. The domination of the main money markets by core central banks is a *sine qua non* for the operations of the private funds, which have garnered enormous volumes of private equity, as well as for the borrowing and lending of commercial banks.

But the early 2020s also made apparent the limits of state power, for the deeper malaise of financialised capitalism is to be found on the side of aggregate supply, manifested in frail profitability, weak productivity growth, zombie firms, and precarious employment. Core state intervention barely touched the side of production. States did not raise the alternative of public ownership over productive capacity, expand public investment in infrastructure, or pose the issue of public ownership over key financial institutions. Above all, core states avoided policies that might provide secure and dignified employment and sought to maintain the balance of power in the workplace in favour of capital.

Even when the wage bills and income statements of private enterprises were brought within the purview of state finances, capitalist property rights were left untouched by core states. Governments paid workers' wages and subsidised enterprise losses but kept away from acquiring equity in productive enterprises. Their overriding concern was to protect the privileges of the narrow elite benefiting from neoliberal financialisation. The result was that intervention triggered further intractable difficulties, including high inflation and vast public debt.

The rise of inflation represents a direct transfer of income from workers' wages to the profits of capital, while also posing a threat to financialisation, since it undermines the value of debt. It is not clear how core states will tackle these disturbances bequeathed by the pandemic shock. Raising the rate of interest to confront inflation runs the risk of inducing a recession that will hurt working people as well as damaging production. High interest rates also exacerbate the burden of debt and raise the spectre of a financial crisis.

The road ahead for capitalist accumulation is daunting, particularly as the ructions of the 2020s were far from being exclusively economic or confined to the core of the world economy. The turmoil cast the sharpest of lights on relations of core and periphery, and on hegemony and imperialism.

Core and periphery, hegemony and imperialism remoulded

At the turn of the twentieth century, classical Marxism defined imperialism in terms of finance capital that sought territorial exclusivity and imposed tariff barriers, while promoting the export of loanable money capital. On this basis, European capitalist powers established enormous colonial empires across the world.

US imperialism after the Second World War took a different form, as controls were applied to the international flows of loanable money capital and industrial capital began to internationalise production. The US empire in the twentieth century was not based on formal colonies but rather on actively shaping the institutional framework of the world economy. Its most significant challenge for decades was geopolitical, not economic, and emanated from the Soviet Union.

Contemporary capitalism presents a still different form of imperialism and hegemony, not least because capitalist relations now dominate the globe – there are no significant non-capitalist areas. The underlying economic foundations of contemporary imperialism are provided by the symbiotic pairing of internationalised productive capital with global portfolio finance.

International production networks, dominated by huge multinationals, shape the division of labour in the world economy. Control takes complex forms and does not necessarily involve property rights over productive capacity abroad. Global portfolio finance, on the other hand, is driven by the risk and return predictions of the managers of private funds and other financial institutions. Money capital flows primarily among core countries, but substantial proportions are directed from core to periphery and even from periphery to periphery.

The pairing of these capitals has not recreated the finance capital of classical Marxism. There is no systematic amalgamation of industrial and bank capital, particularly as internationalised productive capital tends to control huge pools of liquidity available for investment. Neither form of capital seeks territorial exclusivity, and both are global in outlook. What they require is an institutional framework of the world economy conducive to their global expansion and, above all, a reliable form of world money. Imperialism and hegemony in contemporary capitalism cannot be understood independently of these requirements of globally active capitals.

The USA rose to the position of global hegemon when the Soviet Union collapsed in 1991. It took advantage of its historically unique position to influence the institutional framework of the world economy through a range of multilateral institutions, while favouring its own multinationals and financial enterprises. The most important component of its hegemony was the dollar created by the Federal Reserve, acting as international reserve of value, means of payment, and unit of account in the world economy.

For peripheral countries, subordination took subtle and complex forms deriving ultimately from the internationalisation of productive capital, the global reach of financial capital, and the hierarchies of money across the world economy. For peripheral countries, command over domestic money does not have the same meaning and content as for the core, exposed as they are to global capital flows. Moreover, since their currencies are on the lower rungs of the global hierarchy, they have been forced to keep vast reserves of dollars for more than two decades to cope with the pressures of global portfolio finance.

Untrammelled US hegemony came to an end in the 2010s and 2020s as countries that used to be peripheral emerged as contenders. The leading challenger is China, where sustained state intervention, drawing on direct ownership of productive resources and the means of finance, has enabled astonishingly rapid capitalist accumulation. China poses a qualitatively different challenge to US hegemony from that of the Soviet Union, the roots of which are economic and not merely political or military. In this regard, the contest for hegemony resembles the imperialist contests prior to 1914.

And yet, the hegemonic contest is also different from the times of classical imperialism, since the capitals that drive it seek neither territorial command nor the creation of exclusive geographical zones. Multinationals and international financial enterprises, whether they originate in the core or the periphery, have a global outlook. What they seek is a favourable institutional framework in the world market and a reliable form of world money. China's hegemonic challenge focuses on denying the US state its overwhelming power to dictate these conditions.

The difference from the pre-1914 world is also apparent insofar as none of the challengers to the USA comes from the established core powers. The hegemonic prevalence of the USA over the historic centres of capitalist accumulation is intact. Nowhere is that more clearly demonstrated than in Europe, where Germany, the local hegemonic power, even undermined its own pre-eminence by participating in US sanctions against Russia in the Ukraine war. The EU has failed to pose a challenge to the USA either in shaping the framework of the world market, or in providing an alternative form of world money.[10]

The outcome of the emerging hegemonic contests is, however, far from certain. China is wracked by profound internal problems, as capitalist development exacerbates social rifts and the issue of the ownership of means of production continues to divide the economically powerful strata. The ability of the Chinese economy to provide an alternative form of world money is currently very restricted, and will probably remain so as long as the Chinese financial system is under public ownership and capital flows are closely regulated.

The most likely prospect for the years ahead is that of persistent domestic unrest and intensifying hegemonic contests, with a high risk of military conflagration. Alternative strategies are required, and it behoves workers' organisations, social movements, and left-wing political organisations to come up with fresh proposals.

The pressing need for economic and political alternatives

Anti-capitalist and socialist forces face acute difficulties in proposing alternative strategies as the hazards of the interregnum escalate. The deep turmoil of the 2020s barely resolved any of the underlying difficulties of capitalist accumulation, especially those that permeate production.

It is incumbent on the left to tackle the worsening social problems by proposing alternatives that bring that structural change to domestic economies and to the world economy. Structural change means little if it does not aim to oppose and overturn capitalism. Achieving it requires a shift in the balance of class power that would involve unprecedented public economic intervention at the national level as well as profound transformations in international production, trade, and finance.

Economic alternatives are, however, only a part of what is required. For one thing, economic transformation must take into account the sharpening hegemonic contests that raise the prospect of generalised war. For another, economic alternatives must also consider the hollowing out of democracy in both core and periphery during the last several decades.

---

10 In this connection it is worth noting the timely analysis of Michael Hudson; see M. Hudson (2022) 'America Defeats Germany for the Third Time in a Century', 28 February, at michaelhudson.com.

And all alternatives must register the ecological crisis unfolding under the cynical *laissez faire* of both private capital and capitalist states.

Above all, economic transformation in an anti-capitalist and socialist direction cannot avoid the issue of sovereignty, both popular and national. Popular sovereignty amounts to commanding the levers and mechanisms of power across the terrain of social life by workers, the poor, and the broader popular strata. Sovereignty is the ability of these social layers to have a voice on public issues that translates into effective action in neighbourhood, city, and country. It is also the ability to have an effective presence in the workplace, setting the terms of reference for work.

From the perspective of working people, popular sovereignty is integral to democracy; indeed, it is the deeper content of democratic practice, far beyond the formal right to vote. The mechanisms that enable popular sovereignty are, however, available only at a national level, since they involve societal and state institutions that lack an international existence. Popular sovereignty at the international level is a contradiction in terms. What could exist in the international arena is national sovereignty based on popular sovereignty.

The point to stress here is that, from the standpoint of working people and the poor, national sovereignty is not only different from nationalism but in practice negates it. National sovereignty amounts to the lower classes becoming the voice of the nation by possessing the most important levers of domestic power. It means commanding the mechanisms of economic, political, and ideological power, and giving a fundamentally plebeian content to the idea of nation itself. It also means that the poor and the downtrodden arriving across borders would form an integral part of the working class, thus becoming inseparable from the rest of the nation.

Precisely for this reason, national sovereignty backed by popular sovereignty remains the foundation of effective internationalism. The spurious internationalism of contemporary liberal ideology is tantamount to shifting masses of workers across borders without physical protection, guaranteed jobs, secure housing, and access to health and education services. It is the internationalism of capital which translates into establishing productive capacity wherever an enterprise chooses, as well as shifting money freely across borders. This is little more than an ideological framework to facilitate capitalist reproduction.

Workers' internationalism entails respecting the needs and rights of workers across the world, while also protecting the needs, rights, and living conditions of those who live in a country, including newcomers.

The germ – but only the germ – of that stance can be found when workers in one country show solidarity with workers taking action in another. To become a reality, such internationalism requires national sovereignty resting on popular sovereignty and providing foundations for equitable relations across the world. This is the basis for effectively opposing hegemony and imperialist depredations.

A consistent anti-capitalist and socialist agenda on the economy necessarily rests on popular and national sovereignty. It recognises that democracy is fundamental to opposing capitalism from the perspective of workers, the poor, the excluded, and the downtrodden. By the same token, the ruling blocs in core countries – both conservative and liberal – have a manifestly anti-democratic outlook, including imposing emergency measures and constitutional restrictions, cultivating nationalism, and openly using repression.[11]

Democracy is unattainable in societies where a tiny, privileged layer – effectively an oligarchy – sits atop society. The huge inequalities of financialised capitalism, generated by the exploitation of labour and by financial expropriation, prevent democracy from being more than purely formal and procedural.

Financialisation has aggravated the deeply embedded anti-democratic tendencies of capitalism by removing key elements of government policy, including monetary and financial policies, from the electoral realm. The hollowing out of democracy, well attested in core countries, goes together with the gradual demise of the intermediary mechanisms of political representation that give content to democratic participation. The weakening of trade unions, the retreat of communal associations and organisations, and the loss of an effective voice for working people locally and nationally are essential parts of this process.

In proposing alternatives, the left ought to bear in mind the need to demand popular sovereignty and to entrench democracy, thus creating the grounds for effective national sovereignty. The problem is, however, that the left finds itself in a state of historically unprecedented weakness.

---

11 The literature on these issues is vast. See, selectively, L. Canfora (2006) *Democracy in Europe: A History of an Ideology*, translated by S. Jones, Blackwell: Oxford; see further D. Losurdo (2011) [2006] *Liberalism: A Counter-History*, translated by G. Elliott, Verso: London. See also J. Agnoli (2000) 'The Market, the State, and the End of History', translated by W. Bonefeld and S. Soederberg, in W. Bonefeld and K. Psychopedis (eds), *The Politics of Change: Globalization, Ideology and Critique*, Springer Verlag: Berlin, pp. 196–206.

In core countries, despite the growth of an inchoate but popular anti-capitalism in recent decades, the fortunes of the political left languish at a historic nadir. No political formation in the USA, Europe, or Japan is remotely comparable to the socialist and communist parties, or even the anarchist movements, that shaped political life from the 1880s to the 1980s. In individual countries but also at the international level, the left has largely vacated the central political scene.

The emergence of the left was the great political novelty of the long historical period from the French Revolution to the First World War. The left grew by appealing to the broad masses, hailing popular sovereignty, and organising itself in novel and democratic ways. Demanding political freedom and economic equality and fighting against the conservatives and liberals who dominated politics in nineteenth-century Europe, it struggled against exploitation and oppression, war, slavery, colonialism, nationalism, and obscurantism.

Toward the end of the nineteenth and for most of the twentieth century, the left received a sustained input of Marxist political economy, helping it pioneer mass political parties and trade unions. At the peak of its influence, it turned the youth, the women, and the nationally or racially oppressed into political subjects, and led the struggles of peoples in the periphery for independence and sovereignty. Across the world, it was the prime mover in the quest for democracy, combining its socialist vision with the daily struggles of workers for rights and democracy.[12]

The fall of the Soviet Union proved a massive ideological blow that was compounded by the retreat of the organised working class in the face of neoliberal ascendancy. A ferocious ideological campaign has been waged for decades by private enterprises, the mass media, think-tanks, the academy, and an array of state institutions aiming to refashion the human self and society along capitalist principles. Trade unions and cooperative associations – the very substance of intermediary democratic mechanisms – have lost power, influence, and membership.

Today the left appears scarcely connected to working-class struggles and identities. In many core countries, it has lost its moorings among working people, the poor, and the downtrodden, speaking in terms that mean little to its erstwhile adherents. The very meaning of 'left' has

---

12 G. Eley (2002) *Forging Democracy: The History of the Left in Europe, 1850–2000*, Oxford University Press: New York; S. Todd (2014) *The People: The Rise and Fall of the Working Class, 1910–2010*, John Murray: London.

become opaque, often confused with liberal progressivism. It is no longer clear what the left is and what it may contribute to society. To initiate public debate and action on alternatives to capitalist havoc, the left must rebuild itself, creating its own dominant political project and asserting its autonomy from both the conservative and the liberal wings of bourgeois politics.[13]

For democratic and class-based proposals

From the perspective adopted in this book, the left is fundamentally the part of the political spectrum that prioritises equality and freedom, in contrast to the right, which puts forward hierarchy and inequality.[14] Freedom and equality are values that strengthen rather than oppose each other. To begin to provide answers to contemporary problems, the left ought to rediscover its past as a political current that focuses on the exploitative and oppressive nature of capitalism, seeking again to overthrow it by relying on the power of the organised working class and the poor. It needs to delve into its own rich theoretical legacy of proclaiming the merits of the public over the private, and the collective over the individual, without denying space to individual and private life. The left can be nothing if it is not the political formation seeking to transfer power and resources from the few to the many, from the strong to the weak, from the rich to the poor.

These basic distinctions hold at both national and international levels. No genuine formation of the left could advocate democratisation of income, wealth, and power within its own society while at the same time supporting hegemonic and imperialist policies abroad. Equality and freedom should necessarily be demanded both within borders and internationally. The left is essentially counter-hegemonic, aiming for national sovereignty as an indispensable foundation of true internationalism. The famous Marxist dictum 'workers of the world unite' is rooted

---

13 As Immanuel Wallerstein argued, the three conflicting ideologies of liberalism, conservatism, and radicalism have dominated capitalist culture across the world since the French Revolution; see I. Wallerstein (2011) *The Modern World-System*, vol. 4, *Centrist Liberalism Triumphant, 1789–1914*, University of California Press: Berkeley.

14 See Bobbio (1996) [1994] *Left and Right*. On the centuries-long grounding of these values in societies, see E. Todd (2011) *L'Origine des systèmes familiaux, Tome 1 L'Eurasie*, Gallimard: Paris.

in the notion that workers will become the voice of their nation by capturing state power.

As the left lost its historical roots among workers and the poor, a revived right emerged that promotes dreams of a socially stable, healthy, and harmonious capitalism cleansed from oligarchic predators, while 'keeping in their place' women, sexual, and other minorities, and all types of 'deviants'. This current appeals to middle-class layers that feel threatened by the state and big business, and even to layers of the working class that have been shorn of their traditional associations with the left. In international affairs it often embraces realism and shuns imperialist adventures, although it also exploits nationalist feelings cultivated by decades of economic stagnation or decline.

This disgruntled right does not have a counter-hegemonic project and there is no evidence that it intends to form one, but still feeds popular illusions by purloining the discursive weapons abandoned by the left. It has become adept at deploying words such as peace and freedom, as well as denouncing finance, authoritarianism, big business, and the deep state. It may even propose a rhetorical anti-imperialism and mobilise popular anti-war feelings by ascribing war and imperialism to passing perversions or personal vileness instead of systemic factors.

The resurgent right may possibly open space for the eventual return of the left, as it fails to respond adequately to lingering and worsening social problems. But this will not happen automatically, and certainly not without strong agency. The point is that political agency is never a given – it must always be created, and this requires synthetic thinking and concrete, class-based proposals. At a deeper level, the re-emergence of the left could perhaps be helped by what has been called the reaccumulation of real intelligence in the middle and lower social strata as capitalist antinomies worsen.[15]

Above all, the left must leave behind abstruse jargon and talk the everyday language of the great majority of people about the issues that concern them. Dealing with the interregnum requires setting general principles, fixing priorities, and developing an inclusive social programme departing from the need to entrench democracy and to command state power at the national level.

The Pandemic Crisis offers guidance in this respect. The disease

---

15 See E. Todd (2020), *Les luttes de classes en France au xxie siècle*, avec la collaboration de Baptiste Touverey, Éditions du Seuil: Paris, ch. 2.

revealed the appalling state of health systems in several core and peripheral countries as well as the abuses of pharmaceutical enterprises to maximise profits. Heavy investment in public health infrastructure and public provision to cover medical needs are obvious demands. It also became apparent that the burden of reproductive labour and the provision of care services continue to fall heavily on the shoulders of women. Care facilities were shown to be inadequate, and confronting shortages will require public investment.

And yet, focusing demands merely on welfare provision would be entirely inadequate in the current circumstances. As was shown throughout this book, the deeper problems lie on the side of production, and they are inextricably linked to capitalist property rights across society.

For one thing, the Pandemic Crisis cast further light on the extraordinary income and wealth inequality across core and periphery. Confronting inequality requires taxing corporate profits as well as the income and wealth of the richest layers. But reversing the structural causes of inequality would require wholesale restructuring of fundamental property relations in society. In addition to wealth taxes, inheritance taxes, and taxation or outright appropriation of money hidden in tax havens, it would involve selective nationalisation of resources and land redistribution.

For another, high rates of inflation point to the need for strong intervention on the supply side of the economy oriented toward increasing investment, boosting innovation, and accelerating productivity growth. These aims are unachievable without targeted industrial policy that directs investment toward particular sectors, fosters technological development, and raises the skills of the labour force, while creating high-quality employment.

The destructive impact of inflation on the living standards of workers is particularly severe in the sectors of food, transport, energy, and housing. Food production is dominated by multinational corporations operating global production networks that take advantage of cheap labour and vast lands available for cultivation in peripheral countries. They appropriate and exploit natural resources by practising monoculture, using pesticides, genetically modifying plants, and other such practices. The networks are also heavily financialised, and the prices of agricultural commodities are subject to financial speculators in global markets. The outcomes include adulterated and dangerous food, environmental degradation, and extreme insecurity for small producers, especially in the periphery.

State intervention ought to include publicly organised food production that returns land and other natural resources to workers and native populations, improves the quality and diversity of food, and deploys agricultural practices that are friendly to the environment. It is further necessary to ensure that food is more locally supplied: to reduce the distances covered by transport while improving the means of transport. These are complex social decisions that must be made according to the food customs of particular countries. But the underlying principle is the same: preference for locally produced food and efficient transportation to minimise costs and environmental impact.

Similar points hold for energy and housing. Fossil fuels are ecologically destructive, but there will be no effective change without sustained public intervention to put energy production within the public domain. The mechanisms of ESG are entirely inadequate and largely fraudulent in this respect. As for housing, it is the main source of debt for workers and households generally, as well as a major source of financial expropriation of workers by banks and other financial institutions. For broad swathes of the working class in core countries and in several peripheral countries, this increasingly means that finding a place to live has become extremely difficult. Sustained public intervention is necessary to build affordable housing for broad layers of the working class and other social strata which is compatible with ecological requirements.

It is immediately apparent that none of these steps will be taken without democratic planning at national and community levels, with the state and the broader public sector taking a commanding role in production, consumption, and distribution. The balance of power in economic decision making must be altered accordingly, creating social foundations to confront the ecological crisis in a coherent and socially aware way, something that private capital is incapable of doing.

It is equally apparent that none of these steps will be taken without directly challenging the financialisation of the economy. The role of the central bank will have to be altered, leaving behind the sham of 'independence' and supporting the public sector as a democratic planner in command of public money. In this regard, direct credit allocation policies by public banks would be essential to guide resources and finance the structural transformation of the economy.

These tasks also hold for peripheral countries, but they are evidently

more complex. Radical alternative strategies require tackling the exposure of peripheral countries to the pervasive consequences of global
production, trade, and finance, which limit the space for alternative
strategies. Multinationals commanding production networks have
substantial power to demand loose labour and environmental regulations or grant tax benefits. Concerted international action is required to
impose minimum labour, environmental, and taxation standards.

Concerted action is also required in the global financial system,
which leaves peripheral countries exposed to destabilising inflows and
outflows of money capital. The current international financial architecture privileges the interests of private lenders against sovereign debtors
and indebted popular strata, and ensures the dominant position of the
US dollar as world money. Debt forgiveness and external aid ought to be
on the agenda for several countries but, above all, capital inflows should
be controlled by attending to their potential uses and the risks of sudden
reversals.

There are no ready-made blueprints that the left can use today. Only
general principles are available, deriving from the political economy of
contemporary capitalism. But they are powerful tools, if they are applied
sensitively and with attention to the specific needs and characteristics of
each country.

Increasingly intolerable realities call for the left to step forward as an
alternative political power, despite its unprecedented weakness. Only
the left possesses the political values, intellectual tools, and social sensi-
tivities to organise effective resistance to private capital, counter the
divide et impera of leaders, and establish a political presence capable of
delivering popular and national sovereignty. To do so, it must patiently
explain that other political currents are unable to fulfil their promises
for a tamed capitalism, and only a broad anti-capitalist alliance of workers and other popular strata could arrest the never-ending waves of
exploitation, expropriation, and oppression.

A new politics is required that draws on alternative economic and
social strategies, challenges imperial and hegemonic power, and strives
for sovereignty, democracy, and internationalism. If the left fails to
deliver, then historical irrelevance beckons. Even worse for humanity, if
the left fails, there is nothing to stop the steady drift toward social havoc
and war. In the early twentieth century, political revolutionaries posed
the dilemma: socialism or barbarism. Perhaps it is the current generations that will resolve it.

Index